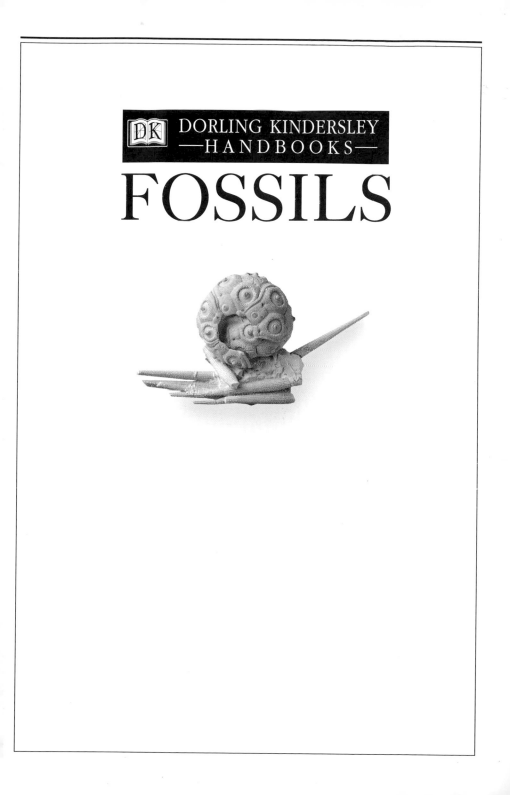

DORLING KINDERSLEY
—HANDBOOKS—

FOSSILS

DORLING KINDERSLEY
—HANDBOOKS—

FOSSILS

CYRIL WALKER
& DAVID WARD

Photography by
COLIN KEATES ABIPP
(The Natural History Museum)

A Dorling Kindersley Book

LONDON, NEW YORK, MUNICH,
MELBOURNE, and DELHI

Editors Susie Behar, Jonathan Metcalf
Art Editors Peter Cross, Clive Hayball
Production Caroline Webber

Scientific Editors Cyril Walker, David Ward

Contributors Dr Andy Gale, David Sealey, Dr Paul Taylor,
Dr Richard Fortey, Dr Brian Rosen, Sam Morris, Dr Ed Jarzembowski, Dr
Neville Hollingworth, Steve Tracey, Dr Chris Duffin, David Ward,
Dr Angela Milner, Cyril Walker, Andy Currant, Miranda Armour-Chelu,
Robert Kruszynski, Dr Jerry Hooker, Mark Crawley

Consultants Dr Chris Cleal,
Dr Peter Forey, Dr Andrew Smith, David Sealey

Illustrations Will Giles, Sandra Pond

First published in Great Britain in 1992
Reprinted with corrections in 2000
by Dorling Kindersley Limited
80 Strand, London WC2R ORL

A Penguin Company

A CIP catalogue record for this book is available
from the British Library
ISBN 0-7513-2796-4

Printed and bound by South China Printing Company in China

CONTENTS

AUTHORS' INTRODUCTION

Fossil collecting is a fascinating hobby which has grown considerably in popularity over the last few decades. Its appeal is understandable: it combines the excitement of discovery with the practical skills of collecting and preparing specimens, and the academic challenge of identifying fossil finds. There are few other branches of science in which a beginner can make a serious contribution to the knowledge of our planet's remarkable pre-history.

In 1910, Sir Robert Falcon Scott embarked on his historic but tragic expedition to the South Pole. On his return from the Pole, Scott and four companions met their death in freak weather conditions. Out of this tragedy came an important scientific discovery: among the personal belongings of the dead explorers, a fossilized seed fern, *Glossopteris*, was found. The existence of this seed fern proved conclusively that the frozen wastes of Antarctica were once part of a fertile continent, and it is known that Scott had recognized the scientific importance of his own find.

FROM COINS TO BONES

Originally the word "fossil" (derived from the Latin word *fossilis*, meaning "to be dug up") referred to anything that had been buried. It included not only the petrified remains of

TRACHYPHYLLIA (CORAL)

plants and animals, but also rocks, minerals, and man-made artefacts, such as coins. It is now used only to refer to the naturally buried and preserved remains of organisms that lived long before historic times.

YEARS OF SPECULATION

Fossils have intrigued people for generations. Greek philosophers regarded them as rather strange, natural phenomena, which formed in the earth, in a similar way to a stalactite or crystal. Martin Luther (1483–1546) believed that fossil finds on mountain tops were evidence of the biblical Flood. In his notebooks, Leonardo da Vinci (1452–1519) suggested that fossils were the petrified remains of once-living organisms. His views, heretical for his era, were withheld until his notebooks were published in the 19th century. The true nature of fossils became slowly apparent in the 17th and 18th

DIPLOMYSTUS (FISH)

HEMICIDARIS
(SEA URCHIN)

CLASSIFICATION

Fossils are usually referred to by their two-part scientific name, although a few have popular or informal names as well. For instance, the oyster *Gryphaea* is often called a "Devil's Toenail" and brachiopods are known as "lamp shells". These names have their uses but lack the precision needed in science; more importantly, they are not internationally accepted and can be confusing. The usual form is to give the scientific name, usually written in italics, followed by the name of the author, the person who first described the species. The first part is the genus, the second part is the species. If the author's name is in brackets, it means that the species has, at a later date, been moved to a different genus. When correctly used, a scientific

centuries. This was aided by the publication of books figuring collections of fossils, and by a wider understanding of natural history. One key observation was that different types of rocks contain different fossils. This fact was of considerable help in the production of the first geological maps and led to the modern sciences of palaeontology (the scientific study of fossils) and stratigraphy (the study of rock strata). Today, palaeontology is concerned only with the remains of animals and plants that lived more than 10,000 years ago.

FIELD TRIP
The authors, David Ward (right) and Cyril Walker (left), in the southern Sahara, examining an exciting fossil find: a scatter of dinosaur bones. Some of the bones found can be seen on page 248.

name refers only to a single type of organism and can be understood by scientists all over the world. The basic unit of classification is the species. There are many and varied definitions, but essentially all members of a species look similar and are able to interbreed. One or more species may be grouped into a genus, linked by features they share. This, along with the family (a group of genera) and the order (a group of families) makes up the pedigree or family tree of an organism. All the stages above "species" are artificial, a man-made classification, and they tend to change depending on current opinion. This can be frustrating to beginner and specialist.

CRINOID STEM

AMBER (FOSSILIZED PLANT RESIN)

AIMS AND LIMITATIONS

This book is intended to assist the collector by illustrating a broad range of fossils, from those most likely to be found, to some of the more spectacular, but less common. The fossils were chosen from the Natural History Museum, London, UK, one of the largest and most diverse collections in the world. Microscopic specimens have not been included. Although many are fascinating and visually stunning, their study is quite specialized. Most major groups of fossils are included, from worms to dinosaurs, from ammonites to man, and from all geological ages and continents. The description of each fossil has been written by experts who work on the many different types of fossil included. Technical terms have been kept to a minimum, but where this has proved difficult, they have been explained in a comprehensive glossary (see pp.312–316).

Many fossils, particularly the larger reptiles and mammals, are only occasionally found whole. This poses a problem in terms of identification. In such cases, small parts of the skeleton have been illustrated.

CALLIOSTOMA (GASTROPOD)

It would be impossible to show a photograph of every type of fossil. However, the range and diversity of specimens contained in this book should enable the collector to find a photograph and description of something sufficiently close to attempt a preliminary identification.

HOMO HABILIS (SKULL OF EARLY MAN)

HOW THIS BOOK WORKS

The main body of the book is divided into three parts: invertebrates, vertebrates, and plants. Within each major division, the main groups are introduced. The genus is the starting point of identification. Usually a typical or relatively common species of the described genus is illustrated. Identifying features are clearly highlighted in annotation. Occasionally, an unusual specimen, but one that makes an interesting point, has been chosen. Each photograph is accompanied by a reconstruction of a typical species of the organism in life. Some of the reconstruction details, such as the colour, are educated guesswork. This annotated example shows a typical page.

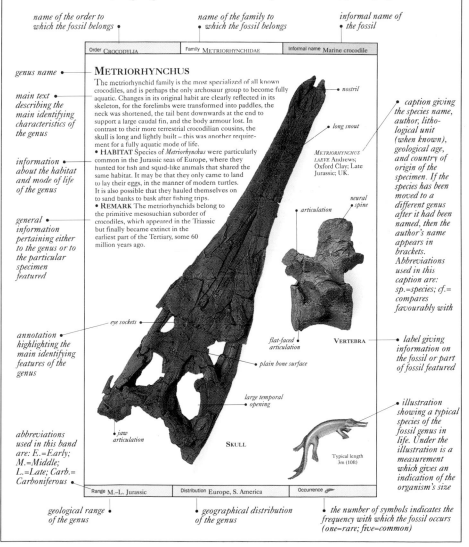

name of the order to which the fossil belongs •

name of the family to • which the fossil belongs

informal name of • the fossil

Order CROCODYLIA

Family METRIORHYNCHIDAE

Informal name Marine crocodile

genus name •

METRIORHYNCHUS

main text • describing the main identifying characteristics of the genus

The metriorhynchid family is the most specialized of all known crocodiles, and is perhaps the only archosaur group to become fully aquatic. Changes in its original habit are clearly reflected in its skeleton, for the forelimbs were transformed into paddles, the neck was shortened, the tail bent downwards at the end to support a large caudal fin, and the body armour lost. In contrast to their more terrestrial crocodilian cousins, the skull is long and lightly built – this was another requirement for a fully aquatic mode of life.

information • about the habitat and mode of life of the genus

• HABITAT Species of *Metriorhynchus* were particularly common in the Jurassic seas of Europe, where they hunted for fish and squid-like animals that shared the same habitat. It may be that they only came to land to lay their eggs, in the manner of modern turtles. It is also possible that they hauled themselves on to sand banks to bask after fishing trips.

general • information pertaining either to the genus or to the particular specimen featured

• REMARK The metriorhynchids belong to the primitive mesosuchian suborder of crocodiles, which appeared in the Triassic but finally became extinct in the earliest part of the Tertiary, some 60 million years ago.

• nostril

• long snout

METRIORHYNCHUS LAEVE Andrews; Oxford Clay; Late Jurassic; UK.

• caption giving the species name, author, lithological unit (when known), geological age, and country of origin of the specimen. If the species has been moved to a different genus after it had been named, then the author's name appears in brackets. Abbreviations used in this caption are: sp.=species; cf.= compares favourably with

neural • spine

• articulation

annotation • highlighting the main identifying features of the genus

eye sockets •

flat-faced • articulation

VERTEBRA

• label giving information on the fossil or part of fossil featured

• plain bone surface

large temporal • opening

• illustration showing a typical species of the fossil genus in life. Under the illustration is a measurement which gives an indication of the organism's size

abbreviations used in this band are: E.=Early; M.=Middle; L.=Late; Carb.= Carboniferous •

jaw • articulation

SKULL

Typical length 3m (10ft)

Range M.–L. Jurassic

Distribution Europe, S. America

Occurrence

geological range • of the genus

• geographical distribution of the genus

• the number of symbols indicates the frequency with which the fossil occurs (one=rare; five=common)

WHAT IS A FOSSIL?

FOSSILS ARE THE REMAINS of long-dead plants and animals that have partly escaped the rotting process and have, after many years, become part of the Earth's crust. A fossil may be the preserved remains of the organism itself, the impression of it in the sediment, or marks made by it in life (known as a trace fossil). For fossilization to occur, rapid burial, usually by water-borne sediment, is required. This is often followed by chemical alteration, where minerals may be added or removed. The replacement by and/or addition of minerals usually aids preservation.

FOSSIL DUNG
Trace fossils are true fossils. This dropping (below left) is probably from an extinct shark. It is usually difficult to relate coprolites to the animal that produced them.

REPTILE FOOTPRINT
While difficult to identify to a particular species, fossil footprints (above) can provide valuable information about the organism's behaviour, such as speed, weight, and mode of life.

HORSE TOOTH
This cheek tooth (below) looks like that of a modern horse, but is actually a fossil. Over the centuries, its organic tissue has been replaced by strengthening mineral salts, ensuring its preservation.

MUMMIFIED FROG
Mummification – the natural drying of an organism – has meant that the frog (right) has progressed part of the way towards becoming a fossil. To ensure proper preservation, it must become entombed in a medium that would guard against further decomposition.

BANDED FLINT
Flints (right) are sometimes mistaken for fossils. During formation, flint can be deposited in bands. With a little weathering and staining, these flints can resemble fossil corals, molluscs, worms, and trilobites.

FOOT-SHAPED
Cretaceous flints come in many forms; this one resembles a human foot (below). *Some flints are crustacean burrow infills; if so they are regarded as trace fossils.*

BIRDS' NEST
The birds' nest (above) is not a fossil; it is a modern nest that has been petrified in a spring.

CLAY BOTTLE
Objects as mundane as a collapsed clay bottle (above) are sometimes mistaken for fossils.

HOW FOSSILIZATION OCCURS

Fossilization is, at best, a risky process which relies on a chain of favourable circumstances. The vast majority of the plants and animals that have ever lived have completely disappeared without trace, leaving no fossil record. With rare exceptions, it is only the skeletal or hard parts of an organism that become fossilized. This often occurs when the organism decaying in the sediment alters the local conditions and promotes the incorporation of mineral salts within its structure, a process known as mineralization. This chemical change often enables the fossil to become more resistant than the surrounding sediment.

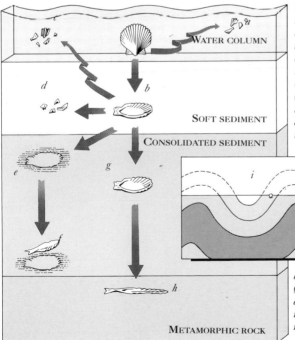

FOSSILIZATION
After death an organism may slowly disintegrate (a) or become buried in soft sediment (b). However, it may be disturbed or digested by sediment-feeding organisms, or current or wave activity may re-expose it (c). As the sediment compacts and the complex chemical reactions of diagenesis occur, the potential fossil may be dissolved (d). But if the sediment is sufficiently consolidated, a mould may be formed (e). Percolating mineral solutions may infill the mould, creating a cast (f). Some enter the sediment relatively unaltered by mineralization (g). If buried and subjected over time to increased temperature and pressure, sedimentary rocks become softened and distorted (metamor-phosed), and ultimately destroyed (h). As rocks are folded, uplifted, and eroded, buried fossils may be exposed on the surface (i).

MODES OF PRESERVATION

TO BECOME preserved as a fossil, some of the normal processes of decay must be permanently arrested. This usually involves isolating the organisms that cause decay from the air or water, and then filling any voids in the hard tissue with additional minerals. The vast majority of fossils are, therefore, found in fresh-water or marine sediments, where oxygen-deprived silt or clay has buried the organism soon after death. If the sediment conditions remain favourable *(see pp.10–11)*, the organism may be preserved as a fossil. In the case of mummification, the arrest of decay is only temporary; a mummified organism will begin to decay as soon as it is exposed to air once again.

Under exceptional circumstances, soft-tissue details may be preserved. Insects in amber and mammoths in ice or tar are well-known examples. In both these cases, the living organism has been caught in the sticky substance (tar or resin) which has then been fossilized, ensuring preservation. If limestone, phosphate, or pyrite is deposited in the sediment surrounding a decaying plant, it forms a "tomb" that may preserve very fine details of the organism. Silicified or otherwise petrified wood can produce spectacular colour effects, although the cell preservation itself is often poor.

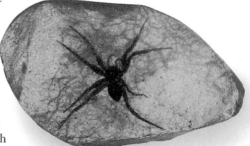

TRAPPED IN AMBER
Amber, the fossilized resin of a plant or tree, sometimes preserves not only the external, but also the internal, structure of an organism. Insects, spiders (above), frogs, and lizards may be preserved in this way.

SILICIFICATION
This is a form of "petrification". Silicified wood (left) can often be found in both terrestrial and freshwater deposits, usually sands and silts. Weathering volcanic ash usually supplies silica, which is gradually incorporated into partially decayed wood. Generally, the cell structure of silicified wood is quite poorly preserved; however, the presence of iron and other minerals can produce some really spectacular colouring.

PHOSPHATIZATION
Bones and teeth (above), *which
normally dissolve on the sea bed
or leach from the sediment, are
more likely to be preserved if large
quantities of phosphates are
present. Phosphatic deposits are a
source of well-preserved fossils and
are often mined commercially.*

MUMMIFICATION
*The dry, sterile atmosphere of a cave
has preserved this moa foot* (above)
*with some soft tissue intact;
usually bones are only preserved
in a fragile state. Mummification
is only a pause in disintegration
and is not true fossilization.*

FREEZING
This Siberian mammoth's hair
(right) *was preserved in
permafrost until recently. Once
thawed, it will decay unless
action is taken, but the hair is
relatively durable.*

TAR AND SAND
*A mixture of tar and sand has
embalmed this beetle* (left). *This
could be stable for thousands, but
not millions, of years.*

LIMESTONE TOMB
*The completeness of this
fragile crinoid, entombed in
limestone* (left), *suggests
that the calcareous nodule
encasing it formed soon
after death.*

PYRITIZATION
*The shell and cham-
bers of this ammonite*
(right) *were replaced
by iron pyrite. This is
often unstable in moist
air, so it must be stored
in very dry conditions.*

GEOLOGICAL TIME CHART

THE PLANET EARTH was formed 4,600 million years ago, with life present for at least 3,850 million years. Although multicellular life appeared over 1,000 million years ago, remains from that period are scarce. The first organisms with hard parts, allowing fossils to become relatively common, appeared about 550 million years ago. Geological time is divided into periods, usually named after the area where the rocks from that period were first exposed: for example, Jurassic is named after the Jura Mountains between France and Switzerland; Devonian after the rocks in Devon, UK. These periods provide a framework which, while estimates of their actual age may alter quite dramatically, allow rocks and fossil remains to be correlated worldwide.

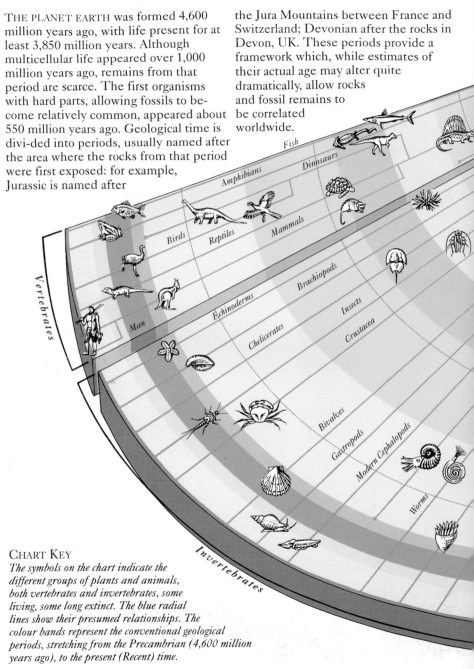

CHART KEY
The symbols on the chart indicate the different groups of plants and animals, both vertebrates and invertebrates, some living, some long extinct. The blue radial lines show their presumed relationships. The colour bands represent the conventional geological periods, stretching from the Precambrian (4,600 million years ago), to the present (Recent) time.

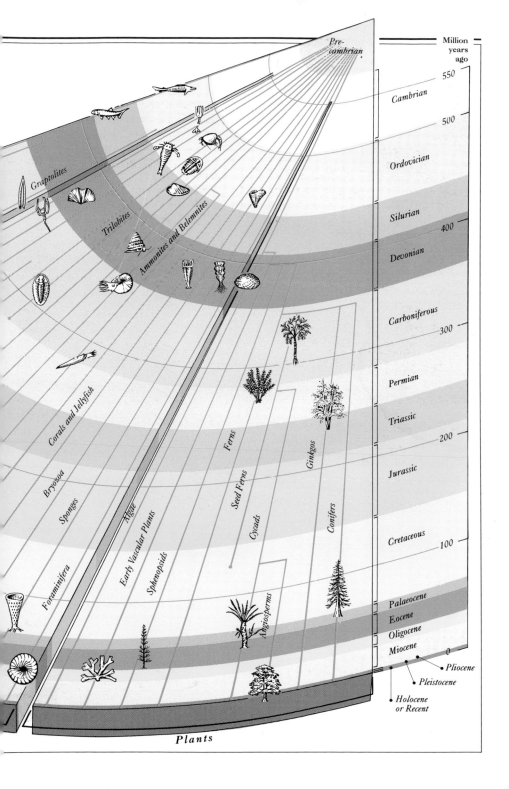

Million
years
ago

Pre-
cambrian

550

Cambrian

500

Ordovician

Silurian

400

Devonian

Carboniferous

300

Permian

Triassic

200

Jurassic

Cretaceous

100

Palaeocene
Eocene
Oligocene
Miocene

0

• *Pliocene*

• *Pleistocene*

• *Holocene*
   or Recent

Graptolites

Trilobites

Ammonites and Belemnites

Corals and Jellyfish

Bryozoa

Sponges

Algae

Early Vascular Plants

Sphenopsids

Ferns

Seed Ferns

Cycads

Ginkgos

Conifers

Angiosperms

Foraminifera

Plants

WHERE TO LOOK

YOU CAN FIND FOSSILS in most places where sedimentary rocks, such as clays, shales, and limestones, are exposed. Exposures of hard rock recover very slowly from collecting and can be disappointing. Artificial exposures, like road cuts or quarries, can be much more productive. Exposures of softer rocks can be good sites, provided they have not been too badly altered by metamorphosis. Inland sections in sands and clays tend to degrade rapidly, become overgrown, and lost. Here temporary exposures are valuable, along with continually eroding river or coastal sections.

Establishing the age of the rocks, with the aid of a geological map, will give you an idea of what sort of fossils to expect. Most libraries have geological guides, but remember that they may be out of date: many an hour has been spent looking for quarries that have been infilled and had houses built on them.

A visit to a local museum is often useful but up-to-date information from other collectors is better. Consider joining a natural history society or a rock and mineral club. They can often gain access to private localities. Most geological societies have a code of conduct relating to collecting, which it is advisable to follow. Wherever you decide to collect fossils, get permission from the authorities.

COASTAL SITES
Wave-washed cliffs and foreshore exposures (above) *are good places to search for fossils. Be aware of the state of the tide when you are rounding headlands. Wear a hard hat to protect you from small stones dislodged by startled seabirds, but remember it will not protect you from larger falling rocks.*

QUARRIES
Supervised parties are usually allowed to collect fossils in quarries (left), *but individuals may be discouraged. Check beforehand whether there are places, usually around active faces, that are out-of-bounds. Hard hats are a normal requirement. The staff often know where the best specimens may be found.*

TRILOBITE
Concoryphe (left), *an
eyeless deep-water genus,
was found in a hard
Cambrian mudstone.*

ARID TERRAINS
*Although erosion is slow in
deserts* (below) *and badlands,
the large areas of exposure that
exist can more than compensate.*

NATIONAL PARKS
*Hammering rocks is often discouraged in areas of
natural beauty and is illegal in most national
parks* (above)*, so please be sensitive. In this way,
fossils will still be there for future generations.*

RUGGED TERRAIN
*Fossils are often concentrated along particular
bedding planes; the combination of a potentially
interesting area and well-stratified rocks make an
ideal hunting ground* (below).

COLLECTING FOSSILS

COLLECTING FOSSILS is a very relaxing and intellectually stimulating hobby, but it is one that can often be frustrated by not having suitable field equipment. It is clearly impossible to cater for all eventualities, but the tools shown below form a basic selection that covers most situations. However, it is always better to leave a fossil in the field than to try to dig it out in a hurry with the wrong tools; this could damage a valuable scientific find.

Occasionally, equipment for plastering is required. You use this to protect fragile fossils before you remove them from the rock. Clean the fossil and expose it as much as possible. Cover it with layers of a separator (wet paper or cling film), followed by layers of plaster bandage. Once the plaster has been set, you can lift the fossil out of the rock face, and then repeat the process on the underside.

Your safety should be a primary concern. Hard hats, goggles, and gloves are essential. Finally, before you set out on an expedition, ask other collectors, who are familiar with the area you intend to visit, exactly what tools you will need.

SAFETY EQUIPMENT
Rocks can be sharp and dangerous. A hard hat is essential if collecting near high rock faces. Goggles will shield your eyes from dust and stones, and gloves will protect your hands.

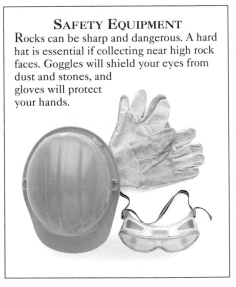

compass

map

long tape measure

MAP AND COMPASS
A geological map and a compass will help you to find fossil localities. Take a long tape measure to record the level of the bed in which you find fossils.

NOTEBOOK AND CAMERA
Record field notes, such as locality, type of rock, and fossils seen, in a sturdy notebook in waterproof ink. A photograph can also prove invaluable.

notebook and pens

hand lens

camera

FIELD TOOLS
For extracting fossils from hard rocks, a sturdy mallet and several guarded chisels are essential equipment. A pick-ended geological hammer is useful on most types of rock. Soft sediments are best tackled with a trowel or a spade.

mallet

geological hammer

trowel

guarded chisels

SIEVE
Use a sieve to separate fossils from sands and gravels. Usually one or two different meshes are needed to avoid losing small fossils.

PLASTERING
Protect fragile fossils in a plaster jacket before removing them from the rock. This prevents them from shattering.

plaster bandages

small brush

large brush

plastic sieve

SPADE
When you are searching for fossils in soft sediments, such as sands, silts, and clays, a narrow-bladed spade, rather than a conventional geological hammer, is the most useful tool for clearing an area around the fossil.

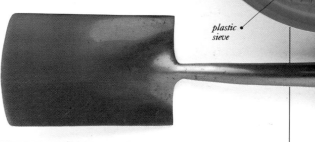

PREPARING YOUR COLLECTION

U NLIKE MOST OUTDOOR activities, fossil collecting does not end when you return from a field trip. A freshly collected specimen usually needs cleaning to remove any adherent matrix. This can be a very simple procedure, such as dusting sand off a specimen, or, it may involve using dilute acids to remove fossils encased in hard rock. For example, you will need acid to remove fossilized teeth from an unconsolidated matrix of shell debris. This is a tricky process that should be first attempted with the guidance of an expert.

Fragile fossils can be strengthened with a dilute solution of consolidant. Use a glue that can be removed, so that a joint can be repositioned later. Plastic boxes are ideal for storing small fossils. Open cardboard trays suit larger specimens. Use glass vials, microscope slides, or even gelatin capsules to house very small specimens.

Each fossil should be labelled. A good method of labelling fossils is to give each fossil a number, which corresponds with a card in a card-file index. The label or card should include the following data: the name, the lithological unit, and the rock's geological age. This should be followed by the locality, its map reference, the county or state, and the date it was collected. A fossil without these details is of little scientific value.

CLEANING FOSSILS
Use a variety of large and small brushes and dental probes to clean the specimen, and to remove small fragments of rock. Chip off more resistant matrix with a lightweight hammer and chisel or with an engraving tool. Handle small or fragile specimens very carefully, preferably with fine forceps. It is a good idea to protect them with a consolidant, so that they will not break up when they are handled or transported.

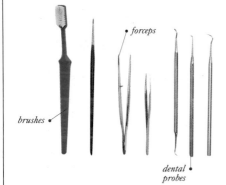

forceps

brushes

dental probes

sieve

dilute acid

engraver

sharks' teeth

SIEVING
Use a stack of stainless steel or brass sieves to separate samples containing small fossils, such as sharks' teeth, into different sizes. Brass sieves are soft and damaged by sea water, and so are not suitable for use in the field.

ORGANIC ACIDS
Use dilute organic acids, e.g. vinegar, to remove the surplus matrix from a calcareous specimen. Practice the procedure on an unimportant fossil first, to avoid damaging a valuable specimen.

plastic boxes

organized
fossil collection

INDEXING

*Store your fossils in individual plastic boxes or
shallow cardboard trays. Label each specimen
carefully. Keep a set of duplicate records in a card-
file system or on computer disc; include details of
the preservatives, glues, and hardeners used.*

card-file
index

labels

computer
disc

MICROSCOPE

*A binocular microscope is useful for
sorting small fossils from a sieved residue, or
examining details of large specimens.*

FROM HOBBY TO SCIENCE

BEGINNERS NORMALLY START by collecting any fossil that comes their way. This is not a bad idea, as there is a lot to learn about the hobby. After a while, however, most collectors specialize in a particular group of fossils, such as trilobites, ammonites, or plant fossils, or perhaps an age or locality.

Initially, most collectors tend to regard fossils merely as objects that are attractive in their own right, a pleasure to admire and own. With time and experience, the specimens themselves become less important and collectors soon realize that their true value lies in the scientific information they represent. Donating specimens to a local or national museum collection is one way a fossil collector can repay any help that he or she has received from museum staff in the past; most museums rely very heavily on the generosity of amateur collectors.

It is no exaggeration to say that palaeontology is one of the few sciences where an amateur is able make a significant contribution to the state of knowledge – indeed, this is probably one of its major attractions as a hobby.

NATIONAL MUSEUMS
These often have an identification service, and good regional and national exhibits of fossils (left), allowing collectors to make their own determinations. Only the best of a vast collection is on display, so try not to be discouraged if your fossils don't quite match in quality. The museum shop will usually have a good selection of books on fossil identification.

LOCAL MUSEUMS
Most museum curators are happy to give advice, discuss the local geology, and help identify problem specimens (right). Their knowledge and enthusiasm has inspired many young collectors to pursue geology as a career. Local museums can also put you in touch with the nearest geological society.

EASY FIND
Shark's teeth are a favourite among fossil collectors. In rocks of the right age, they are quite easy to find.

ERYOPS
MEGALOCEPHALUS
COPE

Most fossil collectors dream of finding something new. This need not be a large and spectacular specimen, like a dinosaur; it is more often a small and apparently insignificant fossil. The skill, for the amateur palaeontologist, lies in recognizing something unusual. If it is a new species, a description is published in a scientific journal, accompanied by a photograph and details of the locality; a procedure that can take several years. The specimen must then be housed in a museum collection. This ensures that all those interested are able to study it. A private collection is not acceptable because it is not open to the public. Parting with a prize specimen can be difficult, but it is necessary if the full potential of the discovery is to be realized.

MUSEUM EXHIBIT
This giant amphibian (above) *is from the Permian of Texas, USA. Magnificent specimens like this, reconstructed by palaeontologists, are a feature of natural history museums worldwide.*

BUYING FOSSILS
You can purchase small fossils, such as molluscs and trilobites, quite cheaply in rock and mineral shops, or at fossil exhibitions. Fish, reptiles, and dinosaurs are also sold on the open market, but usually for considerable sums of money. This means that large vertebrate fossils are often placed out of the price range of most museums, and are, therefore, sadly, lost to the public.

REFERENCE BOOKS
Libraries may house old illustrated monographs. Palaeontology is one of the few branches of science in which something written over a century ago can still be relevant.

FOSSIL IDENTIFICATION KEY

THE FOSSIL RECORD is so vast that to give adequate coverage in a book this size is impossible. Nevertheless, typical examples of most of the more common groups of fossils have been illustrated here. In this way, even if a particular genus is not illustrated, a similar organism will be shown. Over the next eight pages, visual examples of each major group of fossils are given, along with a concise description and the pages of the book where the group is covered in detail. When attempting an identification, it is vital to relate the range of any fossil to the rock in which your particular specimen is found; for instance, you do not find trilobites in the Cretaceous, nor mammals in the Devonian. A look at the geological time chart on pages 14–15 will help you with this. The key is divided into three sections: invertebrates, vertebrates, and plants.

INVERTEBRATES

FORAMINIFERA

Small (some microscopic), multichambered, calcareous objects; either round, discoidal, or ovoid. Usually present in large numbers, they can be rock-forming.
Range Cambrian–Recent

Page: 32

Test of
NUMMULITES

WORMS

Burrows, tracks, or calcareous tubes; usually spiral, cemented to objects. Can be confused with teredinid tubes *(p.111)*, scaphopods *(p.114)*, or corals *(p.50)*.
Range Cambrian–Recent

Tube of
PROLISERPULA

Tubes of
ROTULARIA

Pages: 40–41

SPONGES AND BRYOZOANS

Composed of calcite, silica, or as an outline on a bedding plane. Shaped more like a plant than an animal; irregular, often branching, tree-like; size variable. Sponges are generally thick-walled, with a featureless or coarsely ornamented surface. Bryozoa are usually thin-walled with a delicate pore network; they can encrust other fossils or pebbles. They can be confused with corals *(p.50)* or calcareous algae *(pp.286–287)*.
Range (sponges) Cambrian–Recent
Range (bryozoa) Ordovician–Recent

Skeleton of
RHIZOPOTERION

Pages: 33–39

Skeleton of
RAPHIDONEMA

Skeleton of
CONSTELLARIA

TRACE FOSSILS AND PROBLEMATICA

These encompass tracks, trails, borings, and burrows. Generally they are radiating, feeding, or tubular burrow structures made by worms, arthropods, echinoids, molluscs, or they are walking tracks of arthropods. Terrestrial, shallow lake sediments may show regularly spaced depressions made by "footprints". The systematic position of problematicans is uncertain because they are either poorly preserved or they resemble no modern fossil group.
Range Precambrian–Recent

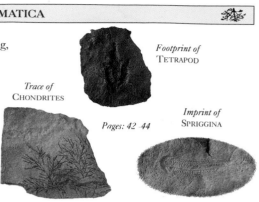

Trace of
CHONDRITES

Footprint of
TETRAPOD

Imprint of
SPRIGGINA

Pages: 42–44

GRAPTOLITES

These are impressions on rocks resembling watch springs, fretsaw blades, or meshwork. "Teeth" may be on one or both sides of stipe, which may be single or multiple. Graptolites may be confused with some plant remains *(pp.286–311)*, or bryozoa *(p.37–41)*, or an oblique section of crinoid stem *(p.168)*.
Range Ordovician–Carboniferous

Skeleton of
RETIOLITES

Pages: 45–49

Skeleton of
DIDYMOGRAPTUS

Skeleton of
PHYLLOGRAPTUS

CORALS

Shapes are very variable: horn-like, tube-like, or tree-like. The skeleton is calcareous. There are one or many calices; each individual calice is divided by a series of radial plates giving a star-like appearance. Calices may be closely abutted or laterally fused in meandering chains (like brain coral, *p.54*). The size of the colony can vary from less than a centimetre to several metres. They can be confused with encrusting bryozoa *(p.36)*, calcareous algae *(p.286)*, serpulid worm tubes *(p.40)*, or sponges *(p.33)*.
Range Ordovician–Recent

Colony of
COLPOPHYLLIA

Pages: 50–55

Colony of
FAVOSITES

Calice of
TRACHYPHYLLIA

ARTHROPODS

Arthropods have segmented bodies with a differentiated anterior end. The body is covered by a cuticle, or shell, that acts as an external skeleton (exoskeleton). The exoskeleton is sometimes strengthened by calcium carbonate or calcium phosphate. Arthropods have a variable number of appendages (legs), which are specialized into locomotory, sensory, or feeding elements. Moulting is a common feature of arthropods – otherwise their growth would be constrained by the external cuticle. Arthropods include the trilobites, the Crustacea (crabs, lobsters, barnacles, and shrimps), the chelicerates (king crabs, scorpions, and spiders), and the Uniramia (millipedes and insects).

TRILOBITES
These possess a flattened, mineralized, calcium carbonate shell, and are preserved in three dimensions or as an impression. The eyes are often fragmented. The thorax may segment.
Range Cambrian–Permian

Internal mould of
OLENELLUS

Pages: 56–65

Exoskeleton of
PHACOPS

CHELICERATES
The body is divided into a fused head, thorax, and abdomen. They can be confused with some trilobites and insects. Rarely found as fossils.
Range Cambrian–Recent

Imprint of
MESOLIMULUS

Pages: 73–75

Body of
DOLOMEDES

CRUSTACEA
Usually the ornamented phosphatic carapace is preserved; sometimes limb fragments, calcareous plates, or bivalved shells, are found.
Range Cambrian–Recent

Imprint of
HYMENOCARIS
Pages: 66–72

Exoskeleton of
ARCHAEOGERYON

INSECTS
These are divided into head, thorax, and abdomen. The adults have six legs and sometimes wings.
Range Devonian–Recent

Exoskeleton of
HYDROPHILUS
Pages: 76–78

Imprint of
PETALURA

BRACHIOPODS

The shells have two symmetrical, calcareous, or chitinous, dissimilar valves. One valve usually bears a hole (pedicle foramen), through which it is attached to the substrate. They are common in older rocks, often in large "nests" of a single species.
Range Cambrian–Recent

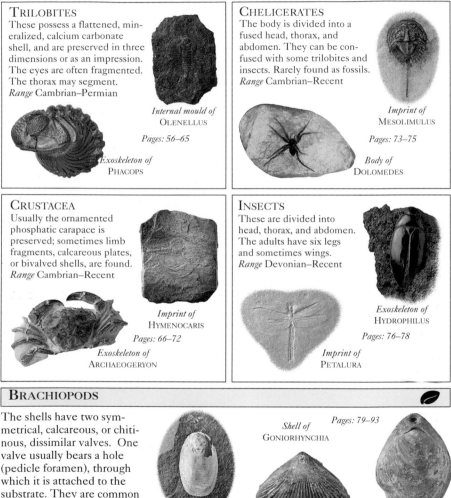

Shell of *Pages: 79–93*
GONIORHYNCHIA

Shell of
LINGULA

Shell of
TEREBRATULA

MOLLUSCS

Molluscs are a very diverse group that includes the chitons, scaphopods, bivalves, gastropods, and cephalopods. Nearly all molluscs have calcium-carbonate shells; only a few genera of gastropods, cephalopods, and nudibranchs lack this. The soft body is rarely preserved, so molluscs are classified by their shell structure. Most are marine; only a few families of bivalve and gastropod have entered fresh water. Some gastropods have become air breathing and colonized the land. They can be filter feeders (most bivalves), herbivores (some gastropods), carnivores (gastropods, cephalopods). One major group, the ammonoids, became extinct at the end of the Cretaceous.

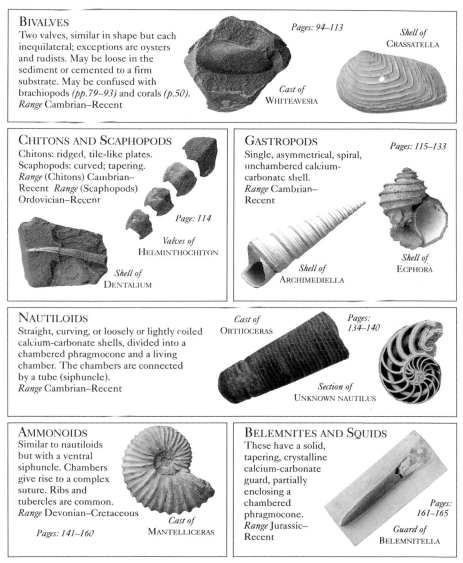

BIVALVES
Two valves, similar in shape but each inequilateral; exceptions are oysters and rudists. May be loose in the sediment or cemented to a firm substrate. May be confused with brachiopods *(pp.79–93)* and corals *(p.50).*
Range Cambrian–Recent

Pages: 94–113

Cast of WHITEAVESIA

Shell of CRASSATELLA

CHITONS AND SCAPHOPODS
Chitons: ridged, tile-like plates. Scaphopods: curved; tapering.
Range (Chitons) Cambrian–Recent *Range* (Scaphopods) Ordovician–Recent

Page: 114

Valves of HELMINTHOCHITON

Shell of DENTALIUM

GASTROPODS
Single, asymmetrical, spiral, unchambered calcium-carbonate shell.
Range Cambrian–Recent

Pages: 115–133

Shell of ARCHIMEDIELLA

Shell of ECPHORA

NAUTILOIDS
Straight, curving, or loosely or lightly coiled calcium-carbonate shells, divided into a chambered phragmocone and a living chamber. The chambers are connected by a tube (siphuncle).
Range Cambrian–Recent

Cast of ORTHOCERAS

Pages: 134–140

Section of UNKNOWN NAUTILUS

AMMONOIDS
Similar to nautiloids but with a ventral siphuncle. Chambers give rise to a complex suture. Ribs and tubercles are common.
Range Devonian–Cretaceous

Pages: 141–160

Cast of MANTELLICERAS

BELEMNITES AND SQUIDS
These have a solid, tapering, crystalline calcium-carbonate guard, partially enclosing a chambered phragmocone.
Range Jurassic–Recent

Pages: 161–165

Guard of BELEMNITELLA

ECHINODERMS ✦

The echinoderms include the echinoids (sea urchins), holothuroids (sea cucumbers), asteroids (starfish), crinoids (sea lilies), as well as the extinct blastoids, cystoids, and carpoids. All have five-rayed symmetry except for some echinoids and carpoids. They possess a complex water vascular system that operates a network of multi-functional tube feet. All are restricted to fully marine environments and thus act as marine indicators. Most possess solid calcite skeletons that fall apart on death; crinoidal debris can be so abundant as to be rock forming *(see p.168)*. Some irregular echinoids *(see Micraster p.185)* have evolved in a manner which makes it possible for them to be used as zone fossils.

CRINOIDS

Comprise a columnar stem, head (or calyx), and arms (pinnules); some species are stemless. On death, they usually disintegrate to isolated calyx ossicles and round, pentagonal, or star-shaped, crystalline-calcite stem segments.
Range Cambrian–Recent

Calyx of MARSUPITES

Pages: 166–174

Calyx of CYATHOCRINITES

ECHINOIDS

The shell or test is composed of thin, loosely cemented, calcite plates. The test may be subspherical and have five-rayed symmetry, or heart-shaped, or dorso-ventrally flattened with a bilateral symmetry (characterized by irregular echinoids). Plates bear spines that may be short and bristle-like or large and club-shaped.
Range Ordovician–Recent

Test of HEMICIDARIS

Pages: 175–185

Test of HEMIASTER

ASTEROIDS

Pages: 186–188

These are five-sided, with margins edged with solid calcitic blocks (ossicles). Occasionally preserved as whole, articulated specimens; more usually found as isolated ossicles.
Range Ordovician–Recent

Cast of TROPIDASTER

OPHIUROIDS

Page: 189

These small, individual ossicles are common in sieved residues; articulated specimens are rare. The central disk of calcite plates has five, snake-like arms. They are common in deep-water sediments.
Range Ordovician–Recent

Skeleton of PALAEOCOMA

BLASTOIDS

Usually intact, compact calyx.
Range Ordovician–Permian

Page: 190

Calyx of PENTREMITES

CYSTOIDS

Short stem, calyx of many small, irregular plates.
Range Cambrian–Permian

Pages: 191–192

Calyx and stem of LEPADOCRINITES

CARPOIDS

Stem short, asymmetrical calyx of small polygonal plates, no arms.

Range Cambrian–Devonian

Page: 193

Calyx of COTHURNOCYSTIS

VERTEBRATES

FISH

Fish are a very diverse group of marine and freshwater vertebrates. The group includes the jawless agnathans, the armoured placoderms, the cartilaginous sharks, rays, and chimaeroids, the spiny acanthodians, and the modern bony fish. All fish possess segmented body musculature, a brain, spinal cord, notochord, terminal mouth, hollow gut, and pharyngeal perforations (usually known as gills). Paired sense organs for smell, sight, balance, and electric fields are also characteristics common to all. The body is usually covered with scales or denticles that may fuse into armoured plates. They all have paired pelvic and pectoral fins, unpaired dorsal and anal fins, and a post-anal tail.

AGNATHANS

Jawless and covered with fine scales. The head may be encased in an armoured shell of fused scales.
Range Late Cambrian–Late Devonian

Head shield of PTERASPIS

Pages: 194–195

PLACODERMS

Heavily armoured with large pectoral fins and sometimes dorsal fin spines. Some have paired bony plates in jaws.
Range Early Devonian–Early Carboniferous

Pages: 196–197

Skeleton of BOTHRIOLEPIS

CHONDRICHTHYANS

Skeletons of sharks, rays, and chimaeroids are rarely preserved articulated. Usually teeth, tooth plates, placoid scales, fin spines, and calcified vertebrae are found. Sharks' teeth have enameloid crowns.
Range Late Silurian–Recent

Pages: 198–207

Tooth of PTYCHODUS

Tooth of STRIATOLAMIA

ACANTHODIANS

Found as isolated scales, teeth, and ornamented fin spines. Fin spines can be confused with those of a shark. Teeth lack enamel.
Range Late Silurian–Early Permian

Page: 208

Skeleton of DIPLACANTHUS

OSTEICHTHYANS

These are found as teeth, bones, scales, fin spines, and otoliths.
Range Late Silurian–Recent

Otolith of CENTROBERYX

Scales of LEPIDOTUS

Pages: 209–220

AMPHIBIANS

The bones are solid or hollow; the skull is composed of fused bony plates. The teeth are simple with no roots. Vertebrae may be unitary or multipartite and have neural canals. Limb bones may bear a variable number of digits.
Range Late Devonian–Recent.

Pages: 221–224

Skeleton of RANA

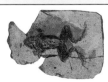

REPTILES

ANAPSIDS

Bones are solid; skulls are without secondary openings. *Range* Early Carboniferous–Recent

Pages: 225–230

Carapace of TRIONYX

DIAPSIDS

Limb bones are usually hollow. Teeth are enamelled with single, long root, set in sockets or fixed to jaws; skulls may be massive and ornamented (crocodiles), or lightly built and loosely ornamented (snakes). Dermal armour, when present, is usually ornate. *Range* Late Carboniferous–Recent

Teeth of LEIODON

Pages: 231–244

Skull of DIPLOCYNODON

DIAPSIDS (DINOSAURS)

Bones are solid, or thick-walled and hollow. Skull is lightly built with fixed quadrate bones; enamelled teeth lie in deep sockets. Hip socket is perforated; head of thigh bone is angled inwards. *Range* Late Triassic–Cretaceous

Jaw of DASPLETOSAURUS

Skull of HETERODONTOSAURUS

Pages: 245–254

Tooth of JOBARIA

SYNAPSIDS

Bones are solid, vertebrae biconcave, neural canal is present. Skull is often massive. Teeth differ. *Range* Late Carboniferous–Jurassic

Pages: 255–257

Skull of CYNOGNATHUS

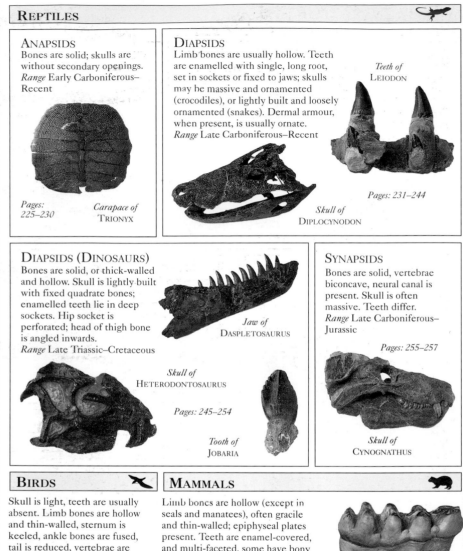

BIRDS

Skull is light, teeth are usually absent. Limb bones are hollow and thin-walled, sternum is keeled, ankle bones are fused, tail is reduced, vertebrae are saddle-shaped with neural canal. *Range* Late Jurassic–Recent

Limb bone of AEPYORNIS

Pages: 258–262

MAMMALS

Limb bones are hollow (except in seals and manatees), often gracile and thin-walled; epiphyseal plates present. Teeth are enamel-covered, and multi-faceted, some have bony roots; incisors, canines, premolars, and molars present. Skull may bear horns or antlers. Lower jaw is a single bone. *Range* Late Triassic–Recent

Pages: 263–285

Tooth of TETRALOPHODON

Skull roof of BISON

PLANTS

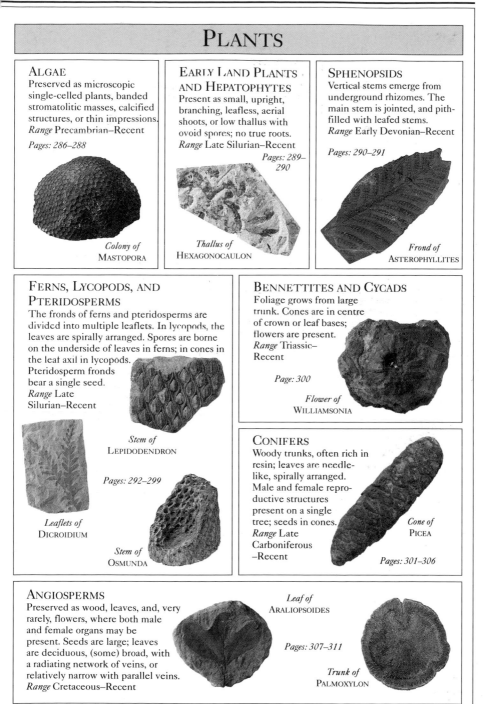

ALGAE
Preserved as microscopic single-celled plants, banded stromatolitic masses, calcified structures, or thin impressions.
Range Precambrian–Recent

Pages: 286–288

Colony of
MASTOPORA

EARLY LAND PLANTS AND HEPATOPHYTES
Present as small, upright, branching, leafless, aerial shoots, or low thallus with ovoid spores; no true roots.
Range Late Silurian–Recent

Pages: 289–290

Thallus of
HEXAGONOCAULON

SPHENOPSIDS
Vertical stems emerge from underground rhizomes. The main stem is jointed, and pith-filled with leafed stems.
Range Early Devonian–Recent

Pages: 290–291

Frond of
ASTEROPHYLLITES

FERNS, LYCOPODS, AND PTERIDOSPERMS
The fronds of ferns and pteridosperms are divided into multiple leaflets. In lycopods, the leaves are spirally arranged. Spores are borne on the underside of leaves in ferns; in cones in the leaf axil in lycopods. Pteridosperm fronds bear a single seed.
Range Late Silurian–Recent

Stem of
LEPIDODENDRON

Pages: 292–299

Leaflets of
DICROIDIUM

Stem of
OSMUNDA

BENNETTITES AND CYCADS
Foliage grows from large trunk. Cones are in centre of crown or leaf bases; flowers are present.
Range Triassic–Recent

Page: 300

Flower of
WILLIAMSONIA

CONIFERS
Woody trunks, often rich in resin; leaves are needle-like, spirally arranged. Male and female reproductive structures present on a single tree; seeds in cones.
Range Late Carboniferous –Recent

Cone of
PICEA

Pages: 301–306

ANGIOSPERMS
Preserved as wood, leaves, and, very rarely, flowers, where both male and female organs may be present. Seeds are large; leaves are deciduous, (some) broad, with a radiating network of veins, or relatively narrow with parallel veins.
Range Cretaceous–Recent

Leaf of
ARALIOPSOIDES

Pages: 307–311

Trunk of
PALMOXYLON

INVERTEBRATES

FORAMINIFERA

F ORAMINIFERANS ARE SMALL, single-celled organisms belonging to the kingdom Protista. Some species secrete a shell, called a test, made of calcium carbonate or (less commonly) chitin. Others construct a test by sticking together particles of sand and debris. Most species live in the sea: planktonic foraminiferans float in the surface waters of the oceans, their dead tests drifting down to the sea bed; benthonic foraminiferans live in or on the sea bottom. Both types occur in large numbers, and rocks may form from their remains. The few large species live in warm, shallow waters.

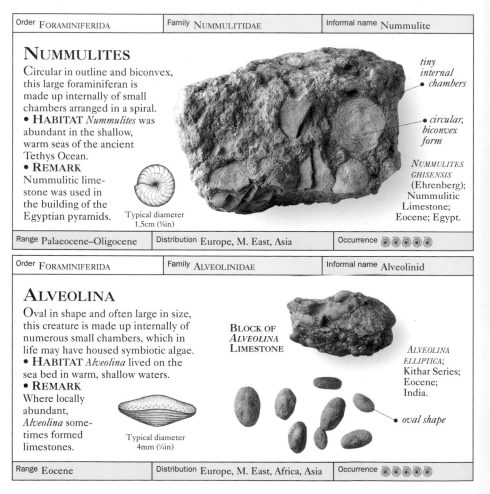

Order FORAMINIFERIDA	Family NUMMULITIDAE	Informal name Nummulite

NUMMULITES
Circular in outline and biconvex, this large foraminiferan is made up internally of small chambers arranged in a spiral.
• HABITAT *Nummulites* was abundant in the shallow, warm seas of the ancient Tethys Ocean.
• REMARK Nummulitic lime-stone was used in the building of the Egyptian pyramids.

Typical diameter
1.5cm (⅝in)

tiny internal chambers

circular, biconvex form

NUMMULITES GHISENSIS (Ehrenberg); Nummulitic Limestone; Eocene; Egypt.

Range Palaeocene–Oligocene	Distribution Europe, M. East, Asia	Occurrence

Order FORAMINIFERIDA	Family ALVEOLINIDAE	Informal name Alveolinid

ALVEOLINA
Oval in shape and often large in size, this creature is made up internally of numerous small chambers, which in life may have housed symbiotic algae.
• HABITAT *Alveolina* lived on the sea bed in warm, shallow waters.
• REMARK Where locally abundant, *Alveolina* some-times formed limestones.

BLOCK OF
ALVEOLINA
LIMESTONE

Typical diameter
4mm (¼in)

ALVEOLINA ELLIPTICA; Kithar Series; Eocene; India.

oval shape

Range Eocene	Distribution Europe, M. East, Africa, Asia	Occurrence

SPONGES

S PONGES ARE PRIMITIVE, sedentary, aquatic animals. Water passes in through their many surface pores to the central cavity of the sac-like body, and out through larger holes. The skeleton, where present, is made up of needle-like spicules, and is either calcareous, siliceous, or horny. Sponges occur as fossils from Cambrian times onwards, and were abundant in the Cretaceous. Stromatoporoids are also believed to be sponges, but archaeocyathids are now thought to be an independent phylum.

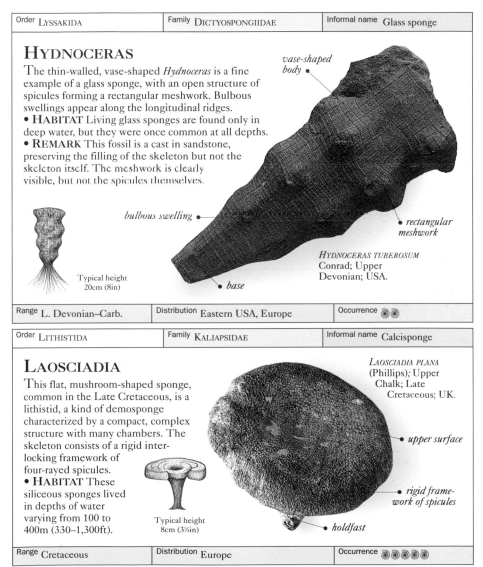

Order LYSSAKIDA	Family DICTYOSPONGIIDAE	Informal name Glass sponge

HYDNOCERAS

The thin-walled, vase-shaped *Hydnoceras* is a fine example of a glass sponge, with an open structure of spicules forming a rectangular meshwork. Bulbous swellings appear along the longitudinal ridges.
• **HABITAT** Living glass sponges are found only in deep water, but they were once common at all depths.
• **REMARK** This fossil is a cast in sandstone, preserving the filling of the skeleton but not the skeleton itself. The meshwork is clearly visible, but not the spicules themselves.

vase-shaped body •

bulbous swelling •

Typical height 20cm (8in)

• rectangular meshwork

HYDNOCERAS TUBEROSUM Conrad; Upper Devonian; USA.

• base

Range L. Devonian–Carb.	Distribution Eastern USA, Europe	Occurrence

Order LITHISTIDA	Family KALIAPSIDAE	Informal name Calcisponge

LAOSCIADIA

This flat, mushroom-shaped sponge, common in the Late Cretaceous, is a lithistid, a kind of demosponge characterized by a compact, complex structure with many chambers. The skeleton consists of a rigid interlocking framework of four-rayed spicules.
• **HABITAT** These siliceous sponges lived in depths of water varying from 100 to 400m (330–1,300ft).

LAOSCIADIA PLANA (Phillips); Upper Chalk; Late Cretaceous; UK.

• upper surface

• rigid framework of spicules

Typical height 8cm (3¼in)

• holdfast

Range Cretaceous	Distribution Europe	Occurrence

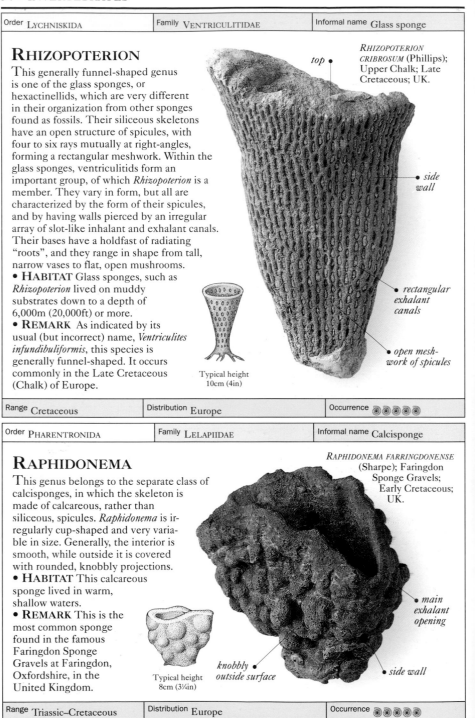

Order LYCHNISKIDA	Family VENTRICULITIDAE	Informal name Glass sponge

RHIZOPOTERION

This generally funnel-shaped genus is one of the glass sponges, or hexactinellids, which are very different in their organization from other sponges found as fossils. Their siliceous skeletons have an open structure of spicules, with four to six rays mutually at right-angles, forming a rectangular meshwork. Within the glass sponges, ventriculitids form an important group, of which *Rhizopoterion* is a member. They vary in form, but all are characterized by the form of their spicules, and by having walls pierced by an irregular array of slot-like inhalant and exhalant canals. Their bases have a holdfast of radiating "roots", and they range in shape from tall, narrow vases to flat, open mushrooms.
• HABITAT Glass sponges, such as *Rhizopoterion* lived on muddy substrates down to a depth of 6,000m (20,000ft) or more.
• REMARK As indicated by its usual (but incorrect) name, *Ventriculites infundibuliformis*, this species is generally funnel-shaped. It occurs commonly in the Late Cretaceous (Chalk) of Europe.

RHIZOPOTERION CRIBROSUM (Phillips); Upper Chalk; Late Cretaceous; UK.

top •

• side wall

• rectangular exhalant canals

• open meshwork of spicules

Typical height 10cm (4in)

Range Cretaceous	Distribution Europe	Occurrence

Order PHARENTRONIDA	Family LELAPIIDAE	Informal name Calcisponge

RAPHIDONEMA

This genus belongs to the separate class of calcisponges, in which the skeleton is made of calcareous, rather than siliceous, spicules. *Raphidonema* is irregularly cup-shaped and very variable in size. Generally, the interior is smooth, while outside it is covered with rounded, knobbly projections.
• HABITAT This calcareous sponge lived in warm, shallow waters.
• REMARK This is the most common sponge found in the famous Faringdon Sponge Gravels at Faringdon, Oxfordshire, in the United Kingdom.

RAPHIDONEMA FARRINGDONENSE (Sharpe); Faringdon Sponge Gravels; Early Cretaceous; UK.

• main exhalant opening

knobbly • outside surface

• side wall

Typical height 8cm (3¼in)

Range Triassic–Cretaceous	Distribution Europe	Occurrence

Order STROMATOPOROIDEA	Family ACTINOSTROMATIDAE	Informal name Stromatoporoid

ACTINOSTROMA

Actinostroma is a typical calcareous, reef-building, blob-like stromatoporoid. Although enigmatic, the genus is thought by some to be the ancestor of modern sclero-sponges. When studied in thin section, it shows a fine structure of thin, concentric layers and radial pillars.
• **HABITAT** This genus commonly lived on, and formed, reefs.
• **REMARK** These organisms were important rock formers, particularly in the Silurian and Devonian.

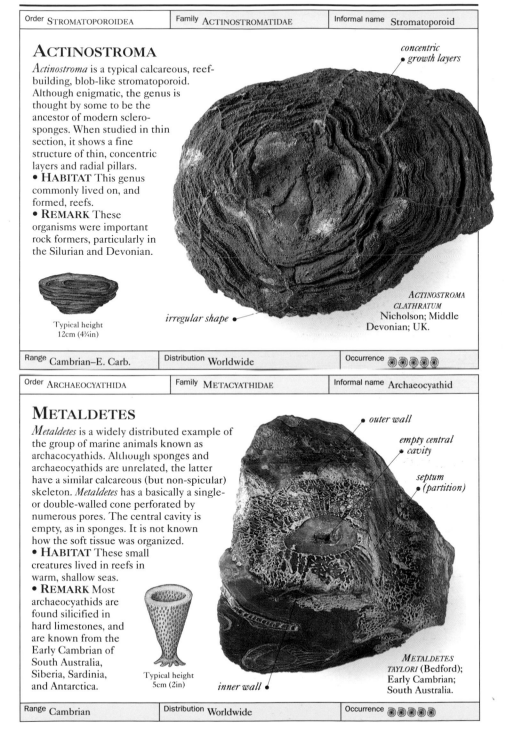

concentric
• *growth layers*

ACTINOSTROMA CLATHRATUM
Nicholson; Middle Devonian; UK.

irregular shape •

Typical height
12cm (4¾in)

Range Cambrian–E. Carb.	Distribution Worldwide	Occurrence

Order ARCHAEOCYATHIDA	Family METACYATHIDAE	Informal name Archaeocyathid

METALDETES

Metaldetes is a widely distributed example of the group of marine animals known as archaeocyathids. Although sponges and archaeocyathids are unrelated, the latter have a similar calcareous (but non-spicular) skeleton. *Metaldetes* has a basically a single- or double-walled cone perforated by numerous pores. The central cavity is empty, as in sponges. It is not known how the soft tissue was organized.
• **HABITAT** These small creatures lived in reefs in warm, shallow seas.
• **REMARK** Most archaeocyathids are found silicified in hard limestones, and are known from the Early Cambrian of South Australia, Siberia, Sardinia, and Antarctica.

• *outer wall*

empty central
• *cavity*

septum
• *(partition)*

METALDETES TAYLORI (Bedford);
Early Cambrian;
South Australia.

Typical height
5cm (2in)

inner wall •

Range Cambrian	Distribution Worldwide	Occurrence

BRYOZOA

BRYOZOANS ARE colonial animals which resemble miniature corals but are more closely related to brachiopods. They range from the Ordovician to the present day. Most bryozoans live on the sea bed and secrete calcareous skeletons. Bryozoan colonies vary in shape – some are sheet-like encrustations on shells and stones, whereas others grow as small trees or net-like fronds. Each colony consists of a few to thousands of connected individuals (zooids). Each zooid has a tubular or box-shaped skeleton.

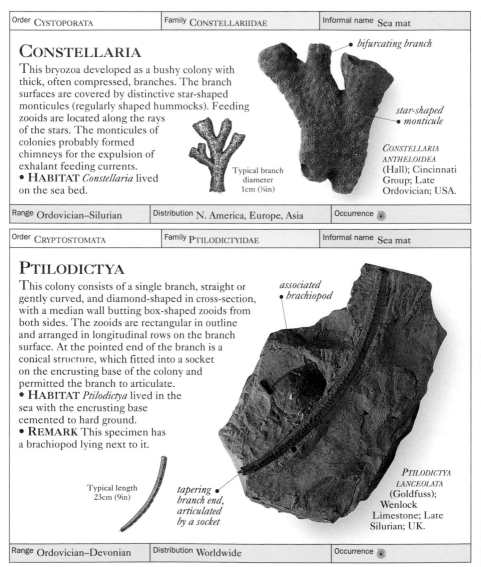

Order CYSTOPORATA	Family CONSTELLARIIDAE	Informal name Sea mat

CONSTELLARIA

This bryozoa developed as a bushy colony with thick, often compressed, branches. The branch surfaces are covered by distinctive star-shaped monticules (regularly shaped hummocks). Feeding zooids are located along the rays of the stars. The monticules of colonies probably formed chimneys for the expulsion of exhalant feeding currents.
• **HABITAT** *Constellaria* lived on the sea bed.

bifurcating branch

star-shaped monticule

Typical branch diameter 1cm (⅜in)

CONSTELLARIA ANTHELOIDEA (Hall); Cincinnati Group; Late Ordovician; USA.

Range Ordovician–Silurian	Distribution N. America, Europe, Asia	Occurrence ◉

Order CRYPTOSTOMATA	Family PTILODICTYIDAE	Informal name Sea mat

PTILODICTYA

This colony consists of a single branch, straight or gently curved, and diamond-shaped in cross-section, with a median wall butting box-shaped zooids from both sides. The zooids are rectangular in outline and arranged in longitudinal rows on the branch surface. At the pointed end of the branch is a conical structure, which fitted into a socket on the encrusting base of the colony and permitted the branch to articulate.
• **HABITAT** *Ptilodictya* lived in the sea with the encrusting base cemented to hard ground.
• **REMARK** This specimen has a brachiopod lying next to it.

associated brachiopod

Typical length 23cm (9in)

tapering branch end, articulated by a socket

PTILODICTYA LANCEOLATA (Goldfuss); Wenlock Limestone; Late Silurian; UK.

Range Ordovician–Devonian	Distribution Worldwide	Occurrence ◉

Order FENESTRATA	Family FENESTELLIDAE	Informal name Lace corals

FENESTELLA

This erect, net-like colony is formed of narrow, regularly-spaced, branches linked by dissepiments. The zooids are arranged in two rows along the branches, with apertures opening on one side only of the planar, folded, or conical colonies. The dissepiments lack zooids. Spinose outgrowths have been developed, especially near the colony base, and were sometimes barbed.

• HABITAT *Fenestella* and similar reticulate bryozoans lived by filtering food from self-generated water currents, which flowed in one direction through the holes in the colony.

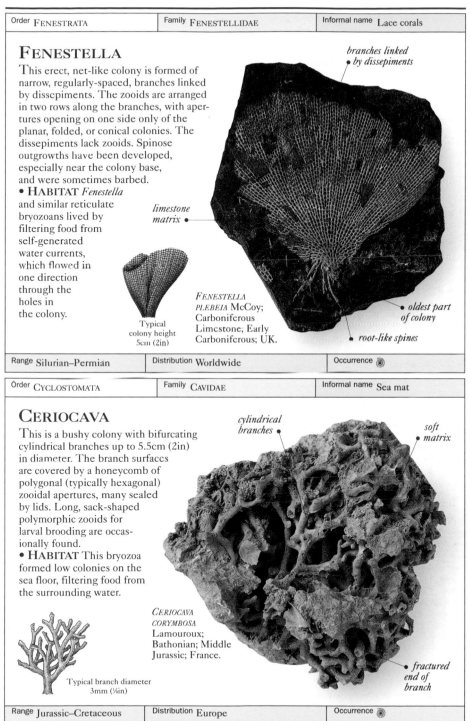

branches linked
• *by dissepiments*

*limestone
matrix* •

Typical
colony height
5cm (2in)

*FENESTELLA
PLEBEIA* McCoy;
Carboniferous
Limestone; Early
Carboniferous; UK.

• *oldest part
of colony*

• *root-like spines*

Range Silurian–Permian	Distribution Worldwide	Occurrence

Order CYCLOSTOMATA	Family CAVIDAE	Informal name Sea mat

CERIOCAVA

This is a bushy colony with bifurcating cylindrical branches up to 5.5cm (2in) in diameter. The branch surfaces are covered by a honeycomb of polygonal (typically hexagonal) zooidal apertures, many sealed by lids. Long, sack-shaped polymorphic zooids for larval brooding are occasionally found.

• HABITAT This bryozoa formed low colonies on the sea floor, filtering food from the surrounding water.

*cylindrical
branches* •

*soft
• matrix*

*CERIOCAVA
CORYMBOSA*
Lamouroux;
Bathonian; Middle
Jurassic; France.

Typical branch diameter
3mm (⅛in)

• *fractured
end of
branch*

Range Jurassic–Cretaceous	Distribution Europe	Occurrence

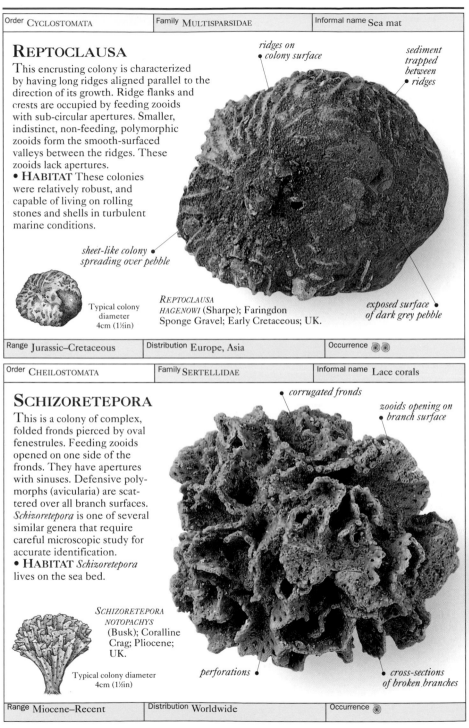

Order CYCLOSTOMATA	Family MULTISPARSIDAE	Informal name Sea mat

REPTOCLAUSA

This encrusting colony is characterized by having long ridges aligned parallel to the direction of its growth. Ridge flanks and crests are occupied by feeding zooids with sub-circular apertures. Smaller, indistinct, non-feeding, polymorphic zooids form the smooth-surfaced valleys between the ridges. These zooids lack apertures.
• **HABITAT** These colonies were relatively robust, and capable of living on rolling stones and shells in turbulent marine conditions.

ridges on colony surface

sediment trapped between ridges

sheet-like colony spreading over pebble

exposed surface of dark grey pebble

Typical colony diameter 4cm (1½in)

REPTOCLAUSA HAGENOWI (Sharpe); Faringdon Sponge Gravel; Early Cretaceous; UK.

Range Jurassic–Cretaceous	Distribution Europe, Asia	Occurrence

Order CHEILOSTOMATA	Family SERTELLIDAE	Informal name Lace corals

SCHIZORETEPORA

This is a colony of complex, folded fronds pierced by oval fenestrules. Feeding zooids opened on one side of the fronds. They have apertures with sinuses. Defensive polymorphs (avicularia) are scattered over all branch surfaces. *Schizoretepora* is one of several similar genera that require careful microscopic study for accurate identification.
• **HABITAT** *Schizoretepora* lives on the sea bed.

corrugated fronds

zooids opening on branch surface

SCHIZORETEPORA NOTOPACHYS (Busk); Coralline Crag; Pliocene; UK.

Typical colony diameter 4cm (1½in)

perforations

cross-sections of broken branches

Range Miocene–Recent	Distribution Worldwide	Occurrence

Order Not Applicable	Family Not Applicable	Informal name Bryozoan limestone

BRYOZOAN LIMESTONE

Some limestones consist predominantly
of fragments of the calcareous skeletons
of bryozoan colonies. Many different
bryozoan species may be present,
often accompanied by broken
mollusc shells and barnacles.
• HABITAT Bryozoan
limestones are especially
common in the shallow-
water deposits of the
Cenozoic Era. Today, they
can be found forming in
subtropical to cold-water
environments, but bryo-
zoan limestones are rarer
in the tropics, where
coral limestones arc found
in great abundance.

branch •
fragments

Width of rock specimen
11cm (4¼in)

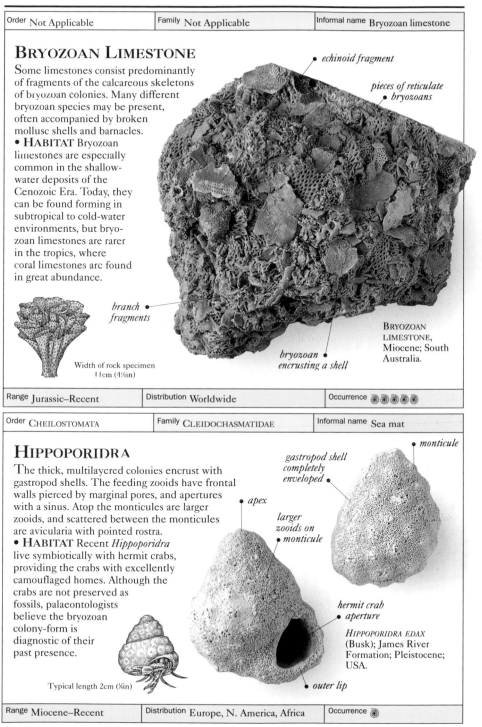

• echinoid fragment

pieces of reticulate
• bryozoans

BRYOZOAN
LIMESTONE,
Miocene; South
Australia.

bryozoan •
encrusting a shell

Range Jurassic–Recent	Distribution Worldwide	Occurrence ◉◉◉◉◉

Order CHEILOSTOMATA	Family CLEIDOCHASMATIDAE	Informal name Sea mat

HIPPOPORIDRA

The thick, multilayered colonies encrust with
gastropod shells. The feeding zooids have frontal
walls pierced by marginal pores, and apertures
with a sinus. Atop the monticules are larger
zooids, and scattered between the monticules
are avicularia with pointed rostra.
• HABITAT Recent *Hippoporidra*
live symbiotically with hermit crabs,
providing the crabs with excellently
camouflaged homes. Although the
crabs are not preserved as
fossils, palaeontologists
believe the bryozoan
colony-form is
diagnostic of their
past presence.

Typical length 2cm (¾in)

• monticule

gastropod shell
completely
enveloped •

• apex

larger
zooids on
• monticule

hermit crab
• aperture

HIPPOPORIDRA EDAX
(Busk); James River
Formation; Pleistocene;
USA.

• outer lip

Range Miocene–Recent	Distribution Europe, N. America, Africa	Occurrence ◉

WORMS

WORM IS A GENERAL NAME applied to representatives of various soft-bodied invertebrate groups. They include the platyhelminthes, nematodes, nemertines, acanthocephalans, annelids, and some hemichordates. Most are unknown or very rare in the fossil record. However, some members of the polychaeta group of segmented worms secrete a dwelling tube made of durable calcite, which is often found attached to fossil shells or pebbles. These are common fossils in certain Mesozoic and Cenozoic rocks.

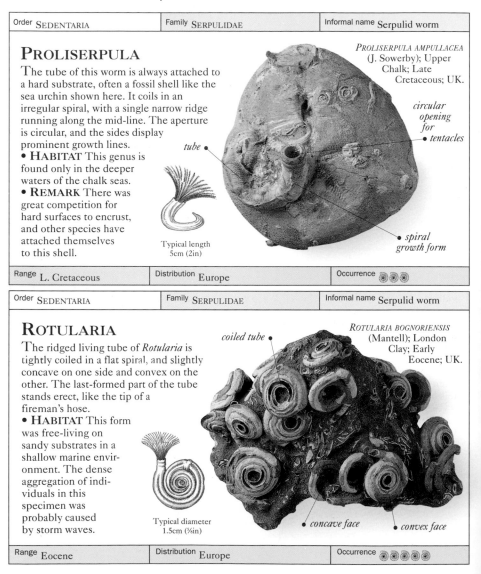

Order SEDENTARIA	Family SERPULIDAE	Informal name Serpulid worm

PROLISERPULA

The tube of this worm is always attached to a hard substrate, often a fossil shell like the sea urchin shown here. It coils in an irregular spiral, with a single narrow ridge running along the mid-line. The aperture is circular, and the sides display prominent growth lines.
• **HABITAT** This genus is found only in the deeper waters of the chalk seas.
• **REMARK** There was great competition for hard surfaces to encrust, and other species have attached themselves to this shell.

tube

Typical length 5cm (2in)

PROLISERPULA AMPULLACEA (J. Sowerby); Upper Chalk; Late Cretaceous; UK.

circular opening for tentacles

spiral growth form

Range L. Cretaceous	Distribution Europe	Occurrence ◉◉◉

Order SEDENTARIA	Family SERPULIDAE	Informal name Serpulid worm

ROTULARIA

The ridged living tube of *Rotularia* is tightly coiled in a flat spiral, and slightly concave on one side and convex on the other. The last-formed part of the tube stands erect, like the tip of a fireman's hose.
• **HABITAT** This form was free-living on sandy substrates in a shallow marine environment. The dense aggregation of individuals in this specimen was probably caused by storm waves.

coiled tube

Typical diameter 1.5cm (⅝in)

ROTULARIA BOGNORIENSIS (Mantell); London Clay; Early Eocene; UK.

concave face

convex face

Range Eocene	Distribution Europe	Occurrence ◉◉◉◉◉

Order SEDENTARIA	Family SERPULIDAE	Informal name Serpulid worm

SERPULA

The tube of this serpulid worm is elongated and rounded in cross-section, tapering slowly to a fine point. It may be gently curved or sharply bent, with a relatively thin wall, ornamented by irregular growth lines. It has a rounded aperture.
• HABITAT Although this genus was not cemented to the substrate, it was not actually mobile.

SERPULA INDISTINCTA (Fleming); Carboniferous Limestone; Early Carboniferous; Northern Ireland.

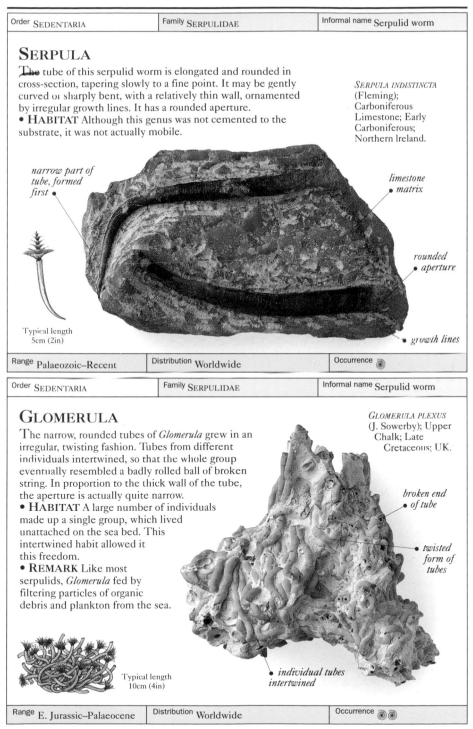

narrow part of tube, formed first •

limestone • matrix

rounded • aperture

Typical length 5cm (2in)

• growth lines

Range Palaeozoic–Recent	Distribution Worldwide	Occurrence

Order SEDENTARIA	Family SERPULIDAE	Informal name Serpulid worm

GLOMERULA

The narrow, rounded tubes of *Glomerula* grew in an irregular, twisting fashion. Tubes from different individuals intertwined, so that the whole group eventually resembled a badly rolled ball of broken string. In proportion to the thick wall of the tube, the aperture is actually quite narrow.
• HABITAT A large number of individuals made up a single group, which lived unattached on the sea bed. This intertwined habit allowed it this freedom.
• REMARK Like most serpulids, *Glomerula* fed by filtering particles of organic debris and plankton from the sea.

GLOMERULA PLEXUS (J. Sowerby); Upper Chalk; Late Cretaceous; UK.

broken end • of tube

• twisted form of tubes

Typical length 10cm (4in)

• individual tubes intertwined

Range E. Jurassic–Palaeocene	Distribution Worldwide	Occurrence

TRACE FOSSILS

T RACE FOSSILS ARE the remains of structures made by animals, preserved in sedimentary rock. They include tracks, trails, borings, and burrows. Since different organisms are able to make the same trace, trace fossils are classified by their shape, rather than by their constructor. Ichnogenera and ichnospecies, from the Greek word *ichnos* (trace), are the usual classifications, but fossils may also be classified by their cause, i.e. feeding, crawling, dwelling, etc., and hence fodinichnia, repichnia, dominichnia.

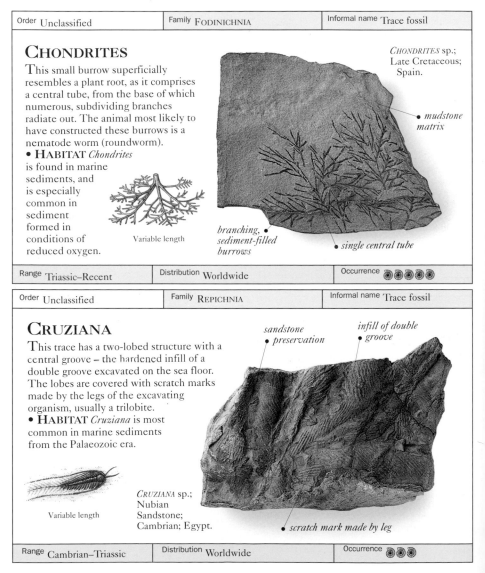

Order Unclassified	Family FODINICHNIA	Informal name Trace fossil

CHONDRITES

This small burrow superficially resembles a plant root, as it comprises a central tube, from the base of which numerous, subdividing branches radiate out. The animal most likely to have constructed these burrows is a nematode worm (roundworm).
• HABITAT *Chondrites* is found in marine sediments, and is especially common in sediment formed in conditions of reduced oxygen.

Variable length

CHONDRITES sp.; Late Cretaceous; Spain.

• *mudstone matrix*

branching, sediment-filled burrows •

• *single central tube*

Range Triassic–Recent	Distribution Worldwide	Occurrence ◉◉◉◉◉

Order Unclassified	Family REPICHNIA	Informal name Trace fossil

CRUZIANA

This trace has a two-lobed structure with a central groove – the hardened infill of a double groove excavated on the sea floor. The lobes are covered with scratch marks made by the legs of the excavating organism, usually a trilobite.
• HABITAT *Cruziana* is most common in marine sediments from the Palaeozoic era.

sandstone • *preservation*

infill of double • *groove*

Variable length

CRUZIANA sp.; Nubian Sandstone; Cambrian; Egypt.

• *scratch mark made by leg*

Range Cambrian–Triassic	Distribution Worldwide	Occurrence ◉◉◉

PROBLEMATICA

SOME FOSSILS CANNOT be placed into major groups of animals or plants with any certainty. Often this is because they represent only a small, obscure part of an organism, but there are others, from strata of the Late Precambrian age, that have completely preserved forms. These have been variously classified as worms, soft corals, jellyfish, etc. However, the true identity of these ancient fossils remains a subject of controversy – some may even be trace fossils – and they are best treated as Problematica.

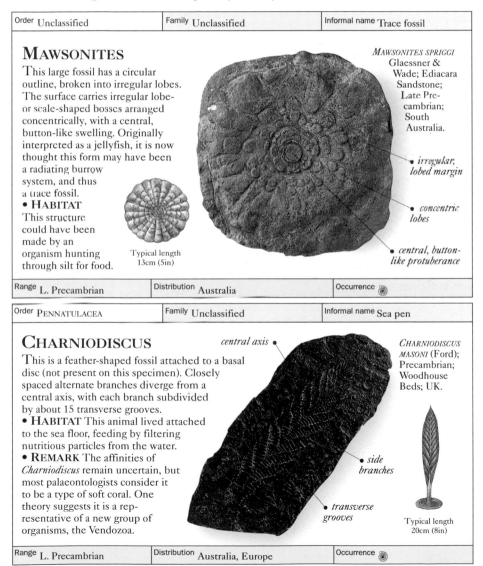

| Order Unclassified | Family Unclassified | Informal name Trace fossil |

MAWSONITES

This large fossil has a circular outline, broken into irregular lobes. The surface carries irregular lobe- or scale-shaped bosses arranged concentrically, with a central, button-like swelling. Originally interpreted as a jellyfish, it is now thought this form may have been a radiating burrow system, and thus a trace fossil.
• HABITAT This structure could have been made by an organism hunting through silt for food.

MAWSONITES SPRIGGI Glaessner & Wade; Ediacara Sandstone; Late Precambrian; South Australia.

• *irregular, lobed margin*
• *concentric lobes*
• *central, button-like protuberance*

Typical length 13cm (5in)

| Range L. Precambrian | Distribution Australia | Occurrence |

| Order PENNATULACEA | Family Unclassified | Informal name Sea pen |

CHARNIODISCUS

This is a feather-shaped fossil attached to a basal disc (not present on this specimen). Closely spaced alternate branches diverge from a central axis, with each branch subdivided by about 15 transverse grooves.
• HABITAT This animal lived attached to the sea floor, feeding by filtering nutritious particles from the water.
• REMARK The affinities of *Charniodiscus* remain uncertain, but most palaeontologists consider it to be a type of soft coral. One theory suggests it is a representative of a new group of organisms, the Vendozoa.

central axis
CHARNIODISCUS MASONI (Ford); Precambrian; Woodhouse Beds; UK.

• *side branches*
• *transverse grooves*

Typical length 20cm (8in)

| Range L. Precambrian | Distribution Australia, Europe | Occurrence |

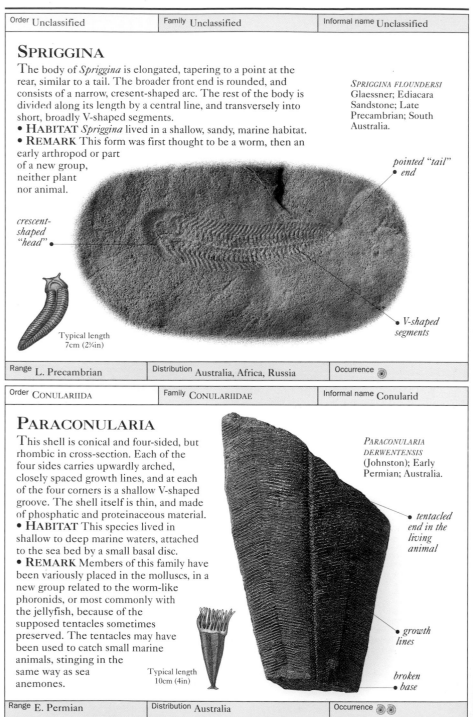

Order Unclassified	Family Unclassified	Informal name Unclassified

SPRIGGINA

The body of *Spriggina* is elongated, tapering to a point at the rear, similar to a tail. The broader front end is rounded, and consists of a narrow, cresent-shaped arc. The rest of the body is divided along its length by a central line, and transversely into short, broadly V-shaped segments.

• **HABITAT** *Spriggina* lived in a shallow, sandy, marine habitat.

• **REMARK** This form was first thought to be a worm, then an early arthropod or part of a new group, neither plant nor animal.

SPRIGGINA FLOUNDERSI Glaessner; Ediacara Sandstone; Late Precambrian; South Australia.

pointed "tail" • end

crescent-shaped "head" •

• V-shaped segments

Range L. Precambrian	Distribution Australia, Africa, Russia	Occurrence

Order CONULARIIDA	Family CONULARIIDAE	Informal name Conularid

PARACONULARIA

This shell is conical and four-sided, but rhombic in cross-section. Each of the four sides carries upwardly arched, closely spaced growth lines, and at each of the four corners is a shallow V-shaped groove. The shell itself is thin, and made of phosphatic and proteinaceous material.

• **HABITAT** This species lived in shallow to deep marine waters, attached to the sea bed by a small basal disc.

• **REMARK** Members of this family have been variously placed in the molluscs, in a new group related to the worm-like phoronids, or most commonly with the jellyfish, because of the supposed tentacles sometimes preserved. The tentacles may have been used to catch small marine animals, stinging in the same way as sea anemones.

PARACONULARIA DERWENTENSIS (Johnston); Early Permian; Australia.

• tentacled end in the living animal

• growth lines

broken • base

Typical length 10cm (4in)

Typical length 7cm (2¾in)

Range E. Permian	Distribution Australia	Occurrence

GRAPTOLITES

G RAPTOLITES ARE AN extinct group of colonial organisms that lived from the Cambrian to the Carboniferous. Their remains can be mistaken for fossil plants as they sometimes resemble fossilized twigs. Each colony had one or more branches (stipes), originating from an individual (sicula). Each subsequent individual was housed within a tubular structure (theca). Geologists find graptolites especially useful in dating rocks.

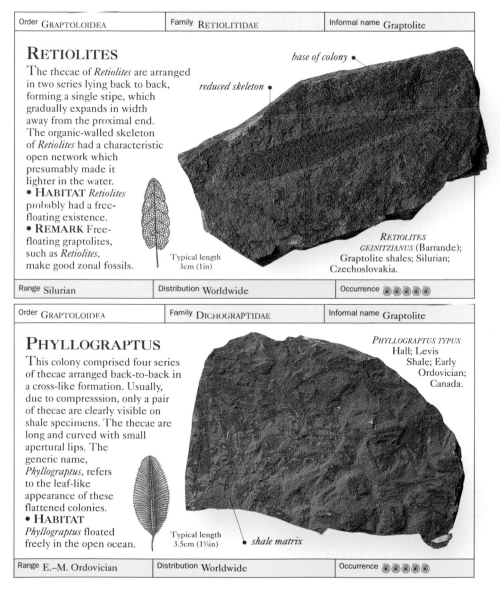

Order GRAPTOLOIDEA	Family RETIOLITIDAE	Informal name Graptolite

RETIOLITES

The thecae of *Retiolites* are arranged in two series lying back to back, forming a single stipe, which gradually expands in width away from the proximal end. The organic-walled skeleton of *Retiolites* had a characteristic open network which presumably made it lighter in the water.
• HABITAT *Retiolites* probably had a free-floating existence.
• REMARK Free-floating graptolites, such as *Retiolites*, make good zonal fossils.

base of colony •

reduced skeleton •

Typical length
3cm (1in)

RETIOLITES GEINITZIANUS (Barrande); Graptolite shales; Silurian; Czechoslovakia.

Range Silurian	Distribution Worldwide	Occurrence ⦿⦿⦿⦿⦿

Order GRAPTOLOIDEA	Family DICHOGRAPTIDAE	Informal name Graptolite

PHYLLOGRAPTUS

This colony comprised four series of thecae arranged back-to-back in a cross-like formation. Usually, due to compresssion, only a pair of thecae are clearly visible on shale specimens. The thecae are long and curved with small apertural lips. The generic name, *Phyllograptus*, refers to the leaf-like appearance of these flattened colonies.
• HABITAT *Phyllograptus* floated freely in the open ocean.

PHYLLOGRAPTUS TYPUS Hall; Levis Shale; Early Ordovician; Canada.

Typical length
3.5cm (1⅜in)

• *shale matrix*

Range E.–M. Ordovician	Distribution Worldwide	Occurrence ⦿⦿⦿⦿⦿

Order GRAPTOLOIDEA	Family DICHOGRAPTIDAE	Informal name Graptolite

EXPANSOGRAPTUS

These were small to large
graptolites with approximately
twenty to several hundred
thecae. Two stipes diverge from
the initial sicula, which is
distinguished by its dorsally
projecting nema (an extension
of the initial sicula) at the point
where the thecae of the two
stipes diverge. The thecae are
usually of relatively simple type,
tubular or with a small apertural
lip. The different species are
distinguished by the number of
thecae per centimetre, and the
width and shape of the stipes.
• HABITAT *Expansograptus*
floated in open seas.

two
extended
• *stipes*

EXPANSOGRAPTUS cf. *NITIDUS*
(Hall); Mytton Formation;
Early Ordovician; UK.

sicula •

Typical length 5cm (2in)

Range E.–M. Ordovician	Distribution Worldwide	Occurrence ◉◉◉◉◉

Order GRAPTOLOIDEA	Family DICHOGRAPTIDAE	Informal name Graptolite

LOGANOGRAPTUS

These were large graptolites: the rapid initial
dichotomies near the sicula produced a colony
with sixteen stipes. These stipes were
evenly separated in life, but
frequently bent in fossils.
The thecae are simple
tubes – about one
per millimetre.
• HABITAT
This genus lived
in the deeper parts
of the Ordo-
vician ocean.

LOGANOGRAPTUS
LOGANI (Hall);
Skiddaw Group; Early
Ordovician; UK.

thecae slowly •
increase in size along stipes

Typical length
20cm (8in)

Range E. Ordovician	Distribution Worldwide	Occurrence ◉◉◉◉◉

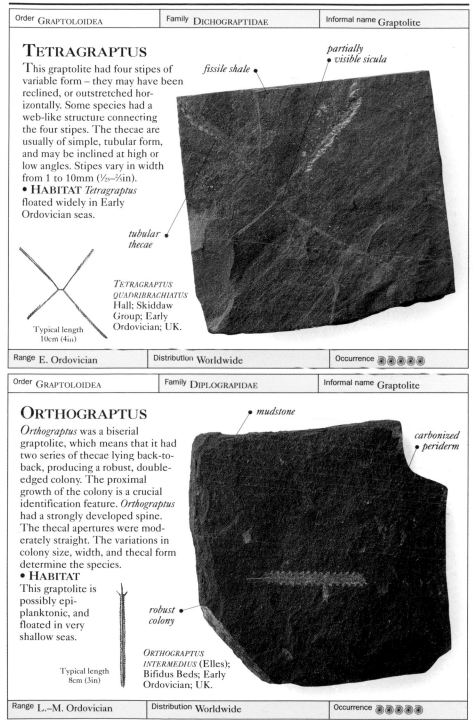

| Order GRAPTOLOIDEA | Family DICHOGRAPTIDAE | Informal name Graptolite |

TETRAGRAPTUS

This graptolite had four stipes of variable form – they may have been reclined, or outstretched horizontally. Some species had a web-like structure connecting the four stipes. The thecae are usually of simple, tubular form, and may be inclined at high or low angles. Stipes vary in width from 1 to 10mm (¹⁄₂₅–²⁄₅in).
• HABITAT *Tetragraptus* floated widely in Early Ordovician seas.

fissile shale

partially visible sicula

tubular thecae

TETRAGRAPTUS QUADRIBRACHIATUS Hall; Skiddaw Group; Early Ordovician; UK.

Typical length 10cm (4in)

| Range E. Ordovician | Distribution Worldwide | Occurrence |

| Order GRAPTOLOIDEA | Family DIPLOGRAPIDAE | Informal name Graptolite |

ORTHOGRAPTUS

Orthograptus was a biserial graptolite, which means that it had two series of thecae lying back-to-back, producing a robust, double-edged colony. The proximal growth of the colony is a crucial identification feature. *Orthograptus* had a strongly developed spine. The thecal apertures were moderately straight. The variations in colony size, width, and thecal form determine the species.
• HABITAT This graptolite is possibly epi-planktonic, and floated in very shallow seas.

mudstone

carbonized periderm

robust colony

ORTHOGRAPTUS INTERMEDIUS (Elles); Bifidus Beds; Early Ordovician; UK.

Typical length 8cm (3in)

| Range L.–M. Ordovician | Distribution Worldwide | Occurrence |

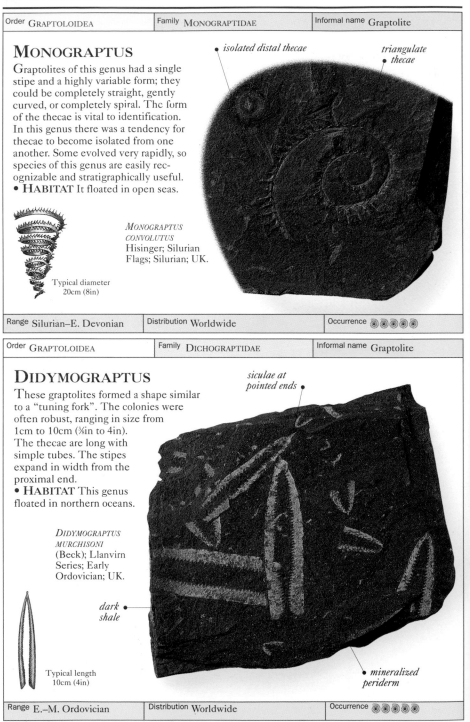

Order GRAPTOLOIDEA	Family MONOGRAPTIDAE	Informal name Graptolite

MONOGRAPTUS

Graptolites of this genus had a single stipe and a highly variable form; they could be completely straight, gently curved, or completely spiral. The form of the thecae is vital to identification. In this genus there was a tendency for thecae to become isolated from one another. Some evolved very rapidly, so species of this genus are easily recognizable and stratigraphically useful.
• HABITAT It floated in open seas.

isolated distal thecae

triangulate thecae

MONOGRAPTUS CONVOLUTUS Hisinger; Silurian Flags; Silurian; UK.

Typical diameter 20cm (8in)

Range Silurian–E. Devonian	Distribution Worldwide	Occurrence

Order GRAPTOLOIDEA	Family DICHOGRAPTIDAE	Informal name Graptolite

DIDYMOGRAPTUS

These graptolites formed a shape similar to a "tuning fork". The colonies were often robust, ranging in size from 1cm to 10cm (⅜in to 4in). The thecae are long with simple tubes. The stipes expand in width from the proximal end.
• HABITAT This genus floated in northern oceans.

siculae at pointed ends

DIDYMOGRAPTUS MURCHISONI (Beck); Llanvirn Series; Early Ordovician; UK.

dark shale

Typical length 10cm (4in)

mineralized periderm

Range E.–M. Ordovician	Distribution Worldwide	Occurrence

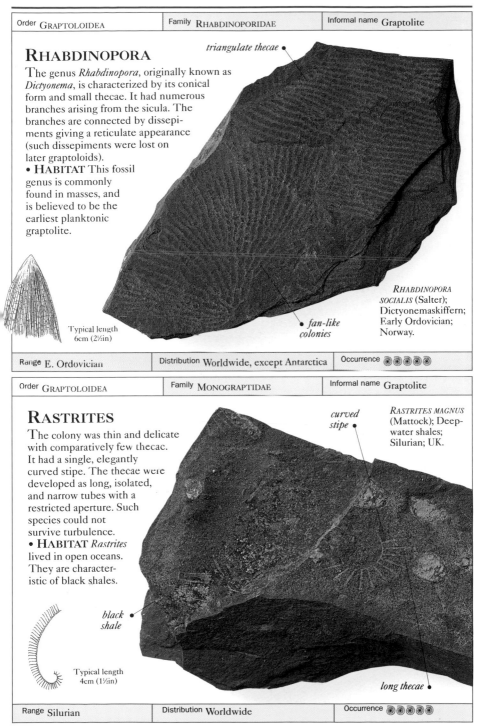

| Order GRAPTOLOIDEA | Family RHABDINOPORIDAE | Informal name Graptolite |

RHABDINOPORA

triangulate thecae •

The genus *Rhabdinopora*, originally known as *Dictyonema*, is characterized by its conical form and small thecae. It had numerous branches arising from the sicula. The branches are connected by dissepiments giving a reticulate appearance (such dissepiments were lost on later graptoloids).
• HABITAT This fossil genus is commonly found in masses, and is believed to be the earliest planktonic graptolite.

Typical length
6cm (2½in)

• fan-like colonies

RHABDINOPORA SOCIALIS (Salter); Dictyonemaskiffern; Early Ordovician; Norway.

| Range E. Ordovician | Distribution Worldwide, except Antarctica | Occurrence ⬤⬤⬤⬤⬤ |

| Order GRAPTOLOIDEA | Family MONOGRAPTIDAE | Informal name Graptolite |

RASTRITES

curved stipe •

RASTRITES MAGNUS (Mattock); Deepwater shales; Silurian; UK.

The colony was thin and delicate with comparatively few thecae. It had a single, elegantly curved stipe. The thecae were developed as long, isolated, and narrow tubes with a restricted aperture. Such species could not survive turbulence.
• HABITAT *Rastrites* lived in open oceans. They are characteristic of black shales.

black shale •

Typical length
4cm (1½in)

long thecae •

| Range Silurian | Distribution Worldwide | Occurrence ⬤⬤⬤⬤⬤ |

CORALS

CORALS ARE MARINE ANIMALS with a sac-like body (polyp), mouth, tentacles, and skeleton. The polyp occupies a circular, polygonal, or elongate cavity (calice), which is generally surrounded by a wall. Calices are usually divided by star-like arrangements of plates (septa), which sometimes have a central structure. The calice wall, if present, forms horn- or tube-like features (corallites), often divided by simple transverse partitions (tabulae) or by series of plates (dissepiments), or both. Polyps may divide to form colonies, with corallites sometimes joined by inter-corallite structures (coenosteum). There are three main coral groups, two extinct (Rugosa, Tabulata), and one extant (Scleractinia).

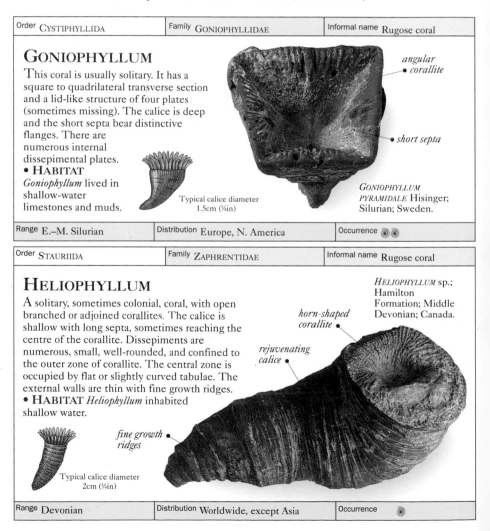

Order CYSTIPHYLLIDA	Family GONIOPHYLLIDAE	Informal name Rugose coral

GONIOPHYLLUM

This coral is usually solitary. It has a square to quadrilateral transverse section and a lid-like structure of four plates (sometimes missing). The calice is deep and the short septa bear distinctive flanges. There are numerous internal dissepimental plates.
• HABITAT *Goniophyllum* lived in shallow-water limestones and muds.

angular corallite

short septa

Typical calice diameter 1.5cm (⅝in)

GONIOPHYLLUM PYRAMIDALE Hisinger; Silurian; Sweden.

Range E.–M. Silurian	Distribution Europe, N. America	Occurrence

Order STAURIIDA	Family ZAPHRENTIDAE	Informal name Rugose coral

HELIOPHYLLUM

A solitary, sometimes colonial, coral, with open branched or adjoined corallites. The calice is shallow with long septa, sometimes reaching the centre of the corallite. Dissepiments are numerous, small, well-rounded, and confined to the outer zone of corallite. The central zone is occupied by flat or slightly curved tabulae. The external walls are thin with fine growth ridges.
• HABITAT *Heliophyllum* inhabited shallow water.

HELIOPHYLLUM sp.; Hamilton Formation; Middle Devonian; Canada.

horn-shaped corallite

rejuvenating calice

fine growth ridges

Typical calice diameter 2cm (¾in)

Range Devonian	Distribution Worldwide, except Asia	Occurrence

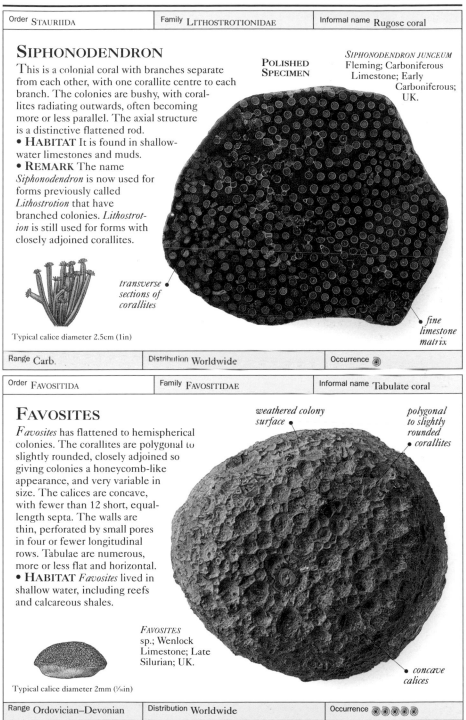

Order STAURIIDA	Family LITHOSTROTIONIDAE	Informal name Rugose coral

SIPHONODENDRON

This is a colonial coral with branches separate from each other, with one corallite centre to each branch. The colonies are bushy, with corallites radiating outwards, often becoming more or less parallel. The axial structure is a distinctive flattened rod.
• HABITAT It is found in shallow-water limestones and muds.
• REMARK The name *Siphonodendron* is now used for forms previously called *Lithostrotion* that have branched colonies. *Lithostrotion* is still used for forms with closely adjoined corallites.

POLISHED SPECIMEN

SIPHONODENDRON JUNCEUM Fleming; Carboniferous Limestone; Early Carboniferous; UK.

transverse sections of corallites

fine limestone matrix

Typical calice diameter 2.5cm (1in)

Range Carb.	Distribution Worldwide	Occurrence

Order FAVOSITIDA	Family FAVOSITIDAE	Informal name Tabulate coral

FAVOSITES

Favosites has flattened to hemispherical colonies. The corallites are polygonal to slightly rounded, closely adjoined so giving colonies a honeycomb-like appearance, and very variable in size. The calices are concave, with fewer than 12 short, equal-length septa. The walls are thin, perforated by small pores in four or fewer longitudinal rows. Tabulae are numerous, more or less flat and horizontal.
• HABITAT *Favosites* lived in shallow water, including reefs and calcareous shales.

weathered colony surface

polygonal to slightly rounded corallites

FAVOSITES sp.; Wenlock Limestone; Late Silurian; UK.

concave calices

Typical calice diameter 2mm (¹⁄₁₆in)

Range Ordovician–Devonian	Distribution Worldwide	Occurrence

Order STAURIIDA	Family AXOPHYLLIDAE	Informal name Rugose coral

ACTINOCYATHUS

This colonial coral has flattened to rounded colonies of closely adjoined polygonal corallites of different sizes in a coarsely honeycomb-like pattern. The calices are concave with a central boss. The septa are thin, often alternating long and short. The axial boss is complex, consisting of a steeply sloping series of small blistery plates arranged in conical form around a small central plate and also intersected by septal plates. The dissepiments are in series, forming a wide outer zone within the corallites, distinctively very large and irregular. In transverse section, the septa appear to be largely absent from the dissepimental zone, but actually form fine ridges running across upper surfaces of dissepiments. The tabulae are flat or concave. The corallites have thin external walls with fine growth ridges, but these are only visible in well preserved specimens when broken along the corallite junctions.

• **HABITAT** *Actinocyathus* lived in shallow-water limestones and muds.

• **REMARK** The name *Actinocyathus* is now used for forms previously called *Lonsdaleia* with closely adjoined corallites. *Lonsdaleia* is still used for openly branched forms.

POLISHED
CROSS-SECTION

variably sized polygonal calices

inner wall

concave calices

outer septal ridges

WEATHERED COLONY SURFACE

ACTINOCYATHUS CRASSICONUS (McCoy); Carboniferous Limestone; Early Carboniferous; UK.

inner septa

Typical calice diameter
6mm (¼in)

Range E. Carb.	Distribution Europe, Asia	Occurrence ⊚⊚⊚⊚⊚⊚

Order FAVOSITIDA	Family HALYSITIDAE	Informal name Tabulate coral

HALYSITES

This colonial coral has its corallites arranged in single series in "pan-pipe" formation, with a minute tube between each corallite. In transverse section they appear chain-like. The chains are straight to curved, dividing and rejoining each other, enclosing cell-like spaces between them. The individual corallites are rounded to elliptical. Septa are absent, or present as a few inconspicuous spines. The walls are thick, the tabulae are numerous, mostly flat and horizontal.
• HABITAT *Halysites* inhabited warm, shallow waters including reefs.

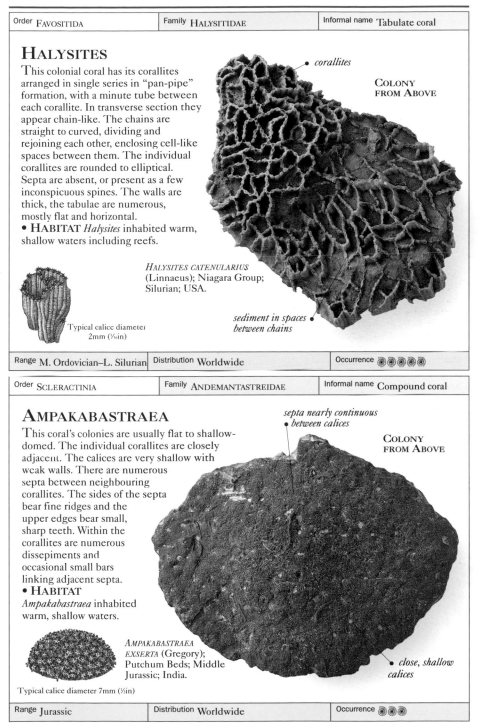

• *corallites*

COLONY
FROM ABOVE

HALYSITES CATENULARIUS
(Linnaeus); Niagara Group;
Silurian; USA.

sediment in spaces •
between chains

Typical calice diameter
2mm (¹⁄₁₆in)

Range M. Ordovician–L. Silurian	Distribution Worldwide	Occurrence

Order SCLERACTINIA	Family ANDEMANTASTREIDAE	Informal name Compound coral

AMPAKABASTRAEA

This coral's colonies are usually flat to shallow-domed. The individual corallites are closely adjacent. The calices are very shallow with weak walls. There are numerous septa between neighbouring corallites. The sides of the septa bear fine ridges and the upper edges bear small, sharp teeth. Within the corallites are numerous dissepiments and occasional small bars linking adjacent septa.
• HABITAT
Ampakabastraea inhabited warm, shallow waters.

septa nearly continuous
• *between calices*

COLONY
FROM ABOVE

AMPAKABASTRAEA
EXSERTA (Gregory);
Putchum Beds; Middle
Jurassic; India.

• *close, shallow*
calices

Typical calice diameter 7mm (¹⁄₄in)

Range Jurassic	Distribution Worldwide	Occurrence

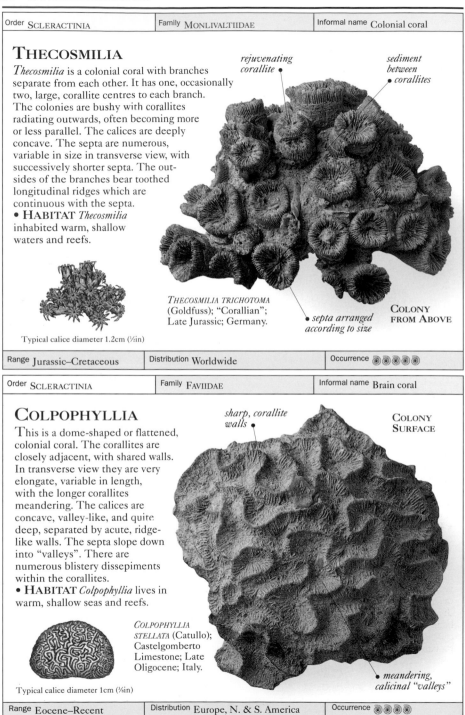

Order SCLERACTINIA	Family MONLIVALTIIDAE	Informal name Colonial coral

THECOSMILIA

Thecosmilia is a colonial coral with branches separate from each other. It has one, occasionally two, large, corallite centres to each branch. The colonies are bushy with corallites radiating outwards, often becoming more or less parallel. The calices are deeply concave. The septa are numerous, variable in size in transverse view, with successively shorter septa. The outsides of the branches bear toothed longitudinal ridges which are continuous with the septa.

• HABITAT *Thecosmilia* inhabited warm, shallow waters and reefs.

rejuvenating corallite

sediment between corallites

THECOSMILIA TRICHOTOMA (Goldfuss); "Corallian"; Late Jurassic; Germany.

septa arranged according to size

COLONY FROM ABOVE

Typical calice diameter 1.2cm (½in)

Range Jurassic–Cretaceous	Distribution Worldwide	Occurrence ◉◉◉◉◉

Order SCLERACTINIA	Family FAVIIDAE	Informal name Brain coral

COLPOPHYLLIA

This is a dome-shaped or flattened, colonial coral. The corallites are closely adjacent, with shared walls. In transverse view they are very elongate, variable in length, with the longer corallites meandering. The calices are concave, valley-like, and quite deep, separated by acute, ridge-like walls. The septa slope down into "valleys". There are numerous blistery dissepiments within the corallites.

• HABITAT *Colpophyllia* lives in warm, shallow seas and reefs.

sharp, corallite walls

COLONY SURFACE

COLPOPHYLLIA STELLATA (Catullo); Castelgomberto Limestone; Late Oligocene; Italy.

meandering, calicinal "valleys"

Typical calice diameter 1cm (⅜in)

Range Eocene–Recent	Distribution Europe, N. & S. America	Occurrence ◉◉◉◉

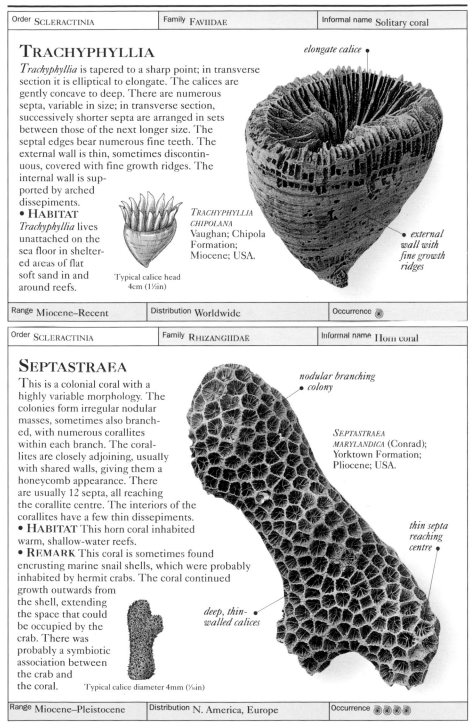

| Order SCLERACTINIA | Family FAVIIDAE | Informal name Solitary coral |

TRACHYPHYLLIA

Trachyphyllia is tapered to a sharp point; in transverse section it is elliptical to elongate. The calices are gently concave to deep. There are numerous septa, variable in size; in transverse section, successively shorter septa are arranged in sets between those of the next longer size. The septal edges bear numerous fine teeth. The external wall is thin, sometimes discontinuous, covered with fine growth ridges. The internal wall is supported by arched dissepiments.

• HABITAT
Trachyphyllia lives unattached on the sea floor in sheltered areas of flat soft sand in and around reefs.

elongate calice

TRACHYPHYLLIA CHIPOLANA Vaughan; Chipola Formation; Miocene; USA.

• *external wall with fine growth ridges*

Typical calice head
4cm (1½in)

| Range Miocene–Recent | Distribution Worldwide | Occurrence |

| Order SCLERACTINIA | Family RHIZANGIIDAE | Informal name Horn coral |

SEPTASTRAEA

This is a colonial coral with a highly variable morphology. The colonies form irregular nodular masses, sometimes also branched, with numerous corallites within each branch. The corallites are closely adjoining, usually with shared walls, giving them a honeycomb appearance. There are usually 12 septa, all reaching the corallite centre. The interiors of the corallites have a few thin dissepiments.
• HABITAT This horn coral inhabited warm, shallow-water reefs.
• REMARK This coral is sometimes found encrusting marine snail shells, which were probably inhabited by hermit crabs. The coral continued growth outwards from the shell, extending the space that could be occupied by the crab. There was probably a symbiotic association between the crab and the coral.

nodular branching colony

SEPTASTRAEA MARYLANDICA (Conrad); Yorktown Formation; Pliocene; USA.

thin septa reaching centre

deep, thin-walled calices

Typical calice diameter 4mm (⅙in)

| Range Miocene–Pleistocene | Distribution N. America, Europe | Occurrence |

TRILOBITES

ALTHOUGH THEY ARE now extinct, these arthropods flourished in the sea, from the Cambrian through to the Permian. They ranged in length from one millimetre to one metre (¹⁄₂₅in–39in). The name, trilobite, derives from their division into three longitudinal lobes: a slightly raised central lobe (the axis), with two flatter pleural lobes on either side. They were also divided into a head shield (cephalon), a thorax of up to 30 segments, and a tail shield (pygidium). The axial region of the head shield (glabella) had cheeks on either side, and often well-developed eyes. Each segment of the thorax had limbs, but these are rarely preserved. Trilobites could roll up (enroll) their external skeletons, probably for defence.

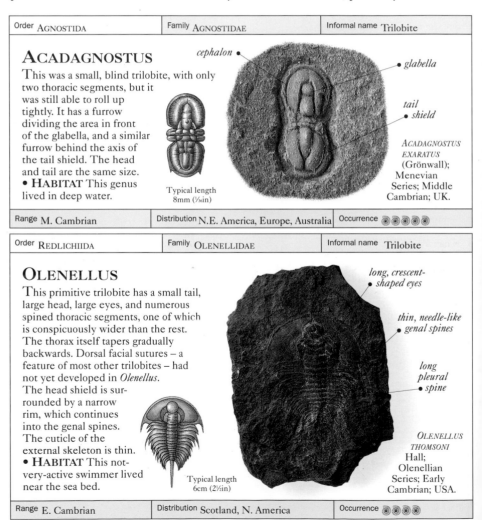

Order AGNOSTIDA	Family AGNOSTIDAE	Informal name Trilobite

ACADAGNOSTUS

This was a small, blind trilobite, with only two thoracic segments, but it was still able to roll up tightly. It has a furrow dividing the area in front of the glabella, and a similar furrow behind the axis of the tail shield. The head and tail are the same size.
• **HABITAT** This genus lived in deep water.

cephalon
glabella
tail shield

Typical length 8mm (¹⁄₃in)

ACADAGNOSTUS EXARATUS (Grönwall); Menevian Series; Middle Cambrian; UK.

Range M. Cambrian	Distribution N.E. America, Europe, Australia	Occurrence ◉◉◉◉◉

Order REDLICHIIDA	Family OLENELLIDAE	Informal name Trilobite

OLENELLUS

This primitive trilobite has a small tail, large head, large eyes, and numerous spined thoracic segments, one of which is conspicuously wider than the rest. The thorax itself tapers gradually backwards. Dorsal facial sutures – a feature of most other trilobites – had not yet developed in *Olenellus*. The head shield is surrounded by a narrow rim, which continues into the genal spines. The cuticle of the external skeleton is thin.
• **HABITAT** This not-very-active swimmer lived near the sea bed.

long, crescent-shaped eyes
thin, needle-like genal spines
long pleural spine

Typical length 6cm (2¹⁄₃in)

OLENELLUS THOMSONI Hall; Olenellian Series; Early Cambrian; USA.

Range E. Cambrian	Distribution Scotland, N. America	Occurrence ◉◉◉◉

Order PTYCHOPARIIDA	Family OLENIDAE	Informal name Trilobite

TRIARTHRUS

The external skeleton of this trilobite is more than twice as long as it is wide. It has a large head shield and a small tail shield. There are no genal spines, but two pairs of deep furrows are visible on the glabella.
• HABITAT *Triarthrus* lived on or near the sea bed.
• REMARK This specimen is one of the rare examples in which the limbs of the trilobite are preserved – the traces of the walking legs may be clearly seen. These were preserved because they were covered at an early stage of burial by a film of iron pyrites, which remains even after the soft tissue has decayed.

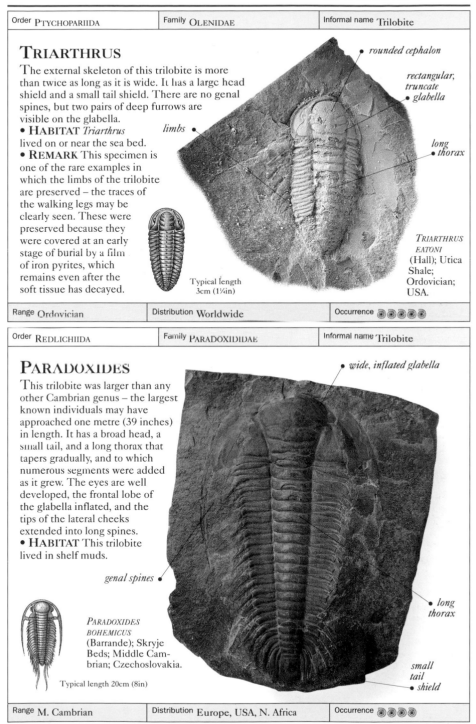

• *rounded cephalon*

rectangular, truncate
• *glabella*

limbs •

long
• *thorax*

TRIARTHRUS EATONI (Hall); Utica Shale; Ordovician; USA.

Typical length 3cm (1¼in)

Range Ordovician	Distribution Worldwide	Occurrence ⬡⬡⬡⬡⬡

Order REDLICHIIDA	Family PARADOXIDIDAE	Informal name Trilobite

PARADOXIDES

This trilobite was larger than any other Cambrian genus – the largest known individuals may have approached one metre (39 inches) in length. It has a broad head, a small tail, and a long thorax that tapers gradually, and to which numerous segments were added as it grew. The eyes are well developed, the frontal lobe of the glabella inflated, and the tips of the lateral cheeks extended into long spines.
• HABITAT This trilobite lived in shelf muds.

• *wide, inflated glabella*

genal spines •

long thorax

PARADOXIDES BOHEMICUS (Barrande); Skryje Beds; Middle Cambrian; Czechoslovakia.

Typical length 20cm (8in)

small tail
• *shield*

Range M. Cambrian	Distribution Europe, USA, N. Africa	Occurrence ⬡⬡⬡⬡

Order REDLICHIIDA	Family XYSTRIDURIDAE	Informal name Trilobite

XYSTRIDURA

This trilobite is broadly oval in outline. Its head section is about twice as wide as it is long, with a well-furrowed glabella and large eyes. The genal angle has extended to form short genal spines. The thorax is divided into 13 segments, with the axis being much narrower than the deeply furrowed pleural lobes. The tail shield is also furrowed, and spines are present around the posterior margin.
• HABITAT *Xystridura* lived on or near the sediment of the sea bed.

XYSTRIDURA SAINT-SMITHII (Chapman); Middle Cambrian; Australia.

large eyes

thorax with short spines

Typical length 6cm (2⅜in)

moderately large tail shield

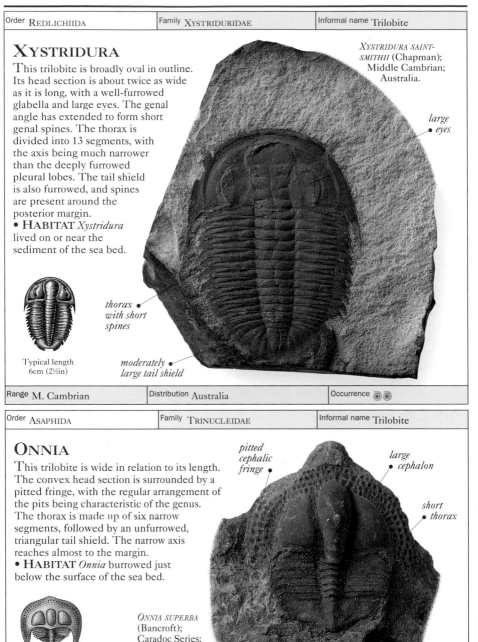

Range M. Cambrian	Distribution Australia	Occurrence

Order ASAPHIDA	Family TRINUCLEIDAE	Informal name Trilobite

ONNIA

This trilobite is wide in relation to its length. The convex head section is surrounded by a pitted fringe, with the regular arrangement of the pits being characteristic of the genus. The thorax is made up of six narrow segments, followed by an unfurrowed, triangular tail shield. The narrow axis reaches almost to the margin.
• HABITAT *Onnia* burrowed just below the surface of the sea bed.

pitted cephalic fringe

large cephalon

short thorax

ONNIA SUPERBA (Bancroft); Caradoc Series; Ordovician; UK.

Typical length 3cm (1¼in)

Range M.–L. Ordovician	Distribution Europe, N. Africa	Occurrence

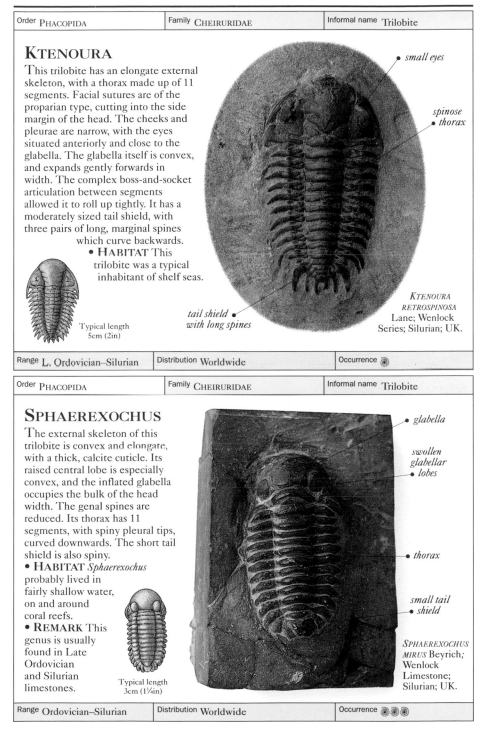

| Order PHACOPIDA | Family CHEIRURIDAE | Informal name Trilobite |

KTENOURA

This trilobite has an elongate external skeleton, with a thorax made up of 11 segments. Facial sutures are of the proparian type, cutting into the side margin of the head. The cheeks and pleurae are narrow, with the eyes situated anteriorly and close to the glabella. The glabella itself is convex, and expands gently forwards in width. The complex boss-and-socket articulation between segments allowed it to roll up tightly. It has a moderately sized tail shield, with three pairs of long, marginal spines which curve backwards.

• HABITAT This trilobite was a typical inhabitant of shelf seas.

small eyes

spinose thorax

Typical length
5cm (2in)

tail shield with long spines

KTENOURA RETROSPINOSA Lane; Wenlock Series; Silurian; UK.

| Range L. Ordovician–Silurian | Distribution Worldwide | Occurrence ● |

| Order PHACOPIDA | Family CHEIRURIDAE | Informal name Trilobite |

SPHAEREXOCHUS

The external skeleton of this trilobite is convex and elongate, with a thick, calcite cuticle. Its raised central lobe is especially convex, and the inflated glabella occupies the bulk of the head width. The genal spines are reduced. Its thorax has 11 segments, with spiny pleural tips, curved downwards. The short tail shield is also spiny.

• HABITAT *Sphaerexochus* probably lived in fairly shallow water, on and around coral reefs.

• REMARK This genus is usually found in Late Ordovician and Silurian limestones.

glabella

swollen glabellar lobes

thorax

small tail shield

Typical length
3cm (1¼in)

SPHAEREXOCHUS MIRUS Beyrich; Wenlock Limestone; Silurian; UK.

| Range Ordovician–Silurian | Distribution Worldwide | Occurrence ● ● ● |

Order ODONTOPLEURIDA	Family ODONTOPLEURIDAE	Informal name Trilobite

SELENOPELTIS

This trilobite has a wide external skeleton, with the head and tail sections short in relation to the thorax. The wide glabella has complex furrows and an inflated central lobe. The genal spines are very long and the pleural tips of each thoracic segment are prolonged into great spines, which project backwards. One similar pair of spines is found on the tail shield.
• HABITAT *Selenopeltis* is thought to have floated freely in ocean waters.

wide glabella

long spinose tips

SELENOPELTIS BUCHI Barrande; Sarká Formation; Ordovician; Czechoslovakia.

Typical length
3.5cm (1⅜in)

short pygidium with few segments

Range E.–M. Ordovician	Distribution Europe, N. Africa	Occurrence

Order PHACOPIDA	Family PHACOPIDAE	Informal name Trilobite

PHACOPS

This trilobite has a convex glabella that expands forwards. The large eyes have fewer lenses than usual, which may have improved optics. The thorax has 12 segments, equipped with facets which facilitate enrollment. The deeply furrowed tail shield is smaller than its head. A sculpture of tubercles ornaments the thick cuticle.
• HABITAT *Phacops* inhabited shallow water in warm seas.

large eye

ENROLLED SPECIMEN

tail tucks beneath head when enrolled

PHACOPS AFRICANUS Burton & Eldredge; Shelf limestones; Devonian; Western Sahara.

tuberculate head

head and tail shield margins

Typical length
4.5cm (1¾in)

Range Devonian	Distribution Worldwide	Occurrence

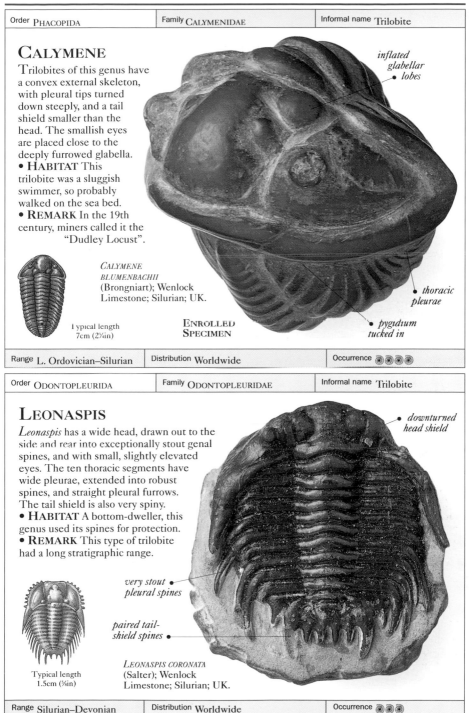

Order PHACOPIDA	Family CALYMENIDAE	Informal name Trilobite

CALYMENE

Trilobites of this genus have a convex external skeleton, with pleural tips turned down steeply, and a tail shield smaller than the head. The smallish eyes are placed close to the deeply furrowed glabella.
• HABITAT This trilobite was a sluggish swimmer, so probably walked on the sea bed.
• REMARK In the 19th century, miners called it the "Dudley Locust".

inflated glabellar lobes

CALYMENE BLUMENBACHII (Brongniart); Wenlock Limestone; Silurian; UK.

Typical length 7cm (2¾in)

ENROLLED SPECIMEN

thoracic pleurae

pygidium tucked in

Range L. Ordovician–Silurian	Distribution Worldwide	Occurrence ◉◉◉◉

Order ODONTOPLEURIDA	Family ODONTOPLEURIDAE	Informal name Trilobite

LEONASPIS

Leonaspis has a wide head, drawn out to the side and rear into exceptionally stout genal spines, and with small, slightly elevated eyes. The ten thoracic segments have wide pleurae, extended into robust spines, and straight pleural furrows. The tail shield is also very spiny.
• HABITAT A bottom-dweller, this genus used its spines for protection.
• REMARK This type of trilobite had a long stratigraphic range.

downturned head shield

very stout pleural spines

paired tail-shield spines

Typical length 1.5cm (⅝in)

LEONASPIS CORONATA (Salter); Wenlock Limestone; Silurian; UK.

Range Silurian–Devonian	Distribution Worldwide	Occurrence ◉◉◉

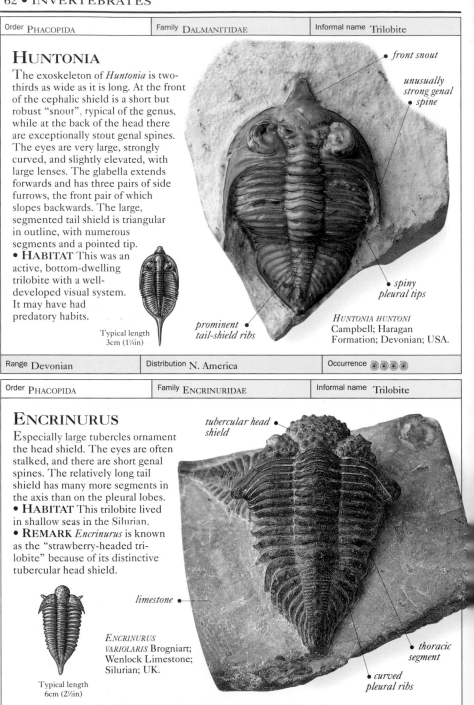

Order PHACOPIDA	Family DALMANITIDAE	Informal name Trilobite

HUNTONIA

The exoskeleton of *Huntonia* is two-thirds as wide as it is long. At the front of the cephalic shield is a short but robust "snout", typical of the genus, while at the back of the head there are exceptionally stout genal spines. The eyes are very large, strongly curved, and slightly elevated, with large lenses. The glabella extends forwards and has three pairs of side furrows, the front pair of which slopes backwards. The large, segmented tail shield is triangular in outline, with numerous segments and a pointed tip.
• HABITAT This was an active, bottom-dwelling trilobite with a well-developed visual system. It may have had predatory habits.

front snout

unusually strong genal spine

spiny pleural tips

Typical length
3cm (1¼in)

prominent tail-shield ribs

HUNTONIA HUNTONI
Campbell; Haragan
Formation; Devonian; USA.

Range Devonian	Distribution N. America	Occurrence

Order PHACOPIDA	Family ENCRINURIDAE	Informal name Trilobite

ENCRINURUS

Especially large tubercles ornament the head shield. The eyes are often stalked, and there are short genal spines. The relatively long tail shield has many more segments in the axis than on the pleural lobes.
• HABITAT This trilobite lived in shallow seas in the Silurian.
• REMARK *Encrinurus* is known as the "strawberry-headed tri-lobite" because of its distinctive tubercular head shield.

tubercular head shield

limestone

ENCRINURUS
VARIOLARIS Brogniart;
Wenlock Limestone;
Silurian; UK.

Typical length
6cm (2½in)

thoracic segment

curved pleural ribs

Range L. Ordovician–Silurian	Distribution Worldwide	Occurrence

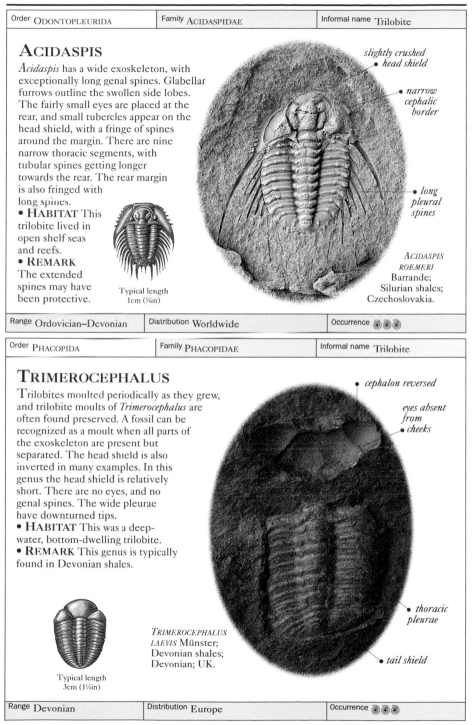

Order ODONTOPLEURIDA	Family ACIDASPIDAE	Informal name Trilobite

ACIDASPIS

Acidaspis has a wide exoskeleton, with exceptionally long genal spines. Glabellar furrows outline the swollen side lobes. The fairly small eyes are placed at the rear, and small tubercles appear on the head shield, with a fringe of spines around the margin. There are nine narrow thoracic segments, with tubular spines getting longer towards the rear. The rear margin is also fringed with long spines.
• **HABITAT** This trilobite lived in open shelf seas and reefs.
• **REMARK** The extended spines may have been protective.

Typical length
1cm (⅜in)

slightly crushed
• *head shield*

• *narrow cephalic border*

• *long pleural spines*

ACIDASPIS ROEMERI Barrande; Silurian shales; Czechoslovakia.

Range Ordovician–Devonian	Distribution Worldwide	Occurrence

Order PHACOPIDA	Family PHACOPIDAE	Informal name Trilobite

TRIMEROCEPHALUS

Trilobites moulted periodically as they grew, and trilobite moults of *Trimerocephalus* are often found preserved. A fossil can be recognized as a moult when all parts of the exoskeleton are present but separated. The head shield is also inverted in many examples. In this genus the head shield is relatively short. There are no eyes, and no genal spines. The wide pleurae have downturned tips.
• **HABITAT** This was a deep-water, bottom-dwelling trilobite.
• **REMARK** This genus is typically found in Devonian shales.

• *cephalon reversed*

eyes absent from
• *cheeks*

TRIMEROCEPHALUS LAEVIS Münster; Devonian shales; Devonian; UK.

• *thoracic pleurae*

• *tail shield*

Typical length
3cm (1¼in)

Range Devonian	Distribution Europe	Occurrence

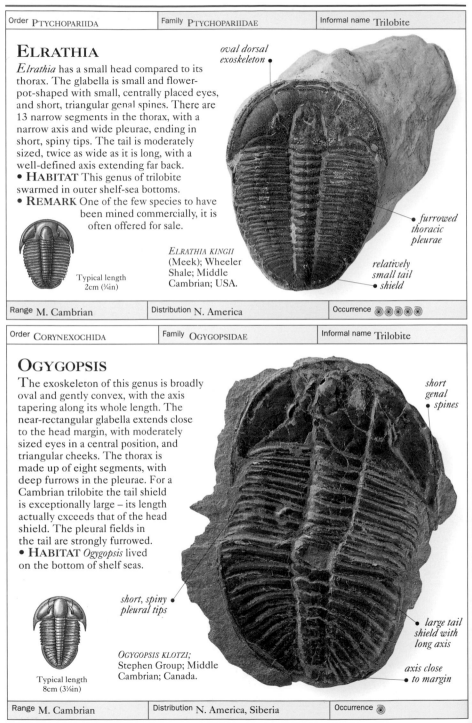

| Order PTYCHOPARIIDA | Family PTYCHOPARIIDAE | Informal name Trilobite |

ELRATHIA

Elrathia has a small head compared to its thorax. The glabella is small and flower-pot-shaped with small, centrally placed eyes, and short, triangular genal spines. There are 13 narrow segments in the thorax, with a narrow axis and wide pleurae, ending in short, spiny tips. The tail is moderately sized, twice as wide as it is long, with a well-defined axis extending far back.
• HABITAT This genus of trilobite swarmed in outer shelf-sea bottoms.
• REMARK One of the few species to have been mined commercially, it is often offered for sale.

oval dorsal exoskeleton

furrowed thoracic pleurae

relatively small tail shield

Typical length 2cm (¾in)

ELRATHIA KINGII (Meek); Wheeler Shale; Middle Cambrian; USA.

| Range M. Cambrian | Distribution N. America | Occurrence |

| Order CORYNEXOCHIDA | Family OGYGOPSIDAE | Informal name Trilobite |

OGYGOPSIS

The exoskeleton of this genus is broadly oval and gently convex, with the axis tapering along its whole length. The near-rectangular glabella extends close to the head margin, with moderately sized eyes in a central position, and triangular cheeks. The thorax is made up of eight segments, with deep furrows in the pleurae. For a Cambrian trilobite the tail shield is exceptionally large – its length actually exceeds that of the head shield. The pleural fields in the tail are strongly furrowed.
• HABITAT *Ogygopsis* lived on the bottom of shelf seas.

short genal spines

short, spiny pleural tips

large tail shield with long axis

axis close to margin

OGYGOPSIS KLOTZI; Stephen Group; Middle Cambrian; Canada.

Typical length 8cm (3⅛in)

| Range M. Cambrian | Distribution N. America, Siberia | Occurrence |

Order CORYNEXOCHIDA	Family SCUTELLUIDAE	Informal name Trilobite

PARALEJURUS

Paralejurus has a convex and nearly semicircular head shield. Subdued dorsal furrows mean that the glabella and the glabellar furrows may be faint or obscure. There are no genal spines, and the eyes are positioned at the rear. In the ten segments of the thorax, the axis is not clearly differentiated from the pleurae. The large and fan-like tail shield has a relatively short axis.
• HABITAT This was an inhabitant of warm shelf seas.
• REMARK This is a sporadically common genus in limestones that accumulated in shallow-water conditions.

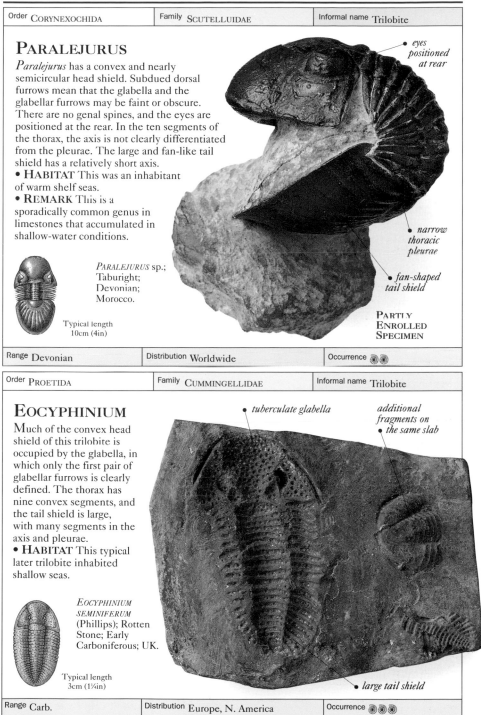

• *eyes positioned at rear*

• *narrow thoracic pleurae*

• *fan-shaped tail shield*

PARTLY
ENROLLED
SPECIMEN

PARALEJURUS sp.;
Taburight;
Devonian;
Morocco.

Typical length
10cm (4in)

Range Devonian	Distribution Worldwide	Occurrence ▦▦

Order PROETIDA	Family CUMMINGELLIDAE	Informal name Trilobite

EOCYPHINIUM

Much of the convex head shield of this trilobite is occupied by the glabella, in which only the first pair of glabellar furrows is clearly defined. The thorax has nine convex segments, and the tail shield is large, with many segments in the axis and pleurae.
• HABITAT This typical later trilobite inhabited shallow seas.

• *tuberculate glabella*

additional fragments on
• *the same slab*

• *large tail shield*

*EOCYPHINIUM
SEMINIFERUM*
(Phillips); Rotten Stone; Early Carboniferous; UK.

Typical length
3cm (1¼in)

Range Carb.	Distribution Europe, N. America	Occurrence ▦▦▦

CRUSTACEA

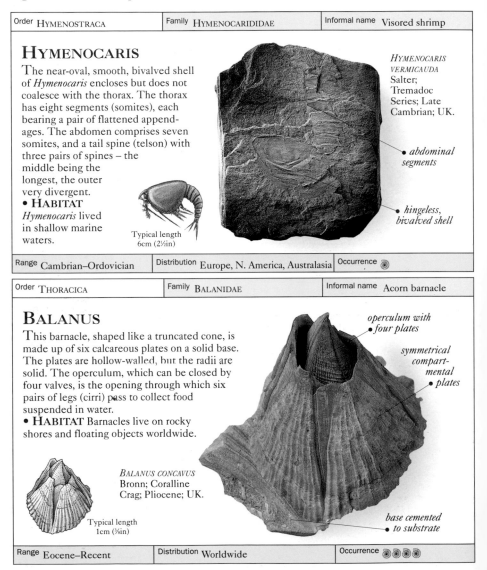

C | RUSTACEA ARE mainly aquatic, carnivorous arthropods, whose body and legs are enclosed by a supporting chitinous shell. The body is divisible into head, thorax, and abdomen, but head and thorax may fuse together into a cephalothorax. The head has two pairs of tactile antennae, and three pairs of limbs with food-handling abilities. The walking legs are divided in two, and may have gills for breathing. The last abdominal appendage may become flattened, to form a tail fan with the end spine.

Order HYMENOSTRACA	Family HYMENOCARIDIDAE	Informal name Visored shrimp

HYMENOCARIS

The near-oval, smooth, bivalved shell of *Hymenocaris* encloses but does not coalesce with the thorax. The thorax has eight segments (somites), each bearing a pair of flattened appendages. The abdomen comprises seven somites, and a tail spine (telson) with three pairs of spines – the middle being the longest, the outer very divergent.
• HABITAT *Hymenocaris* lived in shallow marine waters.

HYMENOCARIS VERMICAUDA Salter; Tremadoc Series; Late Cambrian; UK.

• abdominal segments

• hingeless, bivalved shell

Typical length 6cm (2⅜in)

Range Cambrian–Ordovician	Distribution Europe, N. America, Australasia	Occurrence ◉

Order THORACICA	Family BALANIDAE	Informal name Acorn barnacle

BALANUS

This barnacle, shaped like a truncated cone, is made up of six calcareous plates on a solid base. The plates are hollow-walled, but the radii are solid. The operculum, which can be closed by four valves, is the opening through which six pairs of legs (cirri) pass to collect food suspended in water.
• HABITAT Barnacles live on rocky shores and floating objects worldwide.

operculum with
• four plates

symmetrical compartmental
• plates

BALANUS CONCAVUS Bronn; Coralline Crag; Pliocene; UK.

base cemented
• to substrate

Typical length 1cm (⅜in)

Range Eocene–Recent	Distribution Worldwide	Occurrence ◉◉◉◉

Order DECAPODA	Family CARPILIIDAE	Informal name Mud crab

PALAEOCARPILIUS

The dorsal carapace of *Palaeocarpilius* is egg-like in outline, with a slightly extended front, strongly arched transversely, and more steeply rounded longitudinally. The front and side margins are spiny and the claws are robust, with the right one larger. The legs are long and stout. On the ventral surface, the front curves downwards and backwards to meet the head of the narrow plate in front of the mouth.
• HABITAT The genus was largely tropical, living near the shore.

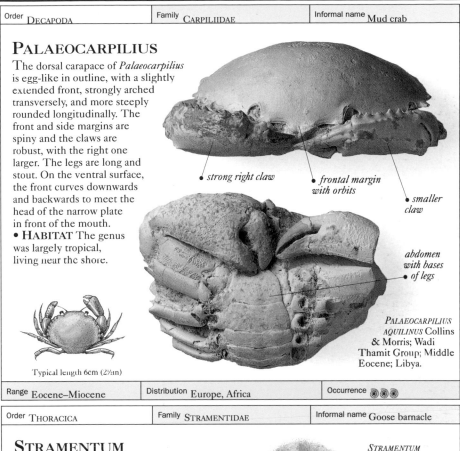

• *strong right claw*

• *frontal margin with orbits*

• *smaller claw*

abdomen with bases • *of legs*

PALAEOCARPILIUS AQUILINUS Collins & Morris; Wadi Thamit Group; Middle Eocene; Libya.

Typical length 6cm (2½in)

Range Eocene–Miocene	Distribution Europe, Africa	Occurrence 〓〓〓

Order THORACICA	Family STRAMENTIDAE	Informal name Goose barnacle

STRAMENTUM

Like most cirripedes, the stalked *Stramentum* remained attached as an adult. It is divided into a capitulum, which contains the body, the mouth parts, and thoracic appendages, and a peduncle or stalk, which contains the gonads. The capitulum is protected by ten calcareous plates. The peduncle is also protected by calcareous plates, but in eight regularly overlapping columns. Each column is surmounted by a plate in the capitulum.
• HABITAT These animals frequently lived attached to the empty shells of ammonites, bivalves, or gastropods lying on the sea floor.
• REMARK It was once believed that these fossils grew into geese.

STRAMENTUM PULCHELLUM (G.B. Sowerby); Middle Chalk; Late Cretaceous; UK.

• *plates enclosing body*

• *plates protecting flexible stalk*

Typical length 2cm (¾in)

• *point of attachment*

Range Cretaceous	Distribution Europe, N. Africa, N. America	Occurrence 〓

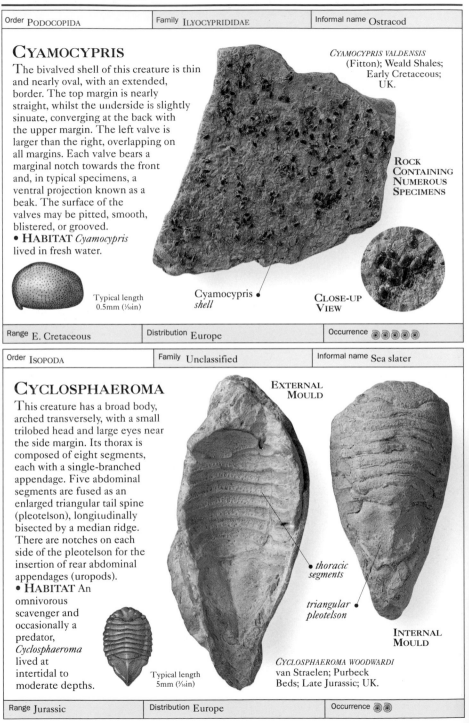

Order PODOCOPIDA	Family ILYOCYPRIDIDAE	Informal name Ostracod

CYAMOCYPRIS

The bivalved shell of this creature is thin and nearly oval, with an extended, border. The top margin is nearly straight, whilst the underside is slightly sinuate, converging at the back with the upper margin. The left valve is larger than the right, overlapping on all margins. Each valve bears a marginal notch towards the front and, in typical specimens, a ventral projection known as a beak. The surface of the valves may be pitted, smooth, blistered, or grooved.
• HABITAT *Cyamocypris* lived in fresh water.

CYAMOCYPRIS VALDENSIS (Fitton); Weald Shales; Early Cretaceous; UK.

ROCK CONTAINING NUMEROUS SPECIMENS

Typical length 0.5mm (⅟₅₀in)

Cyamocypris • *shell*

CLOSE-UP VIEW

Range E. Cretaceous	Distribution Europe	Occurrence ◉◉◉◉◉

Order ISOPODA	Family Unclassified	Informal name Sea slater

CYCLOSPHAEROMA

This creature has a broad body, arched transversely, with a small trilobed head and large eyes near the side margin. Its thorax is composed of eight segments, each with a single-branched appendage. Five abdominal segments are fused as an enlarged triangular tail spine (pleotelson), longitudinally bisected by a median ridge. There are notches on each side of the pleotelson for the insertion of rear abdominal appendages (uropods).
• HABITAT An omnivorous scavenger and occasionally a predator, *Cyclosphaeroma* lived at intertidal to moderate depths.

EXTERNAL MOULD

• *thoracic segments*

triangular • *pleotelson*

INTERNAL MOULD

Typical length 5mm (⅟₅in)

CYCLOSPHAEROMA WOODWARDI van Straelen; Purbeck Beds; Late Jurassic; UK.

Range Jurassic	Distribution Europe	Occurrence ◉◉

| Order DECAPODA | Family ERYONIDAE | Informal name Spiny lobster |

ERYON

The carapace is hexagonal and compressed, with sharp side margins. The front is truncated, with spiny margins at the side, and stalked, well-developed compound eyes. The first to fourth thoracic appendages have claws (chelae); the fifth is sub-chelate. The abdomen is long, flat, and narrow, with a ridge down the middle. It ends in a telson which, with the uropods, forms a tailfan.
• HABITAT *Eryon* lived in quiet, clear-water marine lagoons or in shallow water near to the coastline. Today, the family is found only in the ocean depths.

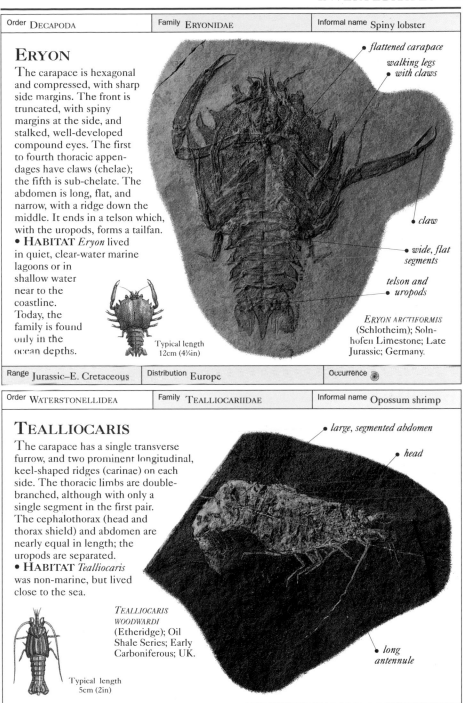

• *flattened carapace*
• *walking legs with claws*

• *claw*

• *wide, flat segments*

• *telson and uropods*

ERYON ARCTIFORMIS (Schlotheim); Solnhofen Limestone; Late Jurassic; Germany.

Typical length 12cm (4¾in)

| Range Jurassic–E. Cretaceous | Distribution Europe | Occurrence |

| Order WATERSTONELLIDEA | Family TEALLIOCARIIDAE | Informal name Opossum shrimp |

TEALLIOCARIS

The carapace has a single transverse furrow, and two prominent longitudinal, keel-shaped ridges (carinae) on each side. The thoracic limbs are double-branched, although with only a single segment in the first pair. The cephalothorax (head and thorax shield) and abdomen are nearly equal in length; the uropods are separated.
• HABITAT *Tealliocaris* was non-marine, but lived close to the sea.

• *large, segmented abdomen*
• *head*

TEALLIOCARIS WOODWARDI (Etheridge); Oil Shale Series; Early Carboniferous; UK.

• *long antennule*

Typical length 5cm (2in)

| Range E. Carb. | Distribution Europe | Occurrence |

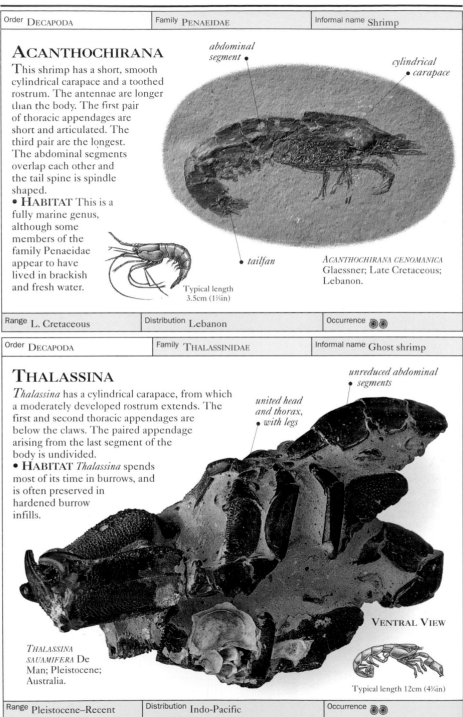

Order DECAPODA	Family PENAEIDAE	Informal name Shrimp

ACANTHOCHIRANA

This shrimp has a short, smooth cylindrical carapace and a toothed rostrum. The antennae are longer than the body. The first pair of thoracic appendages are short and articulated. The third pair are the longest. The abdominal segments overlap each other and the tail spine is spindle shaped.

• HABITAT This is a fully marine genus, although some members of the family Penaeidae appear to have lived in brackish and fresh water.

abdominal segment

cylindrical carapace

tailfan

Typical length 3.5cm (1⅜in)

ACANTHOCHIRANA CENOMANICA Glaessner; Late Cretaceous; Lebanon.

Range L. Cretaceous	Distribution Lebanon	Occurrence

Order DECAPODA	Family THALASSINIDAE	Informal name Ghost shrimp

THALASSINA

Thalassina has a cylindrical carapace, from which a moderately developed rostrum extends. The first and second thoracic appendages are below the claws. The paired appendage arising from the last segment of the body is undivided.

• HABITAT *Thalassina* spends most of its time in burrows, and is often preserved in hardened burrow infills.

unreduced abdominal segments

united head and thorax, with legs

VENTRAL VIEW

THALASSINA SAUAMIFERA De Man; Pleistocene; Australia.

Typical length 12cm (4¾in)

Range Pleistocene–Recent	Distribution Indo-Pacific	Occurrence

Order DECAPODA	Family PALINURIDAE	Informal name Spiny lobster

LINUPARUS

Closely related to the langouste, *Linuparus*
has a carapace compressed from top to
bottom, without a rostrum, but
with three longitudinal
ridges. It has spines, also
compressed, above the
eye sockets and close to
the midline. The base
of the antenna is fused to
the epistome and the side
margin. There are no claws on
the first four legs, and the fifth
leg has a claw only in the female.
The uropods and the telson form
a broad tailfan.
• **HABITAT** These fossils
are found in shallow,
marine seas.

*LINUPARUS
EOCENICUS*
Woods; London
Clay; Early
Eocene; UK.

Typical length
20cm (8in)

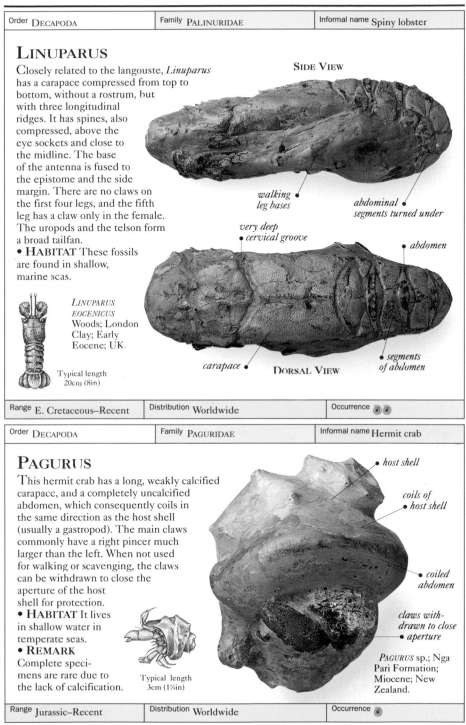

SIDE VIEW

*walking
leg bases*

*very deep
• cervical groove*

*abdominal •
segments turned under*

• abdomen

carapace • DORSAL VIEW

*• segments
of abdomen*

Range E. Cretaceous–Recent	Distribution Worldwide	Occurrence 🔵🔵

Order DECAPODA	Family PAGURIDAE	Informal name Hermit crab

PAGURUS

This hermit crab has a long, weakly calcified
carapace, and a completely uncalcified
abdomen, which consequently coils in
the same direction as the host shell
(usually a gastropod). The main claws
commonly have a right pincer much
larger than the left. When not used
for walking or scavenging, the claws
can be withdrawn to close the
aperture of the host
shell for protection.
• **HABITAT** It lives
in shallow water in
temperate seas.
• **REMARK**
Complete speci-
mens are rare due to
the lack of calcification.

Typical length
3cm (1¼in)

• host shell

*coils of
• host shell*

*• coiled
abdomen*

*claws with-
drawn to close
• aperture*

PAGURUS sp.; Nga
Pari Formation;
Miocene; New
Zealand.

Range Jurassic–Recent	Distribution Worldwide	Occurrence 🔵

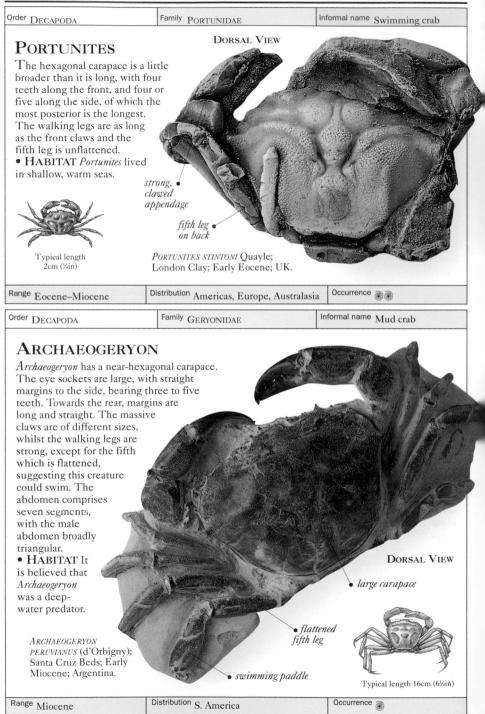

Order DECAPODA	Family PORTUNIDAE	Informal name Swimming crab

PORTUNITES

DORSAL VIEW

The hexagonal carapace is a little broader than it is long, with four teeth along the front, and four or five along the side, of which the most posterior is the longest. The walking legs are as long as the front claws and the fifth leg is unflattened.
• HABITAT *Portunites* lived in shallow, warm seas.

strong, clawed appendage

fifth leg on back

Typical length
2cm (¾in)

PORTUNITES STINTONI Quayle; London Clay; Early Eocene; UK.

Range Eocene–Miocene	Distribution Americas, Europe, Australasia	Occurrence ◉ ◉

Order DECAPODA	Family GERYONIDAE	Informal name Mud crab

ARCHAEOGERYON

Archaeogeryon has a near-hexagonal carapace. The eye sockets are large, with straight margins to the side, bearing three to five teeth. Towards the rear, margins are long and straight. The massive claws are of different sizes, whilst the walking legs are strong, except for the fifth which is flattened, suggesting this creature could swim. The abdomen comprises seven segments, with the male abdomen broadly triangular.
• HABITAT It is believed that *Archaeogeryon* was a deep-water predator.

DORSAL VIEW

large carapace

flattened fifth leg

ARCHAEOGERYON PERUVIANUS (d'Orbigny); Santa Cruz Beds; Early Miocene; Argentina.

swimming paddle

Typical length 16cm (6¼in)

Range Miocene	Distribution S. America	Occurrence ◉

CHELICERATA

T HE CHELICERATES include horse-shoe crabs, spiders, and scorpions. They have bodies divided into a head and thorax shield and an abdomen. Unlike other arthropods, they have no antennae. Of the six pairs of appendages, the first are claws for feeding (chelicerae), the second are for various functions (pedipalps), and the third to sixth are for walking.

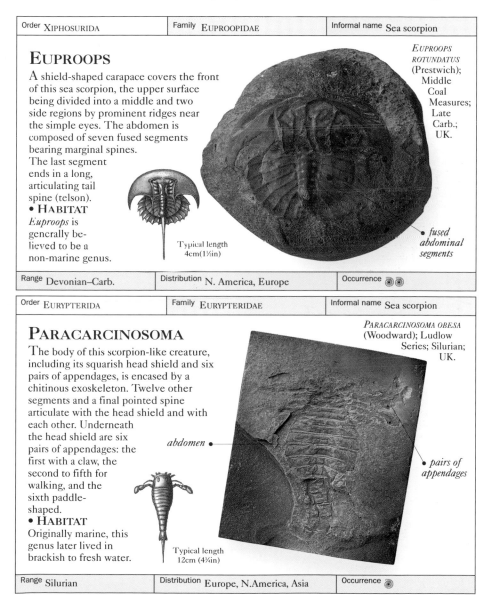

Order XIPHOSURIDA	Family EUPROOPIDAE	Informal name Sea scorpion

EUPROOPS

A shield-shaped carapace covers the front of this sea scorpion, the upper surface being divided into a middle and two side regions by prominent ridges near the simple eyes. The abdomen is composed of seven fused segments bearing marginal spines. The last segment ends in a long, articulating tail spine (telson).
• HABITAT
Euproops is generally be-lieved to be a non-marine genus.

EUPROOPS ROTUNDATUS (Prestwich); Middle Coal Measures; Late Carb.; UK.

Typical length 4cm(1½in)

• *fused abdominal segments*

Range Devonian–Carb.	Distribution N. America, Europe	Occurrence 🔴🔴

Order EURYPTERIDA	Family EURYPTERIDAE	Informal name Sea scorpion

PARACARCINOSOMA

The body of this scorpion-like creature, including its squarish head shield and six pairs of appendages, is encased by a chitinous exoskeleton. Twelve other segments and a final pointed spine articulate with the head shield and with each other. Underneath the head shield are six pairs of appendages: the first with a claw, the second to fifth for walking, and the sixth paddle-shaped.
• HABITAT
Originally marine, this genus later lived in brackish to fresh water.

PARACARCINOSOMA OBESA (Woodward); Ludlow Series; Silurian; UK.

abdomen •

• *pairs of appendages*

Typical length 12cm(4¾in)

Range Silurian	Distribution Europe, N.America, Asia	Occurrence 🔴

| Order LIMULIDA | Family MESOLIMULIDAE | Informal name Horseshoe crab |

MESOLIMULUS

This is the precursor of the living horseshoe crab, so called because the carapace is horseshoe shaped. The upper surface of the carapace is smooth, except for a central ridge and two longitudinal ridges. The eyes are small and widely spaced, lying just outside the longitudinal ridges. The abdomen is unsegmented, but six short spines are ranged around the margin. The abdomen articulates with the carapace, and posteriorly with the long, sharp tail spine (telson).
• HABITAT Modern horseshoe crabs are common along the eastern seaboard of the USA, in the Indian Ocean, and in south-east Asia. They are tolerant of changes in salinity and migrate to lay eggs in shallow, intertidal mud flats. They are relatively omnivorous, living on seaweeds, dead fish, and small crustaceans.

head shield with eyes

fused abdomen with spine

Typical length 12cm (4¾in)

MESOLIMULUS WALCHII (Desmarest); Solnhofen Limestone; Late Jurassic; Germany.

| Range Jurassic–Cretaceous | Distribution Europe, M. East | Occurrence |

| Order SCORPIONIDA | Family PARAISOBUTHIDAE | Informal name Water scorpion |

PARAISOBUTHUS

This aquatic scorpion has abdominal plates divided into two lobes. The first two pairs of coxae (the leg segments nearest to the body) are greatly enlarged into maxillary lobes for feeding. The carapace is squarish, with two well-developed cheeks separated by a deep groove. The stinger is very similar in shape to those of Recent terrestrial scorpions.
• HABITAT These animals were largely aquatic, being able to leave water for only a short time. They are presumed to have been carnivorous, as are modern scorpions, but the stinger may have been used for defence as well as attack.

powerful claws

walking legs

body

long tail

stinger

PARAISOBUTHUS PRANTLI Kjellesvig-Waering; Radnice Group; Late Carboniferous; Czechoslovakia.

Typical length 7cm (2¾in)

| Range L. Carb. | Distribution N. America, Europe | Occurrence |

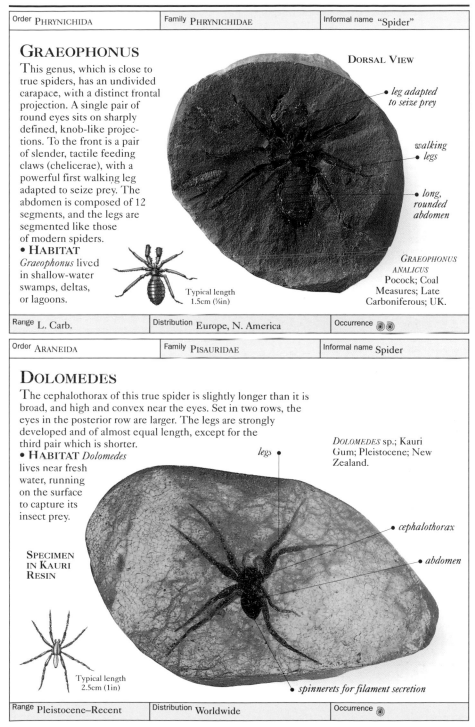

| Order PHRYNICHIDA | Family PHRYNICHIDAE | Informal name "Spider" |

GRAEOPHONUS

This genus, which is close to true spiders, has an undivided carapace, with a distinct frontal projection. A single pair of round eyes sits on sharply defined, knob-like projections. To the front is a pair of slender, tactile feeding claws (chelicerae), with a powerful first walking leg adapted to seize prey. The abdomen is composed of 12 segments, and the legs are segmented like those of modern spiders.

• **HABITAT**
Graeophonus lived in shallow-water swamps, deltas, or lagoons.

DORSAL VIEW

• *leg adapted to seize prey*

walking legs

• *long, rounded abdomen*

GRAEOPHONUS ANALICUS
Pocock; Coal Measures; Late Carboniferous; UK.

Typical length
1.5cm (⅝in)

| Range L. Carb. | Distribution Europe, N. America | Occurrence |

| Order ARANEIDA | Family PISAURIDAE | Informal name Spider |

DOLOMEDES

The cephalothorax of this true spider is slightly longer than it is broad, and high and convex near the eyes. Set in two rows, the eyes in the posterior row are larger. The legs are strongly developed and of almost equal length, except for the third pair which is shorter.

• **HABITAT** *Dolomedes* lives near fresh water, running on the surface to capture its insect prey.

legs •

DOLOMEDES sp.; Kauri Gum; Pleistocene; New Zealand.

• *cephalothorax*

• *abdomen*

SPECIMEN IN KAURI RESIN

Typical length
2.5cm (1in)

• *spinnerets for filament secretion*

| Range Pleistocene–Recent | Distribution Worldwide | Occurrence |

INSECTS

INSECTS ARE TERRESTRIAL and freshwater arthropods, with greater diversity of species than any other animal. Their bodies are divided into head, thorax, and abdomen, with three pairs of walking legs attached to the thorax. The earliest insects, found in the Early Devonian, are wingless. However, the majority are winged, and, by the Late Carboniferous, this group became the first animals to evolve powered flight. Most insects undergo a metamorphosis, with a pupa as a resting stage.

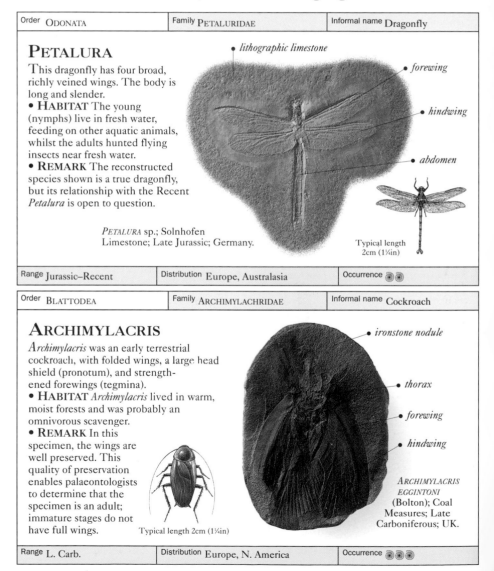

Order ODONATA	Family PETALURIDAE	Informal name Dragonfly

PETALURA

This dragonfly has four broad, richly veined wings. The body is long and slender.
• **HABITAT** The young (nymphs) live in fresh water, feeding on other aquatic animals, whilst the adults hunted flying insects near fresh water.
• **REMARK** The reconstructed species shown is a true dragonfly, but its relationship with the Recent *Petalura* is open to question.

lithographic limestone

forewing

hindwing

abdomen

PETALURA sp.; Solnhofen Limestone; Late Jurassic; Germany.

Typical length 2cm (1¼in)

Range Jurassic–Recent	Distribution Europe, Australasia	Occurrence

Order BLATTODEA	Family ARCHIMYLACHRIDAE	Informal name Cockroach

ARCHIMYLACRIS

Archimylacris was an early terrestrial cockroach, with folded wings, a large head shield (pronotum), and strengthened forewings (tegmina).
• **HABITAT** *Archimylacris* lived in warm, moist forests and was probably an omnivorous scavenger.
• **REMARK** In this specimen, the wings are well preserved. This quality of preservation enables palaeontologists to determine that the specimen is an adult; immature stages do not have full wings.

ironstone nodule

thorax

forewing

hindwing

ARCHIMYLACRIS EGGINTONI (Bolton); Coal Measures; Late Carboniferous; UK.

Typical length 2cm (1¼in)

Range L. Carb.	Distribution Europe, N. America	Occurrence

Order PLECOPTERA	Family MESOLEUCTRIDAE	Informal name Stonefly

MESOLEUCTRA

Mesoleuctra was a slender, aquatic nymph with a terrestrial adult, with folded wings. The nymph had two tails (cerci) and four wing pads.
• **HABITAT** Adults lived amongst stones and foliage, near the streams, rivers, and lakes in which the nymphs lived. The stonefly's diet was probably of small plants, such as lichens and small algae. Today, stonefly nymphs are an important source of food for freshwater fish.
• **REMARK** This specimen was probably buried very quickly in lake sediments, thus preserving the fragile legs. Fossil aquatic insects are relatively rare. More commonly insect-bearing rocks contain terrestrial species, blown into lake sediments.

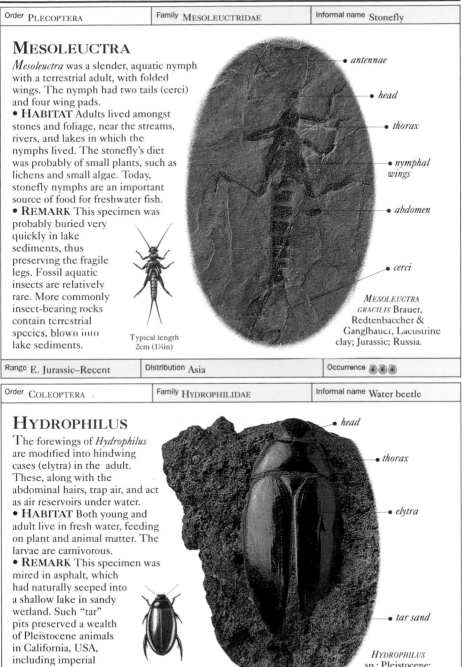

• *antennae*

• *head*

• *thorax*

• *nymphal wings*

• *abdomen*

• *cerci*

MESOLEUCTRA GRACILIS Brauer, Redtenbaccher & Ganglbauer, Lacustrine clay; Jurassic; Russia.

Typical length
2cm (1¼in)

Range E. Jurassic–Recent	Distribution Asia	Occurrence 🐚🐚🐚

Order COLEOPTERA	Family HYDROPHILIDAE	Informal name Water beetle

HYDROPHILUS

The forewings of *Hydrophilus* are modified into hindwing cases (elytra) in the adult. These, along with the abdominal hairs, trap air, and act as air reservoirs under water.
• **HABITAT** Both young and adult live in fresh water, feeding on plant and animal matter. The larvae are carnivorous.
• **REMARK** This specimen was mired in asphalt, which had naturally seeped into a shallow lake in sandy wetland. Such "tar" pits preserved a wealth of Pleistocene animals in California, USA, including imperial mammoths and sabre-toothed cats.

• *head*

• *thorax*

• *elytra*

• *tar sand*

HYDROPHILUS sp.; Pleistocene; Tar sands; USA.

Typical length
2cm (1¼in)

Range Pliocene–Recent	Distribution N. America, Europe	Occurrence 🐚🐚🐚🐚🐚

Order COLEOPTERA	Family TENEBRIONIDAE	Informal name Beetle

BLAPSIUM

This beetle has folded wings with roughly sculptured elytra (compare *Hydrophilus, p.77*). The basal leg segments (coxae) of the hindlegs evidently do not divide the first ventral plate (sternite) of the abdomen. The coxae, which were attached to the thorax by muscles, have dropped out, leaving cavities.

• HABITAT *Blapsium* was an omnivorous scavenger which lived close to the sea. It is found fossilized alongside marine shells.

• REMARK The Stonesfield Slate is famous for its fossils, which are a mixture of marine dwellers, land animals, and plants washed out to sea.

fissile sandstone

thorax

coxal cavities

BLAPSIUM EGERTONI
Westwood; Stonesfield Slate;
Middle Jurassic; UK.

Typical length
2cm (1¼in)

Range Jurassic	Distribution Europe	Occurrence ⬤

Order DIPTERA	Family BIBIONIDAE	Informal name March fly

BIBIO

This insect has only one pair of wings (forewings), folded and developed internally, with the hindwings reduced to balance organs (halteres), characteristic of true flies. The forewings have reduced vein patterns and pigmentation.

• HABITAT March flies typically inhabit grassland, often appearing in spring (hence their name) and visiting flowers.

BIBIO MACULATUS
Heer; Miocene;
Croatia.

limestone

forewing

abdomen

Typical length
2cm (1¼in)

leaf impression

Range Pliocene–Recent	Distribution Europe	Occurrence ⬤⬤

BRACHIOPODS

A LTHOUGH LIVING SPECIES are now rare, brachiopods are common in marine fossiliferous rocks. Over 3,000 genera have been described, from the Cambrian to Recent times, and they form the most abundant fauna in many Palaeozoic rocks. The shell comprises two valves: the pedicle valve on the ventral side, and the smaller brachial valve on the dorsal side. A stalk (pedicle) usually emerges from the rear of the pedicle valve, attaching the brachiopod to the sea floor. The two main groups – the hinged Articulata and the hingeless Inarticulata – are further divided into 12 orders.

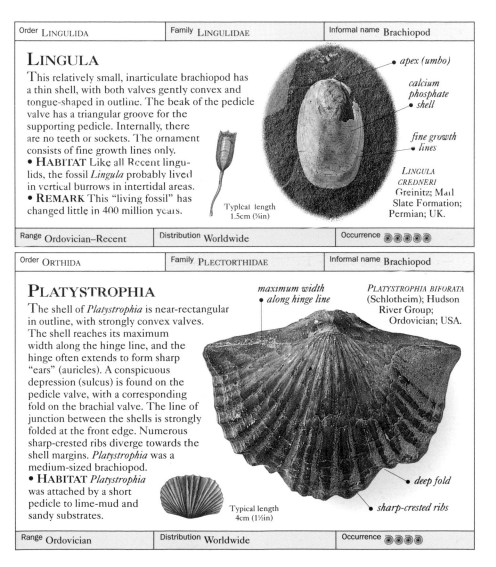

Order LINGULIDA	Family LINGULIDAE	Informal name Brachiopod

LINGULA

This relatively small, inarticulate brachiopod has a thin shell, with both valves gently convex and tongue-shaped in outline. The beak of the pedicle valve has a triangular groove for the supporting pedicle. Internally, there are no teeth or sockets. The ornament consists of fine growth lines only.
• HABITAT Like all Recent lingulids, the fossil *Lingula* probably lived in vertical burrows in intertidal areas.
• REMARK This "living fossil" has changed little in 400 million years.

apex (umbo)

calcium phosphate shell

fine growth lines

LINGULA CREDNERI Greinitz; Mail Slate Formation; Permian; UK.

Typical length 1.5cm (⅝in)

Range Ordovician–Recent	Distribution Worldwide	Occurrence ◉◉◉◉◉

Order ORTHIDA	Family PLECTORTHIDAE	Informal name Brachiopod

PLATYSTROPHIA

The shell of *Platystrophia* is near-rectangular in outline, with strongly convex valves. The shell reaches its maximum width along the hinge line, and the hinge often extends to form sharp "ears" (auricles). A conspicuous depression (sulcus) is found on the pedicle valve, with a corresponding fold on the brachial valve. The line of junction between the shells is strongly folded at the front edge. Numerous sharp-crested ribs diverge towards the shell margins. *Platystrophia* was a medium-sized brachiopod.
• HABITAT *Platystrophia* was attached by a short pedicle to lime-mud and sandy substrates.

maximum width along hinge line

PLATYSTROPHIA BIFORATA (Schlotheim); Hudson River Group; Ordovician; USA.

deep fold

sharp-crested ribs

Typical length 4cm (1½in)

Range Ordovician	Distribution Worldwide	Occurrence ◉◉◉◉

Order ORTHIDA	Family DICOELOSIIDAE	Informal name Brachiopod

DICOELOSIA

The shell of this brachiopod has a characteristic bilobed, near-triangular outline, with a strongly convex pedicle valve and less convex brachial valve. Both valves have a pronounced sulcus, with a strongly incurved beak on the pedicle valve. The hinge line is of variable width, but is generally short. The interarea (between the valves) is medium sized, with an open groove for passage of the pedicle. Numerous fine ribs diverge near the front of the shell.

• HABITAT *Dicoelosia* was attached to bryozoans and shelly fragments in shallow to mid-depths.

twin-lobed pedicle valve

DICOELOSIA BILOBATA (Linnaeus); Wenlock Limestone; Silurian; UK.

Typical length 1.5cm (⅝in)

deep sulcus

ornament of fine ribs

Range Ordovician–Devonian	Distribution Worldwide	Occurrence 🌸🌸🌸🌸🌸

Order STROPHOMENIDA	Family LEPTANIDAE	Informal name Brachiopod

LEPTAENA

This articulate brachiopod had a shell with a semicircular outline, prominent auricles, and a straight hinge line. The pedicle valve is slightly convex and the brachial valve usually flat, except at the front margins where both valves bend almost at right-angles. The surface ornament consists of numerous fine, clustered ribs, and strong, concentric wrinkles (rugae).

• HABITAT *Leptaena* lay on the sea floor with its pedicle valve downwards. The upward-projecting front margin was kept clear of the sediment surface, allowing the brachial valve to be almost completely buried.

• REMARK It is thought that the concentric rugae stabilized the shell in soft substrates. *Leptaena* is usually found with both valves separated in fine-grained limestone shales.

hinge line

LEPTAENA sp.; Longhope Formation; Silurian; USA.

Typical length 4cm (1½in)

sharp bends at front margin

clustered ribs

strong rugae

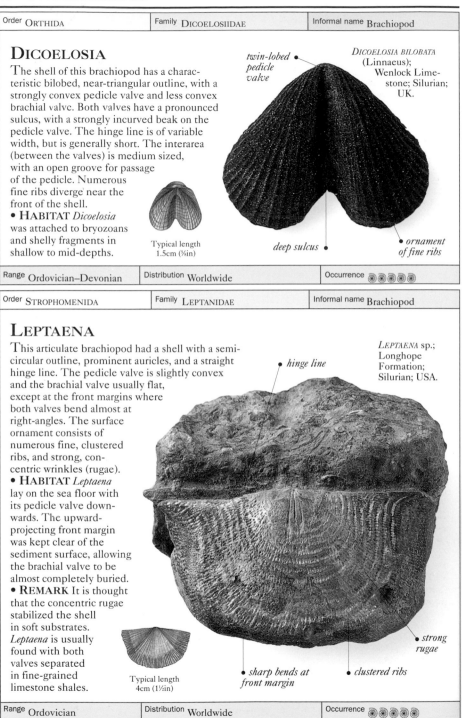

Range Ordovician	Distribution Worldwide	Occurrence 🌸🌸🌸🌸🌸

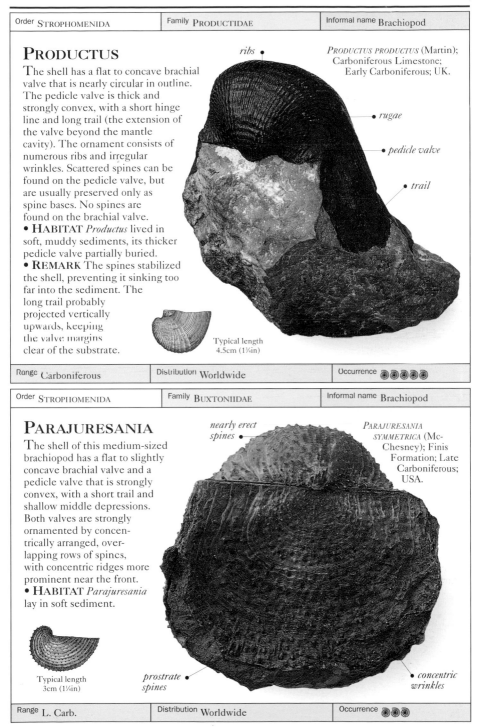

| Order STROPHOMENIDA | Family PRODUCTIDAE | Informal name Brachiopod |

PRODUCTUS

The shell has a flat to concave brachial valve that is nearly circular in outline. The pedicle valve is thick and strongly convex, with a short hinge line and long trail (the extension of the valve beyond the mantle cavity). The ornament consists of numerous ribs and irregular wrinkles. Scattered spines can be found on the pedicle valve, but are usually preserved only as spine bases. No spines are found on the brachial valve.
• **HABITAT** *Productus* lived in soft, muddy sediments, its thicker pedicle valve partially buried.
• **REMARK** The spines stabilized the shell, preventing it sinking too far into the sediment. The long trail probably projected vertically upwards, keeping the valve margins clear of the substrate.

ribs •

PRODUCTUS PRODUCTUS (Martin); Carboniferous Limestone; Early Carboniferous; UK.

• *rugae*

• *pedicle valve*

• *trail*

Typical length
4.5cm (1¾in)

| Range Carboniferous | Distribution Worldwide | Occurrence ●●●●● |

| Order STROPHOMENIDA | Family BUXTONIIDAE | Informal name Brachiopod |

PARAJURESANIA

The shell of this medium-sized brachiopod has a flat to slightly concave brachial valve and a pedicle valve that is strongly convex, with a short trail and shallow middle depressions. Both valves are strongly ornamented by concentrically arranged, overlapping rows of spines, with concentric ridges more prominent near the front.
• **HABITAT** *Parajuresania* lay in soft sediment.

nearly erect spines •

PARAJURESANIA SYMMETRICA (McChesney); Finis Formation; Late Carboniferous; USA.

Typical length
3cm (1¼in)

prostrate • *spines*

• *concentric wrinkles*

| Range L. Carb. | Distribution Worldwide | Occurrence ●●● |

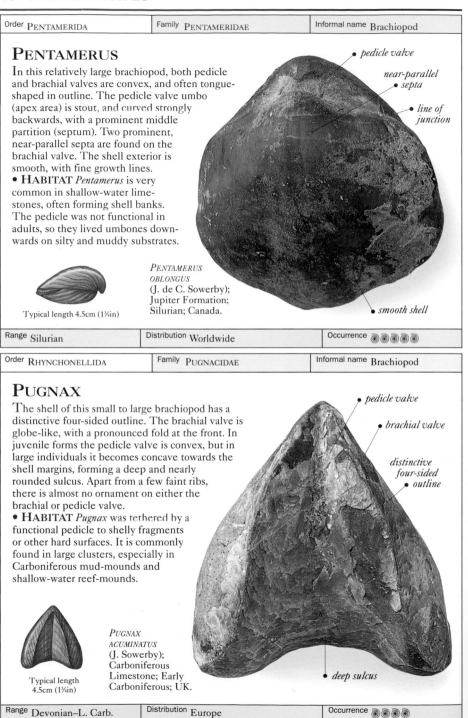

Order PENTAMERIDA	Family PENTAMERIDAE	Informal name Brachiopod

PENTAMERUS

In this relatively large brachiopod, both pedicle and brachial valves are convex, and often tongue-shaped in outline. The pedicle valve umbo (apex area) is stout, and curved strongly backwards, with a prominent middle partition (septum). Two prominent, near-parallel septa are found on the brachial valve. The shell exterior is smooth, with fine growth lines.
• **HABITAT** *Pentamerus* is very common in shallow-water lime-stones, often forming shell banks. The pedicle was not functional in adults, so they lived umbones downwards on silty and muddy substrates.

pedicle valve

near-parallel septa

line of junction

smooth shell

Typical length 4.5cm (1¾in)

PENTAMERUS OBLONGUS (J. de C. Sowerby); Jupiter Formation; Silurian; Canada.

Range Silurian	Distribution Worldwide	Occurrence ◉◉◉◉◉

Order RHYNCHONELLIDA	Family PUGNACIDAE	Informal name Brachiopod

PUGNAX

The shell of this small to large brachiopod has a distinctive four-sided outline. The brachial valve is globe-like, with a pronounced fold at the front. In juvenile forms the pedicle valve is convex, but in large individuals it becomes concave towards the shell margins, forming a deep and nearly rounded sulcus. Apart from a few faint ribs, there is almost no ornament on either the brachial or pedicle valve.
• **HABITAT** *Pugnax* was tethered by a functional pedicle to shelly fragments or other hard surfaces. It is commonly found in large clusters, especially in Carboniferous mud-mounds and shallow-water reef-mounds.

pedicle valve

brachial valve

distinctive four-sided outline

deep sulcus

Typical length 4.5cm (1¾in)

PUGNAX ACUMINATUS (J. Sowerby); Carboniferous Limestone; Early Carboniferous; UK.

Range Devonian–L. Carb.	Distribution Europe	Occurrence ◉◉◉◉

Order RHYNCHONELLIDA	Family PUGNACIDAE	Informal name Brachiopod

PLEUROPUGNOIDES

A relatively small but distinctive brachiopod, *Pleuropugnoides* had a shell that is nearly triangular in outline. The pedicle valve is convex at the back but concave towards the front, developing a large sulcus. The brachial valve is globular, with a broad front fold. The line of junction between the valves (commissure) undulates strongly at the fold crest. Sharp, diverging ribs ornament the shell.

• HABITAT *Pleuropugnoides* lived on Carboniferous reefs.

PLEUROPUGNOIDES PLEURODON (J. Phillips); Carboniferous Limestone; Early Carboniferous; UK.

pedicle valve

sharp ribs

fold in brachial valve

undulating commissure

Typical length 1.5cm (⅝in)

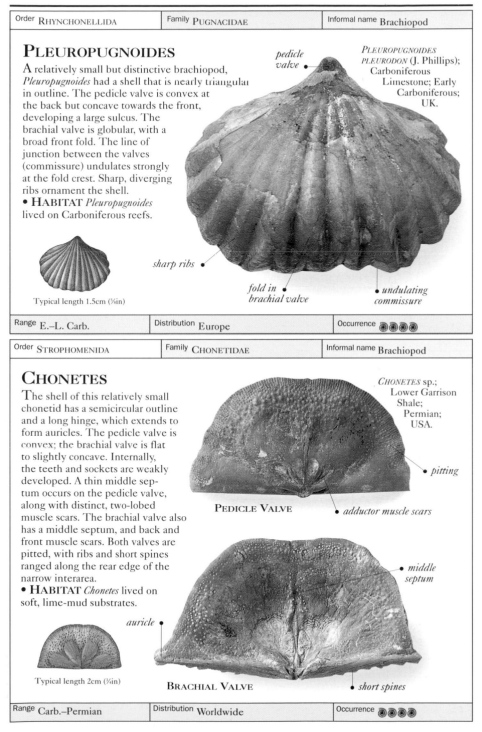

Range E.–L. Carb.	Distribution Europe	Occurrence 🐚🐚🐚🐚

Order STROPHOMENIDA	Family CHONETIDAE	Informal name Brachiopod

CHONETES

The shell of this relatively small chonetid has a semicircular outline and a long hinge, which extends to form auricles. The pedicle valve is convex; the brachial valve is flat to slightly concave. Internally, the teeth and sockets are weakly developed. A thin middle septum occurs on the pedicle valve, along with distinct, two-lobed muscle scars. The brachial valve also has a middle septum, and back and front muscle scars. Both valves are pitted, with ribs and short spines ranged along the rear edge of the narrow interarea.

• HABITAT *Chonetes* lived on soft, lime-mud substrates.

CHONETES sp.; Lower Garrison Shale; Permian; USA.

pitting

PEDICLE VALVE

adductor muscle scars

middle septum

auricle

Typical length 2cm (¾in)

BRACHIAL VALVE

short spines

Range Carb.–Permian	Distribution Worldwide	Occurrence 🐚🐚🐚🐚

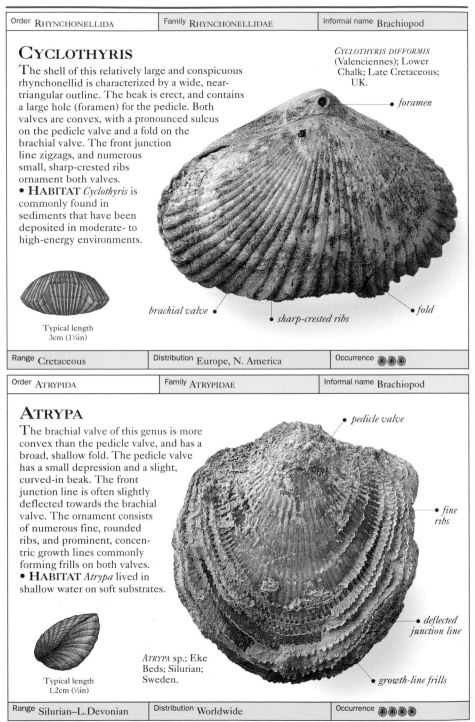

| Order RHYNCHONELLIDA | Family RHYNCHONELLIDAE | Informal name Brachiopod |

CYCLOTHYRIS

The shell of this relatively large and conspicuous rhynchonellid is characterized by a wide, near-triangular outline. The beak is erect, and contains a large hole (foramen) for the pedicle. Both valves are convex, with a pronounced sulcus on the pedicle valve and a fold on the brachial valve. The front junction line zigzags, and numerous small, sharp-crested ribs ornament both valves.
• **HABITAT** *Cyclothyris* is commonly found in sediments that have been deposited in moderate- to high-energy environments.

CYCLOTHYRIS DIFFORMIS (Valenciennes); Lower Chalk; Late Cretaceous; UK.

• *foramen*

brachial valve •

• *sharp-crested ribs*

• *fold*

Typical length
3cm (1¼in)

| Range Cretaceous | Distribution Europe, N. America | Occurrence 🐚🐚🐚 |

| Order ATRYPIDA | Family ATRYPIDAE | Informal name Brachiopod |

ATRYPA

The brachial valve of this genus is more convex than the pedicle valve, and has a broad, shallow fold. The pedicle valve has a small depression and a slight, curved-in beak. The front junction line is often slightly deflected towards the brachial valve. The ornament consists of numerous fine, rounded ribs, and prominent, concentric growth lines commonly forming frills on both valves.
• **HABITAT** *Atrypa* lived in shallow water on soft substrates.

• *pedicle valve*

• *fine ribs*

• *deflected junction line*

ATRYPA sp.; Eke Beds; Silurian; Sweden.

• *growth-line frills*

Typical length
1.2cm (½in)

| Range Silurian–L.Devonian | Distribution Worldwide | Occurrence 🐚🐚🐚🐚 |

| Order SPIRIFERIDA | Family ATHYRIDIDAE | Informal name Brachiopod |

ACTINOCONCHUS

The valves of this distinctive brachiopod are nearly equally convex, and the shell outline is near-circular. Specimens commonly lack a well-developed fold or depression. Broad, thin-layered expansions are developed at growth lines. These are traversed by a series of fine ribs that diverge towards the front margins of the shell.

• **HABITAT** *Actinoconchus* was attached by a short, functional pedicle to hard substrates. The shape of the brachial valve commonly conforms to that of the surface of the substrate.

• **REMARK** The thin-layered expansions on *Actinoconchus* served as camouflage and prevented the shell from sinking into muddy sediments.

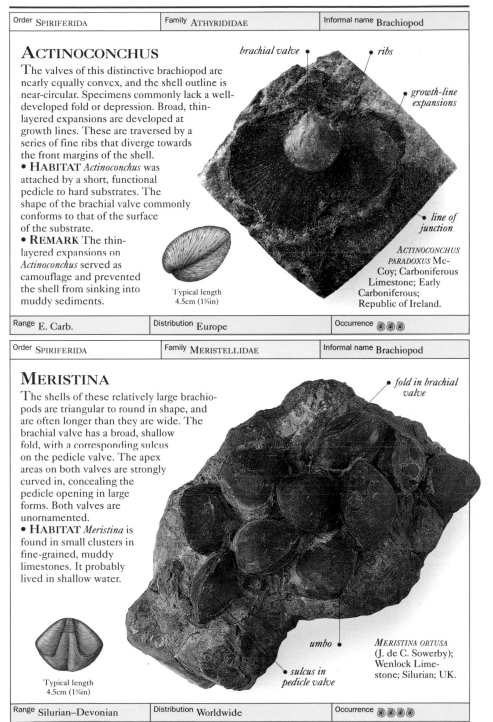

brachial valve •

• ribs

• *growth-line expansions*

• *line of junction*

Typical length
4.5cm (1¾in)

ACTINOCONCHUS PARADOXUS Mc-Coy; Carboniferous Limestone; Early Carboniferous; Republic of Ireland.

| Range E. Carb. | Distribution Europe | Occurrence 🔵🔵🔵 |

| Order SPIRIFERIDA | Family MERISTELLIDAE | Informal name Brachiopod |

MERISTINA

The shells of these relatively large brachiopods are triangular to round in shape, and are often longer than they are wide. The brachial valve has a broad, shallow fold, with a corresponding sulcus on the pedicle valve. The apex areas on both valves are strongly curved in, concealing the pedicle opening in large forms. Both valves are unornamented.

• **HABITAT** *Meristina* is found in small clusters in fine-grained, muddy limestones. It probably lived in shallow water.

• *fold in brachial valve*

umbo •

• *sulcus in pedicle valve*

MERISTINA OBTUSA (J. de C. Sowerby); Wenlock Lime-stone; Silurian; UK.

Typical length
4.5cm (1¾in)

| Range Silurian–Devonian | Distribution Worldwide | Occurrence 🔵🔵🔵🔵 |

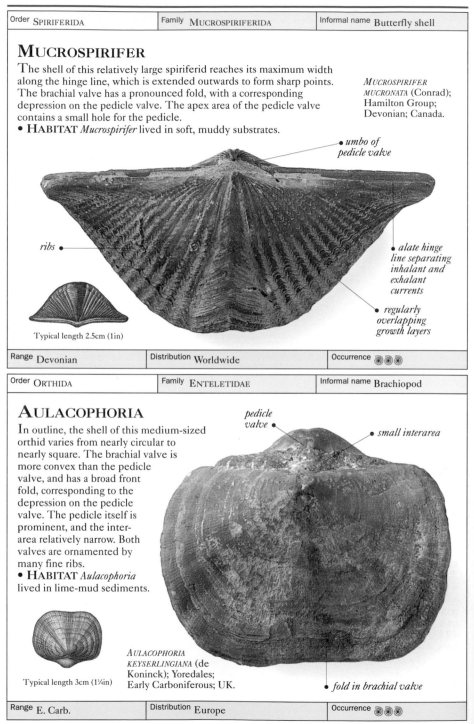

Order SPIRIFERIDA	Family MUCROSPIRIFERIDA	Informal name Butterfly shell

MUCROSPIRIFER

The shell of this relatively large spiriferid reaches its maximum width along the hinge line, which is extended outwards to form sharp points. The brachial valve has a pronounced fold, with a corresponding depression on the pedicle valve. The apex area of the pedicle valve contains a small hole for the pedicle.
• HABITAT *Mucrospirifer* lived in soft, muddy substrates.

MUCROSPIRIFER MUCRONATA (Conrad); Hamilton Group; Devonian; Canada.

umbo of pedicle valve

ribs

alate hinge line separating inhalant and exhalant currents

regularly overlapping growth layers

Typical length 2.5cm (1in)

Range Devonian	Distribution Worldwide	Occurrence 🔘🔘🔘

Order ORTHIDA	Family ENTELETIDAE	Informal name Brachiopod

AULACOPHORIA

In outline, the shell of this medium-sized orthid varies from nearly circular to nearly square. The brachial valve is more convex than the pedicle valve, and has a broad front fold, corresponding to the depression on the pedicle valve. The pedicle itself is prominent, and the inter-area relatively narrow. Both valves are ornamented by many fine ribs.
• HABITAT *Aulacophoria* lived in lime-mud sediments.

pedicle valve

small interarea

AULACOPHORIA KEYSERLINGIANA (de Koninck); Yoredales; Early Carboniferous; UK.

Typical length 3cm (1¼in)

fold in brachial valve

Range E. Carb.	Distribution Europe	Occurrence 🔘🔘🔘

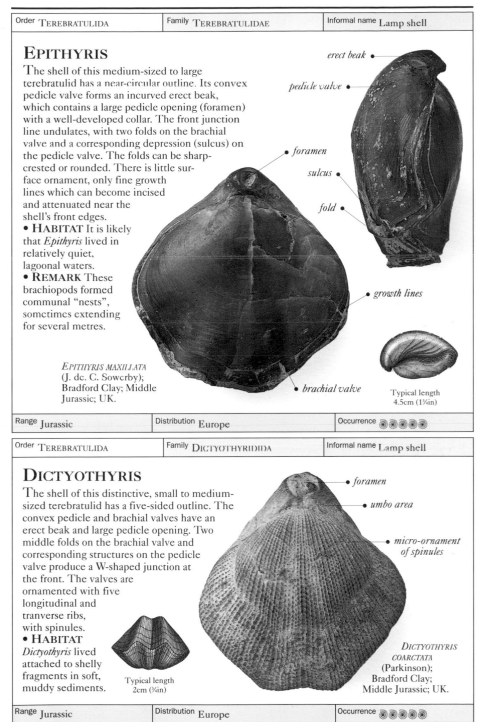

| Order TEREBRATULIDA | Family TEREBRATULIDAE | Informal name Lamp shell |

EPITHYRIS

The shell of this medium-sized to large terebratulid has a near-circular outline. Its convex pedicle valve forms an incurved erect beak, which contains a large pedicle opening (foramen) with a well-developed collar. The front junction line undulates, with two folds on the brachial valve and a corresponding depression (sulcus) on the pedicle valve. The folds can be sharp-crested or rounded. There is little sur-face ornament, only fine growth lines which can become incised and attenuated near the shell's front edges.
• **HABITAT** It is likely that *Epithyris* lived in relatively quiet, lagoonal waters.
• **REMARK** These brachiopods formed communal "nests", sometimes extending for several metres.

erect beak

pedicle valve

foramen

sulcus

fold

growth lines

EPITHYRIS MAXILLATA
(J. de. C. Sowerby);
Bradford Clay; Middle
Jurassic; UK.

brachial valve

Typical length
4.5cm (1¾in)

| Range Jurassic | Distribution Europe | Occurrence ◉◉◉◉◉ |

| Order TEREBRATULIDA | Family DICTYOTHYRIDIDA | Informal name Lamp shell |

DICTYOTHYRIS

The shell of this distinctive, small to medium-sized terebratulid has a five-sided outline. The convex pedicle and brachial valves have an erect beak and large pedicle opening. Two middle folds on the brachial valve and corresponding structures on the pedicle valve produce a W-shaped junction at the front. The valves are ornamented with five longitudinal and tranverse ribs, with spinules.
• **HABITAT** *Dictyothyris* lived attached to shelly fragments in soft, muddy sediments.

foramen

umbo area

micro-ornament of spinules

Typical length
2cm (¾in)

DICTYOTHYRIS COARCTATA
(Parkinson);
Bradford Clay;
Middle Jurassic; UK.

| Range Jurassic | Distribution Europe | Occurrence ◉◉◉◉◉ |

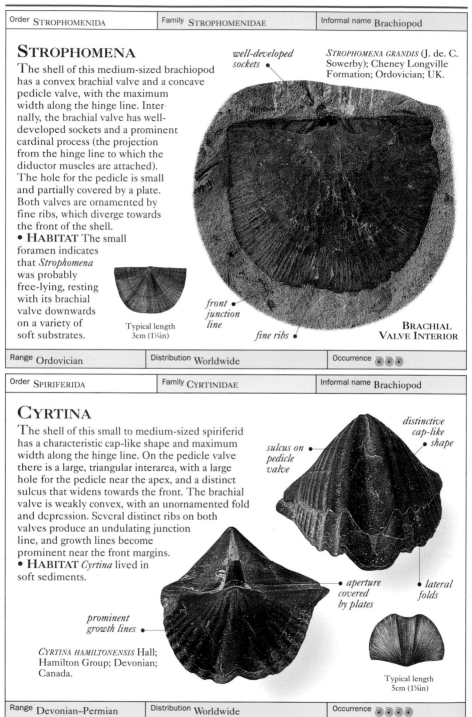

| Order STROPHOMENIDA | Family STROPHOMENIDAE | Informal name Brachiopod |

STROPHOMENA

The shell of this medium-sized brachiopod has a convex brachial valve and a concave pedicle valve, with the maximum width along the hinge line. Internally, the brachial valve has well-developed sockets and a prominent cardinal process (the projection from the hinge line to which the diductor muscles are attached). The hole for the pedicle is small and partially covered by a plate. Both valves are ornamented by fine ribs, which diverge towards the front of the shell.
• HABITAT The small foramen indicates that *Strophomena* was probably free-lying, resting with its brachial valve downwards on a variety of soft substrates.

well-developed sockets

STROPHOMENA GRANDIS (J. de C. Sowerby); Cheney Longville Formation; Ordovician; UK.

Typical length 3cm (1¼in)

front junction line

fine ribs

BRACHIAL VALVE INTERIOR

| Range Ordovician | Distribution Worldwide | Occurrence ◉◉◉ |

| Order SPIRIFERIDA | Family CYRTINIDAE | Informal name Brachiopod |

CYRTINA

The shell of this small to medium-sized spiriferid has a characteristic cap-like shape and maximum width along the hinge line. On the pedicle valve there is a large, triangular interarea, with a large hole for the pedicle near the apex, and a distinct sulcus that widens towards the front. The brachial valve is weakly convex, with an unornamented fold and depression. Several distinct ribs on both valves produce an undulating junction line, and growth lines become prominent near the front margins.
• HABITAT *Cyrtina* lived in soft sediments.

distinctive cap-like shape

sulcus on pedicle valve

prominent growth lines

CYRTINA HAMILTONENSIS Hall; Hamilton Group; Devonian; Canada.

aperture covered by plates

lateral folds

Typical length 5cm (1⅜in)

| Range Devonian–Permian | Distribution Worldwide | Occurrence ◉◉◉◉ |

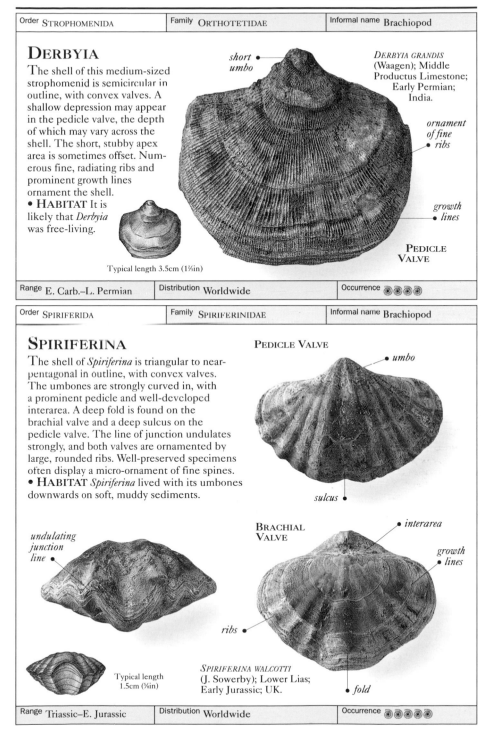

INVERTEBRATES • 89

Order STROPHOMENIDA	Family ORTHOTETIDAE	Informal name Brachiopod

DERBYIA

The shell of this medium-sized strophomenid is semicircular in outline, with convex valves. A shallow depression may appear in the pedicle valve, the depth of which may vary across the shell. The short, stubby apex area is sometimes offset. Numerous fine, radiating ribs and prominent growth lines ornament the shell.
• **HABITAT** It is likely that *Derbyia* was free-living.

short umbo

DERBYIA GRANDIS (Waagen); Middle Productus Limestone; Early Permian; India.

ornament of fine ribs

growth lines

PEDICLE VALVE

Typical length 3.5cm (1⅜in)

Range E. Carb.–L. Permian	Distribution Worldwide	Occurrence

Order SPIRIFERIDA	Family SPIRIFERINIDAE	Informal name Brachiopod

SPIRIFERINA

The shell of *Spiriferina* is triangular to near-pentagonal in outline, with convex valves. The umbones are strongly curved in, with a prominent pedicle and well-developed interarea. A deep fold is found on the brachial valve and a deep sulcus on the pedicle valve. The line of junction undulates strongly, and both valves are ornamented by large, rounded ribs. Well-preserved specimens often display a micro-ornament of fine spines.
• **HABITAT** *Spiriferina* lived with its umbones downwards on soft, muddy sediments.

PEDICLE VALVE

umbo

sulcus

undulating junction line

BRACHIAL VALVE

interarea

growth lines

ribs

Typical length 1.5cm (⅝in)

SPIRIFERINA WALCOTTI (J. Sowerby); Lower Lias; Early Jurassic; UK.

fold

Range Triassic–E. Jurassic	Distribution Worldwide	Occurrence

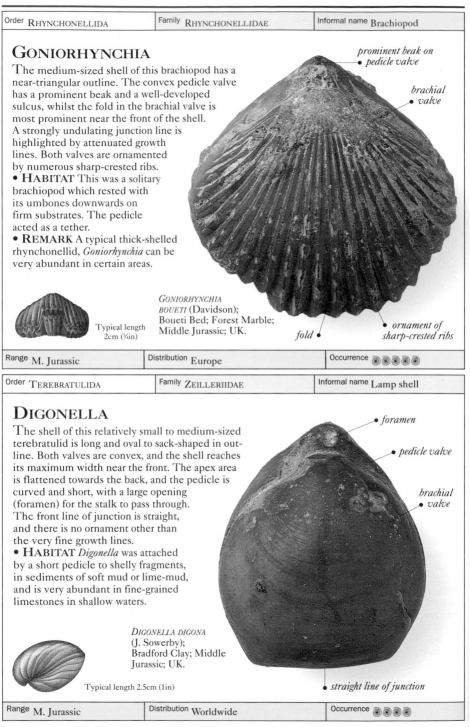

| Order RHYNCHONELLIDA | Family RHYNCHONELLIDAE | Informal name Brachiopod |

GONIORHYNCHIA

The medium-sized shell of this brachiopod has a near-triangular outline. The convex pedicle valve has a prominent beak and a well-developed sulcus, whilst the fold in the brachial valve is most prominent near the front of the shell. A strongly undulating junction line is highlighted by attenuated growth lines. Both valves are ornamented by numerous sharp-crested ribs.
• **HABITAT** This was a solitary brachiopod which rested with its umbones downwards on firm substrates. The pedicle acted as a tether.
• **REMARK** A typical thick-shelled rhynchonellid, *Goniorhynchia* can be very abundant in certain areas.

prominent beak on
• *pedicle valve*

brachial
• *valve*

GONIORHYNCHIA BOUETI (Davidson); Boueti Bed; Forest Marble; Middle Jurassic; UK.

Typical length 2cm (¾in)

fold •

• *ornament of sharp-crested ribs*

| Range M. Jurassic | Distribution Europe | Occurrence ◉◉◉◉◉ |

| Order TEREBRATULIDA | Family ZEILLERIIDAE | Informal name Lamp shell |

DIGONELLA

The shell of this relatively small to medium-sized terebratulid is long and oval to sack-shaped in outline. Both valves are convex, and the shell reaches its maximum width near the front. The apex area is flattened towards the back, and the pedicle is curved and short, with a large opening (foramen) for the stalk to pass through. The front line of junction is straight, and there is no ornament other than the very fine growth lines.
• **HABITAT** *Digonella* was attached by a short pedicle to shelly fragments, in sediments of soft mud or lime-mud, and is very abundant in fine-grained limestones in shallow waters.

• *foramen*

• *pedicle valve*

brachial
• *valve*

DIGONELLA DIGONA (J. Sowerby); Bradford Clay; Middle Jurassic; UK.

Typical length 2.5cm (1in)

• *straight line of junction*

| Range M. Jurassic | Distribution Worldwide | Occurrence ◉◉◉◉ |

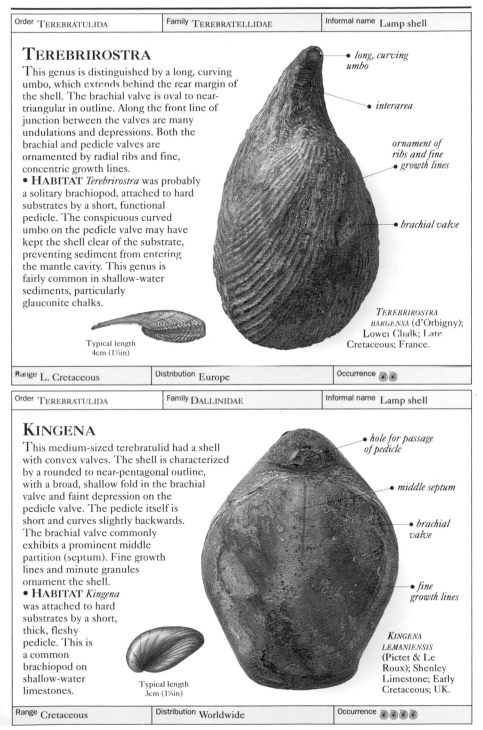

Order TEREBRATULIDA	Family TEREBRATELLIDAE	Informal name Lamp shell

TEREBRIROSTRA

This genus is distinguished by a long, curving umbo, which extends behind the rear margin of the shell. The brachial valve is oval to near-triangular in outline. Along the front line of junction between the valves are many undulations and depressions. Both the brachial and pedicle valves are ornamented by radial ribs and fine, concentric growth lines.
• HABITAT *Terebrirostra* was probably a solitary brachiopod, attached to hard substrates by a short, functional pedicle. The conspicuous curved umbo on the pedicle valve may have kept the shell clear of the substrate, preventing sediment from entering the mantle cavity. This genus is fairly common in shallow-water sediments, particularly glauconite chalks.

• *long, curving umbo*

• *interarea*

ornament of ribs and fine
• *growth lines*

• *brachial valve*

Typical length
4cm (1½in)

TEREBRIROSTRA BARGENSA (d'Orbigny); Lower Chalk; Late Cretaceous; France.

Range L. Cretaceous	Distribution Europe	Occurrence 🌑🌑

Order TEREBRATULIDA	Family DALLINIDAE	Informal name Lamp shell

KINGENA

This medium-sized terebratulid had a shell with convex valves. The shell is characterized by a rounded to near-pentagonal outline, with a broad, shallow fold in the brachial valve and faint depression on the pedicle valve. The pedicle itself is short and curves slightly backwards. The brachial valve commonly exhibits a prominent middle partition (septum). Fine growth lines and minute granules ornament the shell.
• HABITAT *Kingena* was attached to hard substrates by a short, thick, fleshy pedicle. This is a common brachiopod on shallow-water limestones.

• *hole for passage of pedicle*

• *middle septum*

• *brachial valve*

• *fine growth lines*

KINGENA LEMANIENSIS (Pictet & Le Roux); Shenley Limestone; Early Cretaceous; UK.

Typical length
3cm (1¼in)

Range Cretaceous	Distribution Worldwide	Occurrence 🌑🌑🌑🌑

Order ACROTRETIDA	Family CRANIIDAE	Informal name Brachiopod

ANCISTROCRANIA

The shell of this small brachiopod is almost circular in outline, with a straight rear margin. The shape of the pedicle valve conforms to the underlying substrate. Both valves exhibit a well-developed pair of circular muscle scars, accompanied by smaller muscle scars, and both thicken at their front margins. Apart from surface blisters (pustules), the ornament consists of concentric growth lines, and may have provided some form of camouflage.

• HABITAT Most genera in the family are cemented to hard substrates by their pedicle valves.

• REMARK The family appeared in the Early Mesozoic, and is still alive in today's oceans. They are unique in lacking a pedicle.

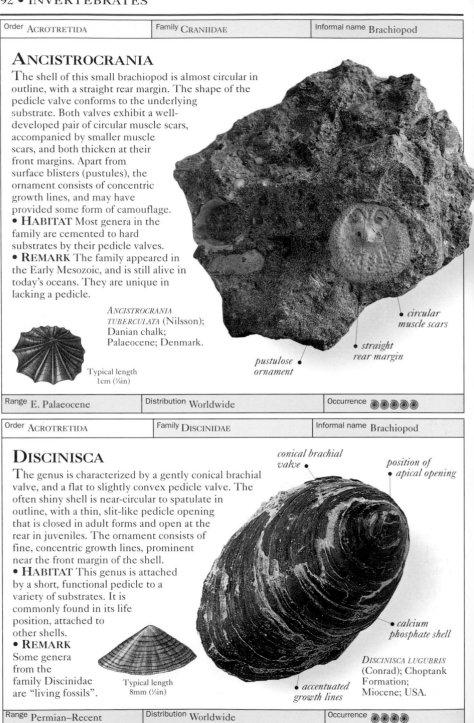

ANCISTROCRANIA TUBERCULATA (Nilsson); Danian chalk; Palaeocene; Denmark.

Typical length 1cm (⅜in)

• *circular muscle scars*

• *straight rear margin*

pustulose • *ornament*

Range E. Palaeocene	Distribution Worldwide	Occurrence ◉◉◉◉◉

Order ACROTRETIDA	Family DISCINIDAE	Informal name Brachiopod

DISCINISCA

The genus is characterized by a gently conical brachial valve, and a flat to slightly convex pedicle valve. The often shiny shell is near-circular to spatulate in outline, with a thin, slit-like pedicle opening that is closed in adult forms and open at the rear in juveniles. The ornament consists of fine, concentric growth lines, prominent near the front margin of the shell.

• HABITAT This genus is attached by a short, functional pedicle to a variety of substrates. It is commonly found in its life position, attached to other shells.

• REMARK Some genera from the family Discinidae are "living fossils".

conical brachial valve •

position of • *apical opening*

• *calcium phosphate shell*

DISCINISCA LUGUBRIS (Conrad); Choptank Formation; Miocene; USA.

Typical length 8mm (⅓in)

• *accentuated growth lines*

Range Permian–Recent	Distribution Worldwide	Occurrence ◉◉◉◉

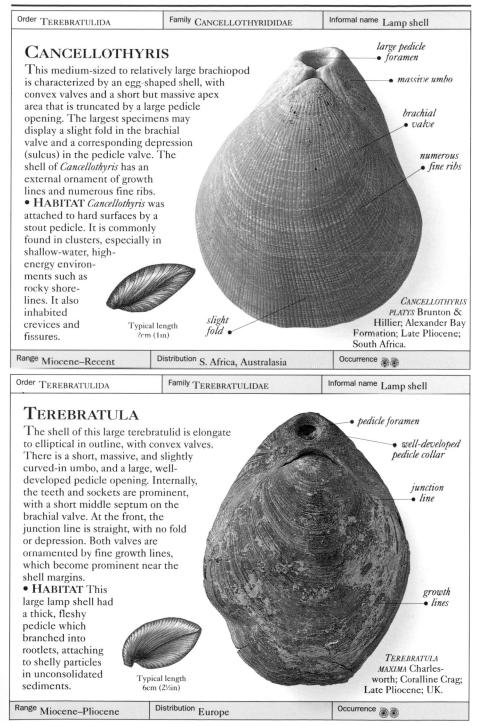

Order TEREBRATULIDA	Family CANCELLOTHYRIDIDAE	Informal name Lamp shell

CANCELLOTHYRIS

This medium-sized to relatively large brachiopod is characterized by an egg-shaped shell, with convex valves and a short but massive apex area that is truncated by a large pedicle opening. The largest specimens may display a slight fold in the brachial valve and a corresponding depression (sulcus) in the pedicle valve. The shell of *Cancellothyris* has an external ornament of growth lines and numerous fine ribs.

• **HABITAT** *Cancellothyris* was attached to hard surfaces by a stout pedicle. It is commonly found in clusters, especially in shallow-water, high-energy environments such as rocky shorelines. It also inhabited crevices and fissures.

large pedicle
• *foramen*

• *massive umbo*

brachial
• *valve*

numerous
• *fine ribs*

Typical length
?cm (1in)

slight
fold •

CANCELLOTHYRIS
PLATYS Brunton &
Hillier; Alexander Bay
Formation; Late Pliocene;
South Africa.

Range Miocene–Recent	Distribution S. Africa, Australasia	Occurrence

Order TEREBRATULIDA	Family TEREBRATULIDAE	Informal name Lamp shell

TEREBRATULA

The shell of this large terebratulid is elongate to elliptical in outline, with convex valves. There is a short, massive, and slightly curved-in umbo, and a large, well-developed pedicle opening. Internally, the teeth and sockets are prominent, with a short middle septum on the brachial valve. At the front, the junction line is straight, with no fold or depression. Both valves are ornamented by fine growth lines, which become prominent near the shell margins.

• **HABITAT** This large lamp shell had a thick, fleshy pedicle which branched into rootlets, attaching to shelly particles in unconsolidated sediments.

• *pedicle foramen*

• *well-developed*
pedicle collar

junction
• *line*

growth
• *lines*

Typical length
6cm (2½in)

TEREBRATULA
MAXIMA Charles-
worth; Coralline Crag;
Late Pliocene; UK.

Range Miocene–Pliocene	Distribution Europe	Occurrence

BIVALVES

BIVALVES ARE MOLLUSCS in which the shells are made up of two valves connected by a ligament of organic material, rarely preserved in fossils. The valves are articulated by a hinge, usually with interlocking teeth. In most cases the valves are closed by two main muscles, whose points of attachment to the shell are marked by distinct scars. Bivalves feed by filtering particles from the water through siphons. Although they possess a foot, they have limited mobility. Many burrow in sediment or bore into stone or wood. Others cement themselves to submerged objects, or attach themselves with a byssus of organic threads. Bivalves are classified by their hinges.

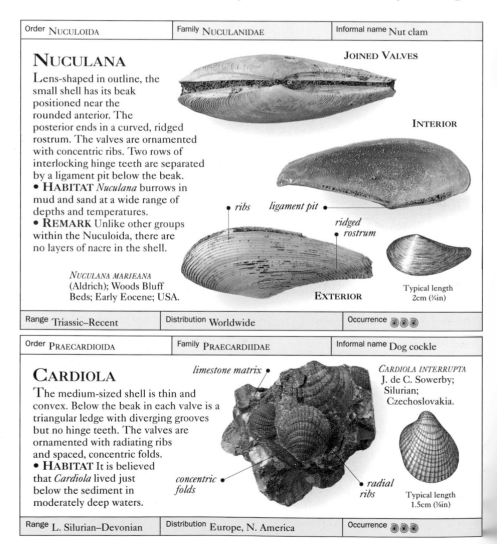

Order NUCULOIDA	Family NUCULANIDAE	Informal name Nut clam

NUCULANA

Lens-shaped in outline, the small shell has its beak positioned near the rounded anterior. The posterior ends in a curved, ridged rostrum. The valves are ornamented with concentric ribs. Two rows of interlocking hinge teeth are separated by a ligament pit below the beak.
• **HABITAT** *Nuculana* burrows in mud and sand at a wide range of depths and temperatures.
• **REMARK** Unlike other groups within the Nuculoida, there are no layers of nacre in the shell.

JOINED VALVES

INTERIOR

• *ribs* *ligament pit* •

ridged rostrum

NUCULANA MARIEANA (Aldrich); Woods Bluff Beds; Early Eocene; USA.

EXTERIOR

Typical length 2cm (¾in)

Range Triassic–Recent	Distribution Worldwide	Occurrence ◉◉◉

Order PRAECARDIOIDA	Family PRAECARDIIDAE	Informal name Dog cockle

CARDIOLA

limestone matrix •

The medium-sized shell is thin and convex. Below the beak in each valve is a triangular ledge with diverging grooves but no hinge teeth. The valves are ornamented with radiating ribs and spaced, concentric folds.
• **HABITAT** It is believed that *Cardiola* lived just below the sediment in moderately deep waters.

CARDIOLA INTERRUPTA J. de C. Sowerby; Silurian; Czechoslovakia.

concentric folds •

• *radial ribs*

Typical length 1.5cm (⅝in)

Range L. Silurian–Devonian	Distribution Europe, N. America	Occurrence ◉◉◉

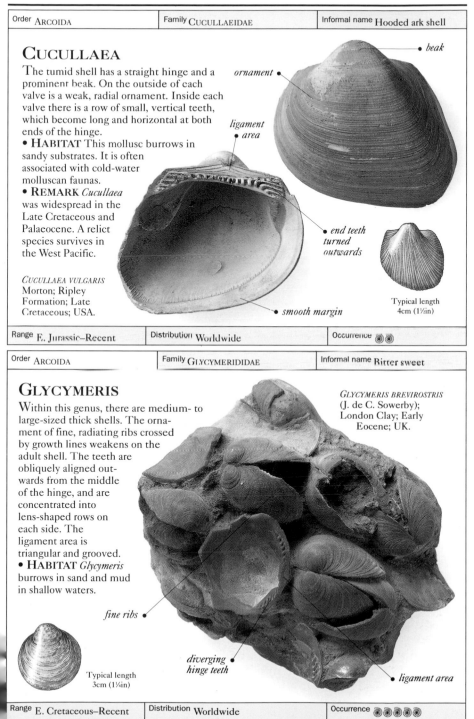

| Order ARCOIDA | Family CUCULLAEIDAE | Informal name Hooded ark shell |

CUCULLAEA

The tumid shell has a straight hinge and a prominent beak. On the outside of each valve is a weak, radial ornament. Inside each valve there is a row of small, vertical teeth, which become long and horizontal at both ends of the hinge.
• **HABITAT** This mollusc burrows in sandy substrates. It is often associated with cold-water molluscan faunas.
• **REMARK** *Cucullaea* was widespread in the Late Cretaceous and Palaeocene. A relict species survives in the West Pacific.

ornament

beak

ligament area

end teeth turned outwards

smooth margin

Typical length
4cm (1½in)

CUCULLAEA VULGARIS
Morton; Ripley
Formation; Late
Cretaceous; USA.

| Range E. Jurassic–Recent | Distribution Worldwide | Occurrence ◑◑ |

| Order ARCOIDA | Family GLYCYMERIDIDAE | Informal name Bitter sweet |

GLYCYMERIS

Within this genus, there are medium- to large-sized thick shells. The ornament of fine, radiating ribs crossed by growth lines weakens on the adult shell. The teeth are obliquely aligned outwards from the middle of the hinge, and are concentrated into lens-shaped rows on each side. The ligament area is triangular and grooved.
• **HABITAT** *Glycymeris* burrows in sand and mud in shallow waters.

GLYCYMERIS BREVIROSTRIS
(J. de C. Sowerby);
London Clay; Early
Eocene; UK.

fine ribs

diverging hinge teeth

ligament area

Typical length
3cm (1¼in)

| Range E. Cretaceous–Recent | Distribution Worldwide | Occurrence ◉◉◉◉◉ |

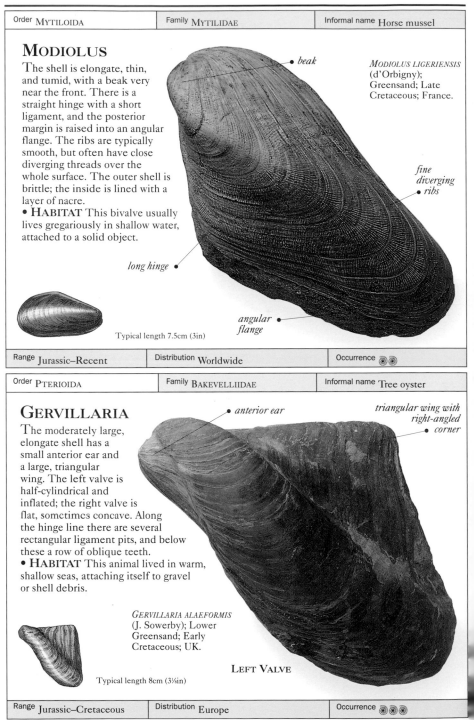

Order MYTILOIDA	Family MYTILIDAE	Informal name Horse mussel

MODIOLUS

The shell is elongate, thin, and tumid, with a beak very near the front. There is a straight hinge with a short ligament, and the posterior margin is raised into an angular flange. The ribs are typically smooth, but often have close diverging threads over the whole surface. The outer shell is brittle; the inside is lined with a layer of nacre.

• **HABITAT** This bivalve usually lives gregariously in shallow water, attached to a solid object.

• *beak*

MODIOLUS LIGERIENSIS (d'Orbigny); Greensand; Late Cretaceous; France.

fine diverging • *ribs*

long hinge •

Typical length 7.5cm (3in)

angular • *flange*

Range Jurassic–Recent	Distribution Worldwide	Occurrence

Order PTERIOIDA	Family BAKEVELLIIDAE	Informal name Tree oyster

GERVILLARIA

The moderately large, elongate shell has a small anterior ear and a large, triangular wing. The left valve is half-cylindrical and inflated; the right valve is flat, sometimes concave. Along the hinge line there are several rectangular ligament pits, and below these a row of oblique teeth.

• **HABITAT** This animal lived in warm, shallow seas, attaching itself to gravel or shell debris.

• *anterior ear*

triangular wing with right-angled • *corner*

GERVILLARIA ALAEFORMIS (J. Sowerby); Lower Greensand; Early Cretaceous; UK.

LEFT VALVE

Typical length 8cm (3⅛in)

Range Jurassic–Cretaceous	Distribution Europe	Occurrence

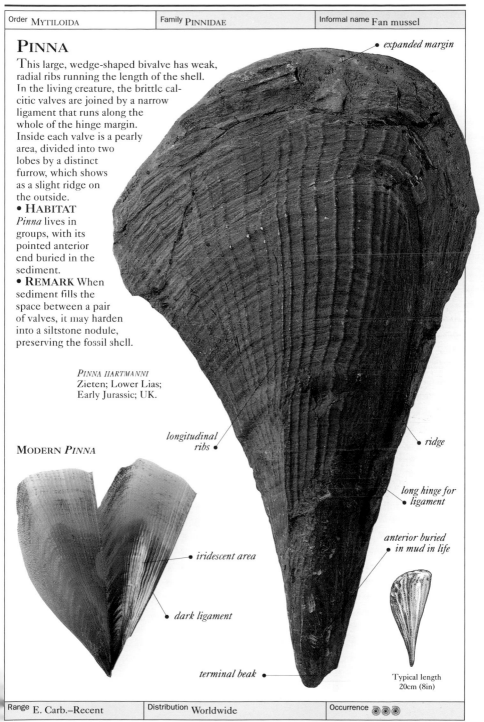

| Order MYTILOIDA | Family PINNIDAE | Informal name Fan mussel |

PINNA

This large, wedge-shaped bivalve has weak, radial ribs running the length of the shell. In the living creature, the brittle calcitic valves are joined by a narrow ligament that runs along the whole of the hinge margin. Inside each valve is a pearly area, divided into two lobes by a distinct furrow, which shows as a slight ridge on the outside.
• **HABITAT** *Pinna* lives in groups, with its pointed anterior end buried in the sediment.
• **REMARK** When sediment fills the space between a pair of valves, it may harden into a siltstone nodule, preserving the fossil shell.

PINNA HARTMANNI Zieten; Lower Lias; Early Jurassic; UK.

MODERN *PINNA*

expanded margin

longitudinal ribs

ridge

long hinge for ligament

anterior buried in mud in life

iridescent area

dark ligament

terminal beak

Typical length 20cm (8in)

| Range E. Carb.–Recent | Distribution Worldwide | Occurrence |

| Order PTERIOIDA | Family INOCERAMIDAE | Informal name Inoceramid oyster |

VOLVICERAMUS

The shell of *Volviceramus* has an outer layer of calcite and an iridescent interior. Its straight hinge has narrow ligament pits. The left valve is large, thick, and spirally coiled, and the right valve sits within it. Concentric ridges are found on both valves, but they are stronger on the right valve.

• HABITAT The growth and habits of this oyster are believed to have been similar to those of the genus *Gryphaea*. (*see p.101*).

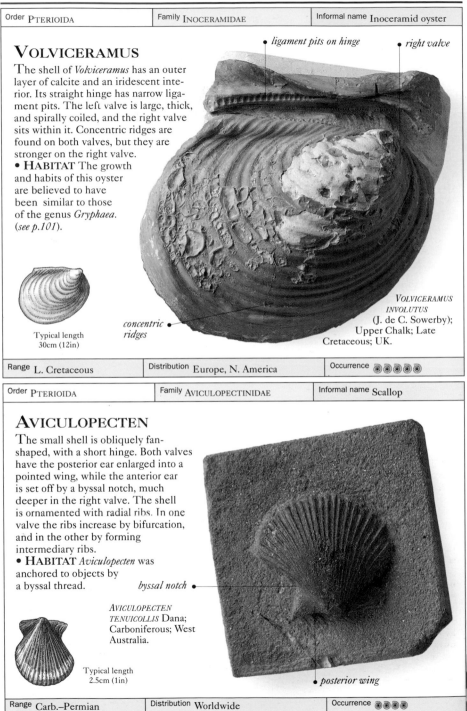

ligament pits on hinge

right valve

VOLVICERAMUS INVOLUTUS (J. de C. Sowerby); Upper Chalk; Late Cretaceous; UK.

Typical length 30cm (12in)

concentric ridges

| Range L. Cretaceous | Distribution Europe, N. America | Occurrence |

| Order PTERIOIDA | Family AVICULOPECTINIDAE | Informal name Scallop |

AVICULOPECTEN

The small shell is obliquely fan-shaped, with a short hinge. Both valves have the posterior ear enlarged into a pointed wing, while the anterior ear is set off by a byssal notch, much deeper in the right valve. The shell is ornamented with radial ribs. In one valve the ribs increase by bifurcation, and in the other by forming intermediary ribs.

• HABITAT *Aviculopecten* was anchored to objects by a byssal thread.

byssal notch

AVICULOPECTEN TENUICOLLIS Dana; Carboniferous; West Australia.

Typical length 2.5cm (1in)

posterior wing

| Range Carb.–Permian | Distribution Worldwide | Occurrence |

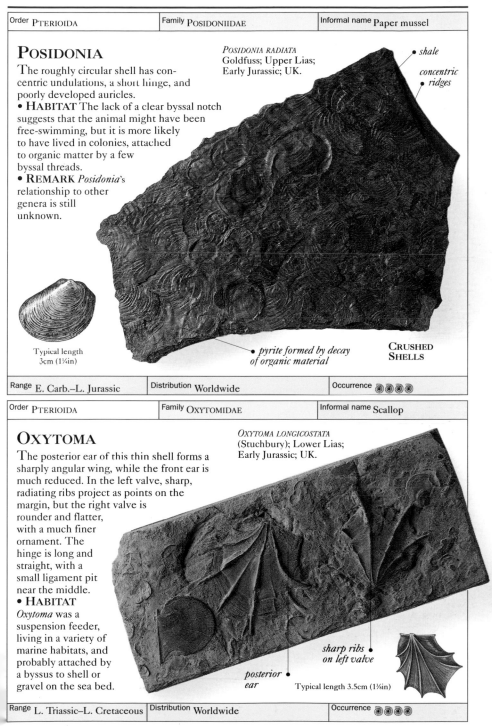

Order PTERIOIDA	Family POSIDONIIDAE	Informal name Paper mussel

POSIDONIA

The roughly circular shell has concentric undulations, a short hinge, and poorly developed auricles.
• **HABITAT** The lack of a clear byssal notch suggests that the animal might have been free-swimming, but it is more likely to have lived in colonies, attached to organic matter by a few byssal threads.
• **REMARK** *Posidonia's* relationship to other genera is still unknown.

POSIDONIA RADIATA
Goldfuss; Upper Lias;
Early Jurassic; UK.

• *shale*

concentric
• *ridges*

Typical length
3cm (1¼in)

• *pyrite formed by decay*
of organic material

**CRUSHED
SHELLS**

Range E. Carb.–L. Jurassic	Distribution Worldwide	Occurrence ◉◉◉◉

Order PTERIOIDA	Family OXYTOMIDAE	Informal name Scallop

OXYTOMA

The posterior ear of this thin shell forms a sharply angular wing, while the front ear is much reduced. In the left valve, sharp, radiating ribs project as points on the margin, but the right valve is rounder and flatter, with a much finer ornament. The hinge is long and straight, with a small ligament pit near the middle.
• **HABITAT**
Oxytoma was a suspension feeder, living in a variety of marine habitats, and probably attached by a byssus to shell or gravel on the sea bed.

OXYTOMA LONGICOSTATA
(Stuchbury); Lower Lias;
Early Jurassic; UK.

sharp ribs •
on left valve

posterior •
ear   Typical length 3.5cm (1⅜in)

Range L. Triassic–L. Cretaceous	Distribution Worldwide	Occurrence ◉◉◉◉

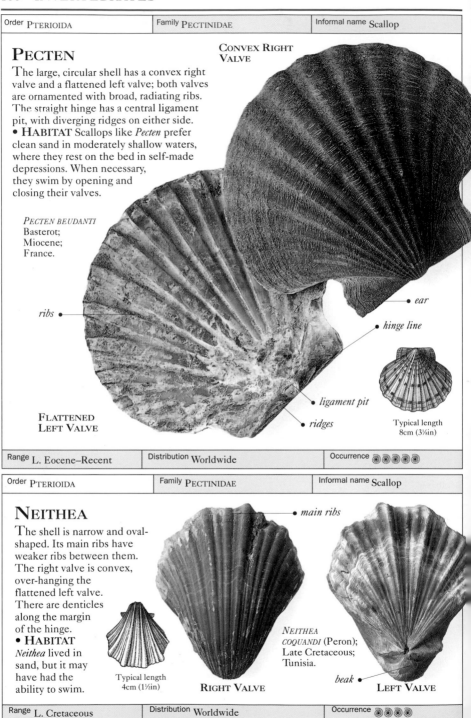

Order PTERIOIDA	Family PECTINIDAE	Informal name Scallop

PECTEN

The large, circular shell has a convex right valve and a flattened left valve; both valves are ornamented with broad, radiating ribs. The straight hinge has a central ligament pit, with diverging ridges on either side.
• HABITAT Scallops like *Pecten* prefer clean sand in moderately shallow waters, where they rest on the bed in self-made depressions. When necessary, they swim by opening and closing their valves.

CONVEX RIGHT VALVE

PECTEN BEUDANTI
Basterot;
Miocene;
France.

ribs •

• ear

• hinge line

FLATTENED LEFT VALVE

• ligament pit

• ridges

Typical length
8cm (3¼in)

Range L. Eocene–Recent	Distribution Worldwide	Occurrence

Order PTERIOIDA	Family PECTINIDAE	Informal name Scallop

NEITHEA

The shell is narrow and oval-shaped. Its main ribs have weaker ribs between them. The right valve is convex, over-hanging the flattened left valve. There are denticles along the margin of the hinge.
• HABITAT *Neithea* lived in sand, but it may have had the ability to swim.

• main ribs

NEITHEA COQUANDI (Peron);
Late Cretaceous;
Tunisia.

Typical length
4cm (1½in)

RIGHT VALVE

beak •

LEFT VALVE

Range L. Cretaceous	Distribution Worldwide	Occurrence

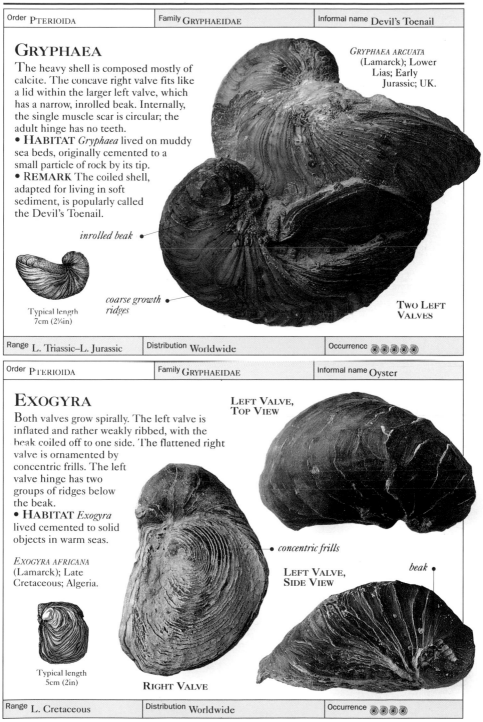

| Order PTERIOIDA | Family GRYPHAEIDAE | Informal name Devil's Toenail |

GRYPHAEA

The heavy shell is composed mostly of calcite. The concave right valve fits like a lid within the larger left valve, which has a narrow, inrolled beak. Internally, the single muscle scar is circular; the adult hinge has no teeth.
• HABITAT *Gryphaea* lived on muddy sea beds, originally cemented to a small particle of rock by its tip.
• REMARK The coiled shell, adapted for living in soft sediment, is popularly called the Devil's Toenail.

GRYPHAEA ARCUATA
(Lamarck); Lower Lias; Early Jurassic; UK.

inrolled beak •

Typical length 7cm (2¾in)

coarse growth ridges •

TWO LEFT VALVES

| Range L. Triassic–L. Jurassic | Distribution Worldwide | Occurrence 🔘🔘🔘🔘🔘 |

| Order PTERIOIDA | Family GRYPHAEIDAE | Informal name Oyster |

EXOGYRA

Both valves grow spirally. The left valve is inflated and rather weakly ribbed, with the beak coiled off to one side. The flattened right valve is ornamented by concentric frills. The left valve hinge has two groups of ridges below the beak.
• HABITAT *Exogyra* lived cemented to solid objects in warm seas.

LEFT VALVE, TOP VIEW

EXOGYRA AFRICANA
(Lamarck); Late Cretaceous; Algeria.

• concentric frills

LEFT VALVE, SIDE VIEW

beak •

Typical length 5cm (2in)

RIGHT VALVE

| Range L. Cretaceous | Distribution Worldwide | Occurrence 🔘🔘🔘🔘 |

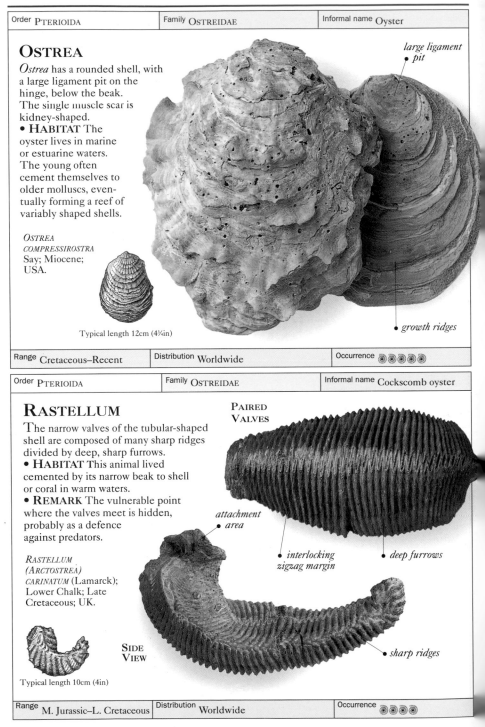

Order PTERIOIDA	Family OSTREIDAE	Informal name Oyster

OSTREA

Ostrea has a rounded shell, with a large ligament pit on the hinge, below the beak. The single muscle scar is kidney-shaped.
• **HABITAT** The oyster lives in marine or estuarine waters. The young often cement themselves to older molluscs, eventually forming a reef of variably shaped shells.

OSTREA COMPRESSIROSTRA Say; Miocene; USA.

large ligament pit

growth ridges

Typical length 12cm (4¾in)

Range Cretaceous–Recent	Distribution Worldwide	Occurrence ✹✹✹✹✹

Order PTERIOIDA	Family OSTREIDAE	Informal name Cockscomb oyster

RASTELLUM

PAIRED VALVES

The narrow valves of the tubular-shaped shell are composed of many sharp ridges divided by deep, sharp furrows.
• **HABITAT** This animal lived cemented by its narrow beak to shell or coral in warm waters.
• **REMARK** The vulnerable point where the valves meet is hidden, probably as a defence against predators.

RASTELLUM (ARCTOSTREA) CARINATUM (Lamarck); Lower Chalk; Late Cretaceous; UK.

attachment area

interlocking zigzag margin

deep furrows

SIDE VIEW

sharp ridges

Typical length 10cm (4in)

Range M. Jurassic–L. Cretaceous	Distribution Worldwide	Occurrence ✹✹✹✹

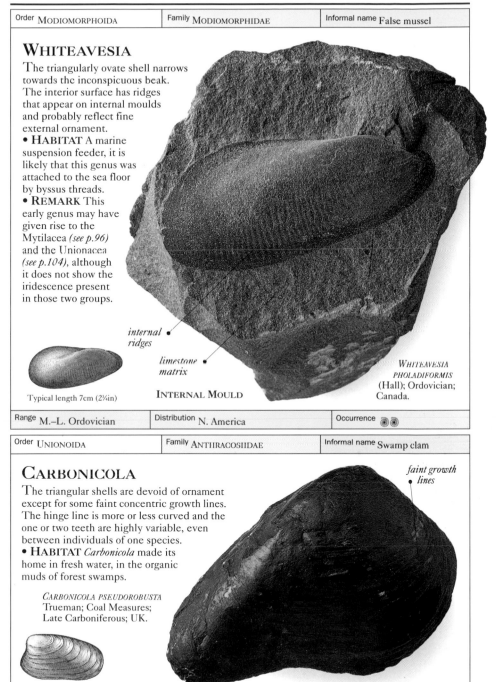

Order MODIOMORPHOIDA	Family MODIOMORPHIDAE	Informal name False mussel

WHITEAVESIA

The triangularly ovate shell narrows towards the inconspicuous beak. The interior surface has ridges that appear on internal moulds and probably reflect fine external ornament.
• **HABITAT** A marine suspension feeder, it is likely that this genus was attached to the sea floor by byssus threads.
• **REMARK** This early genus may have given rise to the Mytilacea *(see p.96)* and the Unionacea *(see p.104)*, although it does not show the iridescence present in those two groups.

internal ridges

limestone matrix

Typical length 7cm (2¾in)

INTERNAL MOULD

WHITEAVESIA PHOLADIFORMIS (Hall); Ordovician; Canada.

Range M.–L. Ordovician	Distribution N. America	Occurrence 🔵🔵

Order UNIONOIDA	Family ANTHRACOSIIDAE	Informal name Swamp clam

CARBONICOLA

The triangular shells are devoid of ornament except for some faint concentric growth lines. The hinge line is more or less curved and the one or two teeth are highly variable, even between individuals of one species.
• **HABITAT** *Carbonicola* made its home in fresh water, in the organic muds of forest swamps.

faint growth lines

CARBONICOLA PSEUDOROBUSTA Trueman; Coal Measures; Late Carboniferous; UK.

Typical length 7cm (2¾in)

Range L. Carb.	Distribution W. Europe	Occurrence 🔵🔵🔵🔵🔵

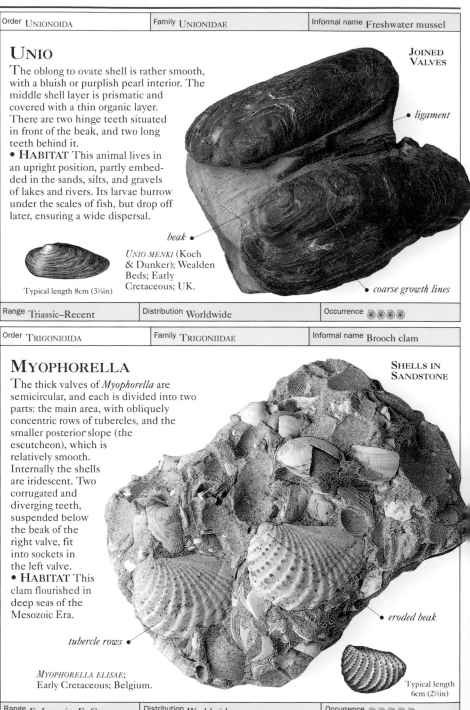

| Order UNIONOIDA | Family UNIONIDAE | Informal name Freshwater mussel |

UNIO

JOINED VALVES

The oblong to ovate shell is rather smooth, with a bluish or purplish pearl interior. The middle shell layer is prismatic and covered with a thin organic layer. There are two hinge teeth situated in front of the beak, and two long teeth behind it.

• **HABITAT** This animal lives in an upright position, partly embedded in the sands, silts, and gravels of lakes and rivers. Its larvae burrow under the scales of fish, but drop off later, ensuring a wide dispersal.

• *ligament*

beak •

UNIO MENKI (Koch & Dunker); Wealden Beds; Early Cretaceous; UK.

Typical length 8cm (3⅛in)

• *coarse growth lines*

| Range Triassic–Recent | Distribution Worldwide | Occurrence 🌑🌑🌑🌑 |

| Order TRIGONIOIDA | Family TRIGONIIDAE | Informal name Brooch clam |

MYOPHORELLA

SHELLS IN SANDSTONE

The thick valves of *Myophorella* are semicircular, and each is divided into two parts: the main area, with obliquely concentric rows of tubercles, and the smaller posterior slope (the escutcheon), which is relatively smooth. Internally the shells are iridescent. Two corrugated and diverging teeth, suspended below the beak of the right valve, fit into sockets in the left valve.

• **HABITAT** This clam flourished in deep seas of the Mesozoic Era.

tubercle rows •

MYOPHORELLA ELISAE; Early Cretaceous; Belgium.

• *eroded beak*

Typical length 6cm (2⅜in)

| Range E. Jurassic–E. Cretaceous | Distribution Worldwide | Occurrence 🌑🌑🌑🌑🌑 |

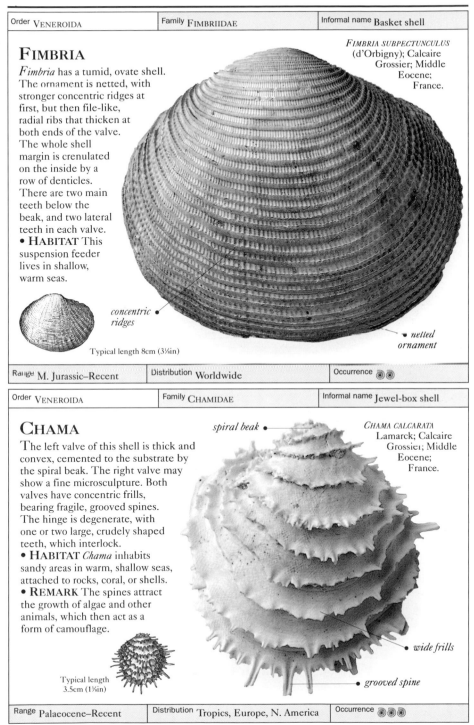

| Order VENEROIDA | Family FIMBRIIDAE | Informal name Basket shell |

FIMBRIA

Fimbria has a tumid, ovate shell. The ornament is netted, with stronger concentric ridges at first, but then file-like, radial ribs that thicken at both ends of the valve. The whole shell margin is crenulated on the inside by a row of denticles. There are two main teeth below the beak, and two lateral teeth in each valve.
• HABITAT This suspension feeder lives in shallow, warm seas.

FIMBRIA SUBPECTUNCULUS (d'Orbigny); Calcaire Grossier; Middle Eocene; France.

concentric • ridges

• netted ornament

Typical length 8cm (3¼in)

| Range M. Jurassic–Recent | Distribution Worldwide | Occurrence ◉◉ |

| Order VENEROIDA | Family CHAMIDAE | Informal name Jewel-box shell |

CHAMA

The left valve of this shell is thick and convex, cemented to the substrate by the spiral beak. The right valve may show a fine microsculpture. Both valves have concentric frills, bearing fragile, grooved spines. The hinge is degenerate, with one or two large, crudely shaped teeth, which interlock.
• HABITAT *Chama* inhabits sandy areas in warm, shallow seas, attached to rocks, coral, or shells.
• REMARK The spines attract the growth of algae and other animals, which then act as a form of camouflage.

spiral beak •

CHAMA CALCARATA Lamarck; Calcaire Grossier; Middle Eocene; France.

• wide frills

• grooved spine

Typical length 3.5cm (1⅜in)

| Range Palaeocene–Recent | Distribution Tropics, Europe, N. America | Occurrence ◉◉◉ |

Order VENEROIDA	Family CARDITIDAE	Informal name False cockle

VENERICOR

The large, thick, oval to triangular shell has a prominent beak. When very young, it has narrow, radial ribs, which may be armed with small tubercles. These soon become smooth, flat ribbons separated by shallow grooves. In each valve the wide, triangular hinge plate bears three massive teeth. The inner shell margin is marked by a row of flat denticles.
• **HABITAT** *Venericor* lived in warm, shallow waters, burrowing into the sand or silt.
• **REMARK** Paired valves in life position are found in large numbers in some strata.

VENERICOR PLANICOSTA (Lamarck); Earnley Formation; Middle Eocene; UK.

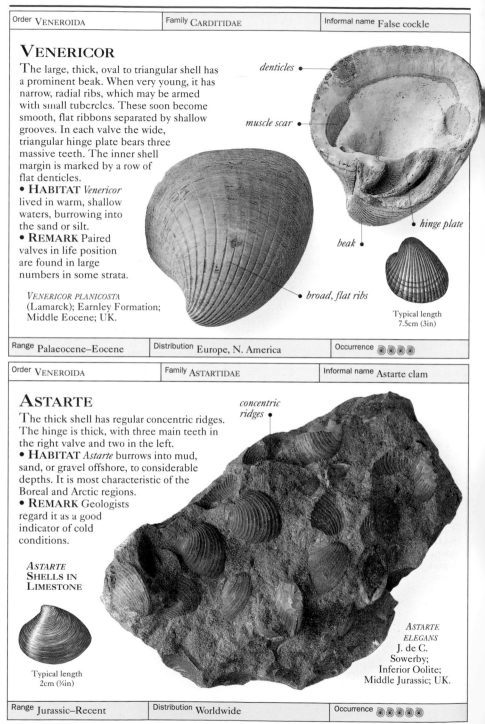

denticles •

muscle scar •

• *hinge plate*

beak •

• *broad, flat ribs*

Typical length 7.5cm (3in)

Range Palaeocene–Eocene	Distribution Europe, N. America	Occurrence ◉◉◉◉

Order VENEROIDA	Family ASTARTIDAE	Informal name Astarte clam

ASTARTE

The thick shell has regular concentric ridges. The hinge is thick, with three main teeth in the right valve and two in the left.
• **HABITAT** *Astarte* burrows into mud, sand, or gravel offshore, to considerable depths. It is most characteristic of the Boreal and Arctic regions.
• **REMARK** Geologists regard it as a good indicator of cold conditions.

concentric ridges •

ASTARTE SHELLS IN LIMESTONE

ASTARTE ELEGANS J. de C. Sowerby; Inferior Oolite; Middle Jurassic; UK.

Typical length 2cm (¾in)

Range Jurassic–Recent	Distribution Worldwide	Occurrence ◉◉◉◉◉

Order VENEROIDA	Family CRASSATELLIDAE	Informal name Clam

CRASSATELLA

The solid rectangular shell has two V-shaped cardinal teeth in the left valve and one in the right, flanked by elongate lateral teeth. There are two muscle scars, which are joined by a roundly curved pallial line. The margins of the valves are finely crenulated. The young valves have strong concentric ridges. These fade out in some species but persist in others.
• HABITAT These clams were common in warm, shallow seas, where they burrowed into soft substrates.
• REMARK Some species of this genus evolved relatively rapidly.

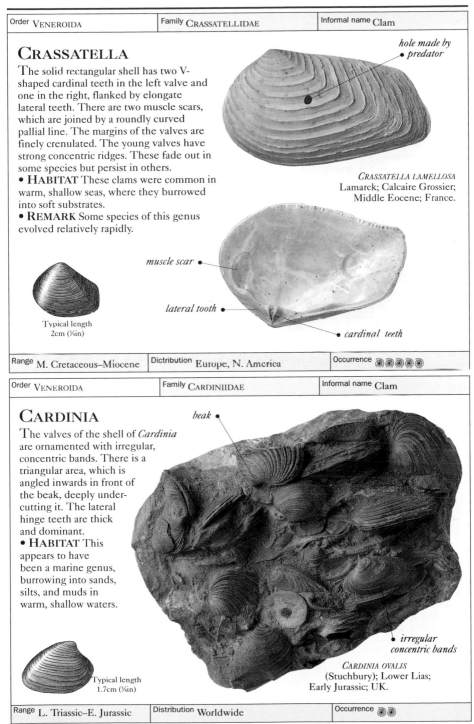

hole made by predator

CRASSATELLA LAMELLOSA
Lamarck; Calcaire Grossier;
Middle Eocene; France.

muscle scar

lateral tooth

cardinal teeth

Typical length
2cm (¾in)

Range M. Cretaceous–Miocene	Distribution Europe, N. America	Occurrence

Order VENEROIDA	Family CARDINIIDAE	Informal name Clam

CARDINIA

The valves of the shell of *Cardinia* are ornamented with irregular, concentric bands. There is a triangular area, which is angled inwards in front of the beak, deeply under-cutting it. The lateral hinge teeth are thick and dominant.
• HABITAT This appears to have been a marine genus, burrowing into sands, silts, and muds in warm, shallow waters.

beak

irregular concentric bands

CARDINIA OVALIS
(Stuchbury); Lower Lias;
Early Jurassic; UK.

Typical length
1.7cm (⅝in)

Range L. Triassic–E. Jurassic	Distribution Worldwide	Occurrence

Order VENEROIDA	Family CARDIIDAE	Informal name Cockle

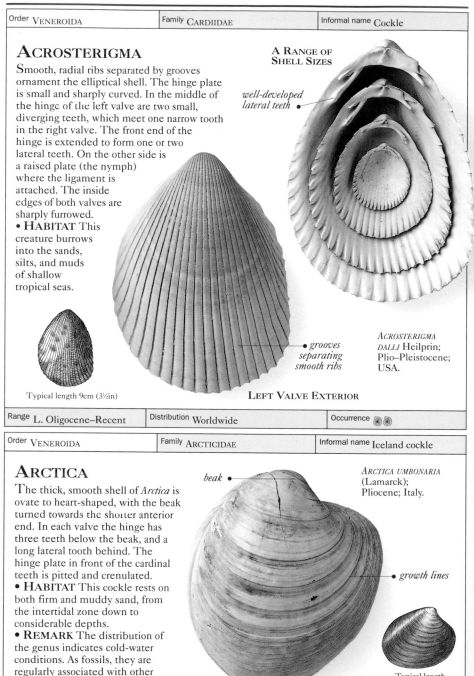

ACROSTERIGMA

Smooth, radial ribs separated by grooves ornament the elliptical shell. The hinge plate is small and sharply curved. In the middle of the hinge of the left valve are two small, diverging teeth, which meet one narrow tooth in the right valve. The front end of the hinge is extended to form one or two lateral teeth. On the other side is a raised plate (the nymph) where the ligament is attached. The inside edges of both valves are sharply furrowed.
• **HABITAT** This creature burrows into the sands, silts, and muds of shallow tropical seas.

A RANGE OF
SHELL SIZES

well-developed lateral teeth

grooves separating smooth ribs

ACROSTERIGMA
DALLI Heilprin;
Plio–Pleistocene;
USA.

Typical length 9cm (3½in)

LEFT VALVE EXTERIOR

Range L. Oligocene–Recent	Distribution Worldwide	Occurrence 🌑🌑

Order VENEROIDA	Family ARCTICIDAE	Informal name Iceland cockle

ARCTICA

The thick, smooth shell of *Arctica* is ovate to heart-shaped, with the beak turned towards the shorter anterior end. In each valve the hinge has three teeth below the beak, and a long lateral tooth behind. The hinge plate in front of the cardinal teeth is pitted and crenulated.
• **HABITAT** This cockle rests on both firm and muddy sand, from the intertidal zone down to considerable depths.
• **REMARK** The distribution of the genus indicates cold-water conditions. As fossils, they are regularly associated with other cold-water molluscs.

beak

ARCTICA UMBONARIA
(Lamarck);
Pliocene; Italy.

growth lines

Typical length
9cm (3½in)

Range L. Cretaceous–Recent	Distribution Europe, N. America	Occurrence 🌑🌑🌑🌑

Order VENEROIDA	Family CORBICULIDAE	Informal name Marsh clam

POLYMESODA

Polymesoda has an oval shell, with weak concentric growth ridges and wrinkles. There are three cardinal teeth below the beak and strong, elongate lateral teeth. Some fossils still show radiating colour bands.
• **HABITAT** This clam lives in tidal marshes and brackish lagoons in tropical and sub-tropical regions.
• **REMARK** European fossils differ from the American forms in details of the teeth and pallial line.

SLAB WITH SHELLS

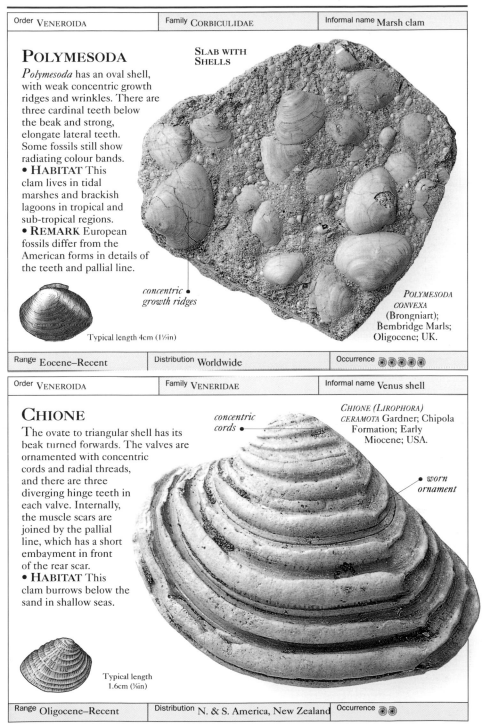

concentric growth ridges

Typical length 4cm (1½in)

POLYMESODA CONVEXA (Brongniart); Bembridge Marls; Oligocene; UK.

Range Eocene–Recent	Distribution Worldwide	Occurrence 🦪🦪🦪🦪🦪

Order VENEROIDA	Family VENERIDAE	Informal name Venus shell

CHIONE

The ovate to triangular shell has its beak turned forwards. The valves are ornamented with concentric cords and radial threads, and there are three diverging hinge teeth in each valve. Internally, the muscle scars are joined by the pallial line, which has a short embayment in front of the rear scar.
• **HABITAT** This clam burrows below the sand in shallow seas.

concentric cords

CHIONE (LIROPHORA) CERAMOTA Gardner; Chipola Formation; Early Miocene; USA.

• *worn ornament*

Typical length 1.6cm (⅝in)

Range Oligocene–Recent	Distribution N. & S. America, New Zealand	Occurrence 🦪🦪

Order MYOIDA	Family MYIDAE	Informal name River clam

POTAMOMYA

The shell is small and rather thin, varying from ovate to wedge-shaped. The surface is smooth, except where roughened by irregular growth lines. In the right valve, the ligament was attached to a central triangular projection; the rear part of this extends to form a narrow oblique tooth. The left valve hinge has a groove which receives this tooth.
• HABITAT *Potamomya* was often abundant in non-marine, silty sands and muds.

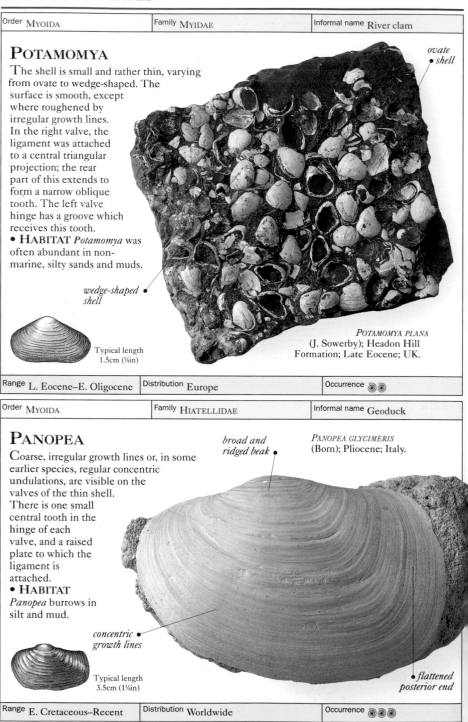

ovate shell

wedge-shaped shell

Typical length 1.5cm (⅝in)

POTAMOMYA PLANA
(J. Sowerby); Headon Hill
Formation; Late Eocene; UK.

Range L. Eocene–E. Oligocene	Distribution Europe	Occurrence

Order MYOIDA	Family HIATELLIDAE	Informal name Geoduck

PANOPEA

Coarse, irregular growth lines or, in some earlier species, regular concentric undulations, are visible on the valves of the thin shell. There is one small central tooth in the hinge of each valve, and a raised plate to which the ligament is attached.
• HABITAT *Panopea* burrows in silt and mud.

broad and ridged beak

PANOPEA GLYCIMERIS
(Born); Pliocene; Italy.

concentric growth lines

Typical length 3.5cm (1⅜in)

flattened posterior end

Range E. Cretaceous–Recent	Distribution Worldwide	Occurrence

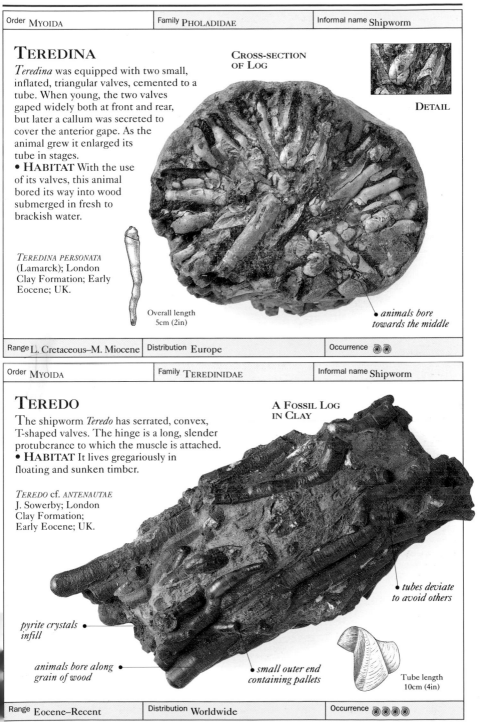

Order MYOIDA	Family PHOLADIDAE	Informal name Shipworm

TEREDINA

Teredina was equipped with two small, inflated, triangular valves, cemented to a tube. When young, the two valves gaped widely both at front and rear, but later a callum was secreted to cover the anterior gape. As the animal grew it enlarged its tube in stages.
• HABITAT With the use of its valves, this animal bored its way into wood submerged in fresh to brackish water.

TEREDINA PERSONATA
(Lamarck); London
Clay Formation; Early
Eocene; UK.

CROSS-SECTION
OF LOG

DETAIL

Overall length
5cm (2in)

• *animals bore
towards the middle*

Range L. Cretaceous–M. Miocene	Distribution Europe	Occurrence

Order MYOIDA	Family TEREDINIDAE	Informal name Shipworm

TEREDO

The shipworm *Teredo* has serrated, convex, T-shaped valves. The hinge is a long, slender protuberance to which the muscle is attached.
• HABITAT It lives gregariously in floating and sunken timber.

TEREDO cf. *ANTENAUTAE*
J. Sowerby; London
Clay Formation;
Early Eocene; UK.

A FOSSIL LOG
IN CLAY

• *tubes deviate
to avoid others*

*pyrite crystals
infill* •

*animals bore along
grain of wood* •

• *small outer end
containing pallets*

Tube length
10cm (4in)

Range Eocene–Recent	Distribution Worldwide	Occurrence

Order HIPPURITOIDA	Family HIPPURITIDAE	Informal name Rudist

HIPPURITES

This genus belongs to an extraordinary group of complex bivalves known as rudists. One valve is conical in shape, enlarging rapidly from the base, where it is cemented to the substrate. The other valve is more or less flat, fitting like a small lid, with two long teeth descending from its inner surface, and two bosses where the muscles were attached. The outside of the cone is corrugated by longitudinal ribs. Internally, the walls are folded, forming vertical pillars, a narrow tooth, and sockets to receive the teeth in the other valve. The structure of the shell allows water to pass through.

• **HABITAT** *Hippurites* lived near corals or on firm sand in warm seas. Although some species were solitary, others were gregarious and may have grouped together to form reefs.

JOINED VALVES

lid-like upper valve

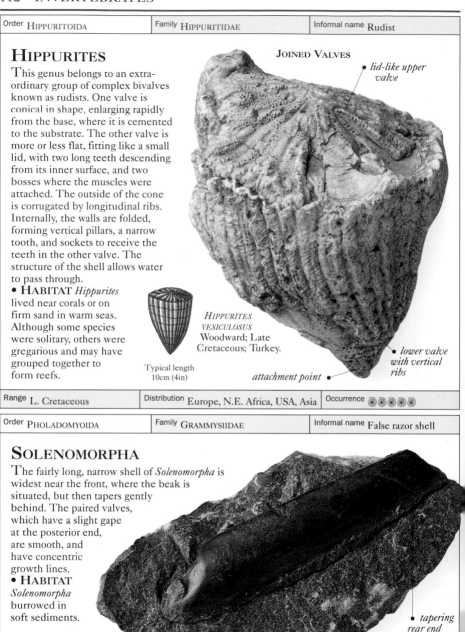

HIPPURITES VESICULOSUS Woodward; Late Cretaceous; Turkey.

Typical length 10cm (4in)

attachment point

lower valve with vertical ribs

Range L. Cretaceous	Distribution Europe, N.E. Africa, USA, Asia	Occurrence ⊛⊛⊛⊛⊛

Order PHOLADOMYOIDA	Family GRAMMYSIIDAE	Informal name False razor shell

SOLENOMORPHA

The fairly long, narrow shell of *Solenomorpha* is widest near the front, where the beak is situated, but then tapers gently behind. The paired valves, which have a slight gape at the posterior end, are smooth, and have concentric growth lines.

• **HABITAT** *Solenomorpha* burrowed in soft sediments.

tapering rear end

SOLENOMORPHA MINOR (McCoy); Carboniferous Limestone; Early Carboniferous; UK.

INTERNAL MOULD

Typical length 1.8cm (¾in)

Range E. Devonian–L. Permian	Distribution Worldwide	Occurrence ⊛⊛⊛

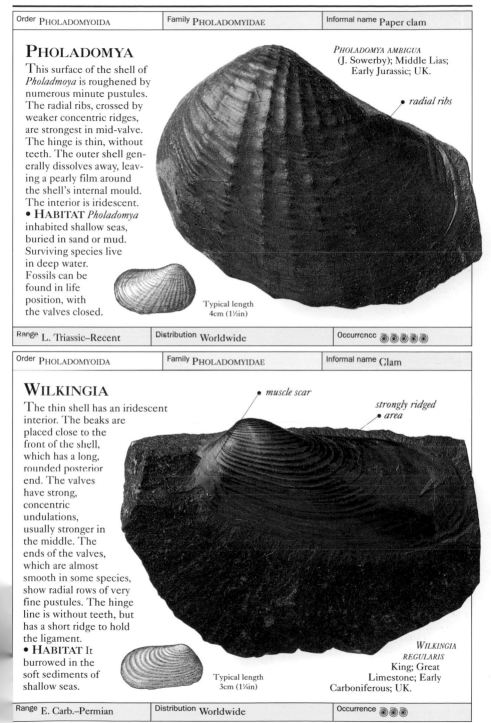

Order PHOLADOMYOIDA	Family PHOLADOMYIDAE	Informal name Paper clam

PHOLADOMYA

This surface of the shell of *Pholadmoya* is roughened by numerous minute pustules. The radial ribs, crossed by weaker concentric ridges, are strongest in mid-valve. The hinge is thin, without teeth. The outer shell generally dissolves away, leaving a pearly film around the shell's internal mould. The interior is iridescent.

• **HABITAT** *Pholadomya* inhabited shallow seas, buried in sand or mud. Surviving species live in deep water. Fossils can be found in life position, with the valves closed.

PHOLADOMYA AMBIGUA (J. Sowerby); Middle Lias; Early Jurassic; UK.

• *radial ribs*

Typical length
4cm (1½in)

Range L. Triassic–Recent	Distribution Worldwide	Occurrence

Order PHOLADOMYOIDA	Family PHOLADOMYIDAE	Informal name Clam

WILKINGIA

The thin shell has an iridescent interior. The beaks are placed close to the front of the shell, which has a long, rounded posterior end. The valves have strong, concentric undulations, usually stronger in the middle. The ends of the valves, which are almost smooth in some species, show radial rows of very fine pustules. The hinge line is without teeth, but has a short ridge to hold the ligament.

• **HABITAT** It burrowed in the soft sediments of shallow seas.

• *muscle scar*

strongly ridged area

WILKINGIA REGULARIS King; Great Limestone; Early Carboniferous; UK.

Typical length
3cm (1¼in)

Range E. Carb.–Permian	Distribution Worldwide	Occurrence

SCAPHOPODS AND CHITONS

T HE SCAPHOPOD SHELL is a tapering tube, open at both ends, with concentric ornament or longitudinal ribs. The larger end contains the animal's head and foot, and is buried in the sediment; the smaller end is often notched and is regularly discarded as the animal grows. Chitons have a powerful foot for gripping hard surfaces, covered by a shell of eight overlapping valves held in place by a scaly or spiny girdle. The valves contain secretory and sense organs, which reach the surface as small pores.

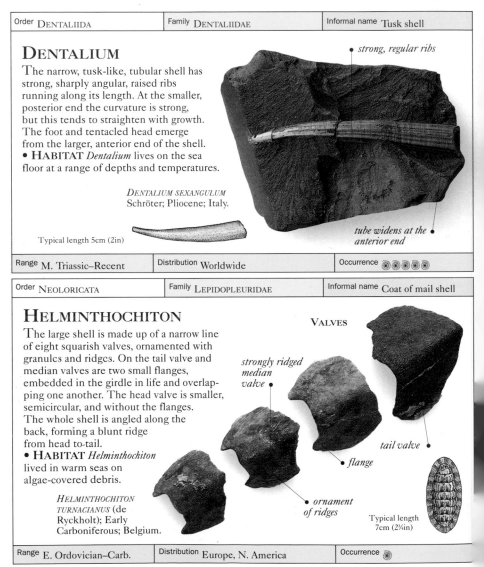

Order DENTALIIDA	Family DENTALIIDAE	Informal name Tusk shell

DENTALIUM

The narrow, tusk-like, tubular shell has strong, sharply angular, raised ribs running along its length. At the smaller, posterior end the curvature is strong, but this tends to straighten with growth. The foot and tentacled head emerge from the larger, anterior end of the shell.
• HABITAT *Dentalium* lives on the sea floor at a range of depths and temperatures.

strong, regular ribs

DENTALIUM SEXANGULUM
Schröter; Pliocene; Italy.

Typical length 5cm (2in)

tube widens at the anterior end

Range M. Triassic–Recent	Distribution Worldwide	Occurrence ◉◉◉◉◉

Order NEOLORICATA	Family LEPIDOPLEURIDAE	Informal name Coat of mail shell

HELMINTHOCHITON

The large shell is made up of a narrow line of eight squarish valves, ornamented with granules and ridges. On the tail valve and median valves are two small flanges, embedded in the girdle in life and overlapping one another. The head valve is smaller, semicircular, and without the flanges. The whole shell is angled along the back, forming a blunt ridge from head to-tail.
• HABITAT *Helminthochiton* lived in warm seas on algae-covered debris.

VALVES

strongly ridged median valve

tail valve

flange

HELMINTHOCHITON TURNACIANUS (de Ryckholt); Early Carboniferous; Belgium.

ornament of ridges

Typical length 7cm (2¾in)

Range E. Ordovician–Carb.	Distribution Europe, N. America	Occurrence ◉

GASTROPODS

GASTROPODS ARE the largest, most successful class of molluscs, and have been able to exploit a wide variety of marine, freshwater, and land habitats. They have a head with eyes and a mouth, a flattened foot for crawling, and viscera that are generally coiled and carried in a spiral shell. A few groups cease the coiling at some stage, and some have abandoned the shell altogether. Shells are composed of calcium carbonate, usually in the form of aragonite, but sometimes in layers of calcite. An inner nacreous layer is characteristic of some more primitive forms, but the organic outer coat of many living gastropods is usually lost in fossils. Some families have an inhalant siphon, emerging through a channel in the aperture.

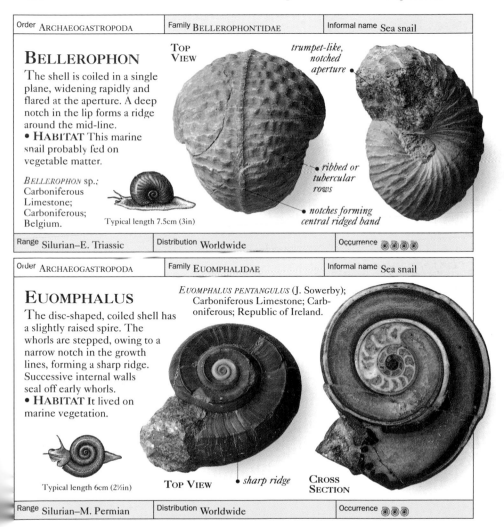

Order ARCHAEOGASTROPODA	Family BELLEROPHONTIDAE	Informal name Sea snail

BELLEROPHON

The shell is coiled in a single plane, widening rapidly and flared at the aperture. A deep notch in the lip forms a ridge around the mid-line.
• **HABITAT** This marine snail probably fed on vegetable matter.

BELLEROPHON sp.;
Carboniferous
Limestone;
Carboniferous;
Belgium.

TOP VIEW

trumpet-like, notched aperture

• *ribbed or tubercular rows*

• *notches forming central ridged band*

Typical length 7.5cm (3in)

Range Silurian–E. Triassic	Distribution Worldwide	Occurrence

Order ARCHAEOGASTROPODA	Family EUOMPHALIDAE	Informal name Sea snail

EUOMPHALUS

The disc-shaped, coiled shell has a slightly raised spire. The whorls are stepped, owing to a narrow notch in the growth lines, forming a sharp ridge. Successive internal walls seal off early whorls.
• **HABITAT** It lived on marine vegetation.

EUOMPHALUS PENTANGULUS (J. Sowerby);
Carboniferous Limestone; Carboniferous; Republic of Ireland.

Typical length 6cm (2½in)

TOP VIEW

• *sharp ridge*

CROSS SECTION

Range Silurian–M. Permian	Distribution Worldwide	Occurrence

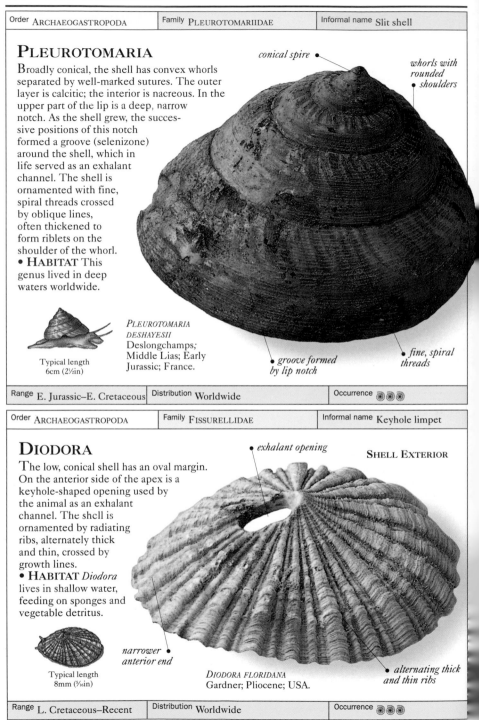

Order ARCHAEOGASTROPODA	Family PLEUROTOMARIIDAE	Informal name Slit shell

PLEUROTOMARIA

Broadly conical, the shell has convex whorls separated by well-marked sutures. The outer layer is calcitic; the interior is nacreous. In the upper part of the lip is a deep, narrow notch. As the shell grew, the successive positions of this notch formed a groove (selenizone) around the shell, which in life served as an exhalant channel. The shell is ornamented with fine, spiral threads crossed by oblique lines, often thickened to form riblets on the shoulder of the whorl.
• **HABITAT** This genus lived in deep waters worldwide.

conical spire •

whorls with rounded shoulders

Typical length
6cm (2⅜in)

PLEUROTOMARIA DESHAYESII
Deslongchamps;
Middle Lias; Early
Jurassic; France.

• *groove formed by lip notch*

• *fine, spiral threads*

Range E. Jurassic–E. Cretaceous	Distribution Worldwide	Occurrence ◉◉◉

Order ARCHAEOGASTROPODA	Family FISSURELLIDAE	Informal name Keyhole limpet

DIODORA

The low, conical shell has an oval margin. On the anterior side of the apex is a keyhole-shaped opening used by the animal as an exhalant channel. The shell is ornamented by radiating ribs, alternately thick and thin, crossed by growth lines.
• **HABITAT** *Diodora* lives in shallow water, feeding on sponges and vegetable detritus.

• *exhalant opening*

SHELL EXTERIOR

narrower anterior end •

Typical length
8mm (⅜in)

DIODORA FLORIDANA
Gardner; Pliocene; USA.

• *alternating thick and thin ribs*

Range L. Cretaceous–Recent	Distribution Worldwide	Occurrence ◉◉◉

Order ARCHAEOGASTROPODA	Family SYMMETROCAPULIDAE	Informal name Cap shell

SYMMETROCAPULUS

This limpet had a large, cap-shaped shell with an oval margin, ornamented with numerous narrow, radiating ribs interrupted by irregular, concentric folds. The first two small whorls are smooth, turned forward, and dextrally coiled, a little to the left of the shell's highest point.

• **HABITAT**
This marine limpet was adapted for grazing on rock surfaces.

beak

coiled apex, now eroded

Typical length
3.5cm (1¼in)

SYMMETROCAPULUS RUGOSUS (J. de C. Sowerby); Inferior Oolite; Middle Jurassic; France.

narrow ribs

short anterior slope

Range Jurassic–Eocene	Distribution Europe, N. America	Occurrence

Order ARCHAEOGASTROPODA	Family PLATYCERATIDAE	Informal name Sea snail

PLATYCERAS

The first few whorls of the shell are loosely coiled but rapidly enlarging, so that the last whorl is inflated and more or less cap-shaped. Sinuous growth lines produce prominent ridges and furrows which indent the shell margin. These had no functional significance but followed the shape of the object on which the animal lived – and so they vary between individuals.

• **HABITAT**
Commensal with crinoids, *Platyceras* shells are occasionally preserved in their life position on the host.

regularly coiled apical whorls

PLATYCERAS HALIOTIS (J. de C. Sowerby); Wenlock Limestone; Silurian; UK.

margin follows shape of substrate

Typical length
2cm (¾in)

inflated body whorl, with ridges

Range Silurian–E. Carb.	Distribution Worldwide	Occurrence

Order ARCHAEOGASTROPODA	Family TROCHIDAE	Informal name Top shell

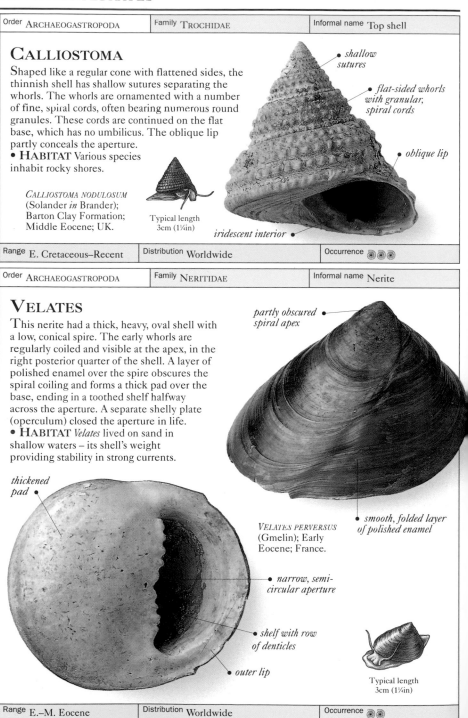

CALLIOSTOMA

Shaped like a regular cone with flattened sides, the thinnish shell has shallow sutures separating the whorls. The whorls are ornamented with a number of fine, spiral cords, often bearing numerous round granules. These cords are continued on the flat base, which has no umbilicus. The oblique lip partly conceals the aperture.
• HABITAT Various species inhabit rocky shores.

CALLIOSTOMA NODULOSUM (Solander *in* Brander); Barton Clay Formation; Middle Eocene; UK.

Typical length 3cm (1¼in)

shallow sutures
flat-sided whorls with granular, spiral cords
oblique lip
iridescent interior

Range E. Cretaceous–Recent	Distribution Worldwide	Occurrence

Order ARCHAEOGASTROPODA	Family NERITIDAE	Informal name Nerite

VELATES

This nerite had a thick, heavy, oval shell with a low, conical spire. The early whorls are regularly coiled and visible at the apex, in the right posterior quarter of the shell. A layer of polished enamel over the spire obscures the spiral coiling and forms a thick pad over the base, ending in a toothed shelf halfway across the aperture. A separate shelly plate (operculum) closed the aperture in life.
• HABITAT *Velates* lived on sand in shallow waters – its shell's weight providing stability in strong currents.

partly obscured spiral apex
thickened pad
smooth, folded layer of polished enamel

VELATES PERVERSUS (Gmelin); Early Eocene; France.

narrow, semi-circular aperture
shelf with row of denticles
outer lip

Typical length 3cm (1¼in)

Range E.–M. Eocene	Distribution Worldwide	Occurrence

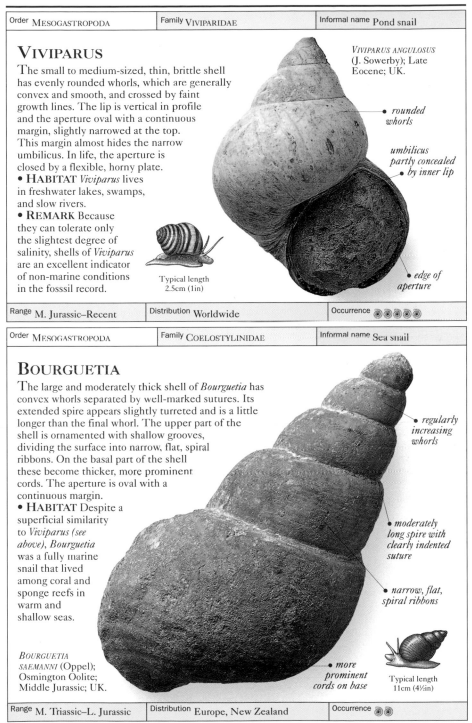

Order MESOGASTROPODA	Family VIVIPARIDAE	Informal name Pond snail

VIVIPARUS

VIVIPARUS ANGULOSUS (J. Sowerby); Late Eocene; UK.

The small to medium-sized, thin, brittle shell has evenly rounded whorls, which are generally convex and smooth, and crossed by faint growth lines. The lip is vertical in profile and the aperture oval with a continuous margin, slightly narrowed at the top. This margin almost hides the narrow umbilicus. In life, the aperture is closed by a flexible, horny plate.

• **HABITAT** *Viviparus* lives in freshwater lakes, swamps, and slow rivers.

• **REMARK** Because they can tolerate only the slightest degree of salinity, shells of *Viviparus* are an excellent indicator of non-marine conditions in the fosssil record.

rounded whorls

umbilicus partly concealed by inner lip

Typical length 2.5cm (1in)

edge of aperture

Range M. Jurassic–Recent	Distribution Worldwide	Occurrence

Order MESOGASTROPODA	Family COELOSTYLINIDAE	Informal name Sea snail

BOURGUETIA

The large and moderately thick shell of *Bourguetia* has convex whorls separated by well-marked sutures. Its extended spire appears slightly turreted and is a little longer than the final whorl. The upper part of the shell is ornamented with shallow grooves, dividing the surface into narrow, flat, spiral ribbons. On the basal part of the shell these become thicker, more prominent cords. The aperture is oval with a continuous margin.

• **HABITAT** Despite a superficial similarity to *Viviparus (see above), Bourguetia* was a fully marine snail that lived among coral and sponge reefs in warm and shallow seas.

regularly increasing whorls

moderately long spire with clearly indented suture

narrow, flat, spiral ribbons

BOURGUETIA SAEMANNI (Oppel); Osmington Oolite; Middle Jurassic; UK.

more prominent cords on base

Typical length 11cm (4¼in)

Range M. Triassic–L. Jurassic	Distribution Europe, New Zealand	Occurrence

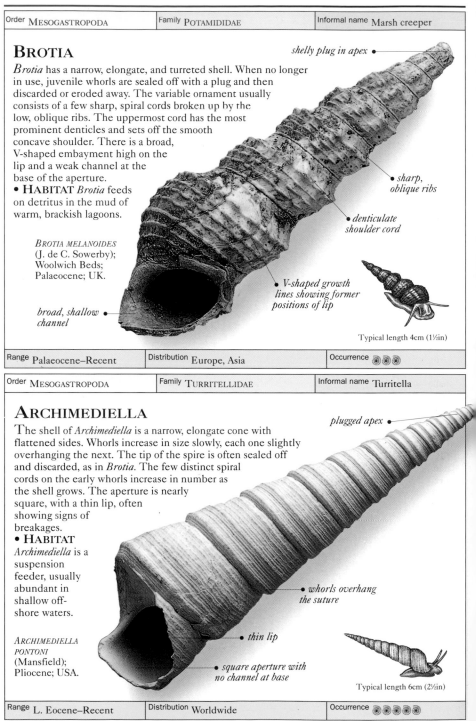

Order MESOGASTROPODA	Family POTAMIDIDAE	Informal name Marsh creeper

BROTIA

shelly plug in apex

Brotia has a narrow, elongate, and turreted shell. When no longer in use, juvenile whorls are sealed off with a plug and then discarded or eroded away. The variable ornament usually consists of a few sharp, spiral cords broken up by the low, oblique ribs. The uppermost cord has the most prominent denticles and sets off the smooth concave shoulder. There is a broad, V-shaped embayment high on the lip and a weak channel at the base of the aperture.
• HABITAT *Brotia* feeds on detritus in the mud of warm, brackish lagoons.

sharp, oblique ribs

denticulate shoulder cord

BROTIA MELANOIDES (J. de C. Sowerby); Woolwich Beds; Palaeocene; UK.

V-shaped growth lines showing former positions of lip

broad, shallow channel

Typical length 4cm (1½in)

Range Palaeocene–Recent	Distribution Europe, Asia	Occurrence ◉◉◉

Order MESOGASTROPODA	Family TURRITELLIDAE	Informal name Turritella

ARCHIMEDIELLA

plugged apex

The shell of *Archimediella* is a narrow, elongate cone with flattened sides. Whorls increase in size slowly, each one slightly overhanging the next. The tip of the spire is often sealed off and discarded, as in *Brotia*. The few distinct spiral cords on the early whorls increase in number as the shell grows. The aperture is nearly square, with a thin lip, often showing signs of breakages.
• HABITAT *Archimediella* is a suspension feeder, usually abundant in shallow off-shore waters.

whorls overhang the suture

ARCHIMEDIELLA PONTONI (Mansfield); Pliocene; USA.

thin lip

square aperture with no channel at base

Typical length 6cm (2½in)

Range L. Eocene–Recent	Distribution Worldwide	Occurrence ◉◉◉◉◉

Order MESOGASTROPODA	Family CAMPANILIDAE	Informal name Giant cerith

CAMPANILE

A giant among gastropods, the shell of *Campanile* can reach a length of 60cm (24in), and if this could be uncoiled it would make a tube over 3m (10ft) long. There may be more than 30 whorls constructed in the animal's lifetime, but the earlier ones are back-filled with shell once they have been evacuated, and are periodically lost by abrasion, leaving the apex sealed. Early whorls are turreted by an upper row of tubercles, with finer cords below. On the last few whorls the ornament deteriorates, leaving a single row of blunt knobs. The large, flared aperture is developed only on fully adult shells. The central pillar (columella) is strengthened by two encircling ridges which are obsolete at the aperture but can be seen clearly when the shell is broken. A calcified outer layer is covered with rows of small pits.

• HABITAT *Campanile* feeds on algae on sandy bottoms in very shallow, warm seas. The tip of the heavy shell trails behind it as it crawls, eventually wearing flat on one side.

• REMARK Only a single species survives today, in the shallow coastal waters off Australia.

SHELL CUT IN HALF

• *secondary thickening*

• *tip worn flat*

CAMPANILE GIGANTEUM (Lamarck); Calcaire Grossier; Middle Eocene; France.

rectangular whorls •

distinct cords on • *spire whorls*

two oblique ridges on columella •

prominent row • *of knobs*

fine, curved growth • *lines*

pitted • *outer layer*

immature • *outer lip*

• *weakening ridges on columella*

• *siphonal channel*

Typical length 30cm (12in)

Range L. Cretaceous–Recent	Distribution Worldwide	Occurrence

| Order MESOGASTROPODA | Family APORRHAIDAE | Informal name Pelican's foot |

TESSAROLAX

The small, biconical, ridged shell of *Tessarolax* was much enlarged by having the extremities drawn out into four slender and delicate, curved spines. The bases of these are connected by an outgrowth of the lip, like the web of a duck's foot.
• HABITAT This creature was probably a detritus feeder, living on muddy sand in moderately deep water.
• REMARK The spines may have helped to prevent the shell sinking into the substrate.

TESSAROLAX FITTONI (Forbes); Lower Greensand; Early Cretaceous; UK.

Typical length 6cm (2⅜in)

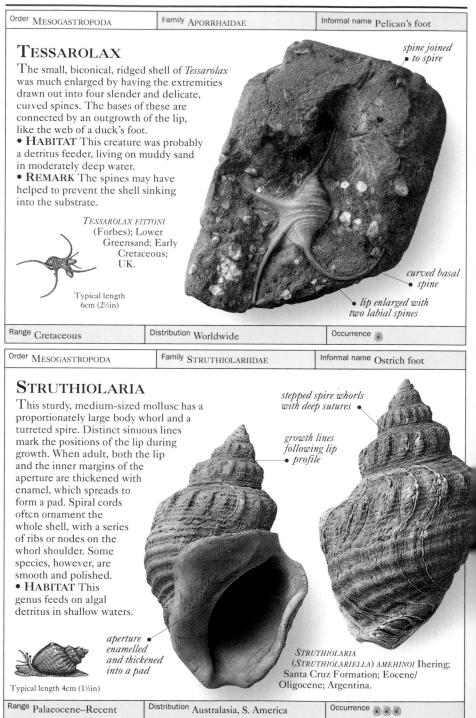

spine joined
• to spire

curved basal
• spine

• lip enlarged with
two labial spines

| Range Cretaceous | Distribution Worldwide | Occurrence ◉ |

| Order MESOGASTROPODA | Family STRUTHIOLARIIDAE | Informal name Ostrich foot |

STRUTHIOLARIA

This sturdy, medium-sized mollusc has a proportionately large body whorl and a turreted spire. Distinct sinuous lines mark the positions of the lip during growth. When adult, both the lip and the inner margins of the aperture are thickened with enamel, which spreads to form a pad. Spiral cords often ornament the whole shell, with a series of ribs or nodes on the whorl shoulder. Some species, however, are smooth and polished.
• HABITAT This genus feeds on algal detritus in shallow waters.

stepped spire whorls
with deep sutures •

growth lines
following lip
• profile

aperture •
enamelled
and thickened
into a pad

STRUTHIOLARIA
(*STRUTHIOLARIELLA*) *AMEHINOI* Ihering;
Santa Cruz Formation; Eocene/
Oligocene; Argentina.

Typical length 4cm (1⅝in)

| Range Palaeocene–Recent | Distribution Australasia, S. America | Occurrence ◉ ◉ ◉ |

Order MESOGASTROPODA	Family STROMBIDAE	Informal name Beak shell

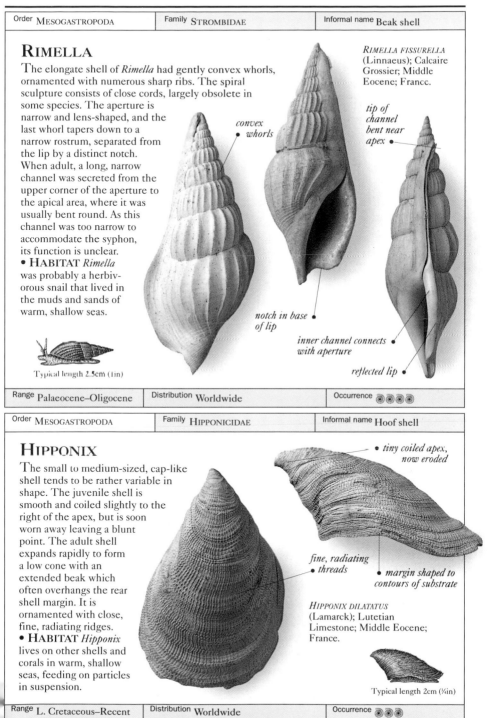

RIMELLA

The elongate shell of *Rimella* had gently convex whorls, ornamented with numerous sharp ribs. The spiral sculpture consists of close cords, largely obsolete in some species. The aperture is narrow and lens-shaped, and the last whorl tapers down to a narrow rostrum, separated from the lip by a distinct notch. When adult, a long, narrow channel was secreted from the upper corner of the aperture to the apical area, where it was usually bent round. As this channel was too narrow to accommodate the syphon, its function is unclear.
• **HABITAT** *Rimella* was probably a herbivorous snail that lived in the muds and sands of warm, shallow seas.

RIMELLA FISSURELLA (Linnaeus); Calcaire Grossier; Middle Eocene; France.

convex whorls •

tip of channel bent near apex •

notch in base of lip •

inner channel connects with aperture •

reflected lip •

Typical length 2.5cm (1in)

Range Palaeocene–Oligocene	Distribution Worldwide	Occurrence ⊛⊛⊛⊛

Order MESOGASTROPODA	Family HIPPONICIDAE	Informal name Hoof shell

HIPPONIX

The small to medium-sized, cap-like shell tends to be rather variable in shape. The juvenile shell is smooth and coiled slightly to the right of the apex, but is soon worn away leaving a blunt point. The adult shell expands rapidly to form a low cone with an extended beak which often overhangs the rear shell margin. It is ornamented with close, fine, radiating ridges.
• **HABITAT** *Hipponix* lives on other shells and corals in warm, shallow seas, feeding on particles in suspension.

• tiny coiled apex, now eroded

fine, radiating • threads

• margin shaped to contours of substrate

HIPPONIX DILATATUS (Lamarck); Lutetian Limestone; Middle Eocene; France.

Typical length 2cm (¾in)

Range L. Cretaceous–Recent	Distribution Worldwide	Occurrence ⊛⊛⊛

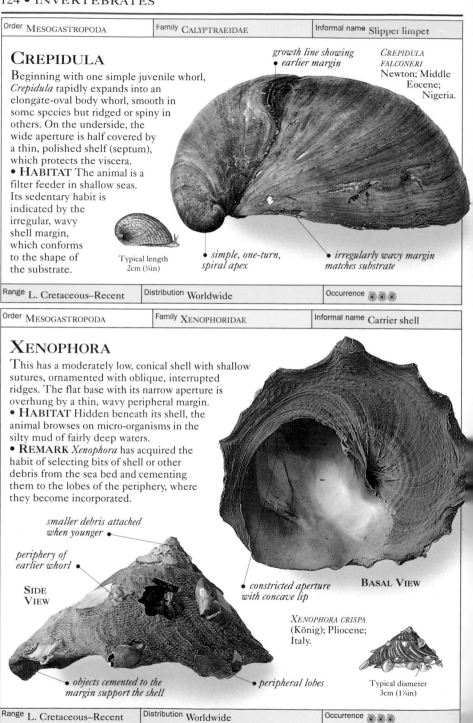

Order MESOGASTROPODA	Family CALYPTRAEIDAE	Informal name Slipper limpet

CREPIDULA

Beginning with one simple juvenile whorl, *Crepidula* rapidly expands into an elongate-oval body whorl, smooth in some species but ridged or spiny in others. On the underside, the wide aperture is half covered by a thin, polished shelf (septum), which protects the viscera.
• HABITAT The animal is a filter feeder in shallow seas. Its sedentary habit is indicated by the irregular, wavy shell margin, which conforms to the shape of the substrate.

growth line showing earlier margin

CREPIDULA FALCONERI Newton; Middle Eocene; Nigeria.

Typical length 2cm (¾in)

• *simple, one-turn, spiral apex*

• *irregularly wavy margin matches substrate*

Range L. Cretaceous–Recent	Distribution Worldwide	Occurrence

Order MESOGASTROPODA	Family XENOPHORIDAE	Informal name Carrier shell

XENOPHORA

This has a moderately low, conical shell with shallow sutures, ornamented with oblique, interrupted ridges. The flat base with its narrow aperture is overhung by a thin, wavy peripheral margin.
• HABITAT Hidden beneath its shell, the animal browses on micro-organisms in the silty mud of fairly deep waters.
• REMARK *Xenophora* has acquired the habit of selecting bits of shell or other debris from the sea bed and cementing them to the lobes of the periphery, where they become incorporated.

smaller debris attached when younger •

periphery of earlier whorl •

SIDE VIEW

• *objects cemented to the margin support the shell*

• *constricted aperture with concave lip*

BASAL VIEW

XENOPHORA CRISPA (König); Pliocene; Italy.

• *peripheral lobes*

Typical diameter 3cm (1¼in)

Range L. Cretaceous–Recent	Distribution Worldwide	Occurrence

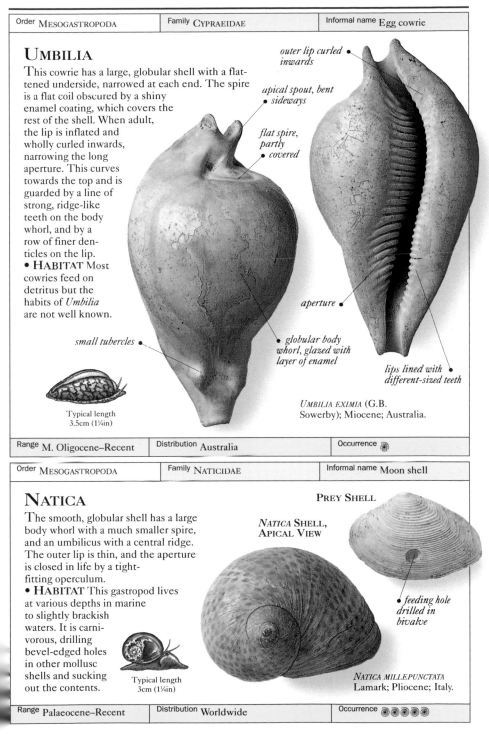

Order MESOGASTROPODA	Family CYPRAEIDAE	Informal name Egg cowrie

UMBILIA

This cowrie has a large, globular shell with a flattened underside, narrowed at each end. The spire is a flat coil obscured by a shiny enamel coating, which covers the rest of the shell. When adult, the lip is inflated and wholly curled inwards, narrowing the long aperture. This curves towards the top and is guarded by a line of strong, ridge-like teeth on the body whorl, and by a row of finer denticles on the lip.
• HABITAT Most cowries feed on detritus but the habits of *Umbilia* are not well known.

outer lip curled inwards

apical spout, bent sideways

flat spire, partly covered

aperture

small tubercles

globular body whorl, glazed with layer of enamel

lips lined with different-sized teeth

Typical length
3.5cm (1¼in)

UMBILIA EXIMIA (G.B. Sowerby); Miocene; Australia.

Range M. Oligocene–Recent	Distribution Australia	Occurrence

Order MESOGASTROPODA	Family NATICIDAE	Informal name Moon shell

NATICA

The smooth, globular shell has a large body whorl with a much smaller spire, and an umbilicus with a central ridge. The outer lip is thin, and the aperture is closed in life by a tight-fitting operculum.
• HABITAT This gastropod lives at various depths in marine to slightly brackish waters. It is carnivorous, drilling bevel-edged holes in other mollusc shells and sucking out the contents.

PREY SHELL

NATICA SHELL, APICAL VIEW

feeding hole drilled in bivalve

Typical length
3cm (1¼in)

NATICA MILLEPUNCTATA Lamark; Pliocene; Italy.

Range Palaeocene–Recent	Distribution Worldwide	Occurrence

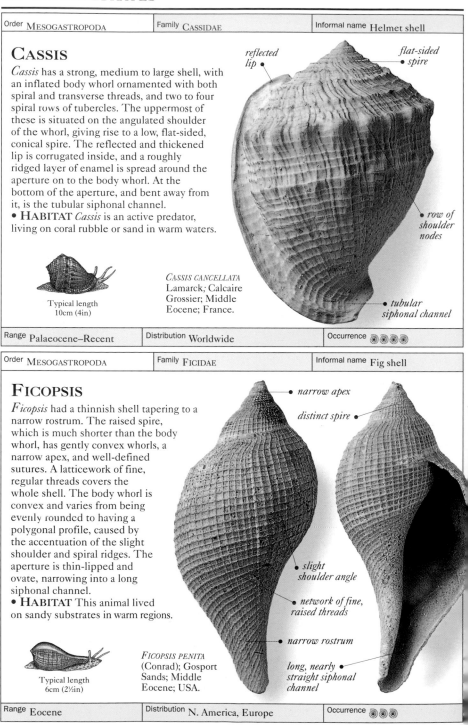

| Order MESOGASTROPODA | Family CASSIDAE | Informal name Helmet shell |

CASSIS

Cassis has a strong, medium to large shell, with an inflated body whorl ornamented with both spiral and transverse threads, and two to four spiral rows of tubercles. The uppermost of these is situated on the angulated shoulder of the whorl, giving rise to a low, flat-sided, conical spire. The reflected and thickened lip is corrugated inside, and a roughly ridged layer of enamel is spread around the aperture on to the body whorl. At the bottom of the aperture, and bent away from it, is the tubular siphonal channel.
• HABITAT *Cassis* is an active predator, living on coral rubble or sand in warm waters.

reflected lip

flat-sided spire

row of shoulder nodes

Typical length
10cm (4in)

CASSIS CANCELLATA Lamarck; Calcaire Grossier; Middle Eocene; France.

tubular siphonal channel

| Range Palaeocene–Recent | Distribution Worldwide | Occurrence |

| Order MESOGASTROPODA | Family FICIDAE | Informal name Fig shell |

FICOPSIS

Ficopsis had a thinnish shell tapering to a narrow rostrum. The raised spire, which is much shorter than the body whorl, has gently convex whorls, a narrow apex, and well-defined sutures. A latticework of fine, regular threads covers the whole shell. The body whorl is convex and varies from being evenly rounded to having a polygonal profile, caused by the accentuation of the slight shoulder and spiral ridges. The aperture is thin-lipped and ovate, narrowing into a long siphonal channel.
• HABITAT This animal lived on sandy substrates in warm regions.

narrow apex

distinct spire

slight shoulder angle

network of fine, raised threads

narrow rostrum

Typical length
6cm (2⅜in)

FICOPSIS PENITA (Conrad); Gosport Sands; Middle Eocene; USA.

long, nearly straight siphonal channel

| Range Eocene | Distribution N. America, Europe | Occurrence |

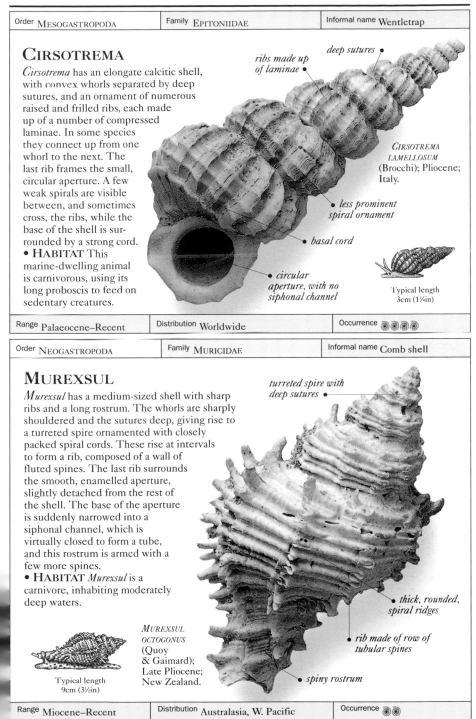

| Order MESOGASTROPODA | Family EPITONIIDAE | Informal name Wentletrap |

CIRSOTREMA

Cirsotrema has an elongate calcitic shell, with convex whorls separated by deep sutures, and an ornament of numerous raised and frilled ribs, each made up of a number of compressed laminae. In some species they connect up from one whorl to the next. The last rib frames the small, circular aperture. A few weak spirals are visible between, and sometimes cross, the ribs, while the base of the shell is surrounded by a strong cord.
• HABITAT This marine-dwelling animal is carnivorous, using its long proboscis to feed on sedentary creatures.

deep sutures

ribs made up of laminae

CIRSOTREMA LAMELLOSUM (Brocchi); Pliocene; Italy.

less prominent spiral ornament

basal cord

circular aperture, with no siphonal channel

Typical length 3cm (1¼in)

| Range Palaeocene–Recent | Distribution Worldwide | Occurrence |

| Order NEOGASTROPODA | Family MURICIDAE | Informal name Comb shell |

MUREXSUL

Murexsul has a medium-sized shell with sharp ribs and a long rostrum. The whorls are sharply shouldered and the sutures deep, giving rise to a turreted spire ornamented with closely packed spiral cords. These rise at intervals to form a rib, composed of a wall of fluted spines. The last rib surrounds the smooth, enamelled aperture, slightly detached from the rest of the shell. The base of the aperture is suddenly narrowed into a siphonal channel, which is virtually closed to form a tube, and this rostrum is armed with a few more spines.
• HABITAT *Murexsul* is a carnivore, inhabiting moderately deep waters.

turreted spire with deep sutures

MUREXSUL OCTOGONUS (Quoy & Gaimard); Late Pliocene; New Zealand.

Typical length 9cm (3½in)

thick, rounded, spiral ridges

rib made of row of tubular spines

spiny rostrum

| Range Miocene–Recent | Distribution Australasia, W. Pacific | Occurrence |

| Order NEOGASTROPODA | Family MURICIDAE | Informal name Sea snail |

ECPHORA

Ecphora is one of the best known and most striking fossil gastropods. The spire of its shell is relatively small and turreted, and the whorls are dominated by two prominent encircling keels which are often grooved along their length. One or two more keels appear on the base of the body whorl. The siphonal channel is sharply bent back from the aperture, and a chain of the spouts of previous channels makes a spiral around the rostrum.
• **HABITAT** This creature was a carnivorous predator, living in shallow waters.

turreted spire •

simple sculpture of strong keels •

• *suture*

• *tubular ends of former channels*

ECPHORA QUADRICOSTATA (Say); Yorktown Formation; Pliocene; USA.

basal wall extension •

Typical length 10cm (4in)

| Range L. Oligocene–Pliocene | Distribution N. America, Europe | Occurrence ◉◉◉◉ |

| Order NEOGASTROPODA | Family BUCCINIDAE | Informal name Whelk |

NEPTUNEA

The shell of this large whelk has rounded whorls separated by deep sutures. Some species coil dextrally, as most gastropods do, but others are typically sinistral. A fairly long and stepped spire leads in to a convex body whorl. The large, ovate aperture has a rather short and broad siphonal channel. If present, ornament is restricted to spiral lines, cords, or keels, although coarse, transverse growth lines may occur.
• **HABITAT** A cold-water carnivore, *Neptunea* preys on bivalves and other invertebrates in moderately to very deep seas.

stepped spire •

NEPTUNEA CONTRARIA (Linnaeus); Red Crag; Late Pliocene; UK.

• *ornament of fine, spiral threads*

• *growth stages*

sinistral coiling •

Typical length 9cm (3½in)

| Range L. Eocene–Recent | Distribution Worldwide | Occurrence ◉◉◉ |

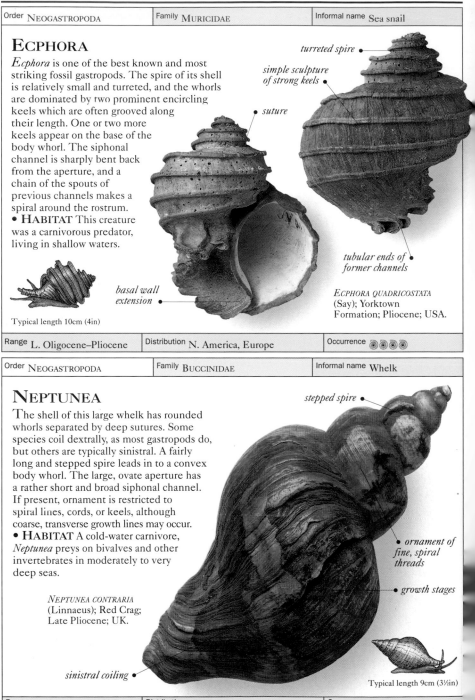

Order NEOGASTROPODA	Family FASCIOLARIIDAE	Informal name Sea snail

CLAVILITHES

Clavilithes had a medium to large, fusiform shell. The young shell begins as a smooth column of equal-sized whorls, developing low ribs crossed by spiral threads. The sculpture soon dies away, leaving only a few spiral lines, and the whorls become flat-sided. A sharp shelf at the top of the whorl gives the spire a stepped shape. The last whorl is usually cup-shaped and the aperture oval.
• **HABITAT** Probably carnivorous, this gastropod was an inhabitant of sand, silt, and mud in moderately deep, warm waters.

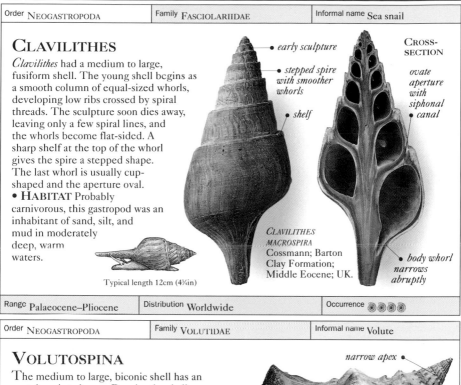

• *early sculpture*

• *stepped spire with smoother whorls*

• *shelf*

CROSS-SECTION

ovate aperture with siphonal canal

CLAVILITHES MACROSPIRA Cossmann; Barton Clay Formation; Middle Eocene; UK.

• *body whorl narrows abruptly*

Typical length 12cm (4¾in)

Range Palaeocene–Pliocene	Distribution Worldwide	Occurrence ◉◉◉◉

Order NEOGASTROPODA	Family VOLUTIDAE	Informal name Volute

VOLUTOSPINA

The medium to large, biconic shell has an acutely pointed apex. Despite the shallow sutures the spire has a turreted appearance, caused by the short ribs which end in sharp spines on the shoulder. The body whorl is ornamented with weak, flat, spiral ribbons, crossed by numerous inconspicuous vertical growth lines. The rather narrow aperture tapers down to an open siphonal channel and the outer lip is not thickened. There are several ridges on the columella, the lowest one being the strongest, and a layer of enamel spreads from the interior on to the body whorl.
• **HABITAT** This creature inhabited sandy or muddy sea beds in warm waters.
• **REMARK** Like other volutes, *Volutospina* was a fast-moving predator.

narrow apex •

• *low ribs with prominent spines*

VOLUTOSPINA LUCTATOR (Solander *in* Brander); Barton Clay Formation; Middle Eocene; UK.

rostrum with • *siphonal channel*

Typical length 7cm (2¾in)

Range L. Cretaceous–Pliocene	Distribution Worldwide	Occurrence ◉◉◉◉◉

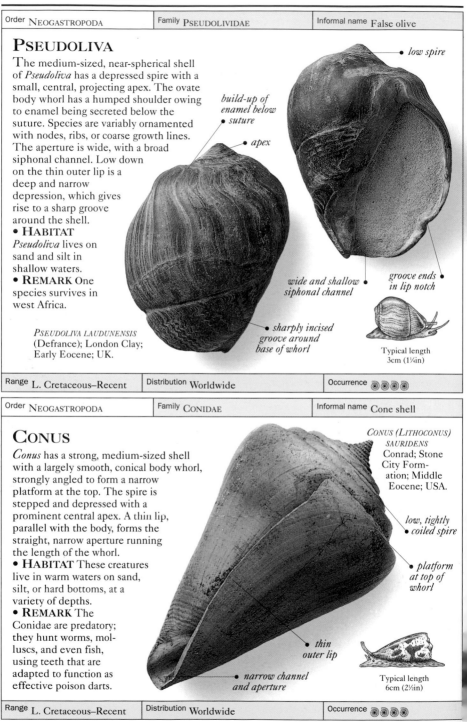

Order NEOGASTROPODA	Family PSEUDOLIVIDAE	Informal name False olive

PSEUDOLIVA

The medium-sized, near-spherical shell of *Pseudoliva* has a depressed spire with a small, central, projecting apex. The ovate body whorl has a humped shoulder owing to enamel being secreted below the suture. Species are variably ornamented with nodes, ribs, or coarse growth lines. The aperture is wide, with a broad siphonal channel. Low down on the thin outer lip is a deep and narrow depression, which gives rise to a sharp groove around the shell.
• **HABITAT** *Pseudoliva* lives on sand and silt in shallow waters.
• **REMARK** One species survives in west Africa.

low spire

build-up of enamel below suture

apex

wide and shallow siphonal channel

groove ends in lip notch

sharply incised groove around base of whorl

PSEUDOLIVA LAUDUNENSIS (Defrance); London Clay; Early Eocene; UK.

Typical length 3cm (1¼in)

Range L. Cretaceous–Recent	Distribution Worldwide	Occurrence ◉◉◉◉

Order NEOGASTROPODA	Family CONIDAE	Informal name Cone shell

CONUS

Conus has a strong, medium-sized shell with a largely smooth, conical body whorl, strongly angled to form a narrow platform at the top. The spire is stepped and depressed with a prominent central apex. A thin lip, parallel with the body, forms the straight, narrow aperture running the length of the whorl.
• **HABITAT** These creatures live in warm waters on sand, silt, or hard bottoms, at a variety of depths.
• **REMARK** The Conidae are predatory; they hunt worms, molluscs, and even fish, using teeth that are adapted to function as effective poison darts.

CONUS (LITHOCONUS) SAURIDENS Conrad; Stone City Form- ation; Middle Eocene; USA.

low, tightly coiled spire

platform at top of whorl

thin outer lip

narrow channel and aperture

Typical length 6cm (2⅜in)

Range L. Cretaceous–Recent	Distribution Worldwide	Occurrence ◉◉◉◉

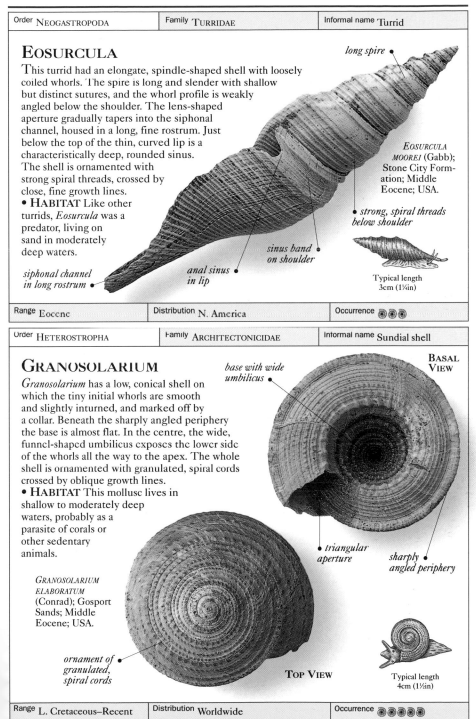

Order NEOGASTROPODA	Family TURRIDAE	Informal name Turrid

EOSURCULA

This turrid had an elongate, spindle-shaped shell with loosely coiled whorls. The spire is long and slender with shallow but distinct sutures, and the whorl profile is weakly angled below the shoulder. The lens-shaped aperture gradually tapers into the siphonal channel, housed in a long, fine rostrum. Just below the top of the thin, curved lip is a characteristically deep, rounded sinus. The shell is ornamented with strong spiral threads, crossed by close, fine growth lines.
• HABITAT Like other turrids, *Eosurcula* was a predator, living on sand in moderately deep waters.

long spire •

EOSURCULA MOOREI (Gabb); Stone City Formation; Middle Eocene; USA.

• *strong, spiral threads below shoulder*

sinus band on shoulder •

siphonal channel in long rostrum •

anal sinus in lip •

Typical length
3cm (1¼in)

Range Eocene	Distribution N. America	Occurrence ⬤⬤⬤

Order HETEROSTROPHA	Family ARCHITECTONICIDAE	Informal name Sundial shell

GRANOSOLARIUM

Granosolarium has a low, conical shell on which the tiny initial whorls are smooth and slightly inturned, and marked off by a collar. Beneath the sharply angled periphery the base is almost flat. In the centre, the wide, funnel-shaped umbilicus exposes the lower side of the whorls all the way to the apex. The whole shell is ornamented with granulated, spiral cords crossed by oblique growth lines.
• HABITAT This mollusc lives in shallow to moderately deep waters, probably as a parasite of corals or other sedentary animals.

base with wide umbilicus •

BASAL VIEW

• *triangular aperture*

sharply angled periphery •

GRANOSOLARIUM ELABORATUM (Conrad); Gosport Sands; Middle Eocene; USA.

ornament of granulated, spiral cords •

TOP VIEW

Typical length
4cm (1½in)

Range L. Cretaceous–Recent	Distribution Worldwide	Occurrence ⬤⬤⬤⬤⬤

Order CEPHALASPIDEA	Family BULLIDAE	Informal name Bubble shell

BULLA

Bulla has a rather thin, almost spherical shell, only one whorl of which is visible. The few tiny initial whorls coil sinistrally, but the shell then resumes dextral coiling. Each whorl wholly encloses the previous one, so that there is no apparent spire. The aperture is at least as long as the shell, and an enamel layer strengthens the columella wall.

• **HABITAT** Unlike some of its nearest relatives, this is a herbivorous animal living on sandy or muddy bottoms in shallow, warm waters.

• **REMARK** An unusual feature of this gastropod is that its body is twice the size of the shell and is unable to withdraw into it.

apical umbilicus •

• top of aperture reaches apex

• near-spherical body whorl

BULLA AMPULLA Linnaeus; Reef limestone; Pleistocene; Red Sea.

• enamel on columella wall

Typical length 2cm (1¼in)

Range L. Jurassic–Recent	Distribution Worldwide	Occurrence 🔘🔘🔘

Order HETEROSTROPHA	Family NERINEIDAE	Informal name Auger shell

NERINEA

Nerinea had a long, narrow shell, typically with concave sides to the whorls and accentuated keels just over the sutures. The apex, only rarely preserved, is a tiny flat coil which stands at right-angles to the axis of the main shell. A characteristic of the genus is a collection of fine ridges and processes on the walls of the small aperture; there may be up to seven of these, best seen in cross-sections.

• **HABITAT** *Nerinea* is often associated with coral reef deposits.

concave whorls between spiral • keels

columella ridges •

NERINEA sp.; Cretaceous; Israel.

• internal ridge

Typical length 6cm (2½in)

• columella ridge visible in aperture

YOUNG SHELL IN CROSS-SECTION

Range E. Jurassic–L. Cretaceous	Distribution Worldwide	Occurrence 🔘🔘🔘🔘

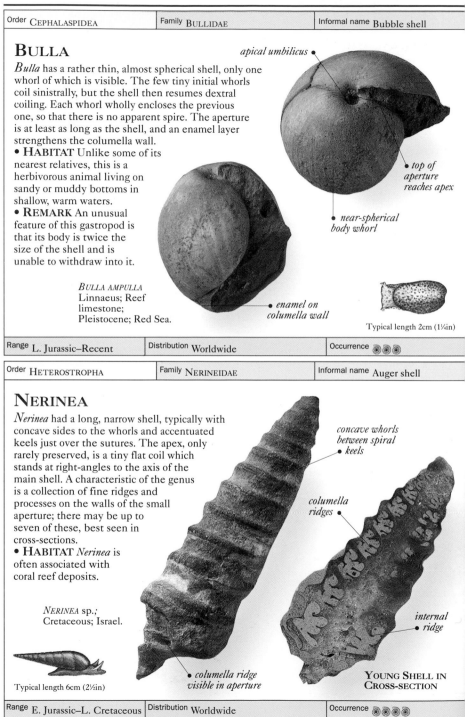

Order BASOMMATOPHORA	Family PLANORBIDAE	Informal name Ramshorn snail

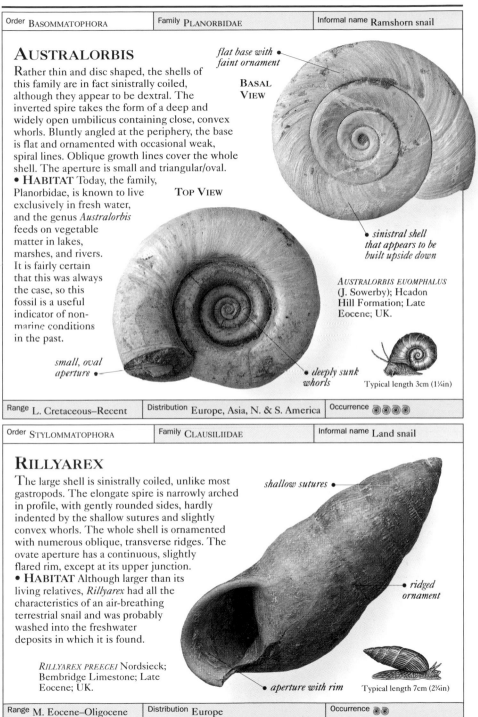

AUSTRALORBIS

Rather thin and disc shaped, the shells of this family are in fact sinistrally coiled, although they appear to be dextral. The inverted spire takes the form of a deep and widely open umbilicus containing close, convex whorls. Bluntly angled at the periphery, the base is flat and ornamented with occasional weak, spiral lines. Oblique growth lines cover the whole shell. The aperture is small and triangular/oval.

• HABITAT Today, the family, Planorbidae, is known to live exclusively in fresh water, and the genus *Australorbis* feeds on vegetable matter in lakes, marshes, and rivers. It is fairly certain that this was always the case, so this fossil is a useful indicator of non-marine conditions in the past.

flat base with •
faint ornament

BASAL
VIEW

TOP VIEW

• *sinistral shell*
that appears to be
built upside down

AUSTRALORBIS EUOMPHALUS (J. Sowerby); Headon Hill Formation; Late Eocene; UK.

small, oval
aperture •

• *deeply sunk*
whorls   Typical length 3cm (1¼in)

Range L. Cretaceous–Recent	Distribution Europe, Asia, N. & S. America	Occurrence ◉◉◉◉

Order STYLOMMATOPHORA	Family CLAUSILIIDAE	Informal name Land snail

RILLYAREX

The large shell is sinistrally coiled, unlike most gastropods. The elongate spire is narrowly arched in profile, with gently rounded sides, hardly indented by the shallow sutures and slightly convex whorls. The whole shell is ornamented with numerous oblique, transverse ridges. The ovate aperture has a continuous, slightly flared rim, except at its upper junction.

• HABITAT Although larger than its living relatives, *Rillyarex* had all the characteristics of an air-breathing terrestrial snail and was probably washed into the freshwater deposits in which it is found.

shallow sutures •

• *ridged*
ornament

RILLYAREX PREECEI Nordsieck; Bembridge Limestone; Late Eocene; UK.

• *aperture with rim*   Typical length 7cm (2¾in)

Range M. Eocene–Oligocene	Distribution Europe	Occurrence ◉◉

NAUTILOIDS

NAUTILOIDS ARE PRIMITIVE, marine cephalopods that possess a shell. They were most abundant in the Palaeozoic Era – 400 million years ago; today, only a single genus survives – the pearly nautilus of the south-west Pacific Ocean. The shell is divided into a body chamber and many smaller chambers. The chambered part of the shell is known as the phragmocone. Nautiloids have heads with well-developed eyes, and grasping tentacles. They swim by squirting water out of the body cavity.

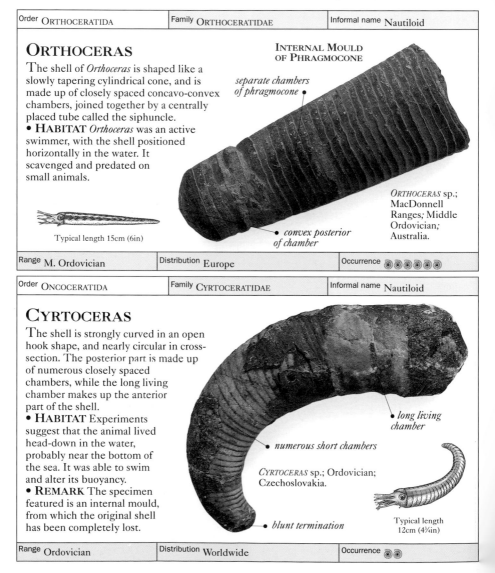

Order ORTHOCERATIDA	Family ORTHOCERATIDAE	Informal name Nautiloid

ORTHOCERAS

The shell of *Orthoceras* is shaped like a slowly tapering cylindrical cone, and is made up of closely spaced concavo-convex chambers, joined together by a centrally placed tube called the siphuncle.
• **HABITAT** *Orthoceras* was an active swimmer, with the shell positioned horizontally in the water. It scavenged and predated on small animals.

INTERNAL MOULD OF PHRAGMOCONE

separate chambers of phragmocone

convex posterior of chamber

ORTHOCERAS sp.; MacDonnell Ranges; Middle Ordovician; Australia.

Typical length 15cm (6in)

Range M. Ordovician	Distribution Europe	Occurrence ◉◉◉◉◉◉

Order ONCOCERATIDA	Family CYRTOCERATIDAE	Informal name Nautiloid

CYRTOCERAS

The shell is strongly curved in an open hook shape, and nearly circular in cross-section. The posterior part is made up of numerous closely spaced chambers, while the long living chamber makes up the anterior part of the shell.
• **HABITAT** Experiments suggest that the animal lived head-down in the water, probably near the bottom of the sea. It was able to swim and alter its buoyancy.
• **REMARK** The specimen featured is an internal mould, from which the original shell has been completely lost.

long living chamber

numerous short chambers

CYRTOCERAS sp.; Ordovician; Czechoslovakia.

blunt termination

Typical length 12cm (4¾in)

Range Ordovician	Distribution Worldwide	Occurrence ◉◉

Order ACTINOCERATIDA	Family HURONIIDAE	Informal name Nautiloid

HURONIA

Shells of this genus have a large, straight siphuncle, with long segments separated by strong constrictions. Complex canals are present. The central canal is very narrow.
• HABITAT This genus lived in shallow seas as a scavenger or predator. It was able to swim and adjust its position in the water column by moving liquid along the siphuncle from chamber to chamber.
• REMARK Only the robust siphuncle of this species is preserved in the specimen. The chambers and outer wall are missing.

HURONIA VERTEBRALIS
Stokes; Ordovician; Canada.

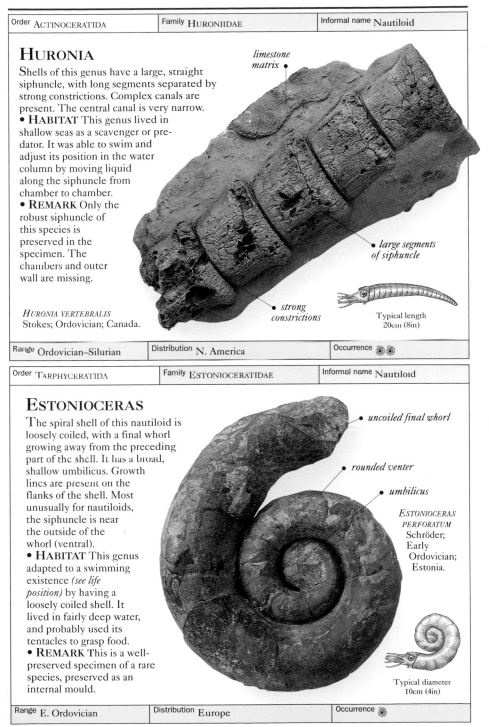

limestone matrix

large segments of siphuncle

strong constrictions

Typical length 20cm (8in)

Range Ordovician–Silurian	Distribution N. America	Occurrence ◉◉

Order TARPHYCERATIDA	Family ESTONIOCERATIDAE	Informal name Nautiloid

ESTONIOCERAS

The spiral shell of this nautiloid is loosely coiled, with a final whorl growing away from the preceding part of the shell. It has a broad, shallow umbilicus. Growth lines are present on the flanks of the shell. Most unusually for nautiloids, the siphuncle is near the outside of the whorl (ventral).
• HABITAT This genus adapted to a swimming existence *(see life position)* by having a loosely coiled shell. It lived in fairly deep water, and probably used its tentacles to grasp food.
• REMARK This is a well-preserved specimen of a rare species, preserved as an internal mould.

uncoiled final whorl

rounded venter

umbilicus

*ESTONIOCERAS
PERFORATUM*
Schröder;
Early
Ordovician;
Estonia.

Typical diameter 10cm (4in)

Range E. Ordovician	Distribution Europe	Occurrence ◉

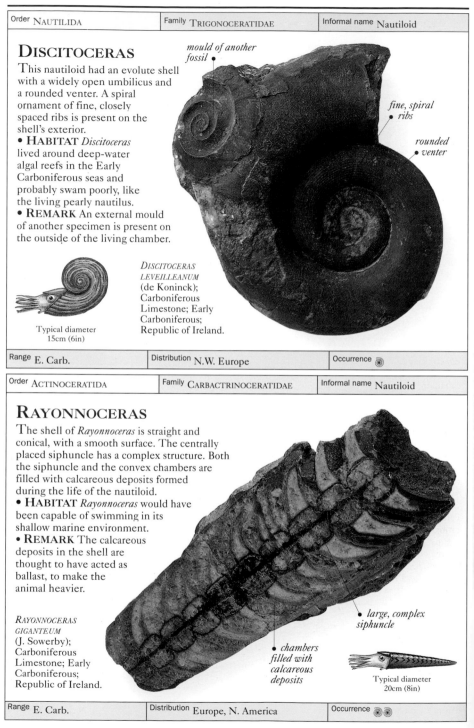

Order NAUTILIDA	Family TRIGONOCERATIDAE	Informal name Nautiloid

DISCITOCERAS

This nautiloid had an evolute shell with a widely open umbilicus and a rounded venter. A spiral ornament of fine, closely spaced ribs is present on the shell's exterior.

• **HABITAT** *Discitoceras* lived around deep-water algal reefs in the Early Carboniferous seas and probably swam poorly, like the living pearly nautilus.

• **REMARK** An external mould of another specimen is present on the outside of the living chamber.

mould of another fossil

fine, spiral ribs

rounded venter

DISCITOCERAS LEVEILLEANUM (de Koninck); Carboniferous Limestone; Early Carboniferous; Republic of Ireland.

Typical diameter 15cm (6in)

Range E. Carb.	Distribution N.W. Europe	Occurrence

Order ACTINOCERATIDA	Family CARBACTRINOCERATIDAE	Informal name Nautiloid

RAYONNOCERAS

The shell of *Rayonnoceras* is straight and conical, with a smooth surface. The centrally placed siphuncle has a complex structure. Both the siphuncle and the convex chambers are filled with calcareous deposits formed during the life of the nautiloid.

• **HABITAT** *Rayonnoceras* would have been capable of swimming in its shallow marine environment.

• **REMARK** The calcareous deposits in the shell are thought to have acted as ballast, to make the animal heavier.

RAYONNOCERAS GIGANTEUM (J. Sowerby); Carboniferous Limestone; Early Carboniferous; Republic of Ireland.

large, complex siphuncle

chambers filled with calcareous deposits

Typical diameter 20cm (8in)

Range E. Carb.	Distribution Europe, N. America	Occurrence

Order NAUTILIDA	Family TRIGONOCERATIDAE	Informal name Nautiloid

VESTINAUTILUS

The shell is notable for its extremely evolute form. It has an open umbilicus and a distinctive mid-flank ridge, which runs along each side, on which the sutures form a forwardly directed V-shaped fold. There are numerous small chambers.
• HABITAT *Vestinautilus* was a poor swimmer, living on the bottom of shelf seas.
• REMARK The specimen is preserved as an internal mould in limestone; the body chamber has broken away. The sutures are well displayed.

VESTINAUTILUS CARINIFEROUS (J. de C. Sowerby); Carboniferous; Locality Unknown.

• *open umbilicus*

• *folded suture*

Typical diameter 6cm (2⅜in)

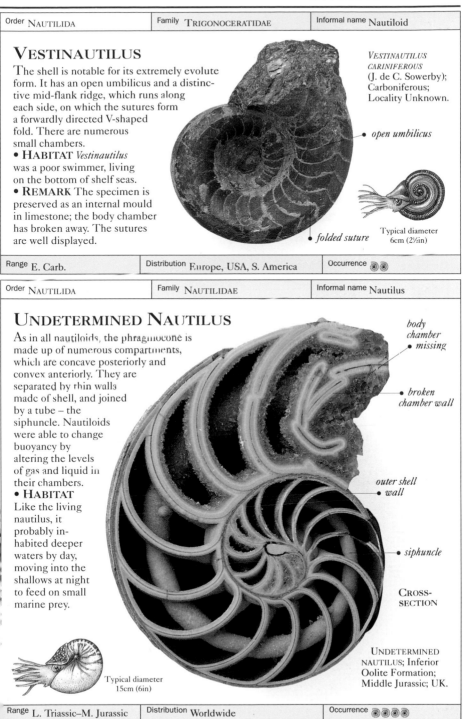

Range E. Carb.	Distribution Europe, USA, S. America	Occurrence ◉◉

Order NAUTILIDA	Family NAUTILIDAE	Informal name Nautilus

UNDETERMINED NAUTILUS

As in all nautiloids, the phragmocone is made up of numerous compartments, which are concave posteriorly and convex anteriorly. They are separated by thin walls made of shell, and joined by a tube – the siphuncle. Nautiloids were able to change buoyancy by altering the levels of gas and liquid in their chambers.
• HABITAT Like the living nautilus, it probably inhabited deeper waters by day, moving into the shallows at night to feed on small marine prey.

body chamber • *missing*

• *broken chamber wall*

outer shell • *wall*

• *siphuncle*

CROSS-SECTION

UNDETERMINED NAUTILUS; Inferior Oolite Formation; Middle Jurassic; UK.

Typical diameter 15cm (6in)

Range L. Triassic–M. Jurassic	Distribution Worldwide	Occurrence ◉◉◉◉

Order NAUTILIDA	Family NAUTILIDAE	Informal name Nautilus

CENOCERAS

The shell form is involute, the umbilicus narrow. The whorl height increases rapidly. The venter is broad and rounded. The suture lines are closely spaced and gently curved, lacking any complex folds. The living chamber occupies about half a whorl. Internally, the numerous chambers have a concavo-convex form in cross-section, and a large siphuncle positioned near the dorsal margin.
• **HABITAT** This marine-dwelling animal fed on small, bottom-dwelling animals.
• **REMARK** Many of the chambers of this specimen are filled with red lime-mud, hardened into limestone. Some are filled with calcite crystals, and many of the walls are broken – probably from the implosion resulting from the shell sinking in deeper water, after the animal died.

broad, rounded
• *venter*

INTERNAL
MOULD

CROSS-
SECTION

• *mud-filled chambers*

narrow •
umbilicus

CENOCERAS sp.;
Inferior Oolite;
Middle Jurassic; UK.

• *simple, curved sutures*

• *broken chamber walls*

numerous concavo-
• *convex chambers*

siphuncle •
joining chambers

• *start of living chamber*

Typical diameter
15cm (6in)

Range L. Triassic–M. Jurassic	Distribution Worldwide	Occurrence ⊛⊛⊛⊛

Order NAUTILIDA	Family NAUTILIDAE	Informal name Nautilus

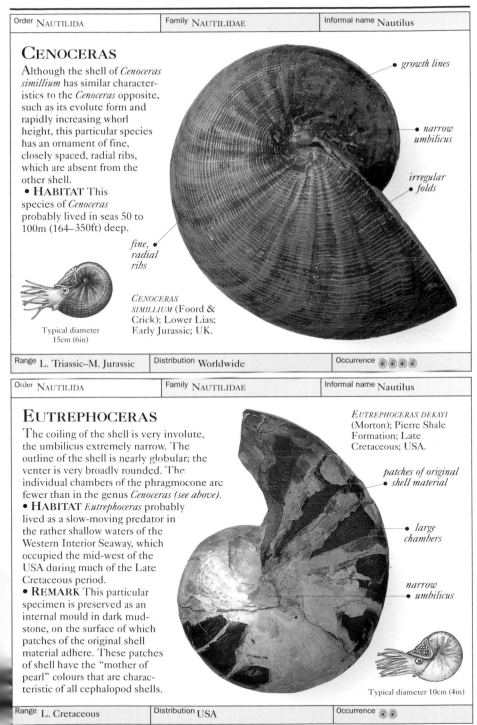

CENOCERAS

Although the shell of *Cenoceras simillium* has similar characteristics to the *Cenoceras* opposite, such as its evolute form and rapidly increasing whorl height, this particular species has an ornament of fine, closely spaced, radial ribs, which are absent from the other shell.

• HABITAT This species of *Cenoceras* probably lived in seas 50 to 100m (164–350ft) deep.

growth lines

narrow umbilicus

irregular folds

fine, radial ribs

CENOCERAS SIMILLIUM (Foord & Crick); Lower Lias; Early Jurassic; UK.

Typical diameter 15cm (6in)

Range L. Triassic–M. Jurassic	Distribution Worldwide	Occurrence 🌑🌑🌑🌑

Order NAUTILIDA	Family NAUTILIDAE	Informal name Nautilus

EUTREPHOCERAS

The coiling of the shell is very involute, the umbilicus extremely narrow. The outline of the shell is nearly globular; the venter is very broadly rounded. The individual chambers of the phragmocone are fewer than in the genus *Cenoceras (see above).*

• HABITAT *Eutrephoceras* probably lived as a slow-moving predator in the rather shallow waters of the Western Interior Seaway, which occupied the mid-west of the USA during much of the Late Cretaceous period.

• REMARK This particular specimen is preserved as an internal mould in dark mud-stone, on the surface of which patches of the original shell material adhere. These patches of shell have the "mother of pearl" colours that are characteristic of all cephalopod shells.

EUTREPHOCERAS DEKAYI (Morton); Pierre Shale Formation; Late Cretaceous; USA.

patches of original shell material

large chambers

narrow umbilicus

Typical diameter 10cm (4in)

Range L. Cretaceous	Distribution USA	Occurrence 🌑🌑

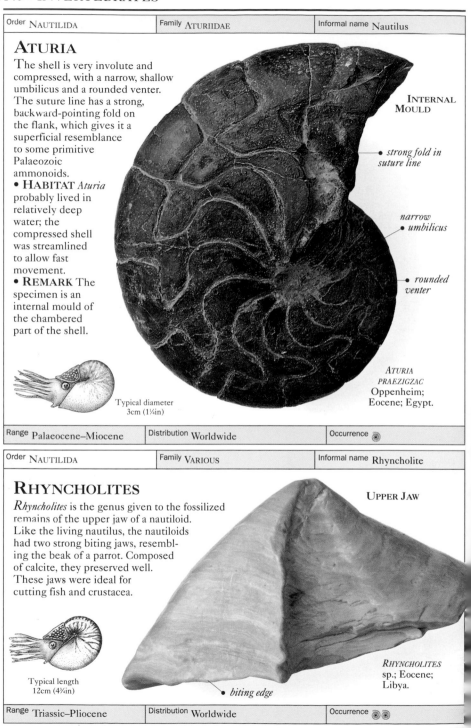

Order NAUTILIDA	Family ATURIIDAE	Informal name Nautilus

ATURIA

The shell is very involute and compressed, with a narrow, shallow umbilicus and a rounded venter. The suture line has a strong, backward-pointing fold on the flank, which gives it a superficial resemblance to some primitive Palaeozoic ammonoids.

• **HABITAT** *Aturia* probably lived in relatively deep water; the compressed shell was streamlined to allow fast movement.

• **REMARK** The specimen is an internal mould of the chambered part of the shell.

INTERNAL
MOULD

• *strong fold in suture line*

narrow
• *umbilicus*

• *rounded venter*

Typical diameter
3cm (1¼in)

*ATURIA
PRAEZIGZAC*
Oppenheim;
Eocene; Egypt.

Range Palaeocene–Miocene	Distribution Worldwide	Occurrence ◉

Order NAUTILIDA	Family VARIOUS	Informal name Rhyncholite

RHYNCHOLITES

Rhyncholites is the genus given to the fossilized remains of the upper jaw of a nautiloid. Like the living nautilus, the nautiloids had two strong biting jaws, resembling the beak of a parrot. Composed of calcite, they preserved well. These jaws were ideal for cutting fish and crustacea.

UPPER JAW

Typical length
12cm (4¾in)

RHYNCHOLITES
sp.; Eocene;
Libya.

• *biting edge*

Range Triassic–Pliocene	Distribution Worldwide	Occurrence ◉◉

AMMONOIDEA

A
MMONOIDS EVOLVED from nauti-loids in the early Devonian period, about 400 million years ago, and were abundant in world seas for the following 370 million years, after which they vanished suddenly at the end of the Cretaceous period. The rapid evolution of ammonoids and their widespread distribution makes them of great value in the subdivision of Late Palaeozoic and Mesozoic time. As a group, they are characterized by the position of the siphuncle (the tube connecting the chambers of the shell), which is near the outside of the shell (ventral). Ammonoidea sutures can be simple, as found in Palaeozoic species, or complex, as found in Mesozoic species. Because they are extinct, we know very little about the soft parts and life habits of the ammonoids. It is rare to find the biting jaws, the tongue-like, rasping radula, or the ink-sacs preserved in living chambers.

Order CLYMENIIDA	Family CLYMENIIDAE	Informal name Clymeniid

CLYMENIA

The evolute shell has a wide, open umbilicus. It is either nearly smooth or it carries weak, gently curved growth lines. The whorl section is compressed, and the venter is rounded. The suture is very simple.

• **HABITAT** This genus lived a predatory existence on or near the floor of Devonian seas.

• **REMARK** One of the more primitive ammonoids, *Clymenia* was locally common in Late Devonian rocks, but not well preserved.

CLYMENIA LAEVIGATA (Münster); Late Devonian; Germany.

limestone matrix •

broad • *umbilicus*

Typical diameter 4cm (1½in)

• *rounded venter*

Range L. Devonian	Distribution Europe, Asia, N. Africa	Occurrence

Order CLYMENIIDA	Family HEXACLYMENIIDAE	Informal name Clymeniid

SOLICLYMENIA

This is an unusually shaped ammonoid, with a very evolute shell which shows distinctive triangular coiling. It has a broad umbilicus and a rounded venter. The simple ribs are closely spaced; the suture is very simple.
• HABITAT It lived in moderately deep water. Although it could swim, its shell shape suggests it spent some time on the sea bed.

simple, close ribs •

evolute shell form •

SOLICLYMENIA PARADOXA (Münster); Late Devonian; Germany.

• *triangular coiling*

Typical length 2cm (¾in)

Range L. Devonian	Distribution Eurasia, N. Africa, N. America	Occurrence 🌑🌑

Order PROLECANITIDA	Family PROLECANITIDAE	Informal name Goniatite

MEROCANITES

The shell of *Merocanites* is evolute and has a broad, open umbilicus; the profile is compressed, the sides parallel. The gently rounded flanks show a suture with several blade-shaped folds (a fairly complex form for Palaeozoic ammonoids). The venter is rounded.
• HABITAT *Merocanites* lived in moderately deep water in the Early Carboniferous seas.
• REMARK The specimen is preserved in dark limestone as an iron-oxide-coated internal mould. The living chamber is not preserved.

complex suture with • *deep folds*

INTERNAL MOULD

• *fine, dark, muddy limestone matrix*

MEROCANITES COMPRESSUS (J. Sowerby); Carboniferous Limestone; Early Carboniferous; UK.

Typical diameter 5cm (2in)

Range E. Carb.	Distribution Europe, Asia, N. America	Occurrence 🌑

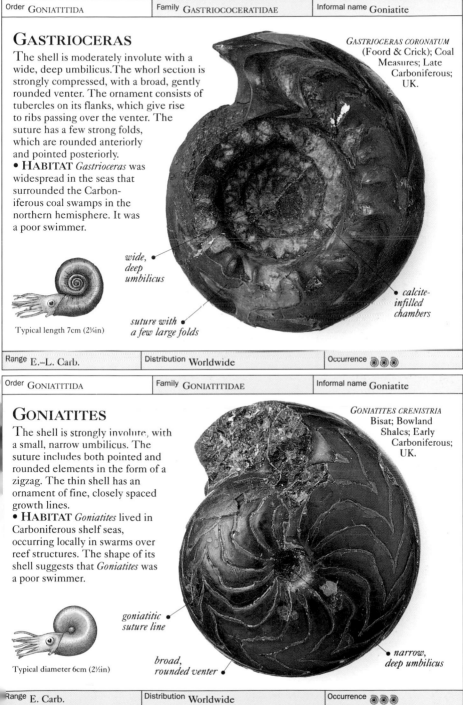

Order GONIATITIDA	Family GASTRIOCOCERATIDAE	Informal name Goniatite

GASTRIOCERAS

The shell is moderately involute with a wide, deep umbilicus. The whorl section is strongly compressed, with a broad, gently rounded venter. The ornament consists of tubercles on its flanks, which give rise to ribs passing over the venter. The suture has a few strong folds, which are rounded anteriorly and pointed posteriorly.

• **HABITAT** *Gastrioceras* was widespread in the seas that surrounded the Carboniferous coal swamps in the northern hemisphere. It was a poor swimmer.

GASTRIOCERAS CORONATUM (Foord & Crick); Coal Measures; Late Carboniferous; UK.

wide, deep umbilicus

calcite-infilled chambers

Typical length 7cm (2¾in)

suture with a few large folds

Range E.–L. Carb.	Distribution Worldwide	Occurrence

Order GONIATITIDA	Family GONIATITIDAE	Informal name Goniatite

GONIATITES

The shell is strongly involute, with a small, narrow umbilicus. The suture includes both pointed and rounded elements in the form of a zigzag. The thin shell has an ornament of fine, closely spaced growth lines.

• **HABITAT** *Goniatites* lived in Carboniferous shelf seas, occurring locally in swarms over reef structures. The shape of its shell suggests that *Goniatites* was a poor swimmer.

GONIATITES CRENISTRIA Bisat; Bowland Shales; Early Carboniferous; UK.

goniatitic suture line

narrow, deep umbilicus

Typical diameter 6cm (2½in)

broad, rounded venter

Range E. Carb.	Distribution Worldwide	Occurrence

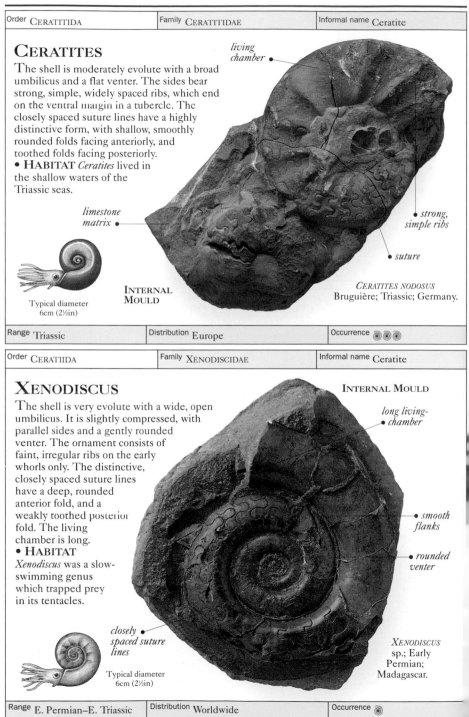

Order CERATITIDA	Family CERATITIDAE	Informal name Ceratite

CERATITES

The shell is moderately evolute with a broad umbilicus and a flat venter. The sides bear strong, simple, widely spaced ribs, which end on the ventral margin in a tubercle. The closely spaced suture lines have a highly distinctive form, with shallow, smoothly rounded folds facing anteriorly, and toothed folds facing posteriorly.
• HABITAT *Ceratites* lived in the shallow waters of the Triassic seas.

living chamber

limestone matrix

Typical diameter 6cm (2½in)

INTERNAL MOULD

strong, simple ribs

suture

CERATITES NODOSUS
Bruguière; Triassic; Germany.

Range Triassic	Distribution Europe	Occurrence

Order CERATIIDA	Family XENODISCIDAE	Informal name Ceratite

XENODISCUS

INTERNAL MOULD

The shell is very evolute with a wide, open umbilicus. It is slightly compressed, with parallel sides and a gently rounded venter. The ornament consists of faint, irregular ribs on the early whorls only. The distinctive, closely spaced suture lines have a deep, rounded anterior fold, and a weakly toothed posterior fold. The living chamber is long.
• HABITAT *Xenodiscus* was a slow-swimming genus which trapped prey in its tentacles.

long living-chamber

smooth flanks

rounded venter

closely spaced suture lines

Typical diameter 6cm (2½in)

XENODISCUS
sp.; Early Permian; Madagascar.

Range E. Permian–E. Triassic	Distribution Worldwide	Occurrence

AMMONITES

A MMONITES ARE A FORM of ammonoid distinguished by their complex suture lines. They were abundant and diverse in the seas of the Mesozoic Era, and they evolved very rapidly to produce numerous species and genera. After a decline in diversity during the Late Cretaceous period, ammonites became extinct at the same time as other marine groups, such as belemnites, and terrestrial groups, such as dinosaurs. As both ammonites and all their close relatives are extinct, scientists know very little about their mode of life. What is known about them has been worked out mostly from experiments with model shells in water tanks.

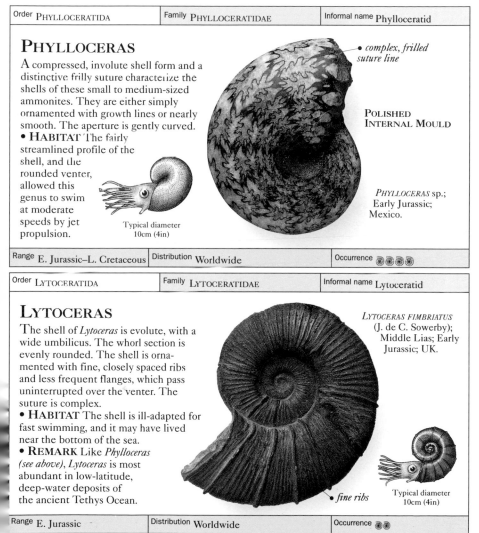

Order PHYLLOCERATIDA	Family PHYLLOCERATIDAE	Informal name Phylloceratid

PHYLLOCERAS

A compressed, involute shell form and a distinctive frilly suture characterize the shells of these small to medium-sized ammonites. They are either simply ornamented with growth lines or nearly smooth. The aperture is gently curved.
• **HABITAT** The fairly streamlined profile of the shell, and the rounded venter, allowed this genus to swim at moderate speeds by jet propulsion.

• *complex, frilled suture line*

POLISHED INTERNAL MOULD

PHYLLOCERAS sp.; Early Jurassic; Mexico.

Typical diameter 10cm (4in)

Range E. Jurassic–L. Cretaceous	Distribution Worldwide	Occurrence ⬤⬤⬤⬤

Order LYTOCERATIDA	Family LYTOCERATIDAE	Informal name Lytoceratid

LYTOCERAS

The shell of *Lytoceras* is evolute, with a wide umbilicus. The whorl section is evenly rounded. The shell is ornamented with fine, closely spaced ribs and less frequent flanges, which pass uninterrupted over the venter. The suture is complex.
• **HABITAT** The shell is ill-adapted for fast swimming, and it may have lived near the bottom of the sea.
• **REMARK** Like *Phylloceras* (see above), *Lytoceras* is most abundant in low-latitude, deep-water deposits of the ancient Tethys Ocean.

LYTOCERAS FIMBRIATUS (J. de C. Sowerby); Middle Lias; Early Jurassic; UK.

• *fine ribs*

Typical diameter 10cm (4in)

Range E. Jurassic	Distribution Worldwide	Occurrence ⬤⬤

Order AMMONITIDA	Family PSILOCERATIDAE	Informal name Ammonite

PSILOCERAS

In many localities around the world, this small, rather smooth genus is taken as the marker of earliest Jurassic time. The Psiloceratidae probably evolved from the *Phylloceras* group *(see p.145)* and retain rather simple sutures. The preservation of original deep pink, pearly shell, crushed flat in shale, is typical of fossil shells found in north Somerset, UK.
• **HABITAT** *Psiloceras* was a moderately capable swimmer.
• **REMARK** This genus was abundant locally in the Early Jurassic period.

• *grey shale matrix*

• *small individuals preserved as nacre shell*

crushed • shells

Typical diameter
7cm (2¾in)

PSILOCERAS PLANORBIS (J. de C. Sowerby); Lower Lias; Early Jurassic; UK.

Range E. Jurassic	Distribution Worldwide	Occurrence 🔘🔘🔘🔘🔘

Order AMMONITIDA	Family AMALTHEIDAE	Informal name Ammonite

AMALTHEUS

Amaltheus is characterized by its very compressed, involute shell, and by the narrow keel which has an ornament resembling a piece of rope. The ornament of the flanks is weak and consists of sickle-shaped ribs or, more rarely, fine, spiral ribs.
• **HABITAT** The streamlined whorl profile and narrow keel suggest that it was quite a good swimmer.
• **REMARK** The genus may have evolved from *Phylloceras (see p.145).*

• *simple s-shaped ribs*

BROWN SANDSTONE MOULD

Typical diameter
7cm (2¾in)

compressed shell • with corded keel

AMALTHEUS STOKESI (J. Sowerby); Middle Lias; Early Jurassic; UK.

Range E. Jurassic	Distribution Worldwide	Occurrence 🔘🔘🔘🔘

Order AMMONITIDA	Family OXYNOTICERATIDAE	Informal name Ammonite

OXYNOTICERAS

This distinctive ammonite is characterized by its strongly compressed, involute shell and knife-sharp keel. The suture line is complex and frilled. The lower specimen has been cut in half to show the septa (pyrite) and the cameral chambers, now filled with yellow calcite. The siphuncle is just visible next to the venter – its characteristic position.
• **HABITAT** The sharp keel would have offered minimum resistance to the water through which *Oxynoticeras* swam, and it is interpreted as one of the fastest-swimming ammonites of all.
• **REMARK** The specimens are internal moulds in bronzy iron pyrites – a common ammonite mode of preservation in clays.

living chamber broken away •

INTERNAL MOULD IN PYRITES

• *involute shell with small umbilicus*

OXYNOTICERAS OXYNOTUM (Quenstedt); Lower Lias; Early Jurassic; UK.

• *cross-section of individual, nearly straight septa*

• *siphuncle just visible on ventral margin of shell*

• *chamber full of yellow calcite*

sharp keel on margin of compressed shell •

PYRITIZED AMMONITE CUT IN HALF

Typical diameter 10cm (4in)

Range E. Jurassic	Distribution Worldwide	Occurrence

Order AMMONITIDA	Family KOSMOCERATIDAE	Informal name Ammonite

KOSMOCERAS

This is a compressed, moderately evolute ammonite. It is very typical of Middle Jurassic deposits. The shell has a complex ornament of bunched ribs and rows of tubercles. The venter is narrow and flat.

• **HABITAT** *Kosmoceras* lived in deeper water and was probably a moderately good swimmer.

• **REMARK** The specimen is preserved in original shell material, crushed in shales.

KOSMOCERAS DUNCANI (J. de C. Sowerby); Oxford Clay; Middle Jurassic; UK.

crushed • nacre shell

Typical diameter
6cm (2⅜in)

Range M. Jurassic	Distribution Worldwide	Occurrence

Order AMMONITIDA	Family PERISPHINCTIDAE	Informal name Ammonite

PAVLOVIA

This is a typical member of the abundant and widespread Late Jurassic family, Perisphinctidae. Members of the family are characterized by open, evolute shell forms, rounded whorl sections, and ornamentation of branching ribs. A long living chamber occupies nearly a whole whorl of the shell. The suture is complex.

• **HABITAT** This genus lived in the extensive Late Jurassic seas.

• branching ribs

evolute • shell form

• umbilicus

PAVLOVIA PRAECOX Spath; Upper Glauconite Series; Late Jurassic; Greenland.

Typical diameter
4cm (1½in)

Range L. Jurassic	Distribution Greenland, northern Europe	Occurrence

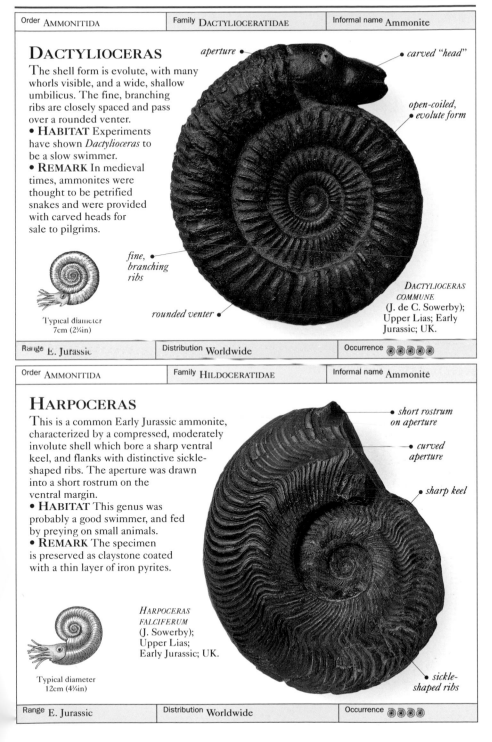

Order AMMONITIDA	Family DACTYLIOCERATIDAE	Informal name Ammonite

DACTYLIOCERAS

aperture •

• carved "head"

The shell form is evolute, with many whorls visible, and a wide, shallow umbilicus. The fine, branching ribs are closely spaced and pass over a rounded venter.
• HABITAT Experiments have shown *Dactylioceras* to be a slow swimmer.
• REMARK In medieval times, ammonites were thought to be petrified snakes and were provided with carved heads for sale to pilgrims.

open-coiled,
• evolute form

fine, •
branching
ribs

rounded venter •

Typical diameter
7cm (2¾in)

*DACTYLIOCERAS
COMMUNE*
(J. de C. Sowerby);
Upper Lias; Early
Jurassic; UK.

Range E. Jurassic	Distribution Worldwide	Occurrence 🌑🌑🌑🌑🌑

Order AMMONITIDA	Family HILDOCERATIDAE	Informal name Ammonite

HARPOCERAS

This is a common Early Jurassic ammonite, characterized by a compressed, moderately involute shell which bore a sharp ventral keel, and flanks with distinctive sickle-shaped ribs. The aperture was drawn into a short rostrum on the ventral margin.
• HABITAT This genus was probably a good swimmer, and fed by preying on small animals.
• REMARK The specimen is preserved as claystone coated with a thin layer of iron pyrites.

• short rostrum
on aperture

• curved
aperture

• sharp keel

*HARPOCERAS
FALCIFERUM*
(J. Sowerby);
Upper Lias;
Early Jurassic; UK.

Typical diameter
12cm (4¾in)

• sickle-
shaped ribs

Range E. Jurassic	Distribution Worldwide	Occurrence 🌑🌑🌑🌑

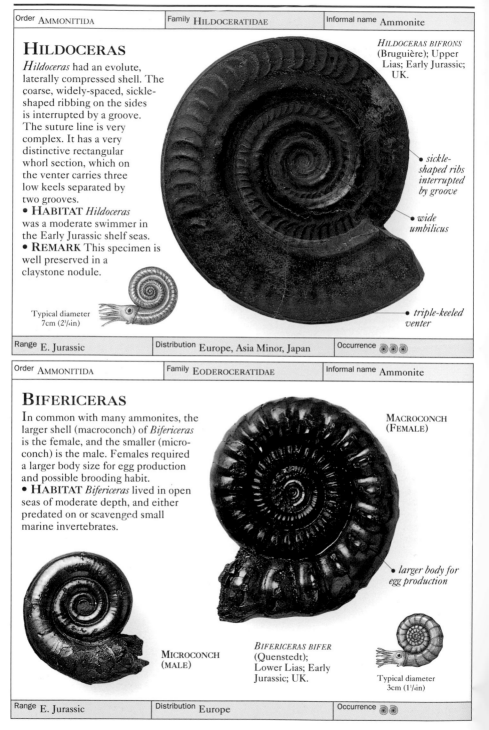

Order AMMONITIDA	Family HILDOCERATIDAE	Informal name Ammonite

HILDOCERAS

Hildoceras had an evolute, laterally compressed shell. The coarse, widely-spaced, sickle-shaped ribbing on the sides is interrupted by a groove. The suture line is very complex. It has a very distinctive rectangular whorl section, which on the venter carries three low keels separated by two grooves.
• HABITAT *Hildoceras* was a moderate swimmer in the Early Jurassic shelf seas.
• REMARK This specimen is well preserved in a claystone nodule.

HILDOCERAS BIFRONS (Bruguière); Upper Lias; Early Jurassic; UK.

• *sickle-shaped ribs interrupted by groove*

• *wide umbilicus*

Typical diameter 7cm (2³/₄in)

• *triple-keeled venter*

Range E. Jurassic	Distribution Europe, Asia Minor, Japan	Occurrence

Order AMMONITIDA	Family EODEROCERATIDAE	Informal name Ammonite

BIFERICERAS

In common with many ammonites, the larger shell (macroconch) of *Bifericeras* is the female, and the smaller (micro-conch) is the male. Females required a larger body size for egg production and possible brooding habit.
• HABITAT *Bifericeras* lived in open seas of moderate depth, and either predated on or scavenged small marine invertebrates.

MACROCONCH (FEMALE)

• *larger body for egg production*

MICROCONCH (MALE)

BIFERICERAS BIFER (Quenstedt); Lower Lias; Early Jurassic; UK.

Typical diameter 3cm (1¹/₄in)

Range E. Jurassic	Distribution Europe	Occurrence

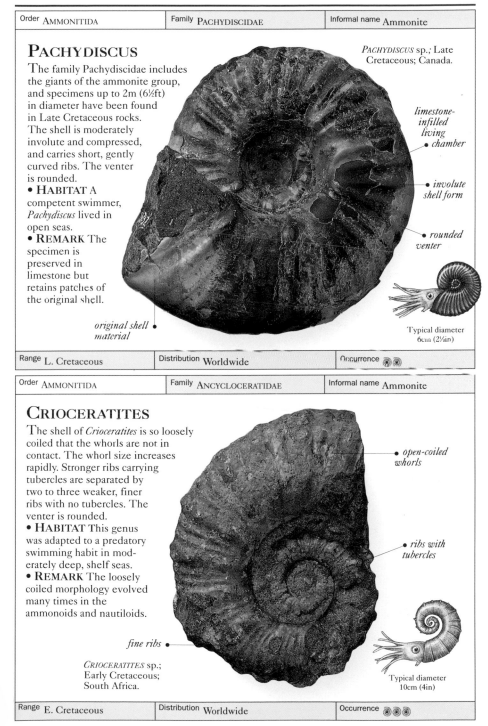

Order AMMONITIDA	Family PACHYDISCIDAE	Informal name Ammonite

PACHYDISCUS

The family Pachydiscidae includes the giants of the ammonite group, and specimens up to 2m (6½ft) in diameter have been found in Late Cretaceous rocks. The shell is moderately involute and compressed, and carries short, gently curved ribs. The venter is rounded.
• **HABITAT** A competent swimmer, *Pachydiscus* lived in open seas.
• **REMARK** The specimen is preserved in limestone but retains patches of the original shell.

PACHYDISCUS sp.; Late Cretaceous; Canada.

limestone-infilled living • *chamber*

• *involute shell form*

• *rounded venter*

original shell • *material*

Typical diameter 6cm (2¼in)

Range L. Cretaceous	Distribution Worldwide	Occurrence

Order AMMONITIDA	Family ANCYCLOCERATIDAE	Informal name Ammonite

CRIOCERATITES

The shell of *Crioceratites* is so loosely coiled that the whorls are not in contact. The whorl size increases rapidly. Stronger ribs carrying tubercles are separated by two to three weaker, finer ribs with no tubercles. The venter is rounded.
• **HABITAT** This genus was adapted to a predatory swimming habit in mod-erately deep, shelf seas.
• **REMARK** The loosely coiled morphology evolved many times in the ammonoids and nautiloids.

• *open-coiled whorls*

• *ribs with tubercles*

fine ribs •

CRIOCERATITES sp.; Early Cretaceous; South Africa.

Typical diameter 10cm (4in)

Range E. Cretaceous	Distribution Worldwide	Occurrence

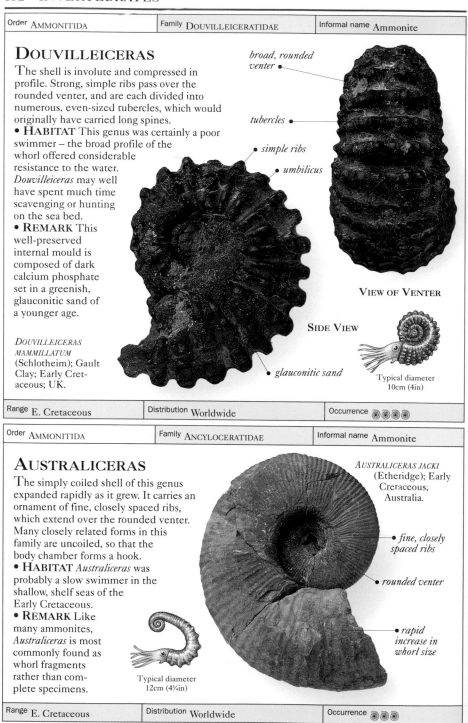

Order AMMONITIDA	Family DOUVILLEICERATIDAE	Informal name Ammonite

DOUVILLEICERAS

The shell is involute and compressed in profile. Strong, simple ribs pass over the rounded venter, and are each divided into numerous, even-sized tubercles, which would originally have carried long spines.
• **HABITAT** This genus was certainly a poor swimmer – the broad profile of the whorl offered considerable resistance to the water. *Douvilleiceras* may well have spent much time scavenging or hunting on the sea bed.
• **REMARK** This well-preserved internal mould is composed of dark calcium phosphate set in a greenish, glauconitic sand of a younger age.

DOUVILLEICERAS MAMMILLATUM (Schlotheim); Gault Clay; Early Cretaceous; UK.

broad, rounded venter •

tubercles •

• *simple ribs*

• *umbilicus*

VIEW OF VENTER

SIDE VIEW

• *glauconitic sand*

Typical diameter 10cm (4in)

Range E. Cretaceous	Distribution Worldwide	Occurrence ◉◉◉◉

Order AMMONITIDA	Family ANCYLOCERATIDAE	Informal name Ammonite

AUSTRALICERAS

The simply coiled shell of this genus expanded rapidly as it grew. It carries an ornament of fine, closely spaced ribs, which extend over the rounded venter. Many closely related forms in this family are uncoiled, so that the body chamber forms a hook.
• **HABITAT** *Australiceras* was probably a slow swimmer in the shallow, shelf seas of the Early Cretaceous.
• **REMARK** Like many ammonites, *Australiceras* is most commonly found as whorl fragments rather than complete specimens.

AUSTRALICERAS JACKI (Etheridge); Early Cretaceous; Australia.

• *fine, closely spaced ribs*

• *rounded venter*

• *rapid increase in whorl size*

Typical diameter 12cm (4¾in)

Range E. Cretaceous	Distribution Worldwide	Occurrence ◉◉◉

Order AMMONITIDA	Family PLACENTICERATIDAE	Informal name Ammonite

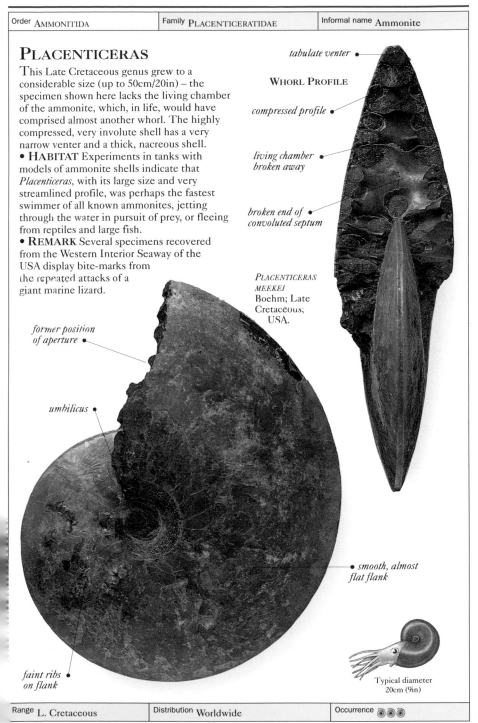

PLACENTICERAS

This Late Cretaceous genus grew to a considerable size (up to 50cm/20in) – the specimen shown here lacks the living chamber of the ammonite, which, in life, would have comprised almost another whorl. The highly compressed, very involute shell has a very narrow venter and a thick, nacreous shell.
• HABITAT Experiments in tanks with models of ammonite shells indicate that *Placenticeras*, with its large size and very streamlined profile, was perhaps the fastest swimmer of all known ammonites, jetting through the water in pursuit of prey, or fleeing from reptiles and large fish.
• REMARK Several specimens recovered from the Western Interior Seaway of the USA display bite-marks from the repeated attacks of a giant marine lizard.

tabulate venter

WHORL PROFILE

compressed profile

living chamber broken away

broken end of convoluted septum

PLACENTICERAS MEEKEI Boehm; Late Cretaceous; USA.

former position of aperture

umbilicus

smooth, almost flat flank

faint ribs on flank

Typical diameter 20cm (9in)

Range L. Cretaceous	Distribution Worldwide	Occurrence

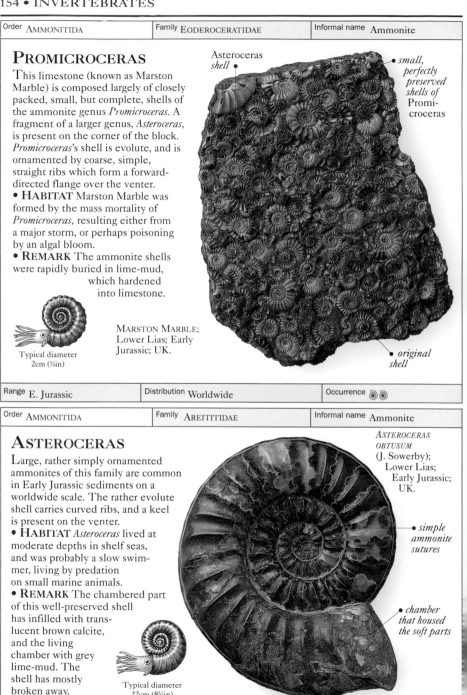

Order AMMONITIDA	Family EODEROCERATIDAE	Informal name Ammonite

PROMICROCERAS

This limestone (known as Marston Marble) is composed largely of closely packed, small, but complete, shells of the ammonite genus *Promicroceras*. A fragment of a larger genus, *Asteroceras*, is present on the corner of the block. *Promicroceras*'s shell is evolute, and is ornamented by coarse, simple, straight ribs which form a forward-directed flange over the venter.
• **HABITAT** Marston Marble was formed by the mass mortality of *Promicroceras*, resulting either from a major storm, or perhaps poisoning by an algal bloom.
• **REMARK** The ammonite shells were rapidly buried in lime-mud, which hardened into limestone.

Asteroceras shell •

• *small, perfectly preserved shells of* Promi-croceras

MARSTON MARBLE;
Lower Lias; Early
Jurassic; UK.

Typical diameter
2cm (¾in)

• *original shell*

Range E. Jurassic	Distribution Worldwide	Occurrence

Order AMMONITIDA	Family AREITITIDAE	Informal name Ammonite

ASTEROCERAS

Large, rather simply ornamented ammonites of this family are common in Early Jurassic sediments on a worldwide scale. The rather evolute shell carries curved ribs, and a keel is present on the venter.
• **HABITAT** *Asteroceras* lived at moderate depths in shelf seas, and was probably a slow swimmer, living by predation on small marine animals.
• **REMARK** The chambered part of this well-preserved shell has infilled with translucent brown calcite, and the living chamber with grey lime-mud. The shell has mostly broken away.

ASTEROCERAS OBTUSUM (J. Sowerby); Lower Lias; Early Jurassic; UK.

• *simple ammonite sutures*

• *chamber that housed the soft parts*

Typical diameter
22cm (8¾in)

Range E. Jurassic	Distribution Worldwide	Occurrence

Order AMMONITIDA	Family ECHIOCERATIDAE	Informal name Ammonite

ECHIOCERAS

The shell is extremely evolute, with numerous visible whorls and a shallow umbilicus. Short, straight ribs are present on the flanks, but do not pass on to the low-keeled venter.

• HABITAT This ammonite inhabited the shelf seas of the Early Jurassic. From the very evolute shell shape it is possible to infer that *Echioceras* was not adapted for fast swimming. It probably scavenged, or caught slow-moving prey.

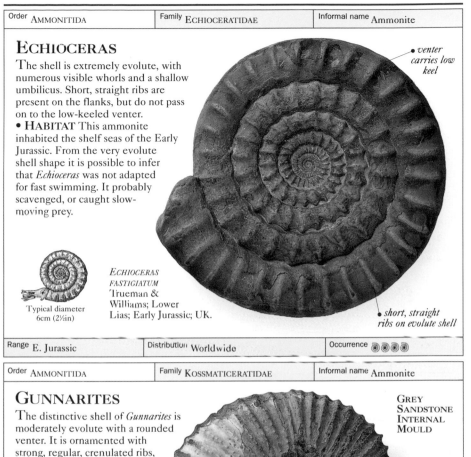

• *venter carries low keel*

• *short, straight ribs on evolute shell*

Typical diameter
6cm (2⅜in)

ECHIOCERAS FASTIGIATUM Trueman & Williams; Lower Lias; Early Jurassic; UK.

Range E. Jurassic	Distribution Worldwide	Occurrence ◉◉◉◉

Order AMMONITIDA	Family KOSSMATICERATIDAE	Informal name Ammonite

GUNNARITES

The distinctive shell of *Gunnarites* is moderately evolute with a rounded venter. It is ornamented with strong, regular, crenulated ribs, which arise from tubercles in the umbilicus.

• HABITAT *Gunnarites* lived in the shelf seas of the Late Cretaceous, and was probably a slow swimmer.

• REMARK This specimen is preserved as an internal mould, along with some of the original shell (yellow-brown).

GREY SANDSTONE INTERNAL MOULD

• *strong, crenulated ribs arise from tubercles*

original shell •

Typical diameter
16cm (6¼in)

GUNNARITES sp.; Marambio Group; Late Cretaceous; Antarctica.

Range L. Cretaceous	Distribution Antarctica, India, Australasia	Occurrence ◉◉

Order AMMONITIDA	Family ACANTHOCERATIDAE	Informal name Ammonite

MANTELLICERAS

The shell is involute, with a fairly small umbilicus. The whorl section is rectangular, the venter flat. Alternately long and short ribs are present on the flanks.

• **HABITAT** *Mantelliceras* and its relatives were probably poor swimmers, since they were not streamlined. They display strong sexual dimorphism in size, with the females (macroconchs) much larger.

• **REMARK** This genus is characteristic of the beginning of the Late Cretaceous in the northern hemisphere.

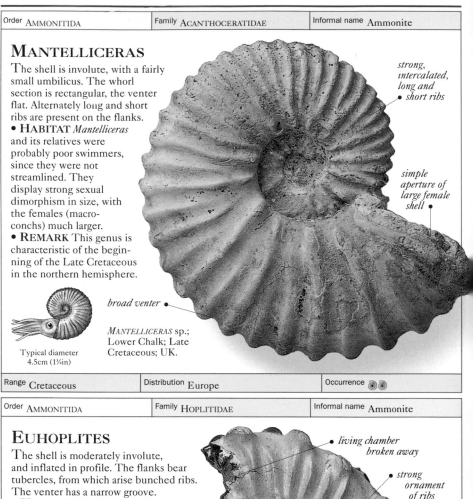

strong, intercalated, long and short ribs

simple aperture of large female shell

broad venter

MANTELLICERAS sp.; Lower Chalk; Late Cretaceous; UK.

Typical diameter 4.5cm (1¾in)

Range Cretaceous	Distribution Europe	Occurrence

Order AMMONITIDA	Family HOPLITIDAE	Informal name Ammonite

EUHOPLITES

The shell is moderately involute, and inflated in profile. The flanks bear tubercles, from which arise bunched ribs. The venter has a narrow groove.

• **HABITAT** The numerous ribs and tubercles, together with the rectangular profile of the whorl, would have offered much resistance to water, and prevented *Euhoplites* from swimming fast.

• **REMARK** In life the shell would have been three times the size of this fragment, which has missing whorls.

living chamber broken away

strong ornament of ribs and tubercles

EUHOPLITES OPALINUS Spath; Gault Clay; Early Cretaceous; UK.

original nacre shell preserved

Typical diameter 3.5cm (1⅜in)

pyrite preservation

Range E. Cretaceous	Distribution Europe	Occurrence

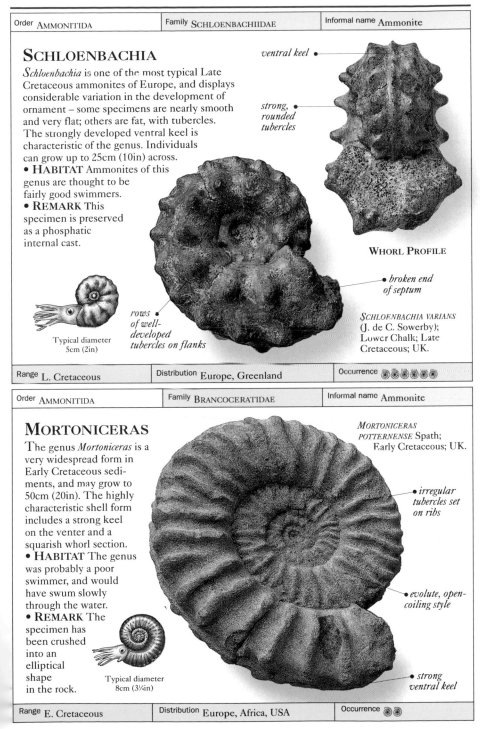

Order AMMONITIDA	Family SCHLOENBACHIIDAE	Informal name Ammonite

SCHLOENBACHIA

Schloenbachia is one of the most typical Late Cretaceous ammonites of Europe, and displays considerable variation in the development of ornament – some specimens are nearly smooth and very flat; others are fat, with tubercles. The strongly developed ventral keel is characteristic of the genus. Individuals can grow up to 25cm (10in) across.

• HABITAT Ammonites of this genus are thought to be fairly good swimmers.

• REMARK This specimen is preserved as a phosphatic internal cast.

ventral keel

strong, rounded tubercles

WHORL PROFILE

broken end of septum

rows of well-developed tubercles on flanks

Typical diameter 5cm (2in)

SCHLOENBACHIA VARANS (J. de C. Sowerby); Lower Chalk; Late Cretaceous; UK.

Range L. Cretaceous	Distribution Europe, Greenland	Occurrence

Order AMMONITIDA	Family BRANCOCERATIDAE	Informal name Ammonite

MORTONICERAS

The genus *Mortoniceras* is a very widespread form in Early Cretaceous sediments, and may grow to 50cm (20in). The highly characteristic shell form includes a strong keel on the venter and a squarish whorl section.

• HABITAT The genus was probably a poor swimmer, and would have swum slowly through the water.

• REMARK The specimen has been crushed into an elliptical shape in the rock.

MORTONICERAS POTTERNENSE Spath; Early Cretaceous; UK.

irregular tubercles set on ribs

evolute, open-coiling style

Typical diameter 8cm (3¼in)

strong ventral keel

Range E. Cretaceous	Distribution Europe, Africa, USA	Occurrence

Order AMMONITIDA	Family DESHAYESITIDAE	Informal name Ammonite

DESHAYESITES

Deshayesites was an evolute, compressed ammonite, whose shell carries a rather simple ornament of sinuous ribs. The ribs pass over the narrow, rounded venter. The genus was common in and absolutely diagnostic of Aptian times.
• **HABITAT** The streamlined profile and weak ornament suggest that this genus was capable of fast movement through the water.
• **REMARK** The specimen is preserved as an internal mould with traces of original shell.

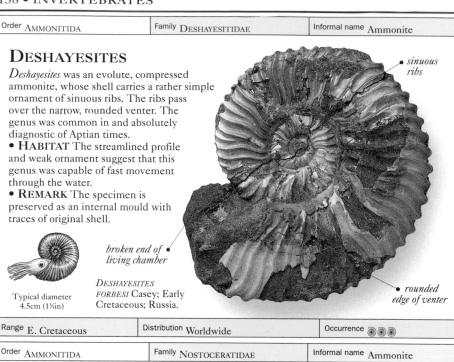

• *sinuous ribs*

broken end of living chamber •

DESHAYESITES FORBESI Casey; Early Cretaceous; Russia.

Typical diameter 4.5cm (1¾in)

• *rounded edge of venter*

Range E. Cretaceous	Distribution Worldwide	Occurrence

Order AMMONITIDA	Family NOSTOCERATIDAE	Informal name Ammonite

NIPPONITES

Of all the Late Cretaceous ammonites that coiled in an irregular fashion, *Nipponites* was the most bizarre. At first sight the shell appears to be an irregular tangle of whorls. On closer inspection, however, it proves to be a 3D network of U's. It possesses a typical complex ammonite suture, and a simple ornament of ribs, and probably evolved from a helically coiled form *(see p.159)*.
• **HABITAT** *Nipponites* probably lived as a planktonic form, drifting through the mid-level or upper waters of the warm Late Cretaceous seas, and feeding on small animals which it caught with its tentacles.

BROWN SANDSTONE INTERNAL MOULD

simple ribs of varying • size

• *apparently irregular coiling pattern*

NIPPONITES MIRABILIS Yabe; Late Cretaceous; Japan.

Typical diameter 6cm (2½in)

Range L. Cretaceous	Distribution Japan, USA	Occurrence

Order AMMONITIDA	Family NOSTOCERATIDAE	Informal name Ammonite

BOSTRYCHOCERAS

In this genus, and in the closely related family Turrilitidae, the coiling of the shell has become helical (like a snail or gastropod), in contrast to the planispiral, flat coiling of most ammonites. Although superficially similar to gastropods, such fossils are readily identifiable as ammonites from the characteristic suture lines. In *Bostrychoceras*, the coiling is loose, so that successive whorls are not in contact. The simple ornament of fine, closely spaced ribs is interrupted on the living chamber by the development of tubercles. The living chamber is U-shaped, and the aperture was directed forwards in life, so that the protruding tentacles would not have been in contact with the sea bed below.

• HABITAT Palaeontologists believe that this genus was probably planktonic, floating in the open ocean, and feeding on small animals in the water column. The very widespread distribution accords quite well with this theory, since ocean-going species are commonly of global occurrence.

• REMARK *Bostrychoceras* is most often found as small pieces of broken whorls, the ornamentation of which allows identification.

YELLOW
LIMESTONE
MOULD

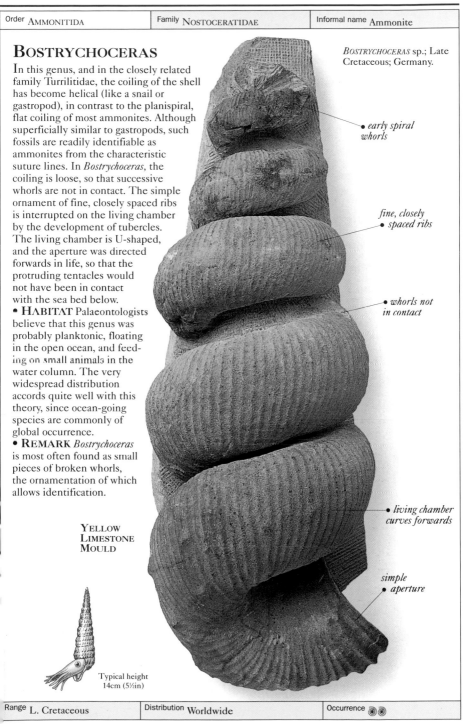

BOSTRYCHOCERAS sp.; Late Cretaceous; Germany.

• *early spiral whorls*

• *fine, closely spaced ribs*

• *whorls not in contact*

• *living chamber curves forwards*

• *simple aperture*

Typical height
14cm (5½in)

Range L. Cretaceous	Distribution Worldwide	Occurrence 🌑🌑

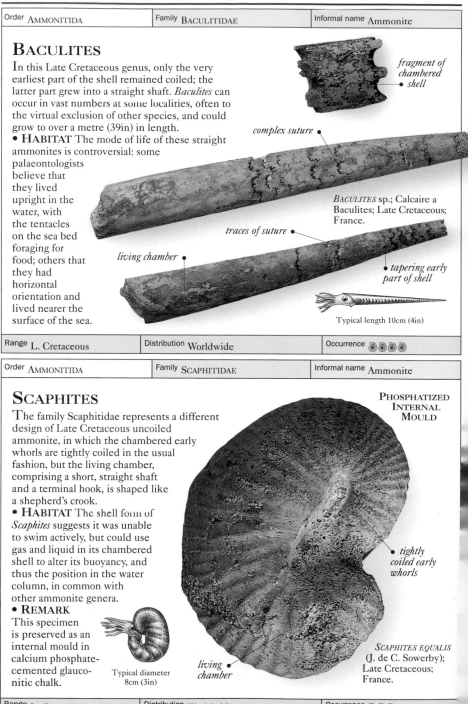

Order AMMONITIDA	Family BACULITIDAE	Informal name Ammonite

BACULITES

In this Late Cretaceous genus, only the very earliest part of the shell remained coiled; the latter part grew into a straight shaft. *Baculites* can occur in vast numbers at some localities, often to the virtual exclusion of other species, and could grow to over a metre (39in) in length.

• HABITAT The mode of life of these straight ammonites is controversial: some palaeontologists believe that they lived upright in the water, with the tentacles on the sea bed foraging for food; others that they had horizontal orientation and lived nearer the surface of the sea.

fragment of chambered shell

complex suture

BACULITES sp.; Calcaire a Baculites; Late Cretaceous; France.

traces of suture

living chamber

tapering early part of shell

Typical length 10cm (4in)

Range L. Cretaceous	Distribution Worldwide	Occurrence ⚫⚫⚫⚫

Order AMMONITIDA	Family SCAPHITIDAE	Informal name Ammonite

SCAPHITES

PHOSPHATIZED INTERNAL MOULD

The family Scaphitidae represents a different design of Late Cretaceous uncoiled ammonite, in which the chambered early whorls are tightly coiled in the usual fashion, but the living chamber, comprising a short, straight shaft and a terminal hook, is shaped like a shepherd's crook.

• HABITAT The shell form of *Scaphites* suggests it was unable to swim actively, but could use gas and liquid in its chambered shell to alter its buoyancy, and thus the position in the water column, in common with other ammonite genera.

• REMARK This specimen is preserved as an internal mould in calcium phosphate-cemented glauco-nitic chalk.

Typical diameter 8cm (3in)

tightly coiled early whorls

living chamber

SCAPHITES EQUALIS (J. de C. Sowerby); Late Cretaceous; France.

Range L. Cretaceous	Distribution Worldwide	Occurrence ⚫⚫⚫

BELEMNITES AND SQUIDS

B ELEMNITES AND SQUIDS belong to a diverse group of cephalopods, which include the living squid, cuttlefish, and octopus. The group is characterized by an internal, chambered shell enclosed entirely by soft, muscular tissues. Many forms have a hard internal support structure, made of calcium carbonate or protein, known as the pen or guard. Belemnites possessed strong, usually cylindrical, calcite guards that preserved well, and occur abundantly in Mesozoic marine rocks. Squids possess an internal support called a pen, which is made of proteinaceous chitin. This is only rarely preserved. However, in a few instances, the soft tissue has been preserved, and an entire squid, complete with tentacles, is recognizable.

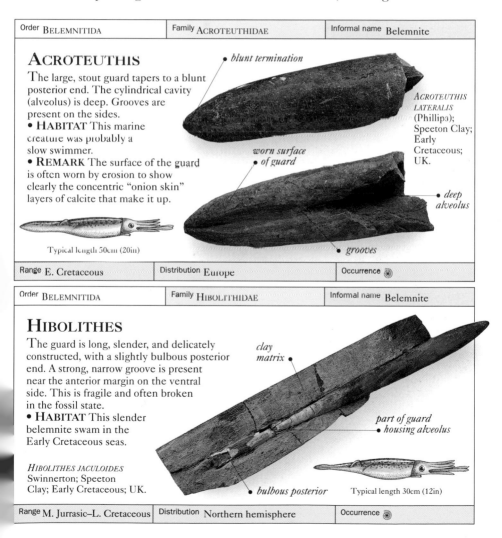

Order BELEMNITIDA	Family ACROTEUTHIDAE	Informal name Belemnite

ACROTEUTHIS

The large, stout guard tapers to a blunt posterior end. The cylindrical cavity (alveolus) is deep. Grooves are present on the sides.
• **HABITAT** This marine creature was probably a slow swimmer.
• **REMARK** The surface of the guard is often worn by erosion to show clearly the concentric "onion skin" layers of calcite that make it up.

blunt termination

worn surface of guard

ACROTEUTHIS
LATERALIS
(Phillips);
Speeton Clay;
Early
Cretaceous;
UK.

deep alveolus

grooves

Typical length 50cm (20in)

Range E. Cretaceous	Distribution Europe	Occurrence

Order BELEMNITIDA	Family HIBOLITHIDAE	Informal name Belemnite

HIBOLITHES

The guard is long, slender, and delicately constructed, with a slightly bulbous posterior end. A strong, narrow groove is present near the anterior margin on the ventral side. This is fragile and often broken in the fossil state.
• **HABITAT** This slender belemnite swam in the Early Cretaceous seas.

HIBOLITHES JACULOIDES
Swinnerton; Speeton
Clay; Early Cretaceous; UK.

clay matrix

part of guard housing alveolus

bulbous posterior

Typical length 30cm (12in)

Range M. Jurrasic–L. Cretaceous	Distribution Northern hemisphere	Occurrence

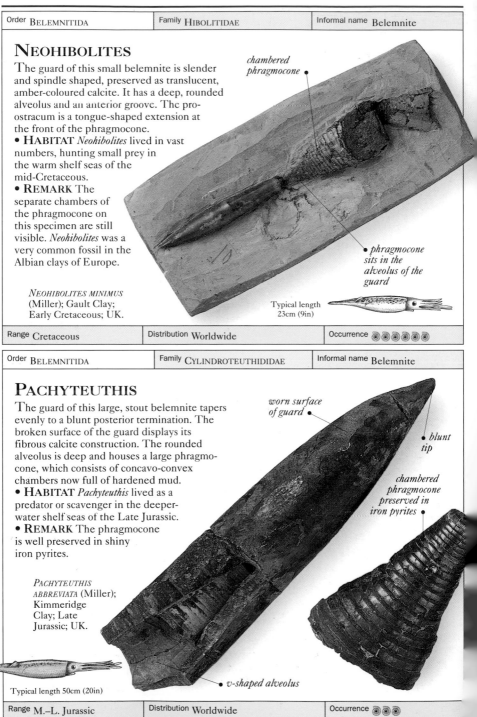

Order BELEMNITIDA	Family HIBOLITIDAE	Informal name Belemnite

NEOHIBOLITES

The guard of this small belemnite is slender and spindle shaped, preserved as translucent, amber-coloured calcite. It has a deep, rounded alveolus and an anterior groove. The pro-ostracum is a tongue-shaped extension at the front of the phragmocone.

• **HABITAT** *Neohibolites* lived in vast numbers, hunting small prey in the warm shelf seas of the mid-Cretaceous.

• **REMARK** The separate chambers of the phragmocone on this specimen are still visible. *Neohibolites* was a very common fossil in the Albian clays of Europe.

chambered phragmocone •

phragmocone • *sits in the alveolus of the guard*

NEOHIBOLITES MINIMUS (Miller); Gault Clay; Early Cretaceous; UK.

Typical length 23cm (9in)

Range Cretaceous	Distribution Worldwide	Occurrence ◉◉◉◉◉

Order BELEMNITIDA	Family CYLINDROTEUTHIDIDAE	Informal name Belemnite

PACHYTEUTHIS

The guard of this large, stout belemnite tapers evenly to a blunt posterior termination. The broken surface of the guard displays its fibrous calcite construction. The rounded alveolus is deep and houses a large phragmocone, which consists of concavo-convex chambers now full of hardened mud.

• **HABITAT** *Pachyteuthis* lived as a predator or scavenger in the deeper-water shelf seas of the Late Jurassic.

• **REMARK** The phragmocone is well preserved in shiny iron pyrites.

worn surface of guard •

• *blunt tip*

chambered phragmocone preserved in iron pyrites •

PACHYTEUTHIS ABBREVIATA (Miller); Kimmeridge Clay; Late Jurassic; UK.

Typical length 50cm (20in)

• *v-shaped alveolus*

Range M.–L. Jurassic	Distribution Worldwide	Occurrence ◉◉◉

| Order BELEMNITIDA | Family BELEMNITELLIDAE | Informal name Belemnite |

BELEMNITELLA

The guard tapers only gently, and is terminated posteriorly by a tip called a mucron. The anterior part of the guard is paper-thin and houses a deep alveolus. The surface of the guard carries a network of intricately branching, shallow grooves, which are probably impressions created by the blood vessels in the soft tissues of the living belemnite.
• HABITAT *Belemnitella* swam in the shallower waters of the Late Cretaceous Chalk sea, and used its hooked tentacles to catch small prey.
• REMARK This is one of the belemnites which survived nearly to the end of the Cretaceous. It occurs in huge numbers at some localities in so-called "belemnite graveyards".

BELEMNITELLA MUCRONATA (Schlotheim); Maastrichtian; Late Cretaceous; Holland.

deep alveolus

impression of veins on surface of guard

point on tip of guard

Typical length 40cm (16in)

| Range L. Cretaceous | Distribution Northern hemisphere | Occurrence |

| Order BELEMNITIDA | Family CYLINDROTEUTHIDIDAE | Informal name Belemnite |

CYLINDROTEUTHIS

The guard is long and cylindrical, and tapers gradually to a posterior point. The chambered phragmocone expands anteriorly.
• HABITAT This genus lived as a predator in the deeper parts of shelf seas.
• REMARK This is one of the largest species of belemnite, growing up to 25cm (10in) in length.

CYLINDROTEUTHIS PUZOSIANA (d'Orbigny); Oxford Clay; Late Jurassic; UK.

apex of guard

alveolus of guard

long, cylindrical guard

Typical length 25cm (10in)

| Range M.–L. Jurassic | Distribution Europe, N. America | Occurrence |

Order Not Applicable	Family Not Applicable	Informal name Belemnite limestone

BELEMNITE LIMESTONE

alveolus • • *concentric growth rings*

This cut and polished piece of
marine shelly limestone shows
several belemnites in different
cross-sections. These illustrate well
the massive construction of the
belemnite guard, composed of the
mineral calcite (calcium carbonate).
The belemnites show fine, radially
arranged, calcite crystals, and
display strong, concentric growth
lines. The V-shaped space at the
anterior end of the guard is called
the alveolus, and housed the
chambered phragmocone, used
for buoyancy control by the
belemnite in life.
• HABITAT These various
belemnites would have had
differing life styles, although all
would have been marine dwellers.
• REMARK The term
"marble" is loosely
applied to any
polished limestone.

BELEMNITE
LIMESTONE;
Jurassic; Germany.

calcite of • *belemnite guards* • *shell fragments in limestone*

Range Cretaceous–Triassic	Distribution Worldwide	Occurrence

Order VAMPYROMORPHA	Family TRACHYTEUTHIDIDAE	Informal name Belemnite

TRACHYTEUTHIS

growth lines on surface •

Only the guard of this genus has
ever been found preserved as a
fossil. The outline is an elongated oval, and a lobe is present on
each side. On the dorsal surface
growth lines are visible.
• HABITAT This animal
probably resembled a cuttlefish
in its life habits, living on the sea
bed and preying on crustaceans.
• REMARK It is open to debate
whether this genus is closer to
the squid or cuttlefish in affinity.

TRACHYTEUTHIS sp.;
Solnhofen Limestone; Late
Jurassic; Germany.

flattened guard resembling cuttlebone •

Typical length 25cm (10in)

• *limestone*

Range L. Jurassic	Distribution Europe	Occurrence

Order BELEMNITIDA	Family BELEMNOTHEUTIDIDAE	Informal name Belemnite

BELEMNOTHEUTIS

arms with small hooks •

• *head region*

The head region carries ten arms, on which hooks are present. The anterior part of the body is called the mantle, and has two fins – very much like a living squid. The hindmost part of the animal is the chambered phragmocone, which tapers posteriorly. At the end, a thin guard is sometimes preserved.

• **HABITAT** *Belemnotheutis* lived in the open sea at a moderate depth, and swam by jet propulsion (water expulsion from the mantle) in exactly the same way as squid do in the present day. It used its hooked and suckered arms to catch prey.

• **REMARK** This specimen displays a very rare phenomenon in the fossil record – the preservation of soft parts, which normally would decay and be completely lost. This type of preservation is caused by rapid burial of the animal in stagnant, oxygen-free water, where scavengers and most bacteria cannot live. The belemnite's soft parts are replaced by calcium phosphate.

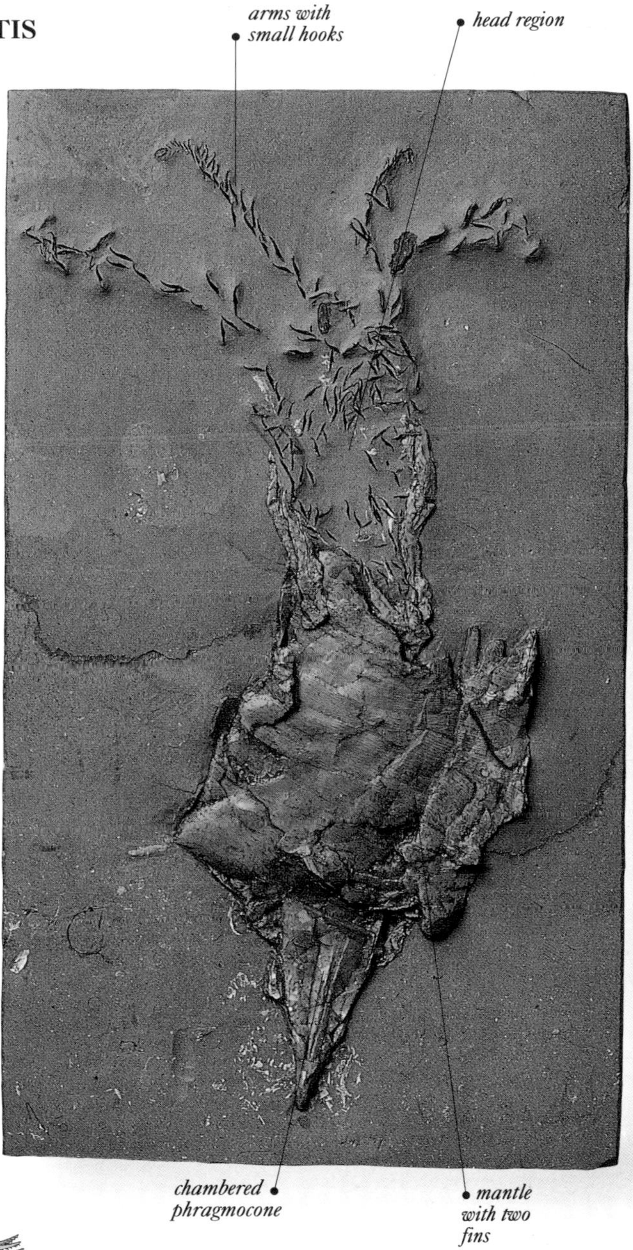

BELEMNOTHEUTIS ANTIQUA Pearce; Oxford Clay; Late Jurassic; UK.

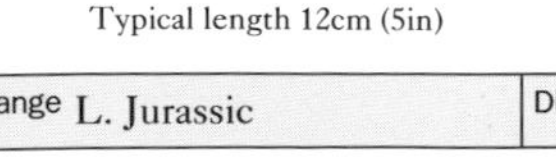

chambered • *phragmocone*

• *mantle with two fins*

Typical length 12cm (5in)

Range L. Jurassic	Distribution Europe	Occurrence ◉

CRINOIDS

C RINOIDS, POPULARLY known as sea lilies and feather stars, possess a massive calcite skeleton, and were so abundant in the Palaeozoic seas that their remains formed vast thicknesses of limestone. Most crinoids are attached to the sea bed by a flexible stem, circular or pentagonal in section, and made up of numerous disc-like plates called columnals. At the top of the stem is a swollen cup or calyx, to which the arms are attached. The arms are used to filter food from the water. Soon after death, the entire skeleton normally falls apart into the small, separate plates called ossicles. In contrast, well-preserved crinoids are rare and beautiful fossils.

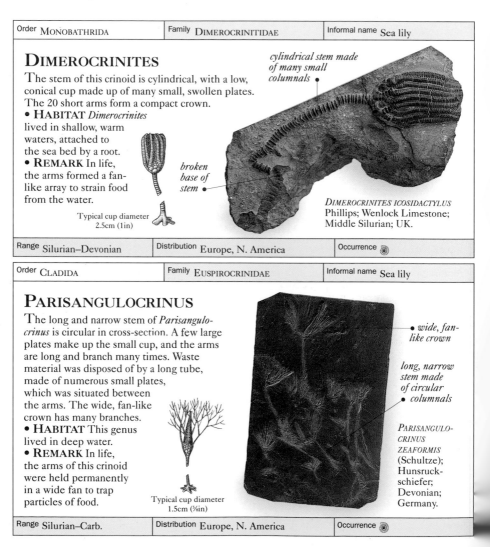

Order MONOBATHRIDA	Family DIMEROCRINITIDAE	Informal name Sea lily

DIMEROCRINITES

The stem of this crinoid is cylindrical, with a low, conical cup made up of many small, swollen plates. The 20 short arms form a compact crown.
• HABITAT *Dimerocrinites* lived in shallow, warm waters, attached to the sea bed by a root.
• REMARK In life, the arms formed a fan-like array to strain food from the water.

cylindrical stem made of many small columnals

broken base of stem

Typical cup diameter 2.5cm (1in)

DIMEROCRINITES ICOSIDACTYLUS Phillips; Wenlock Limestone; Middle Silurian; UK.

Range Silurian–Devonian	Distribution Europe, N. America	Occurrence

Order CLADIDA	Family EUSPIROCRINIDAE	Informal name Sea lily

PARISANGULOCRINUS

The long and narrow stem of *Parisangulo-crinus* is circular in cross-section. A few large plates make up the small cup, and the arms are long and branch many times. Waste material was disposed of by a long tube, made of numerous small plates, which was situated between the arms. The wide, fan-like crown has many branches.
• HABITAT This genus lived in deep water.
• REMARK In life, the arms of this crinoid were held permanently in a wide fan to trap particles of food.

wide, fan-like crown

long, narrow stem made of circular columnals

PARISANGULO-CRINUS ZEAFORMIS (Schultze); Hunsruck-schiefer; Devonian; Germany.

Typical cup diameter 1.5cm (⅝in)

Range Silurian–Carb.	Distribution Europe, N. America	Occurrence

| Order CLADIDA | Family CUPRESSOCRINITIDAE | Informal name Sea lily |

CUPRESSOCRINITES

This robust crinoid has a cylindrical stem, and a large, conical cup made up of ten large plates in two alternating circles. The short arms, five in number, are unbranched and triangular in shape. They fit together closely to form a short, pointed crown.
• HABITAT The very strong form of this species is perhaps related to the rough, current-swept environment in which it lived, in which fragile forms would not have survived.
• REMARK The ancestry and relationships of *Cupressocrinites* are not well understood.

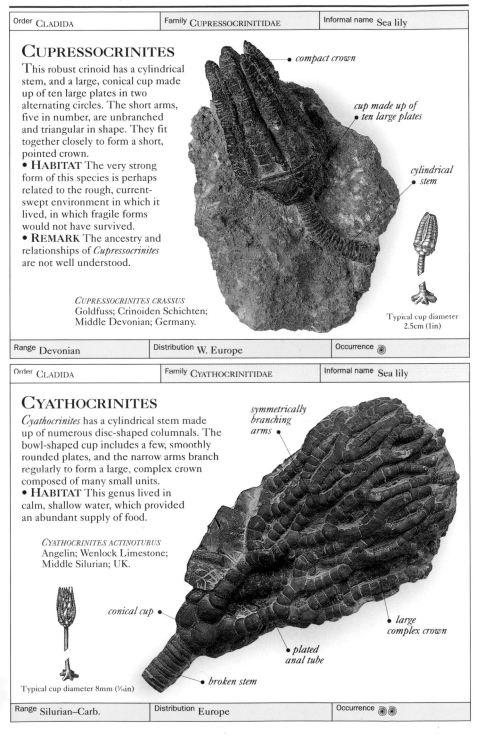

• *compact crown*

cup made up of
• *ten large plates*

cylindrical
• *stem*

CUPRESSOCRINITES CRASSUS
Goldfuss; Crinoiden Schichten;
Middle Devonian; Germany.

Typical cup diameter
2.5cm (1in)

| Range Devonian | Distribution W. Europe | Occurrence |

| Order CLADIDA | Family CYATHOCRINITIDAE | Informal name Sea lily |

CYATHOCRINITES

Cyathocrinites has a cylindrical stem made up of numerous disc-shaped columnals. The bowl-shaped cup includes a few, smoothly rounded plates, and the narrow arms branch regularly to form a large, complex crown composed of many small units.
• HABITAT This genus lived in calm, shallow water, which provided an abundant supply of food.

symmetrically
branching
arms •

CYATHOCRINITES ACTINOTUBUS
Angelin; Wenlock Limestone;
Middle Silurian; UK.

conical cup •

• *large*
complex crown

• *plated*
anal tube

• *broken stem*

Typical cup diameter 8mm (⁵⁄₁₆in)

| Range Silurian–Carb. | Distribution Europe | Occurrence |

Order SAGENOCRINIDA	Family SAGENOCRINIDAE	Informal name Sea lily

SAGENOCRINITES

The stem of *Sagenocrinites* is cylindrical and composed of numerous, very thin columnals. Its crown is very broad and oval in shape. The polygonal plates of the lower arms display clear growth lines and form part of the cup. The free parts of the arms are short and made up of many small plates.
• HABITAT The very compact form of this species suggests that it had adapted to relatively turbulent sea-bed conditions.

SAGENOCRINITES EXPANSUS Phillips; Wenlock Limestone; Middle Silurian; UK.

stem of very thin columnals

short, free arms

broad crown

arm bases forming part of cup

Typical cup diameter 2.5cm (1in)

Range M. Silurian	Distribution Europe, N. America	Occurrence

Order Unclassified	Family Unclassified	Informal name Crinoidal limestone

CLIFTON BLACK ROCK

This striking black limestone contains a length of crinoid stem and many small crinoid ossicles in the background. The structure of the stem is well shown: it is made up of short columnals of even height, and has a large central cavity running along its length, now full of the limestone.
• HABITAT Crinoidal limestone forms from the detritus washed from a reef.
• REMARK The black colour is due to bitumen.

crinoid stem

CLIFTON BLACK ROCK; Carboniferous Limestone; Carboniferous; UK.

large central cavity

Typical cup diameter 4cm (1½in)

Range Carb.	Distribution UK	Occurrence

Order MONOBATHRIDA	Family ACTINOCRINITIDAE	Informal name Sea lily

ACTINOCRINITES

This well-preserved cup is typical of many crinoids of the subclass Camerata. The large, rigid, globular cup is made up of many polygonal plates, clearly outlined on this specimen. These plates are arranged into several rings at the base, above the point of attachment to the stem. Above this point, the plates of the lower arms form a more irregular mosaic pattern, passing out to the five projecting stumps of the arms. The domed upper surface of the cup consists of fairly large plates. The stem is circular and includes many very short columnals. In the Early Carboniferous sea, current action could cause such large drifts of crinoidal debris that they became a major constituent of the limestone. A separate artificial classification has been developed for isolated stem segments.

• HABITAT
Actinocrinites lived on reefs in deep water, anchored to the sea bed by a root-like structure. Its short, simple arms trapped small food particles.

base of free arm

domed top of cup

SIDE VIEW

ACTINOCRINITES PARKINSONI Wright; Carboniferous Limestone; Early Carboniferous; UK.

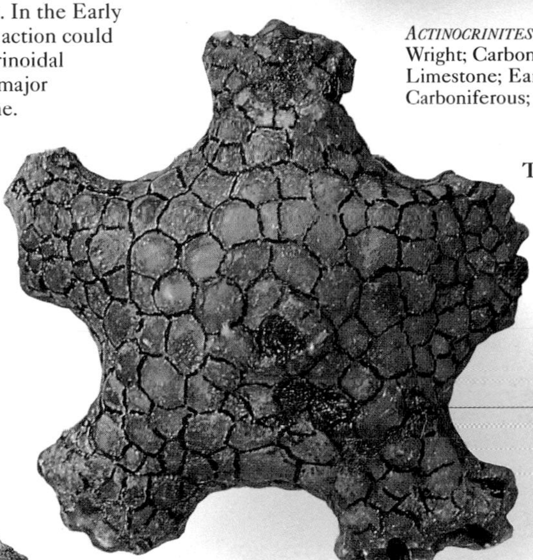

TOP VIEW

curved surface between arms

CRINOIDAL LIMESTONE

polygonal plates

stem segments

Typical cup diameter 4cm (1½in)

Range Carb.	Distribution Worldwide	Occurrence ◉◉◉◉◉

Order ROVEACRINIDA	Family SACCOCOMIDAE	Informal name Feather star

SACCOCOMA

This is a delicately constructed, stemless crinoid, with a small, globular cup. The arms branch once to give a total of ten. The lower parts of the arms have small wing-like extensions; the upper parts have long, narrow side-branches.
• HABITAT *Saccocoma* was free-living, and probably able to tolerate variations in salinity.
• REMARK This species is one of the most common fossils in the Solnhofen Limestone.

globular cup

branched arms

SACCOCOMA TENELLUM (Goldfuss); Solnhofen Limestone; Late Jurassic; Germany.

Typical cup diameter 2cm (¾in)

Range L. Jurassic	Distribution Worldwide	Occurrence ⊛⊛⊛⊛⊛

Order CYRTOCRINIDA	Family HEMICRINIDAE	Informal name Sea lily

HEMICRINUS

This curiously shaped crinoid has arms set at right-angles to its cup, which is shaped like a spoon. The stem-like extension is actually formed from elongated cup plates, and attached directly to a holdfast.
• HABITAT *Hemicrinus* lived attached to pebbles by a holdfast, and inhabited shallow, turbulent waters.
• REMARK The cyrtocrinids are squat, compact crinoids, locally common in Cret-aceous rocks.

end of cup

arm attachment point

point of attachment to root

elongated base of cup

HEMICRINUS CANON (Seeley); Hunstanton Red Rock; Early Cretaceous; UK.

Typical cup diameter 8mm (⁵⁄₁₆in)

Range L. Jurassic–E. Cretaceous	Distribution Europe	Occurrence ⊛⊛

Order COMATULIDA	Family PTEROCOMIDAE	Informal name Feather star

PTEROCOMA

This comatulid or feather star has a small cup, which bears ten long, feather-like arms of equal length. Each of these has a row of little branches (pinnules) on either side. It possessed a stem only in the earliest stages of development.
• HABITAT *Pterocoma* was a free-swimming crinoid, advancing with graceful movements of the arms, like its living relatives.
• REMARK Comatulids are rarely found as entire specimens.

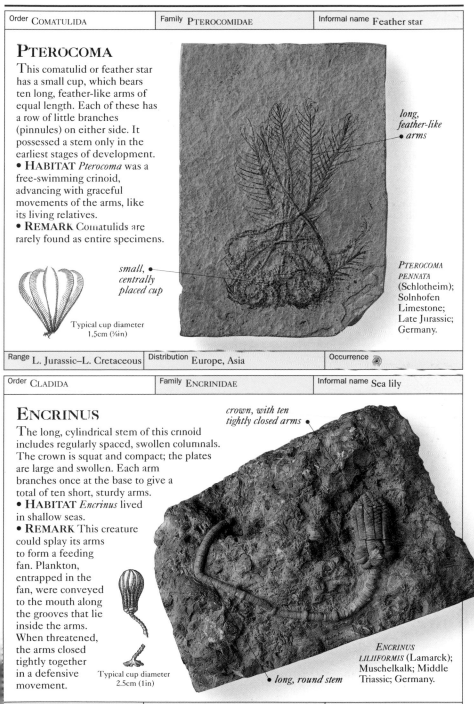

long, feather-like arms

small, centrally placed cup

Typical cup diameter
1.5cm (⅝in)

PTEROCOMA PENNATA (Schlotheim); Solnhofen Limestone; Late Jurassic; Germany.

Range L. Jurassic–L. Cretaceous	Distribution Europe, Asia	Occurrence

Order CLADIDA	Family ENCRINIDAE	Informal name Sea lily

ENCRINUS

The long, cylindrical stem of this crinoid includes regularly spaced, swollen columnals. The crown is squat and compact; the plates are large and swollen. Each arm branches once at the base to give a total of ten short, sturdy arms.
• HABITAT *Encrinus* lived in shallow seas.
• REMARK This creature could splay its arms to form a feeding fan. Plankton, entrapped in the fan, were conveyed to the mouth along the grooves that lie inside the arms. When threatened, the arms closed tightly together in a defensive movement.

crown, with ten tightly closed arms

Typical cup diameter
2.5cm (1in)

long, round stem

ENCRINUS LILIIFORMIS (Lamarck); Muschelkalk; Middle Triassic; Germany.

Range M. Triassic	Distribution Europe	Occurrence

Order ISOCRINIDA	Family PENTACRITINIDAE	Informal name Sea lily

PENTACRINITES

This distinctive crinoid has a long, pentagonal stem, with no
root structure at the base. Regularly spaced whorls of fine
branches (cirri) arise from the stem. The cup is
small and inconspicuous, and the fan-
shaped crown is made up of multi-
branched arms and many small
pinnules (branches).

• **HABITAT** Masses of
Pentacrinites are
commonly found
preserved under
large pieces of fossil
wood, leading to
the belief that it
was pseudopelagic
(living in the open
sea), in colonies
attached to the
underside of floating
logs. The dispersed
debris is locally
abundant around
logs and formed
thin sheets of
limestone.

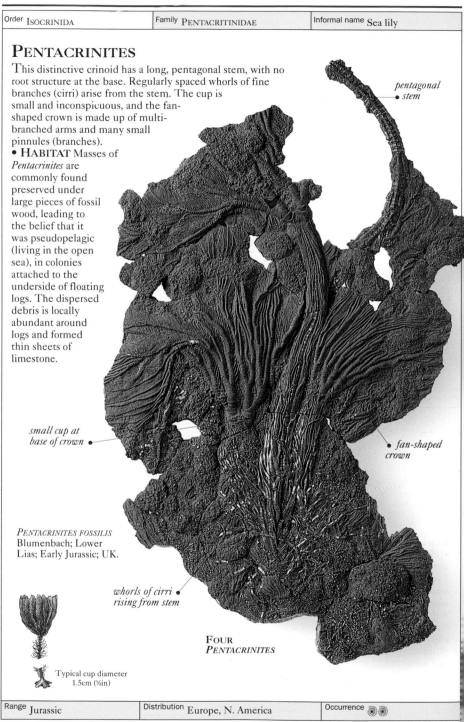

*pentagonal
• stem*

*small cup at
base of crown* •

*• fan-shaped
crown*

PENTACRINITES FOSSILIS
Blumenbach; Lower
Lias; Early Jurassic; UK.

*whorls of cirri •
rising from stem*

FOUR
PENTACRINITES

Typical cup diameter
1.5cm (⅝in)

Range Jurassic	Distribution Europe, N. America	Occurrence

Order MILLERICRINIDA	Family APIOCRINITIDAE	Informal name Sea lily

APIOCRINITES

This stoutly constructed crinoid has a narrow, cylindrical, tapering stem with a conical, irregularly shaped root cemented at the base. The bulbous cup is made up of enlarged columnals, two cycles of cup plates, and the bases of the arms. The arms branch once, symmetrically, to give an elegant fan-shaped crown with ten arms in total.
• HABITAT *Apiocrinites* lived attached to hard, current-swept pavements on the Jurassic sea floor. It filtered food from the water with its arms.
• REMARK Remains of this species are found most commonly as separate discoidal cup plates or columnals. The surface of the stem and the holdfast are often colonized by bryozoa and serpulid worms.

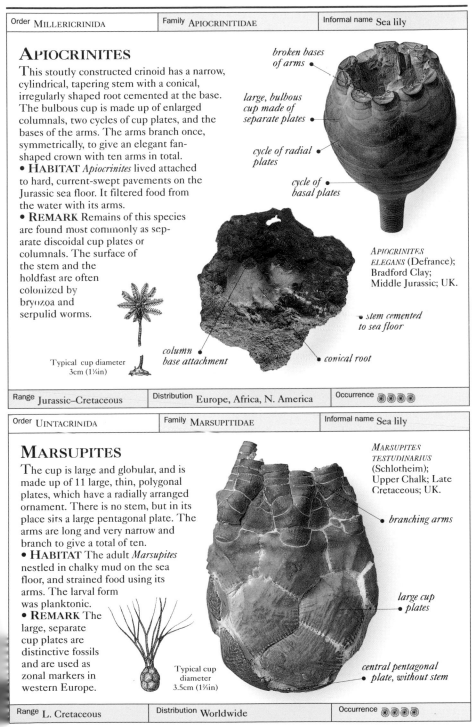

broken bases of arms

large, bulbous cup made of separate plates

cycle of radial plates

cycle of basal plates

APIOCRINITES ELEGANS (Defrance); Bradford Clay; Middle Jurassic; UK.

stem cemented to sea floor

column base attachment

conical root

Typical cup diameter 3cm (1¼in)

Range Jurassic–Cretaceous	Distribution Europe, Africa, N. America	Occurrence

Order UINTACRINIDA	Family MARSUPITIDAE	Informal name Sea lily

MARSUPITES

The cup is large and globular, and is made up of 11 large, thin, polygonal plates, which have a radially arranged ornament. There is no stem, but in its place sits a large pentagonal plate. The arms are long and very narrow and branch to give a total of ten.
• HABITAT The adult *Marsupites* nestled in chalky mud on the sea floor, and strained food using its arms. The larval form was planktonic.
• REMARK The large, separate cup plates are distinctive fossils and are used as zonal markers in western Europe.

MARSUPITES TESTUDINARIUS (Schlotheim); Upper Chalk; Late Cretaceous; UK.

branching arms

large cup plates

central pentagonal plate, without stem

Typical cup diameter 3.5cm (1⅜in)

Range L. Cretaceous	Distribution Worldwide	Occurrence

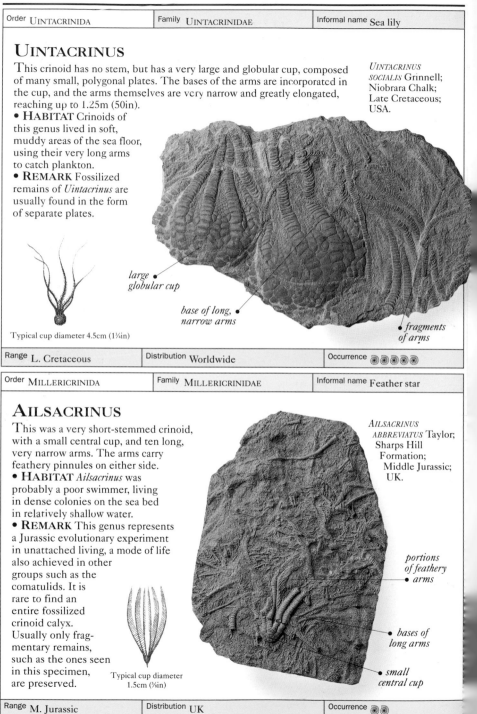

Order UINTACRINIDA	Family UINTACRINIDAE	Informal name Sea lily

UINTACRINUS

This crinoid has no stem, but has a very large and globular cup, composed of many small, polygonal plates. The bases of the arms are incorporated in the cup, and the arms themselves are very narrow and greatly elongated, reaching up to 1.25m (50in).

UINTACRINUS SOCIALIS Grinnell; Niobrara Chalk; Late Cretaceous; USA.

• **HABITAT** Crinoids of this genus lived in soft, muddy areas of the sea floor, using their very long arms to catch plankton.
• **REMARK** Fossilized remains of *Uintacrinus* are usually found in the form of separate plates.

large globular cup

base of long, narrow arms

fragments of arms

Typical cup diameter 4.5cm (1¾in)

Range L. Cretaceous	Distribution Worldwide	Occurrence

Order MILLERICRINIDA	Family MILLERICRINIDAE	Informal name Feather star

AILSACRINUS

This was a very short-stemmed crinoid, with a small central cup, and ten long, very narrow arms. The arms carry feathery pinnules on either side.

AILSACRINUS ABBREVIATUS Taylor; Sharps Hill Formation; Middle Jurassic; UK.

• **HABITAT** *Ailsacrinus* was probably a poor swimmer, living in dense colonies on the sea bed in relatively shallow water.
• **REMARK** This genus represents a Jurassic evolutionary experiment in unattached living, a mode of life also achieved in other groups such as the comatulids. It is rare to find an entire fossilized crinoid calyx. Usually only frag-mentary remains, such as the ones seen in this specimen, are preserved.

portions of feathery arms

bases of long arms

small central cup

Typical cup diameter 1.5cm (⅝in)

Range M. Jurassic	Distribution UK	Occurrence

ECHINOIDS

T HE ECHINOIDS possess a rigid, globular skeleton (test) made up of columns of thin, calcite plates (ambulacrals and interambulacrals). The plates known as ambulacrals have small pores for tube feet. All plates have swollen tubercles for the ball-and-socket articulation of spines, which are used for defence and sometimes for walking. Regular echinoids, which forage on the sea bed, show radial symmetry; irregular echinoids, which usually burrow in soft sea beds, show bilateral symmetry.

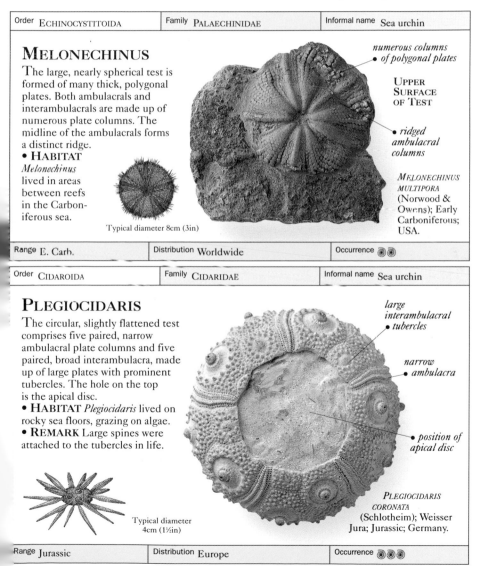

Order ECHINOCYSTITOIDA	Family PALAECHINIDAE	Informal name Sea urchin

MELONECHINUS

The large, nearly spherical test is formed of many thick, polygonal plates. Both ambulacrals and interambulacrals are made up of numerous plate columns. The midline of the ambulacrals forms a distinct ridge.
• HABITAT *Melonechinus* lived in areas between reefs in the Carboniferous sea.

Typical diameter 8cm (3in)

numerous columns
• of polygonal plates

UPPER
SURFACE
OF TEST

• ridged ambulacral columns

MELONECHINUS MULTIPORA (Norwood & Owens); Early Carboniferous; USA.

Range E. Carb.	Distribution Worldwide	Occurrence

Order CIDAROIDA	Family CIDARIDAE	Informal name Sea urchin

PLEGIOCIDARIS

The circular, slightly flattened test comprises five paired, narrow ambulacral plate columns and five paired, broad interambulacra, made up of large plates with prominent tubercles. The hole on the top is the apical disc.
• HABITAT *Plegiocidaris* lived on rocky sea floors, grazing on algae.
• REMARK Large spines were attached to the tubercles in life.

Typical diameter 4cm (1½in)

large interambulacral • tubercles

narrow • ambulacra

• position of apical disc

PLEGIOCIDARIS CORONATA (Schlotheim); Weisser Jura; Jurassic; Germany.

Range Jurassic	Distribution Europe	Occurrence

Order ARCHAEOCIDAROIDA	Family ARCHAEOCIDARIDAE	Informal name Sea urchin

ARCHAEOCIDARIS

The large test, which retains many spines on its surface, is crushed flat. The paired ambulacral columns are narrow, and the broad interambulacra are made up of four columns of plates, each of which carries a single, centrally placed tubercle. A long, narrow spine articulates with each large tubercle. Short spines form a felt-like covering over much of the test. The teeth and jaws are present on the underside, but are dissociated.

ARCHAEOCIDARIS WHATLEYENSIS Lewis & Ensom; Carboniferous Limestone; Early Carboniferous; UK.

• HABITAT The genus was probably an omnivorous browser, living on the open sea floor, protected by its long spines.

scattered elements of jaw system

long, narrow spine

large tubercle

small, fine spines

LOWER SURFACE OF TEST

position of mouth

UPPER SURFACE OF TEST

ambulacral column

smooth spines

felt-like covering of fine spines

position of apical disc

Typical diameter 8cm (3in)

Range E. Carb.–Permian	Distribution Worldwide	Occurrence

Order CIDAROIDA	Family PSYCHOCIDARIDAE	Informal name Sea urchin

TYLOCIDARIS

The small test is circular in outline and slightly flattened. The ten columns of large interambulacral tubercles carry massive, club-shaped defensive spines. The central aperture on the base housed the jaw mechanism (known as Aristotle's Lantern) in life.

• HABITAT *Tylocidaris* lived as an omnivorous grazer on shells and sponges on the Chalk sea floor.

• REMARK Isolated spines and fragments of the test are quite common Chalk fossils.

Typical diameter 3cm (1¼in)

large, club-shaped spines

• underside

large interambulacral tubercles

• *position of mouth opening*

TYLOCIDARIS CLAVIGERA (König); Upper Chalk; Late Cretaceous; UK.

Range L. Cretaceous–Eocene	Distribution Europe, N. America	Occurrence

Order CIDAROIDA	Family CIDARIDAE	Informal name Sea urchin

TEMNOCIDARIS

The nearly spherical test is made up of five paired columns of large interambulacral plates, each with a large conspicuous tubercle. The five paired ambulacral columns are narrow and sinuous. The large, spindle-shaped spines attached to the large interambulacral tubercles had a rough, thorny surface in life.

• HABITAT *Temnocidaris* lived on the Chalk sea floor. It was an omnivorous scavenger, using its sharp teeth to rasp food.

• REMARK *Temnocidaris* is very rarely preserved in its entirety. The apical disc is missing in this specimen.

TEMNOCIDARIS SCEPTRIFERA (Mantell); Upper Chalk; Late Cretaceous; UK.

narrow • *ambulacrum*

large interambulacral • *tubercle*

position • *of apical disc*

large primary • *spine*

Typical diameter 4.5cm (1¾in)

Range L. Cretaceous	Distribution Europe	Occurrence

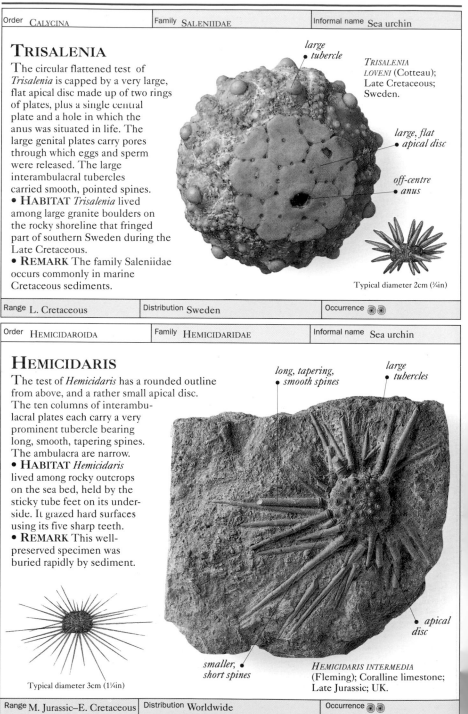

Order CALYCINA	Family SALENIIDAE	Informal name Sea urchin

TRISALENIA

The circular flattened test of *Trisalenia* is capped by a very large, flat apical disc made up of two rings of plates, plus a single central plate and a hole in which the anus was situated in life. The large genital plates carry pores through which eggs and sperm were released. The large interambulacral tubercles carried smooth, pointed spines.
• HABITAT *Trisalenia* lived among large granite boulders on the rocky shoreline that fringed part of southern Sweden during the Late Cretaceous.
• REMARK The family Saleniidae occurs commonly in marine Cretaceous sediments.

large tubercle

TRISALENIA LOVENI (Cotteau); Late Cretaceous; Sweden.

large, flat apical disc

off-centre anus

Typical diameter 2cm (¾in)

Range L. Cretaceous	Distribution Sweden	Occurrence 🔘🔘

Order HEMICIDAROIDA	Family HEMICIDARIDAE	Informal name Sea urchin

HEMICIDARIS

The test of *Hemicidaris* has a rounded outline from above, and a rather small apical disc. The ten columns of interambulacral plates each carry a very prominent tubercle bearing long, smooth, tapering spines. The ambulacra are narrow.
• HABITAT *Hemicidaris* lived among rocky outcrops on the sea bed, held by the sticky tube feet on its underside. It grazed hard surfaces using its five sharp teeth.
• REMARK This well-preserved specimen was buried rapidly by sediment.

long, tapering, smooth spines

large tubercles

apical disc

smaller, short spines

HEMICIDARIS INTERMEDIA (Fleming); Coralline limestone; Late Jurassic; UK.

Typical diameter 3cm (1¼in)

Range M. Jurassic–E. Cretaceous	Distribution Worldwide	Occurrence 🔘🔘

Order PHYMOSOMATOIDA	Family PHYMOSOMATIDAE	Informal name Sea urchin

PHYMOSOMA

The test is circular and flattened. The areas occupied by both the apical disc and the membrane around the mouth are very broad. The ambulacral and interambulacral tubercles are about the same size, and in life bore tapering, smooth, cylindrical or flattened spines. Isolated spines are common Chalk fossils.
• HABITAT *Phymosoma* lived on the Chalk sea floor, grazing on hard surfaces to obtain algae, sponges, and other soft organisms.

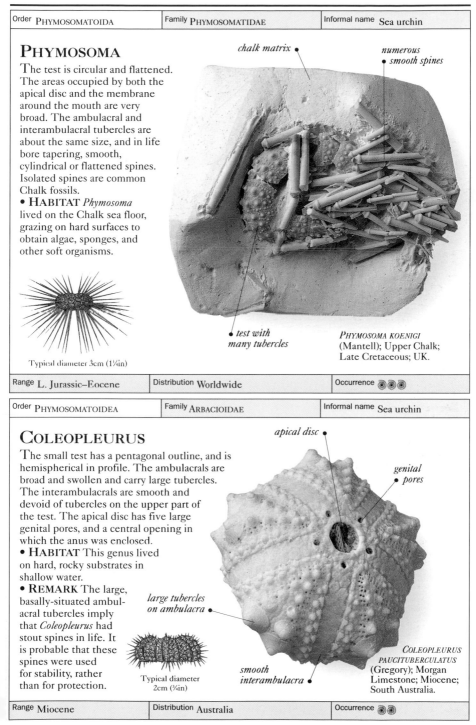

chalk matrix

numerous smooth spines

test with many tubercles

Typical diameter 3cm (1¼in)

PHYMOSOMA KOENIGI (Mantell); Upper Chalk; Late Cretaceous; UK.

Range L. Jurassic–Eocene	Distribution Worldwide	Occurrence ◉◉◉

Order PHYMOSOMATOIDEA	Family ARBACIOIDAE	Informal name Sea urchin

COLEOPLEURUS

The small test has a pentagonal outline, and is hemispherical in profile. The ambulacrals are broad and swollen and carry large tubercles. The interambulacrals are smooth and devoid of tubercles on the upper part of the test. The apical disc has five large genital pores, and a central opening in which the anus was enclosed.
• HABITAT This genus lived on hard, rocky substrates in shallow water.
• REMARK The large, basally-situated ambulacral tubercles imply that *Coleopleurus* had stout spines in life. It is probable that these spines were used for stability, rather than for protection.

apical disc

genital pores

large tubercles on ambulacra

Typical diameter 2cm (¾in)

smooth interambulacra

COLEOPLEURUS PAUCITUBERCULATUS (Gregory); Morgan Limestone; Miocene; South Australia.

Range Miocene	Distribution Australia	Occurrence ◉◉

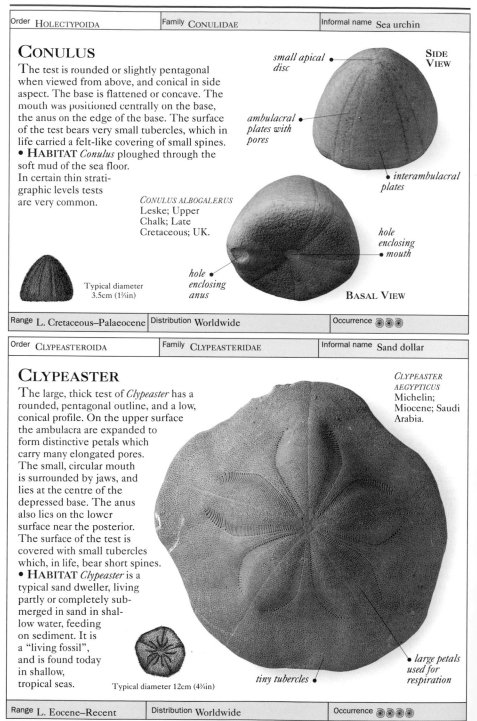

Order HOLECTYPOIDA	Family CONULIDAE	Informal name Sea urchin

CONULUS

The test is rounded or slightly pentagonal when viewed from above, and conical in side aspect. The base is flattened or concave. The mouth was positioned centrally on the base, the anus on the edge of the base. The surface of the test bears very small tubercles, which in life carried a felt-like covering of small spines.
• **HABITAT** *Conulus* ploughed through the soft mud of the sea floor. In certain thin stratigraphic levels tests are very common.

CONULUS ALBOGALERUS Leske; Upper Chalk; Late Cretaceous; UK.

small apical disc

SIDE VIEW

ambulacral plates with pores

interambulacral plates

hole enclosing mouth

Typical diameter 3.5cm (1⅜in)

hole enclosing anus

BASAL VIEW

Range L. Cretaceous–Palaeocene	Distribution Worldwide	Occurrence

Order CLYPEASTEROIDA	Family CLYPEASTERIDAE	Informal name Sand dollar

CLYPEASTER

The large, thick test of *Clypeaster* has a rounded, pentagonal outline, and a low, conical profile. On the upper surface the ambulacra are expanded to form distinctive petals which carry many elongated pores. The small, circular mouth is surrounded by jaws, and lies at the centre of the depressed base. The anus also lies on the lower surface near the posterior. The surface of the test is covered with small tubercles which, in life, bear short spines.
• **HABITAT** *Clypeaster* is a typical sand dweller, living partly or completely submerged in sand in shallow water, feeding on sediment. It is a "living fossil", and is found today in shallow, tropical seas.

CLYPEASTER AEGYPTICUS Michelin; Miocene; Saudi Arabia.

large petals used for respiration

tiny tubercles

Typical diameter 12cm (4¾in)

Range L. Eocene–Recent	Distribution Worldwide	Occurrence

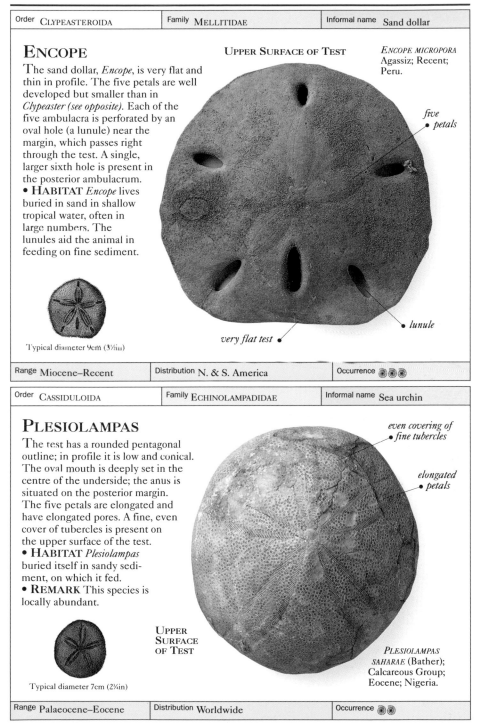

Order CLYPEASTEROIDA	Family MELLITIDAE	Informal name Sand dollar

ENCOPE

The sand dollar, *Encope*, is very flat and thin in profile. The five petals are well developed but smaller than in *Clypeaster (see opposite)*. Each of the five ambulacra is perforated by an oval hole (a lunule) near the margin, which passes right through the test. A single, larger sixth hole is present in the posterior ambulacrum.
• HABITAT *Encope* lives buried in sand in shallow tropical water, often in large numbers. The lunules aid the animal in feeding on fine sediment.

UPPER SURFACE OF TEST

ENCOPE MICROPORA
Agassiz; Recent; Peru.

five petals

lunule

very flat test

Typical diameter 9cm (3½in)

Range Miocene–Recent	Distribution N. & S. America	Occurrence

Order CASSIDULOIDA	Family ECHINOLAMPADIDAE	Informal name Sea urchin

PLESIOLAMPAS

The test has a rounded pentagonal outline; in profile it is low and conical. The oval mouth is deeply set in the centre of the underside; the anus is situated on the posterior margin. The five petals are elongated and have elongated pores. A fine, even cover of tubercles is present on the upper surface of the test.
• HABITAT *Plesiolampas* buried itself in sandy sediment, on which it fed.
• REMARK This species is locally abundant.

even covering of fine tubercles

elongated petals

UPPER SURFACE OF TEST

PLESIOLAMPAS SAHARAE (Bather); Calcareous Group; Eocene; Nigeria.

Typical diameter 7cm (2¾in)

Range Palaeocene–Eocene	Distribution Worldwide	Occurrence

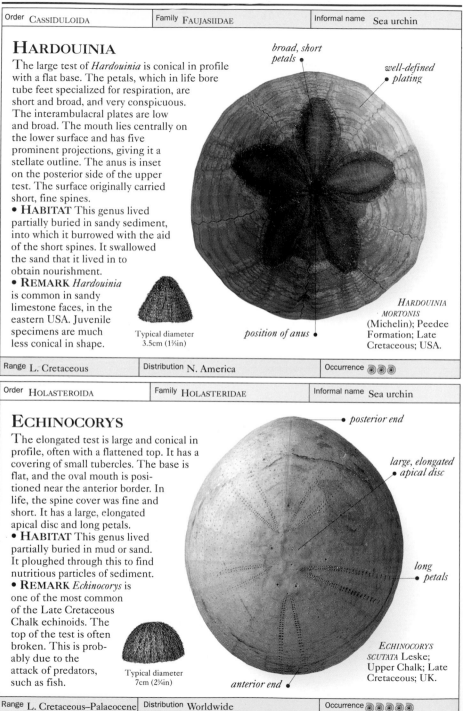

Order CASSIDULOIDA	Family FAUJASIIDAE	Informal name Sea urchin

HARDOUINIA

The large test of *Hardouinia* is conical in profile with a flat base. The petals, which in life bore tube feet specialized for respiration, are short and broad, and very conspicuous. The interambulacral plates are low and broad. The mouth lies centrally on the lower surface and has five prominent projections, giving it a stellate outline. The anus is inset on the posterior side of the upper test. The surface originally carried short, fine spines.

• **HABITAT** This genus lived partially buried in sandy sediment, into which it burrowed with the aid of the short spines. It swallowed the sand that it lived in to obtain nourishment.

• **REMARK** *Hardouinia* is common in sandy limestone faces, in the eastern USA. Juvenile specimens are much less conical in shape.

broad, short petals

well-defined plating

position of anus

Typical diameter
3.5cm (1⅜in)

HARDOUINIA MORTONIS (Michelin); Peedee Formation; Late Cretaceous; USA.

Range L. Cretaceous	Distribution N. America	Occurrence ⦿⦿⦿

Order HOLASTEROIDA	Family HOLASTERIDAE	Informal name Sea urchin

ECHINOCORYS

The elongated test is large and conical in profile, often with a flattened top. It has a covering of small tubercles. The base is flat, and the oval mouth is positioned near the anterior border. In life, the spine cover was fine and short. It has a large, elongated apical disc and long petals.

• **HABITAT** This genus lived partially buried in mud or sand. It ploughed through this to find nutritious particles of sediment.

• **REMARK** *Echinocorys* is one of the most common of the Late Cretaceous Chalk echinoids. The top of the test is often broken. This is probably due to the attack of predators, such as fish.

posterior end

large, elongated apical disc

long petals

Typical diameter
7cm (2¾in)

anterior end

ECHINOCORYS SCUTATA Leske; Upper Chalk; Late Cretaceous; UK.

Range L. Cretaceous–Palaeocene	Distribution Worldwide	Occurrence ⦿⦿⦿⦿⦿

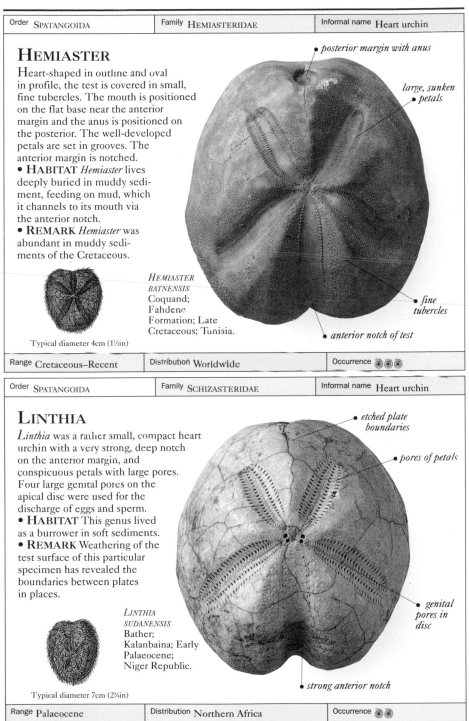

| Order SPATANGOIDA | Family HEMIASTERIDAE | Informal name Heart urchin |

HEMIASTER

Heart-shaped in outline and oval in profile, the test is covered in small, fine tubercles. The mouth is positioned on the flat base near the anterior margin and the anus is positioned on the posterior. The well-developed petals are set in grooves. The anterior margin is notched.
• HABITAT *Hemiaster* lives deeply buried in muddy sediment, feeding on mud, which it channels to its mouth via the anterior notch.
• REMARK *Hemiaster* was abundant in muddy sediments of the Cretaceous.

posterior margin with anus

large, sunken petals

fine tubercles

anterior notch of test

HEMIASTER BATNENSIS Coquand; Fahdene Formation; Late Cretaceous; Tunisia.

Typical diameter 4cm (1½in)

| Range Cretaceous–Recent | Distribution Worldwide | Occurrence ⬤⬤⬤ |

| Order SPATANGOIDA | Family SCHIZASTERIDAE | Informal name Heart urchin |

LINTHIA

Linthia was a rather small, compact heart urchin with a very strong, deep notch on the anterior margin, and conspicuous petals with large pores. Four large genital pores on the apical disc were used for the discharge of eggs and sperm.
• HABITAT This genus lived as a burrower in soft sediments.
• REMARK Weathering of the test surface of this particular specimen has revealed the boundaries between plates in places.

etched plate boundaries

pores of petals

genital pores in disc

strong anterior notch

LINTHIA SUDANENSIS Bather; Kalanbaina; Early Palaeocene; Niger Republic.

Typical diameter 7cm (2¾in)

| Range Palaeocene | Distribution Northern Africa | Occurrence ⬤⬤ |

Order SPATANGOIDA	Family SCHIZASTERIDAE	Informal name Heart urchin

SCHIZASTER

The anterior petal in the heart urchin, *Schizaster*, is deeply inset and enlarged. The pores, which in life bear respiratory tube feet, are very conspicuous on the petals.
• **HABITAT** *Schizaster* lives deeply buried in muds. It uses its long tube feet as a funnel-like connection to the sea bed. *Schizaster* feeds on fine particles of sediment.
• **REMARK** This group of entire and broken individuals probably represents a storm-swept residue – the result of waves scouring deeply buried urchins from their burrows. Most specimens are preserved as internal moulds, as the shell usually breaks away.

BLOCK WITH COMPLETE AND BROKEN HEART URCHINS

well-developed petals

clay matrix

pores for respiratory tube feet

SCHIZASTER BRANDERIANUS Forbes; Barton Beds; Middle Eocene; UK.

large anterior petal

Typical diameter 2.5cm (1in)

Range Eocene–Recent	Distribution Worldwide	Occurrence

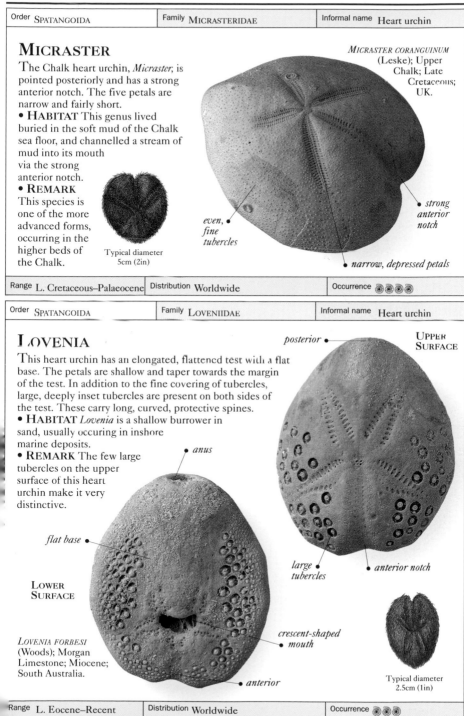

| Order SPATANGOIDA | Family MICRASTERIDAE | Informal name Heart urchin |

MICRASTER

The Chalk heart urchin, *Micraster*, is pointed posteriorly and has a strong anterior notch. The five petals are narrow and fairly short.
• **HABITAT** This genus lived buried in the soft mud of the Chalk sea floor, and channelled a stream of mud into its mouth via the strong anterior notch.
• **REMARK** This species is one of the more advanced forms, occurring in the higher beds of the Chalk.

MICRASTER CORANGUINUM (Leske); Upper Chalk; Late Cretaceous; UK.

Typical diameter 5cm (2in)

even, fine tubercles

strong anterior notch

narrow, depressed petals

| Range L. Cretaceous–Palaeocene | Distribution Worldwide | Occurrence ◉◉◉◉ |

| Order SPATANGOIDA | Family LOVENIIDAE | Informal name Heart urchin |

LOVENIA

This heart urchin has an elongated, flattened test with a flat base. The petals are shallow and taper towards the margin of the test. In addition to the fine covering of tubercles, large, deeply inset tubercles are present on both sides of the test. These carry long, curved, protective spines.
• **HABITAT** *Lovenia* is a shallow burrower in sand, usually occuring in inshore marine deposits.
• **REMARK** The few large tubercles on the upper surface of this heart urchin make it very distinctive.

posterior

UPPER SURFACE

anus

flat base

LOWER SURFACE

LOVENIA FORBESI (Woods); Morgan Limestone; Miocene; South Australia.

large tubercles

anterior notch

crescent-shaped mouth

anterior

Typical diameter 2.5cm (1in)

| Range L. Eocene–Recent | Distribution Worldwide | Occurrence ◉◉◉ |

ASTEROIDS

T HE ASTEROIDS, which include many of the species popularly called starfish, are common marine animals and have a long history extending back into the Ordovician. Most have five arms, although some species have more. The mouth is centrally placed on the underside, and five ambulacral grooves, floored by ambulacral and adambulacral ossicles, run along the midline of each arm. The grooves house the soft, muscular tube feet, which are used for walking, burrowing, and manipulating prey. Asteroids are rarely preserved as complete specimens.

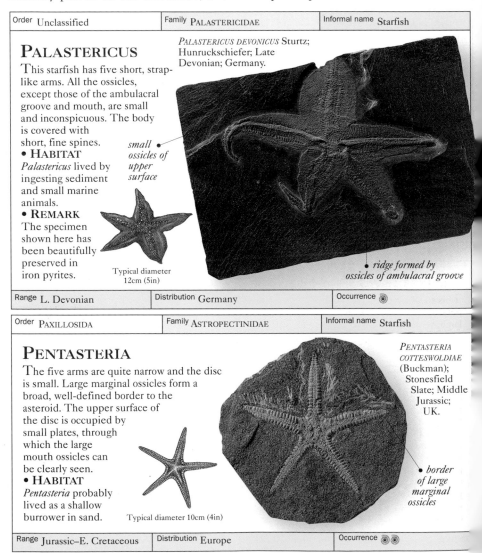

Order Unclassified	Family PALASTERICIDAE	Informal name Starfish

PALASTERICUS

This starfish has five short, strap-like arms. All the ossicles, except those of the ambulacral groove and mouth, are small and inconspicuous. The body is covered with short, fine spines.
• **HABITAT**
Palastericus lived by ingesting sediment and small marine animals.
• **REMARK**
The specimen shown here has been beautifully preserved in iron pyrites.

PALASTERICUS DEVONICUS Sturtz; Hunruckschiefer; Late Devonian; Germany.

small ossicles of upper surface •

Typical diameter 12cm (5in)

• *ridge formed by ossicles of ambulacral groove*

Range L. Devonian	Distribution Germany	Occurrence ⬤

Order PAXILLOSIDA	Family ASTROPECTINIDAE	Informal name Starfish

PENTASTERIA

The five arms are quite narrow and the disc is small. Large marginal ossicles form a broad, well-defined border to the asteroid. The upper surface of the disc is occupied by small plates, through which the large mouth ossicles can be clearly seen.
• **HABITAT**
Pentasteria probably lived as a shallow burrower in sand.

PENTASTERIA COTTESWOLDIAE (Buckman); Stonesfield Slate; Middle Jurassic; UK.

• *border of large marginal ossicles*

Typical diameter 10cm (4in)

Range Jurassic–E. Cretaceous	Distribution Europe	Occurrence ⬤ ⬤

Order Unclassified	Family STENASTERIDAE	Informal name Starfish

STENASTER

This small and enigmatic form has been variously classified as an ophiuroid and an asteroid. The five arms are short, the disc rather broad in form. The broad ambulacral ossicles extend across the width of the arm.
• HABITAT This was a marine-dwelling animal.
• REMARK The Starfish Bed at Girvan in Scotland, UK, formerly yielded a large number of beautifully preserved starfish and other fossils. These starfish were present as natural moulds, where the calcite skeletons had dissolved. A storm was probably responsible for the rapid deposition of sand which smothered the animals. *Stenaster* is a starfish with poorly understood relationships to other asteroids.

STENASTER OBTUSUS (Forbes); Drummock Group; Ordovician; UK.

rows of
• ossicles

LOWER SURFACE OF STARFISH

UPPER SURFACE OF STARFISH

Typical diameter
4cm (1½in)

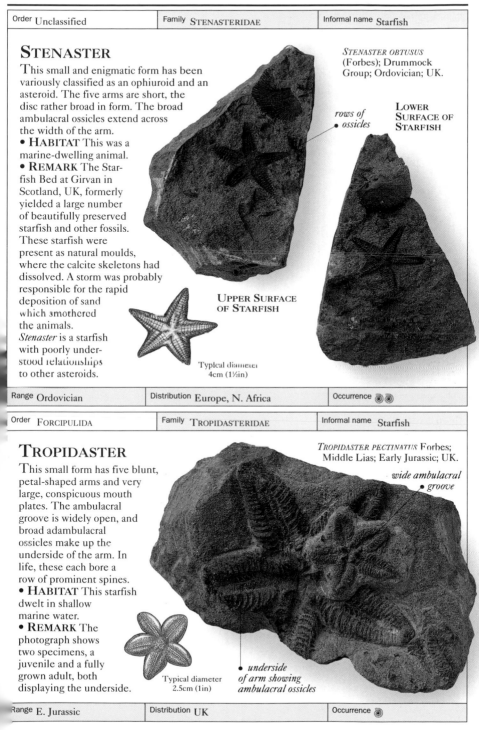

Range Ordovician	Distribution Europe, N. Africa	Occurrence

Order FORCIPULIDA	Family TROPIDASTERIDAE	Informal name Starfish

TROPIDASTER

This small form has five blunt, petal-shaped arms and very large, conspicuous mouth plates. The ambulacral groove is widely open, and broad adambulacral ossicles make up the underside of the arm. In life, these each bore a row of prominent spines.
• HABITAT This starfish dwelt in shallow marine water.
• REMARK The photograph shows two specimens, a juvenile and a fully grown adult, both displaying the underside.

TROPIDASTER PECTINATUS Forbes; Middle Lias; Early Jurassic; UK.

wide ambulacral • *groove*

Typical diameter
2.5cm (1in)

• *underside of arm showing ambulacral ossicles*

Range E. Jurassic	Distribution UK	Occurrence

Order VALVATIDA	Family GONIASTERIDAE	Informal name Starfish

METOPASTER

The arms are very short and the disc is large (the body resembles a pentagonal biscuit). The marginal ossicles are large, few in number, and conspicuous; in life they bore small, granular spines. The marginals, which form the tips of the arms, are elongated and triangular. The disc was covered with small, polygonal ossicles.

• HABITAT Like its living relatives, *Metopaster* probably lived as a sediment feeder or scavenger on the Chalk sea floor.

• REMARK Marginal ossicles of this genus are common fossils.

Typical diameter 5cm (2in)

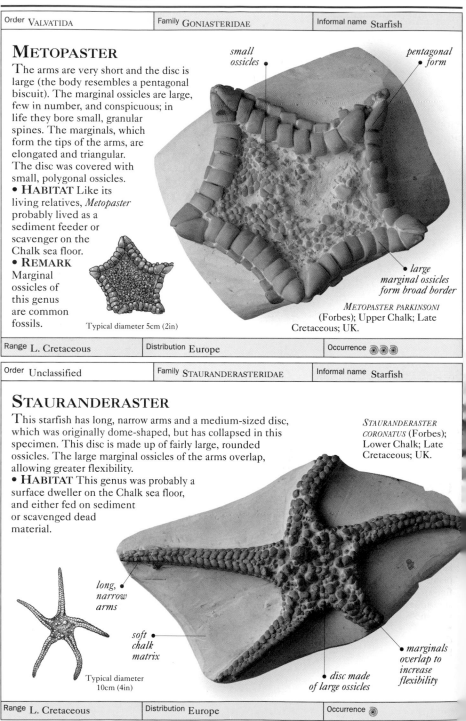

small ossicles

pentagonal form

large marginal ossicles form broad border

METOPASTER PARKINSONI (Forbes); Upper Chalk; Late Cretaceous; UK.

Range L. Cretaceous	Distribution Europe	Occurrence 🔘🔘🔘

Order Unclassified	Family STAURANDERASTERIDAE	Informal name Starfish

STAURANDERASTER

This starfish has long, narrow arms and a medium-sized disc, which was originally dome-shaped, but has collapsed in this specimen. This disc is made up of fairly large, rounded ossicles. The large marginal ossicles of the arms overlap, allowing greater flexibility.

• HABITAT This genus was probably a surface dweller on the Chalk sea floor, and either fed on sediment or scavenged dead material.

STAURANDERASTER CORONATUS (Forbes); Lower Chalk; Late Cretaceous; UK.

long, narrow arms

soft chalk matrix

marginals overlap to increase flexibility

disc made of large ossicles

Typical diameter 10cm (4in)

Range L. Cretaceous	Distribution Europe	Occurrence 🔘

OPHIUROIDEA

T HE OPHIUROIDS ARE commonly called starfish or brittle stars. Closely related to echinoids they possess five long, often fragile, arms which radiate from a flat, nearly circular disc. These arms are very flexible, and quite different in structure from those of asteroids. They consist of a central column of vertebrae, covered by four rows of plates. The ambulacral groove is covered in ophiuroids. Today, ophiuroids occur in vast masses on the sea floor; similar quantities are found in the fossil state.

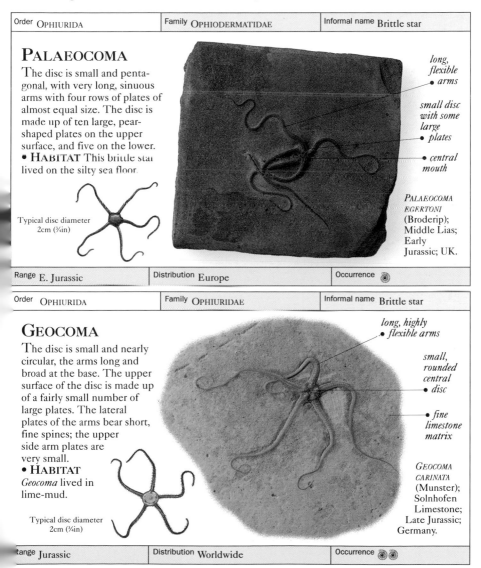

Order OPHIURIDA	Family OPHIODERMATIDAE	Informal name Brittle star

PALAEOCOMA

The disc is small and pentagonal, with very long, sinuous arms with four rows of plates of almost equal size. The disc is made up of ten large, pear-shaped plates on the upper surface, and five on the lower.
• HABITAT This brittle star lived on the silty sea floor.

Typical disc diameter
2cm (¾in)

long, flexible arms

small disc with some large plates

central mouth

PALAEOCOMA EGERTONI (Broderip); Middle Lias; Early Jurassic; UK.

Range E. Jurassic	Distribution Europe	Occurrence

Order OPHIURIDA	Family OPHIURIDAE	Informal name Brittle star

GEOCOMA

The disc is small and nearly circular, the arms long and broad at the base. The upper surface of the disc is made up of a fairly small number of large plates. The lateral plates of the arms bear short, fine spines; the upper side arm plates are very small.
• HABITAT
Geocoma lived in lime-mud.

Typical disc diameter
2cm (¾in)

long, highly flexible arms

small, rounded central disc

fine limestone matrix

GEOCOMA CARINATA (Munster); Solnhofen Limestone; Late Jurassic; Germany.

Range Jurassic	Distribution Worldwide	Occurrence

BLASTOIDS

T HE BLASTOIDS ARE a small, well-defined group of echinoderms, which in life were attached to the substrate by a thin stem, and in which the compact theca is shaped like a rosebud. The theca is made up of three circles of five plates, known as basals, radials, and deltoids. The five columns of ambulacral plates are V-shaped, bearing short brachioles used for filtering food from the water. These fossils are locally common from the Silurian to the Permian, in marine shales and limestones.

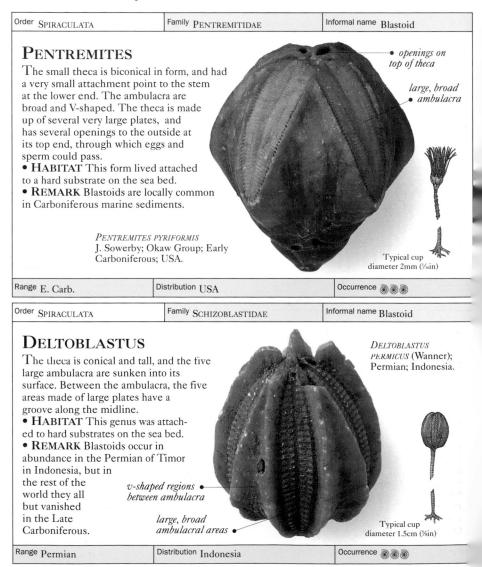

Order SPIRACULATA	Family PENTREMITIDAE	Informal name Blastoid

PENTREMITES

The small theca is biconical in form, and had a very small attachment point to the stem at the lower end. The ambulacra are broad and V-shaped. The theca is made up of several very large plates, and has several openings to the outside at its top end, through which eggs and sperm could pass.
• **HABITAT** This form lived attached to a hard substrate on the sea bed.
• **REMARK** Blastoids are locally common in Carboniferous marine sediments.

PENTREMITES PYRIFORMIS
J. Sowerby; Okaw Group; Early
Carboniferous; USA.

• *openings on top of theca*

large, broad • ambulacra

Typical cup
diameter 2mm (1/16in)

Range E. Carb.	Distribution USA	Occurrence

Order SPIRACULATA	Family SCHIZOBLASTIDAE	Informal name Blastoid

DELTOBLASTUS

The theca is conical and tall, and the five large ambulacra are sunken into its surface. Between the ambulacra, the five areas made of large plates have a groove along the midline.
• **HABITAT** This genus was attach-ed to hard substrates on the sea bed.
• **REMARK** Blastoids occur in abundance in the Permian of Timor in Indonesia, but in the rest of the world they all but vanished in the Late Carboniferous.

*DELTOBLASTUS
PERMICUS* (Wanner);
Permian; Indonesia.

v-shaped regions • between ambulacra

large, broad ambulacral areas •

Typical cup
diameter 1.5cm (5/8in)

Range Permian	Distribution Indonesia	Occurrence

CYSTOIDS

C YSTOIDS SUPERFICIALLY resembled crinoids in that they were attached to the substrate by a stem, and possessed a swollen theca made up of a variable number of plates. Cystoids, however, did not have true arms. Instead they filtered food from the water by means of short, unbranched limbs called brachioles. In addition, they had special pore structures on the plates, which were used for respiration. Cystoides are only found very occasionally, in Ordovician to Devonian rocks.

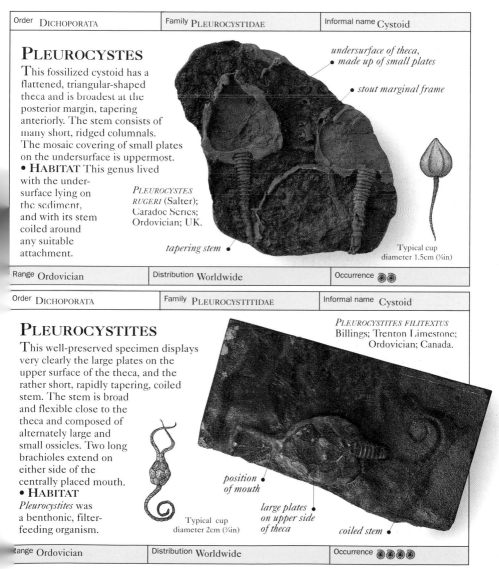

Order DICHOPORATA	Family PLEUROCYSTIDAE	Informal name Cystoid

PLEUROCYSTES

This fossilized cystoid has a flattened, triangular-shaped theca and is broadest at the posterior margin, tapering anteriorly. The stem consists of many short, ridged columnals. The mosaic covering of small plates on the undersurface is uppermost.
• **HABITAT** This genus lived with the under-surface lying on the sediment, and with its stem coiled around any suitable attachment.

undersurface of theca, made up of small plates

stout marginal frame

PLEUROCYSTES RUGERI (Salter); Caradoc Series; Ordovician; UK.

tapering stem

Typical cup diameter 1.5cm (⅝in)

Range Ordovician	Distribution Worldwide	Occurrence 🦠🦠

Order DICHOPORATA	Family PLEUROCYSTITIDAE	Informal name Cystoid

PLEUROCYSTITES

This well-preserved specimen displays very clearly the large plates on the upper surface of the theca, and the rather short, rapidly tapering, coiled stem. The stem is broad and flexible close to the theca and composed of alternately large and small ossicles. Two long brachioles extend on either side of the centrally placed mouth.
• **HABITAT** *Pleurocystites* was a benthonic, filter-feeding organism.

PLEUROCYSTITES FILITEXTUS Billings; Trenton Limestone; Ordovician; Canada.

position of mouth

large plates on upper side of theca

coiled stem

Typical cup diameter 2cm (¾in)

Range Ordovician	Distribution Worldwide	Occurrence 🦠🦠🦠

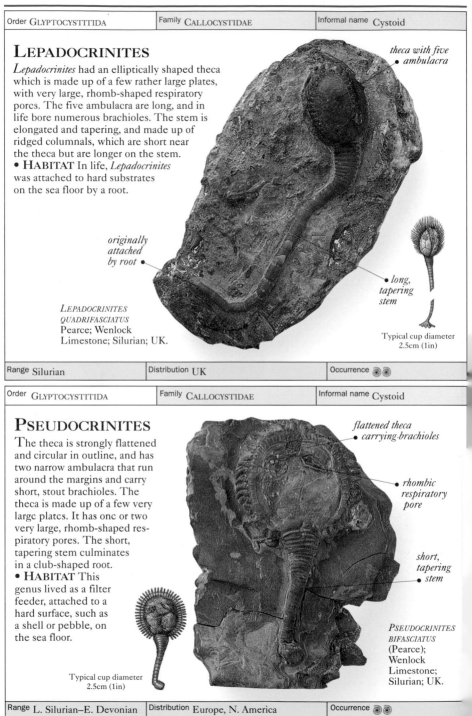

Order GLYPTOCYSTITIDA	Family CALLOCYSTIDAE	Informal name Cystoid

LEPADOCRINITES

Lepadocrinites had an elliptically shaped theca which is made up of a few rather large plates, with very large, rhomb-shaped respiratory pores. The five ambulacra are long, and in life bore numerous brachioles. The stem is elongated and tapering, and made up of ridged columnals, which are short near the theca but are longer on the stem.
• HABITAT In life, *Lepadocrinites* was attached to hard substrates on the sea floor by a root.

theca with five
• ambulacra

originally attached by root •

• long, tapering stem

LEPADOCRINITES QUADRIFASCIATUS
Pearce; Wenlock Limestone; Silurian; UK.

Typical cup diameter
2.5cm (1in)

Range Silurian	Distribution UK	Occurrence 🌑🌑

Order GLYPTOCYSTITIDA	Family CALLOCYSTIDAE	Informal name Cystoid

PSEUDOCRINITES

The theca is strongly flattened and circular in outline, and has two narrow ambulacra that run around the margins and carry short, stout brachioles. The theca is made up of a few very large plates. It has one or two very large, rhomb-shaped respiratory pores. The short, tapering stem culminates in a club-shaped root.
• HABITAT This genus lived as a filter feeder, attached to a hard surface, such as a shell or pebble, on the sea floor.

flattened theca
• carrying brachioles

• rhombic respiratory pore

short, tapering • stem

PSEUDOCRINITES BIFASCIATUS
(Pearce); Wenlock Limestone; Silurian; UK.

Typical cup diameter
2.5cm (1in)

Range L. Silurian–E. Devonian	Distribution Europe, N. America	Occurrence 🌑🌑

CARPOIDS

T HE CARPOIDS ARE a small but diverse group of Cambrian to Devonian animals. They possessed a skeleton with the distinctive fine calcite structure of echinoderms, but without a trace of their five-fold symmetry *(see pp.175–185).* They are probably ancestral to both the echinoderms and the chordates. Carpoids were free living, being able to move on the sea bed, and had a large head and a short, flexible tail. Gill slits (like those in fish) are conspicuous in some carpoid forms.

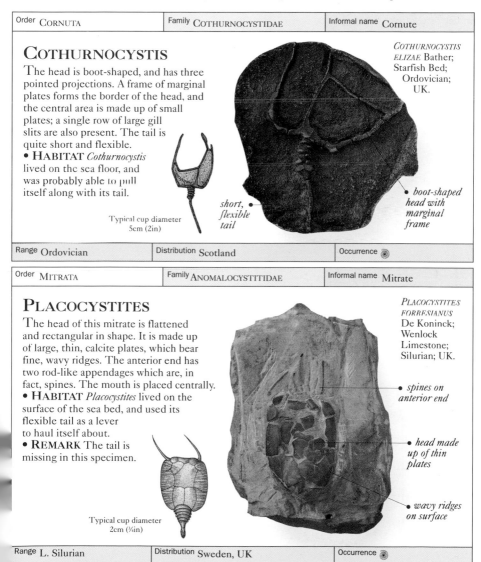

Order CORNUTA	Family COTHURNOCYSTIDAE	Informal name Cornute

COTHURNOCYSTIS

The head is boot-shaped, and has three pointed projections. A frame of marginal plates forms the border of the head, and the central area is made up of small plates; a single row of large gill slits are also present. The tail is quite short and flexible.
• **HABITAT** *Cothurnocystis* lived on the sea floor, and was probably able to pull itself along with its tail.

Typical cup diameter
5cm (2in)

short, flexible tail

COTHURNOCYSTIS ELIZAE Bather; Starfish Bed; Ordovician; UK.

• *boot-shaped head with marginal frame*

Range Ordovician	Distribution Scotland	Occurrence ◉

Order MITRATA	Family ANOMALOCYSTITIDAE	Informal name Mitrate

PLACOCYSTITES

The head of this mitrate is flattened and rectangular in shape. It is made up of large, thin, calcite plates, which bear fine, wavy ridges. The anterior end has two rod-like appendages which are, in fact, spines. The mouth is placed centrally.
• **HABITAT** *Placocystites* lived on the surface of the sea bed, and used its flexible tail as a lever to haul itself about.
• **REMARK** The tail is missing in this specimen.

Typical cup diameter
2cm (¾in)

PLACOCYSTITES FORRESIANUS De Koninck; Wenlock Limestone; Silurian; UK.

• *spines on anterior end*

• *head made up of thin plates*

• *wavy ridges on surface*

Range L. Silurian	Distribution Sweden, UK	Occurrence ◉

VERTEBRATES

AGNATHANS

THESE PRIMITIVE, jawless fishes have an ancient lineage, represented today by the lampreys and hagfishes. Living forms have funnel-like, suctional mouths with rasping, horny teeth, used for scraping flesh. Unlike jawed vertebrates, agnathan gills face inwards from the gill arches. They have no paired fins. Most of the extinct forms were tadpole-shaped, swam by undulating their tails, and had thick plates and scales for armour. They first appeared in marine waters, then spread to fresh and brackish waters, dominating the Silurian and Devonian periods.

Order HETEROSTRACI	Family PTERASPIDAE	Informal name Pteraspid

PTERASPIS

The flattened head region of *Pteraspis* was enclosed by massive, bony plates, which may have been formed by scales fusing together. It had one middle dorsal plate, one rostral plate, and one ventral plate, plus a smaller lateral series. The plates were punctuated by sensory canals. The mouth, situated on the underside, was flanked by small plates which may have assisted suctional bottom feeding. The eyes were small and placed along the sides. The tail, with its larger lower lobe, caused upward driving of the head when rising from the bottom. A massive bony carapace may have acted as a phosphate store during times of shortage.
• **HABITAT** Fossil remains of *Pteraspis* are often found in marine and freshwater deposits.

long rostrum

PTERASPIS ROSTRATA
Agassiz; Old Red
Sandstone;
Devonian;
UK.

HEAD SHIELD

growth lines

immovable lateral plate

bony dorsal shield

dorsal spine base

Typical length
25cm (10in)

Range E. Devonian	Distribution Europe, Asia, N. America	Occurrence

| Order OSTEOSTRACI | Family CEPHALASPIDAE | Informal name Cephalaspid |

CEPHALASPIS

The small freshwater fish, *Cephalaspis*, had a bony dorsal head shield, with overlapping scales covering the rest of its body. The eyes were sited on top, close to the midline, with the mouth on the underside. A middle dorsal area and two lateral areas of polygonal plates are thought to represent sensory areas.
• HABITAT *Cephalaspis* inhabited freshwater pools or streams.

CEPHALASPIS WHITEI
Stensio; Old Red Sandstone; Devonian; UK.

• *sensory plate area*

• *eye socket*

• *cornua directed towards the back*

• *notch*

Typical length
22cm (8¾in)

HEAD SHIELD

| Range E. Devonian | Distribution Europe | Occurrence |

| Order ANASPIDA | Family BIRKENIIDAE | Informal name Anaspid |

BIRKENIA

The spindle-shaped body of this small fish is armoured by deep, overlapping, articulated scales arranged in rows. A row of ridge scales runs along the top. The terminal mouth forms a vertical slit, surrounded by the smaller, less organized cranial scales.
• HABITAT *Birkenia* was a freshwater genus.

BIRKENIA ELEGANS Traquair;
Slot Burn Formation; Middle Silurian; UK.

long, spindle-shaped body •

• *dorsal scales*

tail scales •

• *head*

• *terminal mouth*

Typical length 6cm (2⅜in) • *deep body scales*

| Range M. Silurian | Distribution Europe | Occurrence |

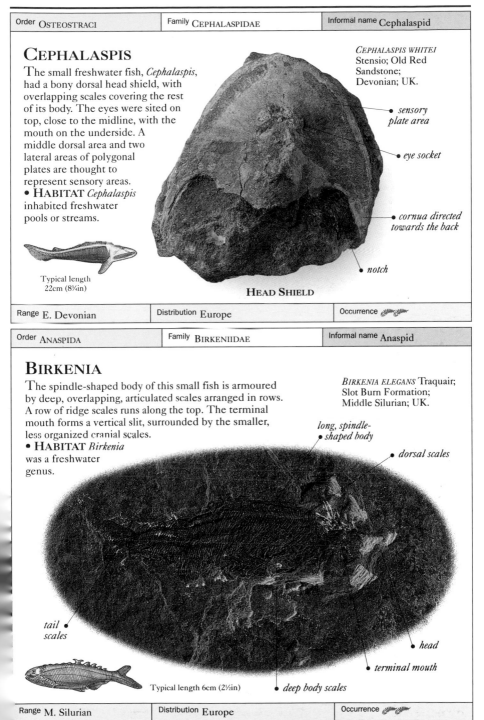

PLACODERMS

THE PLACODERMS FORMED a diverse group of now-extinct fishes that had primitive jaws armed with slicing plates. Typically, these fish lived on the sea bed. They had a heavily armoured head shield connected to a trunk shield which covered the anterior part of the body. The rest of the body and tail was covered by small scales. The moderate to large eyes were protected by a circlet of bony plates. Placoderms lived in marine and fresh water, from the Late Silurian to the Early Carboniferous. Most were moderately sized, but some grew to 6m (20ft) in length.

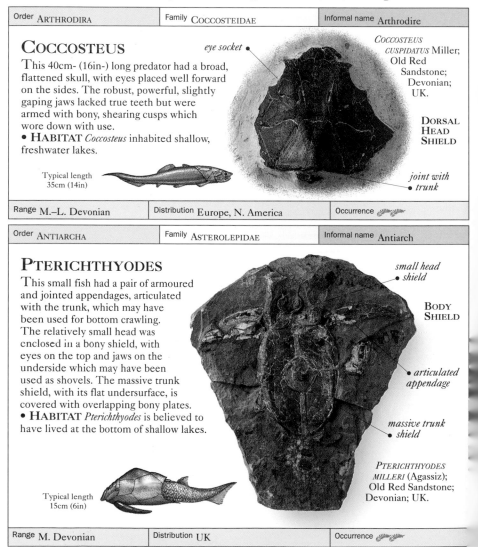

Order ARTHRODIRA	Family COCCOSTEIDAE	Informal name Arthrodire

COCCOSTEUS

This 40cm- (16in-) long predator had a broad, flattened skull, with eyes placed well forward on the sides. The robust, powerful, slightly gaping jaws lacked true teeth but were armed with bony, shearing cusps which wore down with use.
• HABITAT *Coccosteus* inhabited shallow, freshwater lakes.

eye socket •

COCCOSTEUS CUSPIDATUS Miller; Old Red Sandstone; Devonian; UK.

DORSAL HEAD SHIELD

Typical length 35cm (14in)

joint with • *trunk*

Range M.–L. Devonian	Distribution Europe, N. America	Occurrence

Order ANTIARCHA	Family ASTEROLEPIDAE	Informal name Antiarch

PTERICHTHYODES

This small fish had a pair of armoured and jointed appendages, articulated with the trunk, which may have been used for bottom crawling. The relatively small head was enclosed in a bony shield, with eyes on the top and jaws on the underside which may have been used as shovels. The massive trunk shield, with its flat undersurface, is covered with overlapping bony plates.
• HABITAT *Pterichthyodes* is believed to have lived at the bottom of shallow lakes.

small head • *shield*

BODY SHIELD

• *articulated appendage*

massive trunk • *shield*

PTERICHTHYODES MILLERI (Agassiz); Old Red Sandstone; Devonian; UK.

Typical length 15cm (6in)

Range M. Devonian	Distribution UK	Occurrence

Order PTYCTODONTIDA	Family PTYCTODONTIDAE	Informal name Ptyctodont

RHAMPHODOPSIS

The head and trunk armour of this genus was more restricted than in other placoderms; only a few plates covered the upper head and cheek region, while a short trunk girdle bearing just three spines was located just behind it. The unarmoured rear of the trunk ended in a whiplash tail. Paired plates of teeth were carried on both jaws.

RHAMPHODOPSIS THREIPLANDI Watson; Old Red Sandstone; Middle Devonian; UK.

• HABITAT This genus lived in fresh water.

short dorsal • spine

Typical length 15cm (6in)

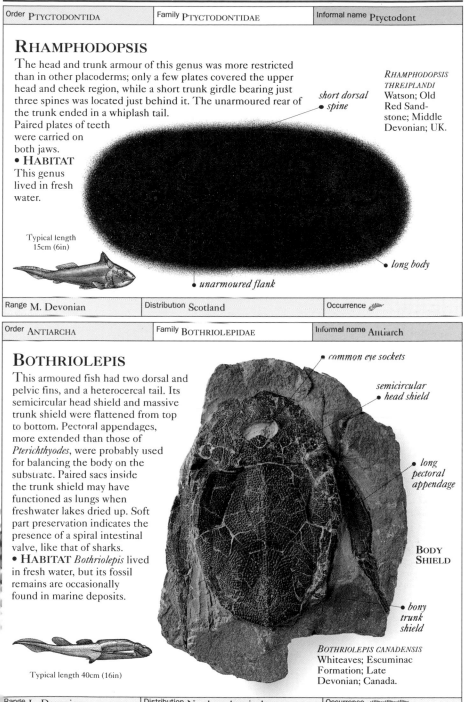

• *long body*

• *unarmoured flank*

Range M. Devonian	Distribution Scotland	Occurrence

Order ANTIARCHA	Family BOTHRIOLEPIDAE	Informal name Antiarch

BOTHRIOLEPIS

This armoured fish had two dorsal and pelvic fins, and a heterocercal tail. Its semicircular head shield and massive trunk shield were flattened from top to bottom. Pectoral appendages, more extended than those of *Pterichthyodes*, were probably used for balancing the body on the substrate. Paired sacs inside the trunk shield may have functioned as lungs when freshwater lakes dried up. Soft part preservation indicates the presence of a spiral intestinal valve, like that of sharks.

• HABITAT *Bothriolepis* lived in fresh water, but its fossil remains are occasionally found in marine deposits.

• *common eye sockets*

semicircular • *head shield*

• *long pectoral appendage*

BODY SHIELD

• *bony trunk shield*

BOTHRIOLEPIS CANADENSIS Whiteaves; Escuminac Formation; Late Devonian; Canada.

Typical length 40cm (16in)

Range L. Devonian	Distribution Northern hemisphere	Occurrence

CHONDRICHTHYANS

CREATURES OF THIS CLASS are characterized by a cartilaginous skeleton made up of tiny, calcified prisms. Living examples include the sharks, skates, rays, and rabbitfishes. Cartilage is not usually preserved, so common fossils tend to be teeth, scales, and dorsal-fin spines. Sharks' teeth are continuously replaced from behind, being shed from the jaw margin or lost during feeding. Trace fossils *(see p.42)* ascribed to the group include spirally coiled faecal remains and intestines. Chondrichthyans diversified from Devonian origins to become very common in today's seas.

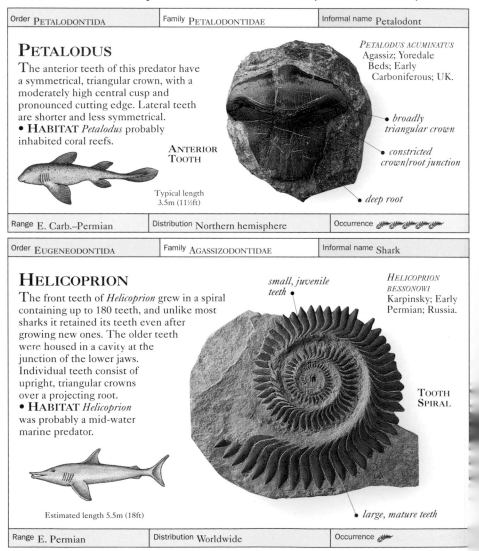

Order PETALODONTIDA	Family PETALODONTIDAE	Informal name Petalodont

PETALODUS
The anterior teeth of this predator have a symmetrical, triangular crown, with a moderately high central cusp and pronounced cutting edge. Lateral teeth are shorter and less symmetrical.
• HABITAT *Petalodus* probably inhabited coral reefs.

PETALODUS ACUMINATUS Agassiz; Yoredale Beds; Early Carboniferous; UK.

ANTERIOR TOOTH

Typical length 3.5m (11½ft)

• *broadly triangular crown*
• *constricted crown/root junction*
• *deep root*

Range E. Carb.–Permian	Distribution Northern hemisphere	Occurrence

Order EUGENEODONTIDA	Family AGASSIZODONTIDAE	Informal name Shark

HELICOPRION
The front teeth of *Helicoprion* grew in a spiral containing up to 180 teeth, and unlike most sharks it retained its teeth even after growing new ones. The older teeth were housed in a cavity at the junction of the lower jaws. Individual teeth consist of upright, triangular crowns over a projecting root.
• HABITAT *Helicoprion* was probably a mid-water marine predator.

small, juvenile teeth •

HELICOPRION BESSONOWI Karpinsky; Early Permian; Russia.

TOOTH SPIRAL

Estimated length 5.5m (18ft)

• *large, mature teeth*

Range E. Permian	Distribution Worldwide	Occurrence

Order HYBODONTIFORMES	Family ACRODONTIDAE	Informal name Hybodont shark

ACRODUS

The dorsal fin of this hybodont shark was supported by an extended spine, with coarse longitudinal ridges (costae) on the side walls and a trailing edge covered with small, tooth-like projections. A long basal part, inserted into the soft tissues of the back, was supported by a fin cartilage. The fin itself cut through the water and prevented rolling during swimming. The underslung mouth was armed with a battery of robust teeth for crushing its food. Coarse ridges of each individual tooth radiate from the crown centre, providing additional abrasion. Anterior and posterior teeth are small; lateral teeth have greatly expanded crowns supported on robust roots.
• HABITAT *Acrodus* was a slow-swimming marine shark, living close to the sea bottom on a diet of molluscs and crustaceans.

ACRODUS NOBILIS
Agassiz; Lower Lias; Early Jurassic; UK.

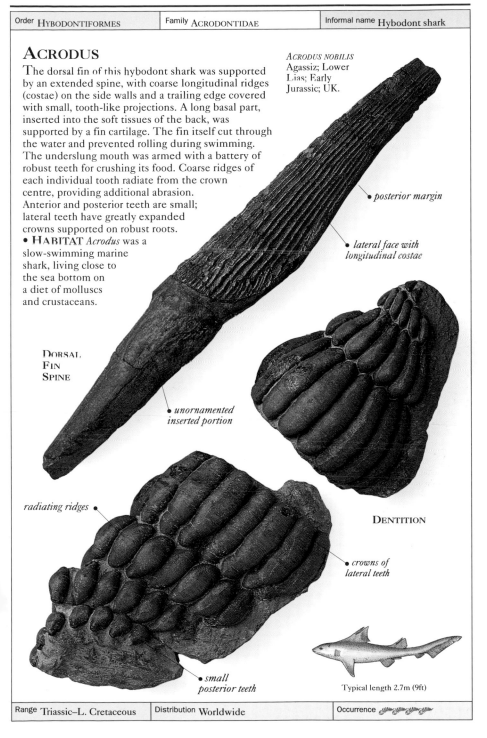

• *posterior margin*

• *lateral face with longitudinal costae*

DORSAL FIN SPINE

• *unornamented inserted portion*

radiating ridges •

DENTITION

• *crowns of lateral teeth*

• *small posterior teeth*

Typical length 2.7m (9ft)

Range Triassic–L. Cretaceous	Distribution Worldwide	Occurrence

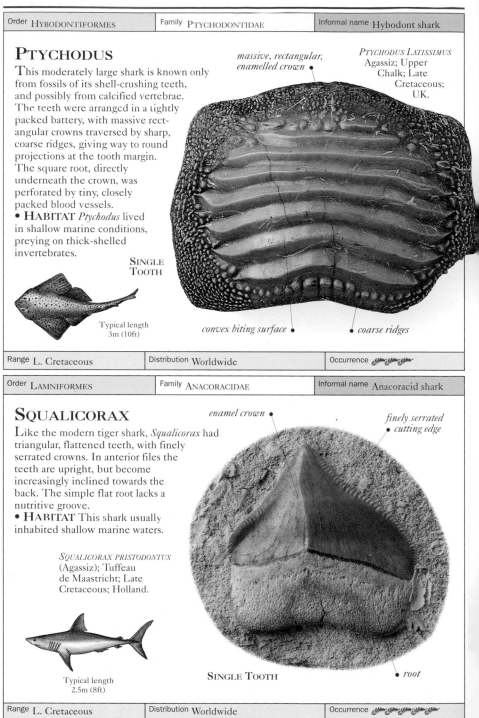

| Order HYBODONTIFORMES | Family PTYCHODONTIDAE | Informal name Hybodont shark |

PTYCHODUS

This moderately large shark is known only
from fossils of its shell-crushing teeth,
and possibly from calcified vertebrae.
The teeth were arranged in a tightly
packed battery, with massive rectangular crowns traversed by sharp,
coarse ridges, giving way to round
projections at the tooth margin.
The square root, directly
underneath the crown, was
perforated by tiny, closely
packed blood vessels.
• HABITAT *Ptychodus* lived
in shallow marine conditions,
preying on thick-shelled
invertebrates.

massive, rectangular, enamelled crown •

PTYCHODUS LATISSIMUS
Agassiz; Upper
Chalk; Late
Cretaceous;
UK.

SINGLE
TOOTH

Typical length
3m (10ft)

convex biting surface •   • *coarse ridges*

| Range L. Cretaceous | Distribution Worldwide | Occurrence |

| Order LAMNIFORMES | Family ANACORACIDAE | Informal name Anacoracid shark |

SQUALICORAX

Like the modern tiger shark, *Squalicorax* had
triangular, flattened teeth, with finely
serrated crowns. In anterior files the
teeth are upright, but become
increasingly inclined towards the
back. The simple flat root lacks a
nutritive groove.
• HABITAT This shark usually
inhabited shallow marine waters.

enamel crown •

finely serrated
• *cutting edge*

SQUALICORAX PRISTODONTUS
(Agassiz); Tuffeau
de Maastricht; Late
Cretaceous; Holland.

SINGLE TOOTH

• *root*

Typical length
2.5m (8ft)

| Range L. Cretaceous | Distribution Worldwide | Occurrence |

Order HEXANCHIFORMES	Family PALAEOSPINACIDAE	Informal name Palaeospinacid shark

SYNECHODUS

This was a small, probably slow-swimming shark, similar in shape to a dogfish. It had a weakly calcified braincase, with a short snout, and underslung mouth containing multi-pointed teeth. These were ornamented by vertical ridges, with crowns displaced in relation to the tongue. The high, central cusp was flanked by up to four pairs of lower, lateral cusplets. Teeth at the front were upright and symmetrical, whereas towards the back symmetry decreased, cusplets became shorter, and central cusps became more inclined. The side walls of the short, dorsal-fin spine were smooth and enamelled, with round enamel projections at the base. Vertebrae were calcified and spool shaped, with a central perforation for the skeletal rod (notochord). Scales were simple and non-growing.
• HABITAT *Synechodus* lived in shallow, marine environments, feeding on small fish and thin-shelled, bottom-dwelling invertebrates.

SYNECHODUS ENNISKILLENI Duffin &Ward; Lower Lias; Early Jurassic; UK.

meeting-point of lower jaws

teeth of lower jaw

skeleton of gill arch

vertebral column

dorsal-fin spine

displaced vertebral centra

PARTIAL SKELETON

Typical length 2.5m (8ft)

Range E. Triassic–Palaeocene	Distribution Worldwide	Occurrence

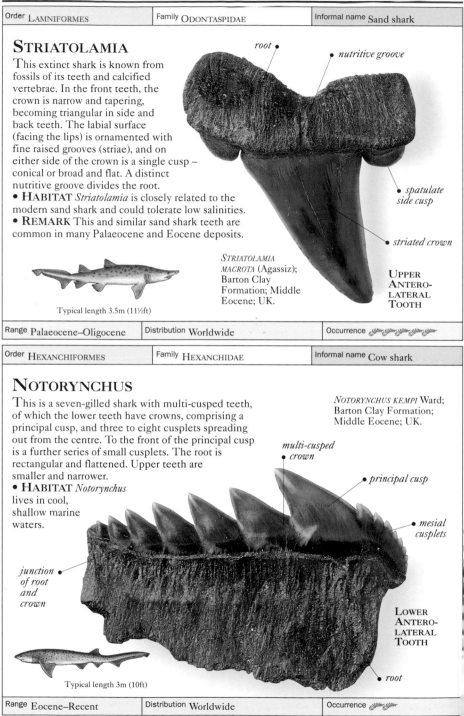

| Order LAMNIFORMES | Family ODONTASPIDAE | Informal name Sand shark |

STRIATOLAMIA

This extinct shark is known from fossils of its teeth and calcified vertebrae. In the front teeth, the crown is narrow and tapering, becoming triangular in side and back teeth. The labial surface (facing the lips) is ornamented with fine raised grooves (striae), and on either side of the crown is a single cusp – conical or broad and flat. A distinct nutritive groove divides the root.

• HABITAT *Striatolamia* is closely related to the modern sand shark and could tolerate low salinities.

• REMARK This and similar sand shark teeth are common in many Palaeocene and Eocene deposits.

root

nutritive groove

spatulate side cusp

striated crown

STRIATOLAMIA MACROTA (Agassiz); Barton Clay Formation; Middle Eocene; UK.

UPPER ANTERO-LATERAL TOOTH

Typical length 3.5m (11½ft)

| Range Palaeocene–Oligocene | Distribution Worldwide | Occurrence |

| Order HEXANCHIFORMES | Family HEXANCHIDAE | Informal name Cow shark |

NOTORYNCHUS

This is a seven-gilled shark with multi-cusped teeth, of which the lower teeth have crowns, comprising a principal cusp, and three to eight cusplets spreading out from the centre. To the front of the principal cusp is a further series of small cusplets. The root is rectangular and flattened. Upper teeth are smaller and narrower.

• HABITAT *Notorynchus* lives in cool, shallow marine waters.

NOTORYNCHUS KEMPI Ward; Barton Clay Formation; Middle Eocene; UK.

multi-cusped crown

principal cusp

mesial cusplets

junction of root and crown

LOWER ANTERO-LATERAL TOOTH

root

Typical length 3m (10ft)

| Range Eocene–Recent | Distribution Worldwide | Occurrence |

Order LAMNIFORMES	Family OTODONTIDAE	Informal name Mackerel shark

CARCHAROCLES

The genus *Carcharocles* is an extinct lineage of sharks characterized by massively constructed teeth with serrated cutting edges. An estimated 13m (42½ft) long, it was one of the planet's largest predators. The crowns of its razor-sharp teeth are triangular, with or without cusplets at the side, and the roots massive, without a nutritive groove. There were approximately 24 teeth in the upper jaw and 20 in the lower. The species *Carcharocles megalodon* was the youngest and largest of the lineage, and had no side cusplets.

• **HABITAT** *Carcharocles* lived in warm seas, and its teeth are most abundant in deposits rich in marine mammals, its probable prey.

• **REMARK** This genus is often confused with the modern white shark, *Carcharodon*, because of their apparent, but in fact only superficial, similarities in lifestyle and prey; the two are only distantly related. Serrated teeth, similar to those of *Carcharocles*, often appear in large carnivores.

CARCHAROCLES MEGALODON (Agassiz); Yorktown Formation; Early Pliocene; USA.

FIRST OR SECOND UPPER RIGHT TOOTH

• shrinkage crack in root

• crown

• serrated cutting edge

EIGHTH LOWER LEFT TOOTH

almost • symmetrical shape

no side • cusplets

• mesial cutting edge

enamel •

• distal cutting • edge

crown inclined • away from the centre

• massively constructed root

TENTH LOWER RIGHT TOOTH

Typical length 13m (42½ft)

Range E. Eocene–Pliocene	Distribution Worldwide	Occurrence

Order CARCHARINIFORMES	Family CARCHARINIDAE	Informal name Tiger shark

GALEOCERDO

The tooth of this shark consists of a crown with a finely serrated cusp and more coarsely serrated blade. The root bears a shallow groove and several vascular openings (foraminae).
• **HABITAT** This genus inhabits coastal waters.

GALEOCERDO CUVIER
(Peron & LeSueur);
Yorktown Formation;
Early Pliocene; USA.

Typical length 5m (16½ft)

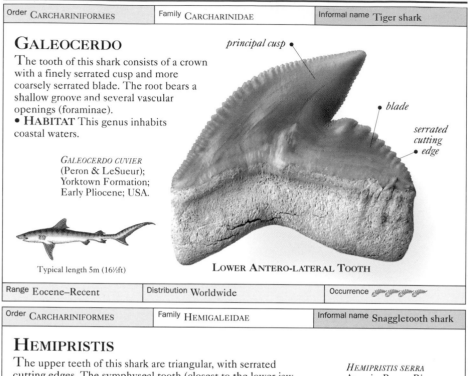

principal cusp

blade

serrated cutting edge

LOWER ANTERO-LATERAL TOOTH

Range Eocene–Recent	Distribution Worldwide	Occurrence

Order CARCHARINIFORMES	Family HEMIGALEIDAE	Informal name Snaggletooth shark

HEMIPRISTIS

The upper teeth of this shark are triangular, with serrated cutting edges. The symphyseal tooth (closest to the lower jaw junction) is almost symmetrical, whilst side teeth become increasingly inclined away from the centre. Lower teeth are slimmer, with V-shaped roots. The symphyseal tooth has few serrations, but lateral teeth become progressively serrated and broad.
• **HABITAT** *Hemipristis* lived in warm coastal waters.
• **REMARK** Many fossil sharks, like *Hemipristis*, have differing upper and lower teeth.

HEMIPRISTIS SERRA
Agassiz; Pungo River
Formation; Middle
Miocene; USA.

RECONSTRUCTED DENTITION

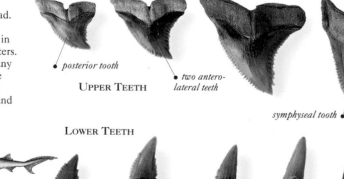

posterior tooth

two antero-lateral teeth

UPPER TEETH

symphyseal tooth

LOWER TEETH

Typical length 5m (16½ft)

posterior tooth

three antero-lateral teeth

symphyseal tooth

Range Eocene–Recent	Distribution Worldwide	Occurrence

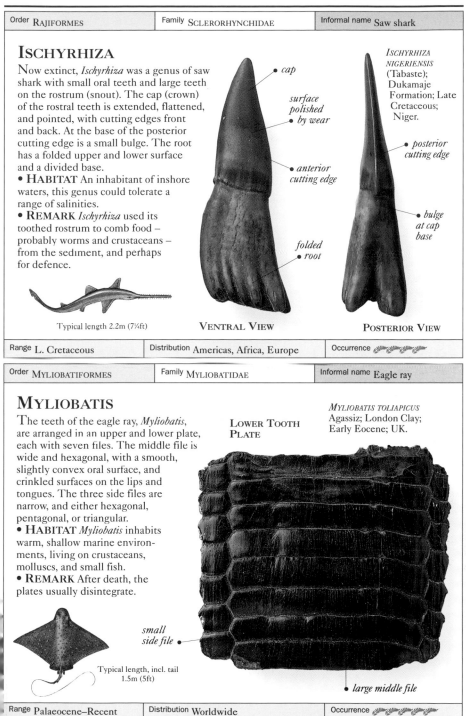

| Order RAJIFORMES | Family SCLERORHYNCHIDAE | Informal name Saw shark |

ISCHYRHIZA

Now extinct, *Ischyrhiza* was a genus of saw shark with small oral teeth and large teeth on the rostrum (snout). The cap (crown) of the rostral teeth is extended, flattened, and pointed, with cutting edges front and back. At the base of the posterior cutting edge is a small bulge. The root has a folded upper and lower surface and a divided base.
• **HABITAT** An inhabitant of inshore waters, this genus could tolerate a range of salinities.
• **REMARK** *Ischyrhiza* used its toothed rostrum to comb food – probably worms and crustaceans – from the sediment, and perhaps for defence.

ISCHYRHIZA NIGERIENSIS (Tabaste); Dukamaje Formation; Late Cretaceous; Niger.

• *cap*

surface polished by wear

• *anterior cutting edge*

• *posterior cutting edge*

• *bulge at cap base*

folded root

Typical length 2.2m (7¼ft)

VENTRAL VIEW

POSTERIOR VIEW

| Range L. Cretaceous | Distribution Americas, Africa, Europe | Occurrence |

| Order MYLIOBATIFORMES | Family MYLIOBATIDAE | Informal name Eagle ray |

MYLIOBATIS

The teeth of the eagle ray, *Myliobatis*, are arranged in an upper and lower plate, each with seven files. The middle file is wide and hexagonal, with a smooth, slightly convex oral surface, and crinkled surfaces on the lips and tongues. The three side files are narrow, and either hexagonal, pentagonal, or triangular.
• **HABITAT** *Myliobatis* inhabits warm, shallow marine environments, living on crustaceans, molluscs, and small fish.
• **REMARK** After death, the plates usually disintegrate.

LOWER TOOTH PLATE

MYLIOBATIS TOLIAPICUS Agassiz; London Clay; Early Eocene; UK.

small side file •

Typical length, incl. tail 1.5m (5ft)

• *large middle file*

| Range Palaeocene–Recent | Distribution Worldwide | Occurrence |

Order MYLIOBATIFORMES	Family DASYATIDAE	Informal name Stingray

HELIOBATIS

Heliobatis was a stingray with a rounded disc, pointed snout, and long, barbed tail. A series of hooked, dermal denticles ran along the dorsal midline. The whip-like tail was armed with up to three barbed spines. The 90 pectoral-fin rays almost met in front of the skull, with the 16 pelvic-fin rays completing the circle behind. The teeth were small and tetrahedral, with a relatively flat occlusal surface. Males had a pair of pelvic claspers. The tail consisted of between 170 and 190 fully calcified vertebrae.

• **HABITAT** Living in freshwater streams and lakes, this stingray probably fed on crayfish, prawns, and other invertebrates.

• **REMARK** When not feeding, *Heliobatis* would lie partially buried in soft sediment. The poisonous tail spines could inflict serious injury to any potential predator.

HELIOBATIS RADIANS
Marsh; Green
River Formation;
Early Eocene; USA.

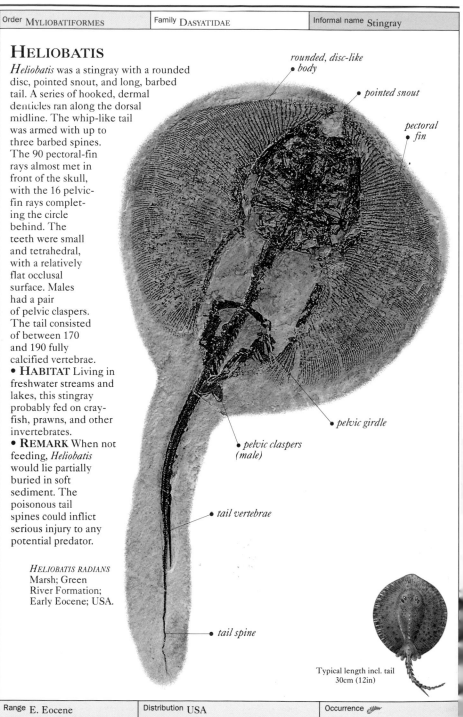

rounded, disc-like body

pointed snout

pectoral fin

pelvic girdle

pelvic claspers (male)

tail vertebrae

tail spine

Typical length incl. tail
30cm (12in)

Range E. Eocene	Distribution USA	Occurrence

Order CHIMAERIFORMES	Family COCHLIODONTIDAE	Informal name Rabbitfish

SANDALODUS

Although known only from isolated tooth plates, this fish is believed to have reached up to 2m (6½ft) in length. The lower teeth are curved strongly inwards; the upper teeth are extended triangles in outline, with pointed anterior ends, and broad, rounded posterior ends. The biting surface is traversed by longitudinal ridges, giving the upper surface of the plate an undulating cross-section. Vertical pillars of hard dentine rise from the tooth plate surface.
• **HABITAT** *Sandalodus* used its teeth to crush thick-shelled invertebrates – and perhaps corals – in warm, shallow, shelf seas.

SANDALODUS MORRISII Davis; Carboniferous Limestone; Early Carboniferous; UK.

UPPER TOOTH PLATE

• *grinding surface*

• *posterior*

Estimated length 2m (6½ft)

Range Carb.	Distribution Europe	Occurrence

Order CHIMAERIFORMES	Family EDAPHODONTIDAE	Informal name Rabbitfish

EDAPHODON

This rabbitfish is known only from isolated tooth plates. The dentition consisted of one pair of lower tooth plates and two pairs of upper tooth plates. The crushing surface of each bony plate is made up of localized areas of specialized dentine (tritors), consisting of hard dentine pillars positioned normally to the tooth plate surface. These were effective in dealing with thick-shelled marine invertebrates.
• **HABITAT** Modern rabbitfish inhabit shallow to deep, cool marine waters.

anterior tip •

LOWER TOOTH PLATE

EDAPHODON BUCKLANDI Agassiz; Bracklesham Beds; Middle Eocene; UK.

• *midline of jaw*

Typical length 1.1m (3½ft)

central specialized • *crushing area*

Range Cretaceous–Pliocene	Distribution Worldwide	Occurrence

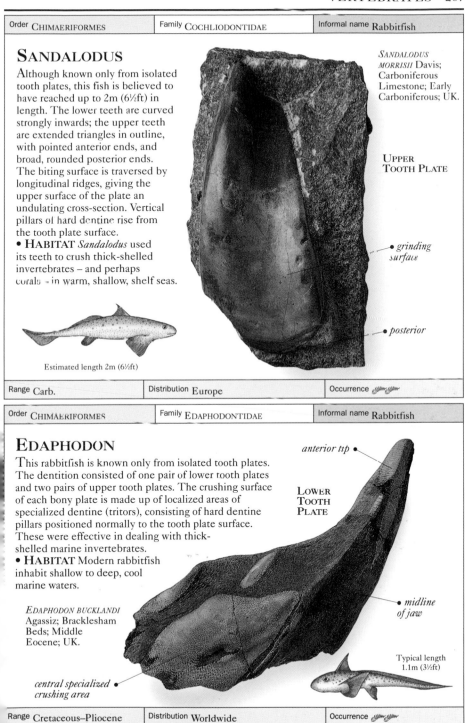

ACANTHODIANS

T HESE FISHES WERE among the earliest known gnathostomes, and flourished in the Devonian. They varied in size from 10cm (4in) to over 2m (6½ft), and were active swimmers with long, tapered bodies protected by scales. A strongly heterocercal tail provided considerable thrust when swimming, and all paired and median fins (except the tail) had strong, immovable spines on their leading edges. The gills were covered by a large scale (operculum), and the teeth often developed in whorls.

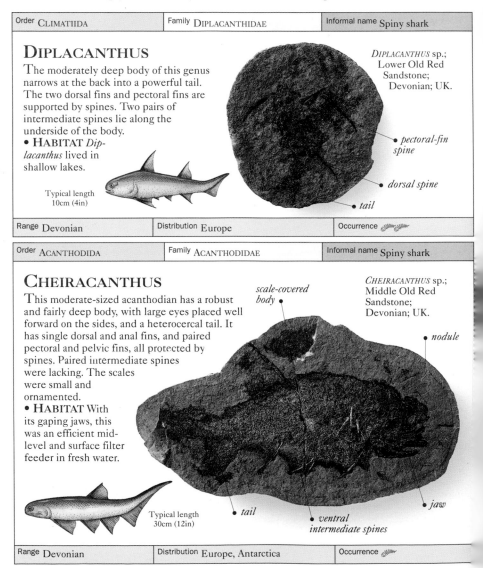

Order CLIMATIIDA	Family DIPLACANTHIDAE	Informal name Spiny shark

DIPLACANTHUS

The moderately deep body of this genus narrows at the back into a powerful tail. The two dorsal fins and pectoral fins are supported by spines. Two pairs of intermediate spines lie along the underside of the body.
• HABITAT *Diplacanthus* lived in shallow lakes.

Typical length 10cm (4in)

DIPLACANTHUS sp.; Lower Old Red Sandstone; Devonian; UK.

• *pectoral-fin spine*
• *dorsal spine*
• *tail*

Range Devonian	Distribution Europe	Occurrence

Order ACANTHODIDA	Family ACANTHODIDAE	Informal name Spiny shark

CHEIRACANTHUS

This moderate-sized acanthodian has a robust and fairly deep body, with large eyes placed well forward on the sides, and a heterocercal tail. It has single dorsal and anal fins, and paired pectoral and pelvic fins, all protected by spines. Paired intermediate spines were lacking. The scales were small and ornamented.
• HABITAT With its gaping jaws, this was an efficient mid-level and surface filter feeder in fresh water.

scale-covered body •

CHEIRACANTHUS sp.; Middle Old Red Sandstone; Devonian; UK.

• *nodule*

Typical length 30cm (12in)

• *tail*
• *ventral intermediate spines*
• *jaw*

Range Devonian	Distribution Europe, Antarctica	Occurrence

OSTEICHTHYANS

F ISH BELONGING TO this class are characterized by a bony internal skeleton. Two subgroups can be identified by their fin structure: the actinopterygians had fins supported by bony rods (radials), while the sarcopterygians had fleshy fins, which were supported by a single bone at the base. Actinopterygians (Devonian to Recent) are very diverse, and include the majority of present-day marine and freshwater fishes. The sarcopterygians dominated during the Devonian and include the lungfish and coelacanths.

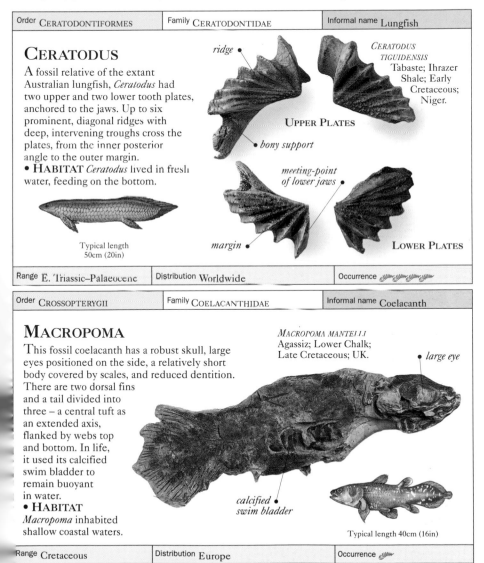

Order CERATODONTIFORMES	Family CERATODONTIDAE	Informal name Lungfish

CERATODUS

A fossil relative of the extant Australian lungfish, *Ceratodus* had two upper and two lower tooth plates, anchored to the jaws. Up to six prominent, diagonal ridges with deep, intervening troughs cross the plates, from the inner posterior angle to the outer margin.
• HABITAT *Ceratodus* lived in fresh water, feeding on the bottom.

ridge

CERATODUS TIGUIDENSIS
Tabaste; Ihrazer Shale; Early Cretaceous; Niger.

UPPER PLATES

bony support

meeting-point of lower jaws

Typical length 50cm (20in)

margin

LOWER PLATES

Range E. Triassic–Palaeocene	Distribution Worldwide	Occurrence

Order CROSSOPTERYGII	Family COELACANTHIDAE	Informal name Coelacanth

MACROPOMA

This fossil coelacanth has a robust skull, large eyes positioned on the side, a relatively short body covered by scales, and reduced dentition. There are two dorsal fins and a tail divided into three – a central tuft as an extended axis, flanked by webs top and bottom. In life, it used its calcified swim bladder to remain buoyant in water.
• HABITAT *Macropoma* inhabited shallow coastal waters.

MACROPOMA MANTELLI
Agassiz; Lower Chalk; Late Cretaceous; UK.

large eye

calcified swim bladder

Typical length 40cm (16in)

Range Cretaceous	Distribution Europe	Occurrence

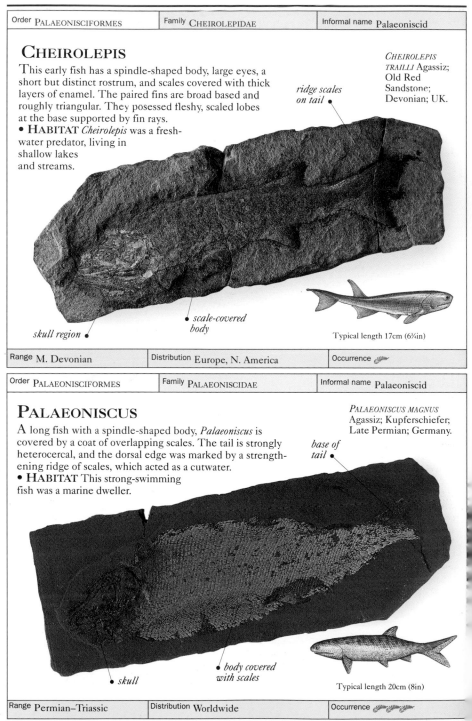

Order PALAEONISCIFORMES	Family CHEIROLEPIDAE	Informal name Palaeoniscid

CHEIROLEPIS

This early fish has a spindle-shaped body, large eyes, a short but distinct rostrum, and scales covered with thick layers of enamel. The paired fins are broad based and roughly triangular. They posessed fleshy, scaled lobes at the base supported by fin rays.
• HABITAT *Cheirolepis* was a freshwater predator, living in shallow lakes and streams.

CHEIROLEPIS TRAILLI Agassiz; Old Red Sandstone; Devonian; UK.

ridge scales on tail •

skull region •

• *scale-covered body*

Typical length 17cm (6¾in)

Range M. Devonian	Distribution Europe, N. America	Occurrence

Order PALAEONISCIFORMES	Family PALAEONISCIDAE	Informal name Palaeoniscid

PALAEONISCUS

A long fish with a spindle-shaped body, *Palaeoniscus* is covered by a coat of overlapping scales. The tail is strongly heterocercal, and the dorsal edge was marked by a strengthening ridge of scales, which acted as a cutwater.
• HABITAT This strong-swimming fish was a marine dweller.

PALAEONISCUS MAGNUS Agassiz; Kupferschiefer; Late Permian; Germany.

base of tail •

• *body covered with scales*

• *skull*

Typical length 20cm (8in)

Range Permian–Triassic	Distribution Worldwide	Occurrence

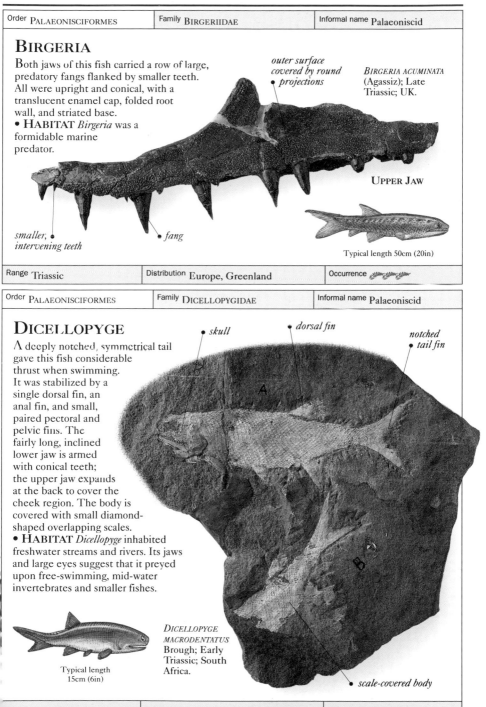

| Order PALAEONISCIFORMES | Family BIRGERIIDAE | Informal name Palaeoniscid |

BIRGERIA

Both jaws of this fish carried a row of large, predatory fangs flanked by smaller teeth. All were upright and conical, with a translucent enamel cap, folded root wall, and striated base.
• HABITAT *Birgeria* was a formidable marine predator.

outer surface covered by round projections

BIRGERIA ACUMINATA (Agassiz); Late Triassic; UK.

UPPER JAW

smaller, intervening teeth

fang

Typical length 50cm (20in)

| Range Triassic | Distribution Europe, Greenland | Occurrence |

| Order PALAEONISCIFORMES | Family DICELLOPYGIDAE | Informal name Palaeoniscid |

DICELLOPYGE

A deeply notched, symmetrical tail gave this fish considerable thrust when swimming. It was stabilized by a single dorsal fin, an anal fin, and small, paired pectoral and pelvic fins. The fairly long, inclined lower jaw is armed with conical teeth; the upper jaw expands at the back to cover the cheek region. The body is covered with small diamond-shaped overlapping scales.
• HABITAT *Dicellopyge* inhabited freshwater streams and rivers. Its jaws and large eyes suggest that it preyed upon free-swimming, mid-water invertebrates and smaller fishes.

skull

dorsal fin

notched tail fin

DICELLOPYGE MACRODENTATUS Brough; Early Triassic; South Africa.

Typical length 15cm (6in)

scale-covered body

| Range E. Triassic | Distribution S. Africa | Occurrence |

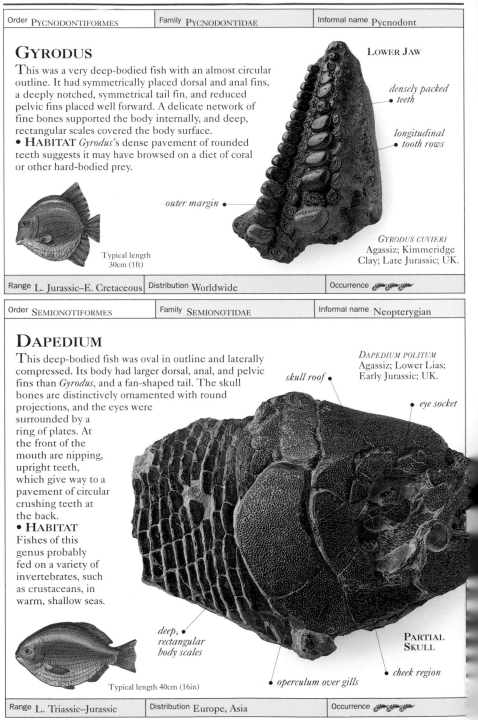

Order PYCNODONTIFORMES	Family PYCNODONTIDAE	Informal name Pycnodont

GYRODUS

This was a very deep-bodied fish with an almost circular outline. It had symmetrically placed dorsal and anal fins, a deeply notched, symmetrical tail fin, and reduced pelvic fins placed well forward. A delicate network of fine bones supported the body internally, and deep, rectangular scales covered the body surface.

• HABITAT *Gyrodus's* dense pavement of rounded teeth suggests it may have browsed on a diet of coral or other hard-bodied prey.

LOWER JAW

densely packed teeth

longitudinal tooth rows

outer margin

GYRODUS CUVIERI
Agassiz; Kimmeridge
Clay; Late Jurassic; UK.

Typical length
30cm (1ft)

Range L. Jurassic–E. Cretaceous	Distribution Worldwide	Occurrence

Order SEMIONOTIFORMES	Family SEMIONOTIDAE	Informal name Neopterygian

DAPEDIUM

This deep-bodied fish was oval in outline and laterally compressed. Its body had larger dorsal, anal, and pelvic fins than *Gyrodus*, and a fan-shaped tail. The skull bones are distinctively ornamented with round projections, and the eyes were surrounded by a ring of plates. At the front of the mouth are nipping, upright teeth, which give way to a pavement of circular crushing teeth at the back.

• HABITAT Fishes of this genus probably fed on a variety of invertebrates, such as crustaceans, in warm, shallow seas.

DAPEDIUM POLITUM
Agassiz; Lower Lias;
Early Jurassic; UK.

skull roof

eye socket

deep, rectangular body scales

PARTIAL
SKULL

cheek region

operculum over gills

Typical length 40cm (16in)

Range L. Triassic–Jurassic	Distribution Europe, Asia	Occurrence

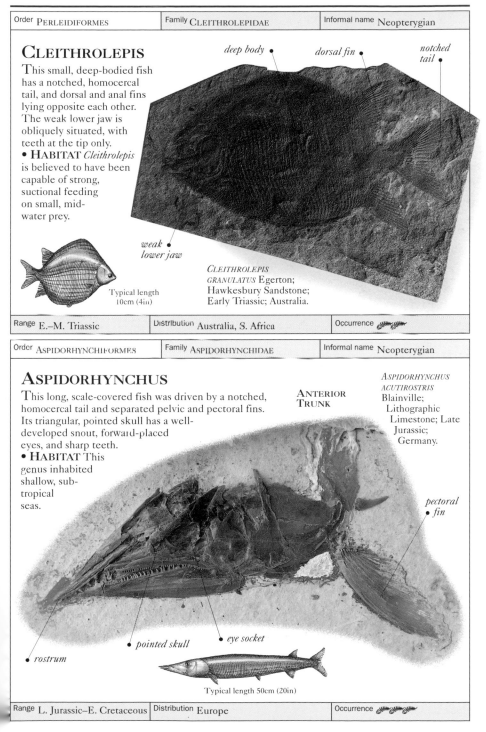

| Order PERLEIDIFORMES | Family CLEITHROLEPIDAE | Informal name Neopterygian |

CLEITHROLEPIS

This small, deep-bodied fish has a notched, homocercal tail, and dorsal and anal fins lying opposite each other. The weak lower jaw is obliquely situated, with teeth at the tip only.
• HABITAT *Cleithrolepis* is believed to have been capable of strong, suctional feeding on small, mid-water prey.

deep body • dorsal fin • notched tail •

weak • lower jaw

CLEITHROLEPIS GRANULATUS Egerton; Hawkesbury Sandstone; Early Triassic; Australia.

Typical length 10cm (4in)

| Range E.–M. Triassic | Distribution Australia, S. Africa | Occurrence |

| Order ASPIDORHYNCHIFORMES | Family ASPIDORHYNCHIDAE | Informal name Neopterygian |

ASPIDORHYNCHUS

This long, scale-covered fish was driven by a notched, homocercal tail and separated pelvic and pectoral fins. Its triangular, pointed skull has a well-developed snout, forward-placed eyes, and sharp teeth.
• HABITAT This genus inhabited shallow, sub-tropical seas.

ANTERIOR TRUNK

ASPIDORHYNCHUS ACUTIROSTRIS Blainville; Lithographic Limestone; Late Jurassic; Germany.

pectoral • fin

• rostrum

• pointed skull   • eye socket

Typical length 50cm (20in)

| Range L. Jurassic–E. Cretaceous | Distribution Europe | Occurrence |

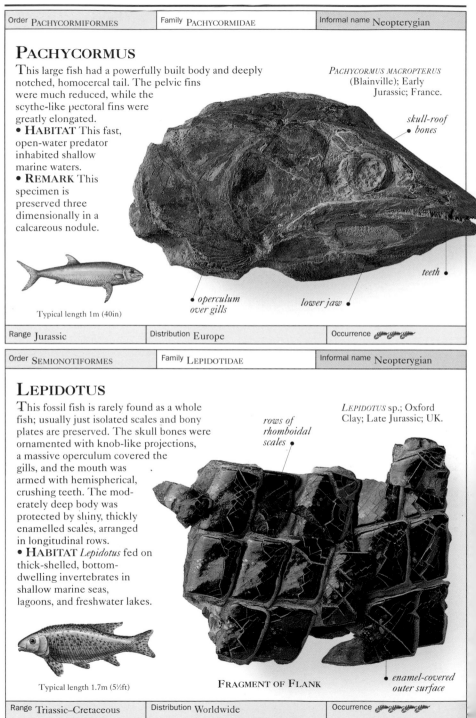

Order PACHYCORMIFORMES	Family PACHYCORMIDAE	Informal name Neopterygian

PACHYCORMUS

This large fish had a powerfully built body and deeply notched, homocercal tail. The pelvic fins were much reduced, while the scythe-like pectoral fins were greatly elongated.

PACHYCORMUS MACROPTERUS (Blainville); Early Jurassic; France.

- **HABITAT** This fast, open-water predator inhabited shallow marine waters.
- **REMARK** This specimen is preserved three dimensionally in a calcareous nodule.

skull-roof bones

teeth

Typical length 1m (40in)

operculum over gills

lower jaw

Range Jurassic	Distribution Europe	Occurrence

Order SEMIONOTIFORMES	Family LEPIDOTIDAE	Informal name Neopterygian

LEPIDOTUS

This fossil fish is rarely found as a whole fish; usually just isolated scales and bony plates are preserved. The skull bones were ornamented with knob-like projections, a massive operculum covered the gills, and the mouth was armed with hemispherical, crushing teeth. The moderately deep body was protected by shiny, thickly enamelled scales, arranged in longitudinal rows.

rows of rhomboidal scales

LEPIDOTUS sp.; Oxford Clay; Late Jurassic; UK.

- **HABITAT** *Lepidotus* fed on thick-shelled, bottom-dwelling invertebrates in shallow marine seas, lagoons, and freshwater lakes.

Typical length 1.7m (5½ft)

FRAGMENT OF FLANK

enamel-covered outer surface

Range Triassic–Cretaceous	Distribution Worldwide	Occurrence

Order ELOPIFORMES	Family PHYLLODONTIDAE	Informal name Elopiform

PHYLLODUS

This fish is known primarily from its convex tooth plates. The oval central teeth are the largest, and are organized into a rough, longitudinal row, in the middle. These are flanked by long, slightly smaller crowns, giving way at the sides to almost con-centric rows of smaller, near-circular teeth, and occasional ovoid teeth.

• HABITAT *Phyllodus* probably fed on thick-shelled, bottom-dwelling marine invertebrates, such as molluscs. As the fossil fish is also found in lagoonal and brackish deposits, it is believed that it may have been able to tolerate salinity.

• REMARK The affinities of the genus to other genera are uncertain.

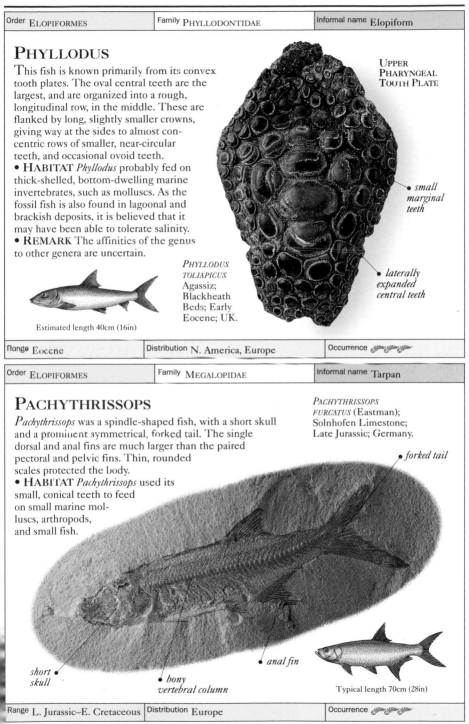

UPPER
PHARYNGEAL
TOOTH PLATE

• *small marginal teeth*

• *laterally expanded central teeth*

PHYLLODUS TOLIAPICUS Agassiz; Blackheath Beds; Early Eocene; UK.

Estimated length 40cm (16in)

Range Eocene	Distribution N. America, Europe	Occurrence

Order ELOPIFORMES	Family MEGALOPIDAE	Informal name Tarpan

PACHYTHRISSOPS

Pachythrissops was a spindle-shaped fish, with a short skull and a prominent symmetrical, forked tail. The single dorsal and anal fins are much larger than the paired pectoral and pelvic fins. Thin, rounded scales protected the body.

• HABITAT *Pachythrissops* used its small, conical teeth to feed on small marine mol-luscs, arthropods, and small fish.

PACHYTHRISSOPS FURCATUS (Eastman); Solnhofen Limestone; Late Jurassic; Germany.

• *forked tail*

short skull •

• *bony vertebral column*

• *anal fin*

Typical length 70cm (28in)

Range L. Jurassic–E. Cretaceous	Distribution Europe	Occurrence

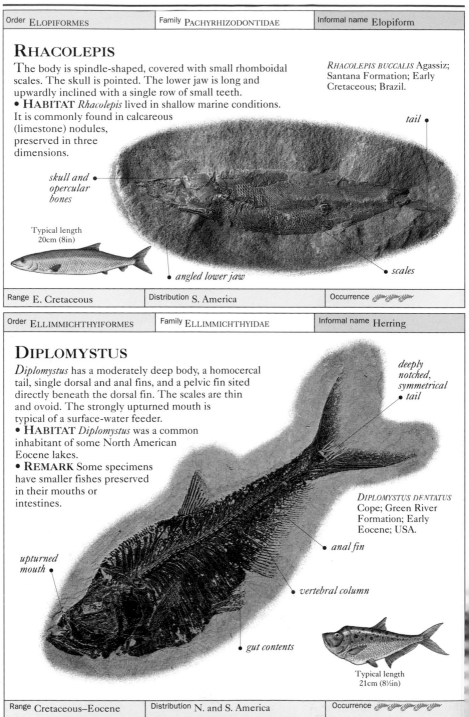

Order ELOPIFORMES	Family PACHYRHIZODONTIDAE	Informal name Elopiform

RHACOLEPIS

The body is spindle-shaped, covered with small rhomboidal scales. The skull is pointed. The lower jaw is long and upwardly inclined with a single row of small teeth.
• HABITAT *Rhacolepis* lived in shallow marine conditions. It is commonly found in calcareous (limestone) nodules, preserved in three dimensions.

RHACOLEPIS BUCCALIS Agassiz; Santana Formation; Early Cretaceous; Brazil.

tail •

skull and • opercular bones

Typical length 20cm (8in)

• *angled lower jaw*

• *scales*

Range E. Cretaceous	Distribution S. America	Occurrence

Order ELLIMMICHTHYIFORMES	Family ELLIMMICHTHYIDAE	Informal name Herring

DIPLOMYSTUS

Diplomystus has a moderately deep body, a homocercal tail, single dorsal and anal fins, and a pelvic fin sited directly beneath the dorsal fin. The scales are thin and ovoid. The strongly upturned mouth is typical of a surface-water feeder.
• HABITAT *Diplomystus* was a common inhabitant of some North American Eocene lakes.
• REMARK Some specimens have smaller fishes preserved in their mouths or intestines.

deeply notched, symmetrical • *tail*

DIPLOMYSTUS DENTATUS Cope; Green River Formation; Early Eocene; USA.

• *anal fin*

upturned mouth •

• *vertebral column*

• *gut contents*

Typical length 21cm (8½in)

Range Cretaceous–Eocene	Distribution N. and S. America	Occurrence

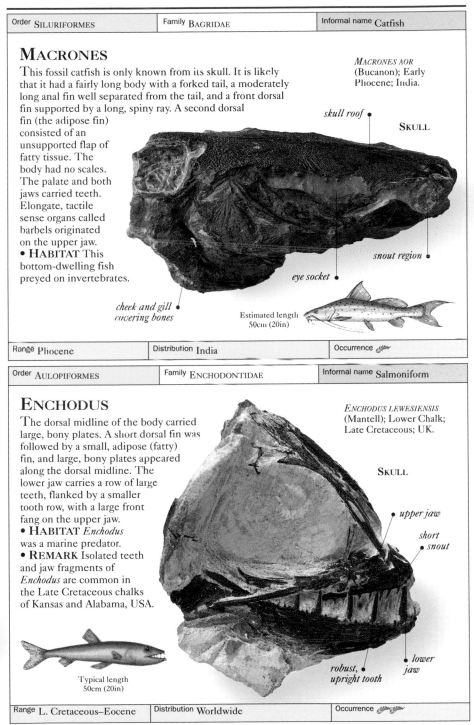

Order SILURIFORMES	Family BAGRIDAE	Informal name Catfish

MACRONES

This fossil catfish is only known from its skull. It is likely that it had a fairly long body with a forked tail, a moderately long anal fin well separated from the tail, and a front dorsal fin supported by a long, spiny ray. A second dorsal fin (the adipose fin) consisted of an unsupported flap of fatty tissue. The body had no scales. The palate and both jaws carried teeth. Elongate, tactile sense organs called barbels originated on the upper jaw.
• **HABITAT** This bottom-dwelling fish preyed on invertebrates.

MACRONES AOR
(Bucanon); Early Pliocene; India.

skull roof •

SKULL

snout region •

eye socket •

cheek and gill covering bones •

Estimated length 50cm (20in)

Range Pliocene	Distribution India	Occurrence

Order AULOPIFORMES	Family ENCHODONTIDAE	Informal name Salmoniform

ENCHODUS

The dorsal midline of the body carried large, bony plates. A short dorsal fin was followed by a small, adipose (fatty) fin, and large, bony plates appeared along the dorsal midline. The lower jaw carries a row of large teeth, flanked by a smaller tooth row, with a large front fang on the upper jaw.
• **HABITAT** *Enchodus* was a marine predator.
• **REMARK** Isolated teeth and jaw fragments of *Enchodus* are common in the Late Cretaceous chalks of Kansas and Alabama, USA.

ENCHODUS LEWESIENSIS
(Mantell); Lower Chalk; Late Cretaceous; UK.

SKULL

• upper jaw

short
• snout

• lower
jaw

robust, •
upright tooth

Typical length 50cm (20in)

Range L. Cretaceous–Eocene	Distribution Worldwide	Occurrence

Order CYPRINIFORMES	Family CYPRINIDAE	Informal name Dace

LEUCISCUS

This dace has a small, but extended, body, small fins, relatively large scales and a forked tail. It is a specialized herbivore with toothless jaws. The front vertebrae and ribs (known as the Weberian ossicles) are movable and, by transmitting vibrations from the swim bladder to the inner ear, improve sensitivity to high frequency sound. When injured, modern species of *Leuciscus* release a chemical from epidermal alarm cells, eliciting a fright reaction in related fish, causing them to scatter and swim to the bottom.

• HABITAT *Leuciscus* inhabits freshwater streams and lakes.

• REMARK This specimen shows a mass mortality, with subsequent irregular alignment of the bodies by the action of currents.

LEUCISCUS PACHECOI
Gomez; Miocene;
Spain.

small but extended body

forked tail

head

fine-grained freshwater marl

fine vertebral column

Typical length
9cm (3½in)

Range Oligocene–Recent	Distribution N. America, Asia, Africa	Occurrence

Order BERYCIFORMES	Family BERYCIDAE	Informal name Alfonsino

CENTROBERYX

Some fossil fish, like this one, may be identified by their otoliths, which are concentrically laminated, aragonitic structures located in the inner ear. Otoliths are embedded in ciliated sense organs. They detect changes in body position. Of the three pairs, the sacculith (shown) is the largest.
• HABITAT *Centroberyx* lived in shoals in moderately deep oceans.

• *dorsal rim*

• *sulcus*

OTOLITH

Typical length
60cm (24in)

*CENTROBERYX
EOCENICUS*
(Frost); London
Clay; Early
Eocene; UK.

• *typical orange colour*

Range L. Cretaceous–Oligocene	Distribution Worldwide	Occurrence

Order BERYCIFORMES	Family TRACHICHTHYIDAE	Informal name Slimehead

HOPLOPTERYX

Hoplopteryx has a dorsal fin supported by nine unjointed, bony fin rays, a deeply forked, homocercal tail, a moderately developed anal fin, and a pelvic fin located well forward. The snout is quite short, the eyes fairly large, and both jaws of the upturned mouth hold small teeth.
• HABITAT This was a marine fish, living in shallow chalk seas.

*HOPLOPTERYX
LEWESIENSIS*
(Mantell); Lower
Chalk; Late
Cretaceous; UK.

• *fin rays*

• *vertebral column*

eye socket •

bones
covering gills

small
pectoral fin

Typical length 27cm (10½in)

Range L. Cretaceous	Distribution Northern hemisphere	Occurrence

Order PERCIFORMES	Family POMACENTRIDAE	Informal name Perch

PRISCACARA

This fossil perch has a deep, oval body protected by dorsal and anal spines, and a fan-shaped tail. It has a slightly upturned, protruding lower jaw. The two jaws, as well as the enlarged bones in the mouth, are covered with fine teeth.
• HABITAT *Priscacara* lived in freshwater streams and lakes, feeding on snails and crustaceans.

PRISCACARA LIOPS
Cope; Green River Formation; Middle Eocene; USA.

stout dorsal • spines

• vertebrae

• eye socket

unforked tail fin •

• lower jaw

Typical length
15cm (6in)

Range Eocene	Distribution N. America	Occurrence

Order PERCIFORMES	Family SCOMBRIDAE	Informal name Mackerel

WETHERELLUS

Although known from the cranial skeleton only, this marine perch is thought to have been around 25cm (10in) long. Its moderately large eye, containing sclerotic plates, is centrally placed in the shallow skull. The jaws are armed with a row of upright, pointed teeth, flanked by a smaller, marginal series.
• HABITAT *Wetherellus* lived in moderately deep oceans.
• REMARK This skull is preserved in a phosphatic nodule.

WETHERELLUS CRISTATUS Casier; London Clay; Early Eocene; UK.

eye socket •

• sclerotic ring

upper • jaw

• operculum over gill

gaping • lower jaw

Estimated length
25cm (10in)

Range E. Eocene	Distribution Europe	Occurrence

AMPHIBIANS

A MPHIBIANS WERE THE first vertebrates to colonize the land, over 400 million years ago. Although they were able to live on land, their eggs were laid in water, hence they were only semi-terrestrial. From the Late Carboniferous period onwards the evolution of fossil amphibians followed two major pathways. One led to modern groups – frogs, salamanders, and caecilians. The second pathway gave rise to reptiles, which developed a waterproof egg, allowing them to breed on land and so become completely terrestrial, unlike today's semi-terrestrial amphibians.

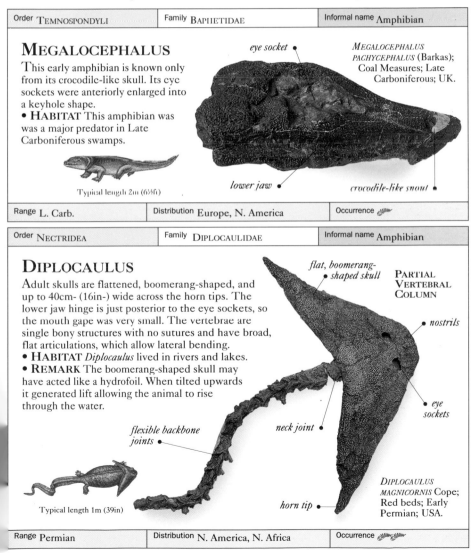

| Order TEMNOSPONDYLI | Family BAPHETIDAE | Informal name Amphibian |

MEGALOCEPHALUS

This early amphibian is known only from its crocodile-like skull. Its eye sockets were anteriorly enlarged into a keyhole shape.
• HABITAT This amphibian was was a major predator in Late Carboniferous swamps.

Typical length 2m (6½ft)

eye socket •
lower jaw •
crocodile-like snout •

MEGALOCEPHALUS PACHYCEPHALUS (Barkas); Coal Measures; Late Carboniferous; UK.

| Range L. Carb. | Distribution Europe, N. America | Occurrence |

| Order NECTRIDEA | Family DIPLOCAULIDAE | Informal name Amphibian |

DIPLOCAULUS

Adult skulls are flattened, boomerang-shaped, and up to 40cm- (16in-) wide across the horn tips. The lower jaw hinge is just posterior to the eye sockets, so the mouth gape was very small. The vertebrae are single bony structures with no sutures and have broad, flat articulations, which allow broad lateral bending.
• HABITAT Diplocaulus lived in rivers and lakes.
• REMARK The boomerang-shaped skull may have acted like a hydrofoil. When tilted upwards it generated lift allowing the animal to rise through the water.

flexible backbone joints •
Typical length 1m (39in)

flat, boomerang-shaped skull
PARTIAL VERTEBRAL COLUMN

• nostrils
neck joint •
• eye sockets
horn tip •

DIPLOCAULUS MAGNICORNIS Cope; Red beds; Early Permian; USA.

| Range Permian | Distribution N. America, N. Africa | Occurrence |

Order TEMNOSPONDYLI	Family BRANCHIOSAURIDAE	Informal name Amphibian

APATEON

This small, neotenous amphibian resembles a salamander. Its skull usually measures between 8 and 24mm (⁵⁄₁₆–1in) in length. The posterior region of the skull behind the eyes is very short. There were three pairs of long, feathery external gills. The ribs were very reduced and the bones of the wrists and ankles are unossified. The hand had four fingers. The tail bore a long, deep fin.
• HABITAT *Apateon* was a totally aquatic amphibian, inhabiting semi-permanent lakes and ponds.
• REMARK Fluctuations in seasonal conditions caused mass deaths of thousands of individuals. These are now preserved in fine-grained, freshwater limestones.

APATEON PEDESTRIS
Meyer; Freshwater limestone; Early Permian; Germany.

• *short skull*

• *feathery external gills*

• *body outline*

• *tail fin*

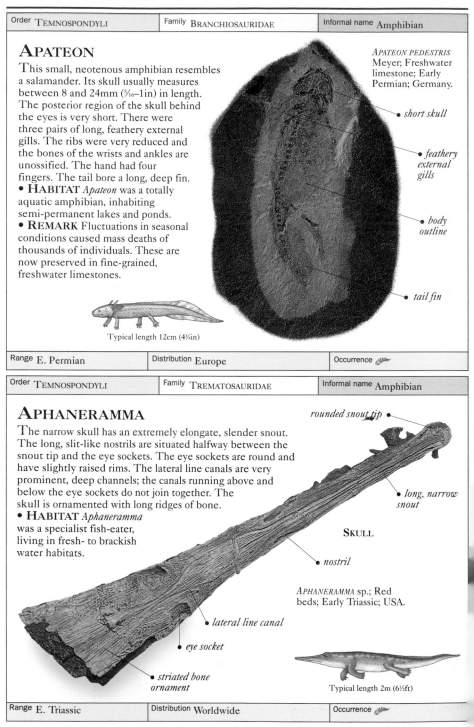

Typical length 12cm (4¾in)

Range E. Permian	Distribution Europe	Occurrence

Order TEMNOSPONDYLI	Family TREMATOSAURIDAE	Informal name Amphibian

APHANERAMMA

The narrow skull has an extremely elongate, slender snout. The long, slit-like nostrils are situated halfway between the snout tip and the eye sockets. The eye sockets are round and have slightly raised rims. The lateral line canals are very prominent, deep channels; the canals running above and below the eye sockets do not join together. The skull is ornamented with long ridges of bone.
• HABITAT *Aphaneramma* was a specialist fish-eater, living in fresh- to brackish water habitats.

rounded snout tip •

• *long, narrow snout*

SKULL

• *nostril*

APHANERAMMA sp.; Red beds; Early Triassic; USA.

• *lateral line canal*

• *eye socket*

• *striated bone ornament*

Typical length 2m (6½ft)

Range E. Triassic	Distribution Worldwide	Occurrence

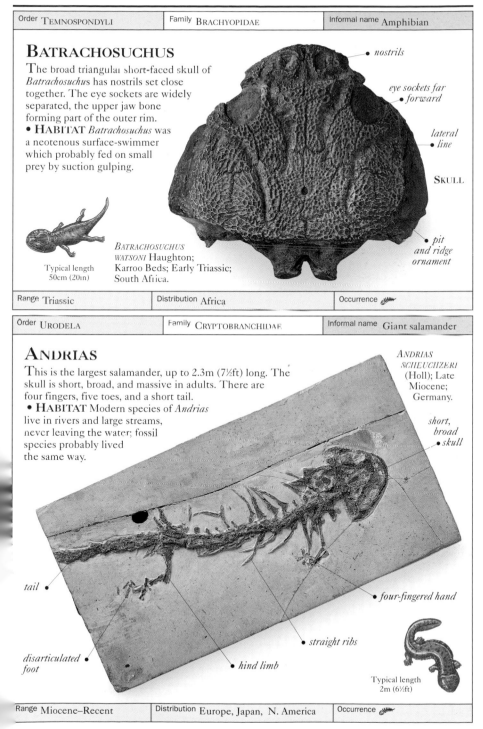

Order TEMNOSPONDYLI	Family BRACHYOPIDAE	Informal name Amphibian

BATRACHOSUCHUS

The broad triangular short-faced skull of *Batrachosuchus* has nostrils set close together. The eye sockets are widely separated, the upper jaw bone forming part of the outer rim.
• HABITAT *Batrachosuchus* was a neotenous surface-swimmer which probably fed on small prey by suction gulping.

nostrils

eye sockets far forward

lateral line

SKULL

pit and ridge ornament

Typical length
50cm (20in)

BATRACHOSUCHUS WATSONI Haughton;
Karroo Beds; Early Triassic;
South Africa.

Range Triassic	Distribution Africa	Occurrence

Order URODELA	Family CRYPTOBRANCHIDAE	Informal name Giant salamander

ANDRIAS

This is the largest salamander, up to 2.3m (7½ft) long. The skull is short, broad, and massive in adults. There are four fingers, five toes, and a short tail.
• HABITAT Modern species of *Andrias* live in rivers and large streams, never leaving the water; fossil species probably lived the same way.

ANDRIAS SCHEUCHZERI (Holl); Late Miocene; Germany.

short, broad skull

tail

four-fingered hand

disarticulated foot

hind limb

straight ribs

Typical length
2m (6½ft)

Range Miocene–Recent	Distribution Europe, Japan, N. America	Occurrence

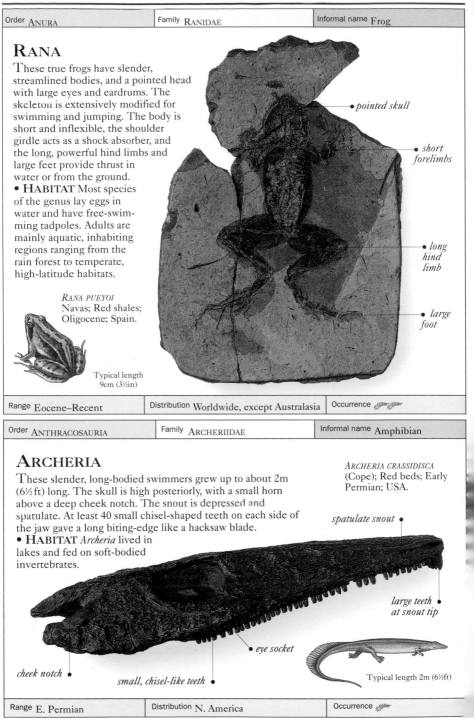

Order ANURA	Family RANIDAE	Informal name Frog

RANA

These true frogs have slender, streamlined bodies, and a pointed head with large eyes and eardrums. The skeleton is extensively modified for swimming and jumping. The body is short and inflexible, the shoulder girdle acts as a shock absorber, and the long, powerful hind limbs and large feet provide thrust in water or from the ground.
• HABITAT Most species of the genus lay eggs in water and have free-swimming tadpoles. Adults are mainly aquatic, inhabiting regions ranging from the rain forest to temperate, high-latitude habitats.

pointed skull

short forelimbs

long hind limb

large foot

RANA PUEYOI
Navas; Red shales; Oligocene; Spain.

Typical length
9cm (3½in)

Range Eocene–Recent	Distribution Worldwide, except Australasia	Occurrence

Order ANTHRACOSAURIA	Family ARCHERIIDAE	Informal name Amphibian

ARCHERIA

These slender, long-bodied swimmers grew up to about 2m (6½ft) long. The skull is high posteriorly, with a small horn above a deep cheek notch. The snout is depressed and spatulate. At least 40 small chisel-shaped teeth on each side of the jaw gave a long biting-edge like a hacksaw blade.
• HABITAT *Archeria* lived in lakes and fed on soft-bodied invertebrates.

ARCHERIA CRASSIDISCA
(Cope); Red beds; Early Permian; USA.

spatulate snout

large teeth at snout tip

eye socket

cheek notch

small, chisel-like teeth

Typical length 2m (6½ft)

Range E. Permian	Distribution N. America	Occurrence

ANAPSID REPTILES

T HE CLASS REPTILIA is divided into three subclasses (the Anapsida, Diapsida, and Synapsida), according to the number of openings in the skull roof and the configuration of the associated skull bones behind the eye sockets. In the Anapsida there are no such openings, indicating they were amongst the first reptiles. The early forms, which first appeared about 300 million years ago, were usually small, lizard-like creatures. However, they are significant because they gave rise to the reptiles that produced birds and mammals, as well as the dinosaurs that ruled the world in the Mesozoic Era. Turtles are traditionally placed within the Anapsida subclass, despite appearing some 30 million years after the other anapsids became extinct.

Order CAPTORHINIDA	Family PROCOLOPHONIDAE	Informal name Procolophonid

PROCOLOPHON

Evolving from the early members of the anapsid line, the lizard-like, triangular-headed procolophonids retained many primitive features in their skeletons. For example, the skull has an obvious "third eye", which is more in keeping with the anapsids' amphibian ancestors, while the jaws and palate have numerous rows of simple teeth. The heavy limbs and relatively massive fore- and hind-limb girdles indicate slow movement and a sprawling gait.
• HABITAT All appear to have been land-living vegetarians.
• REMARK The family first appeared in the Early Triassic, but failed to survive beyond it.

PROCOLOPHON TRIGONICEPS Owen; Karoo Formation; Early Triassic; South Africa.

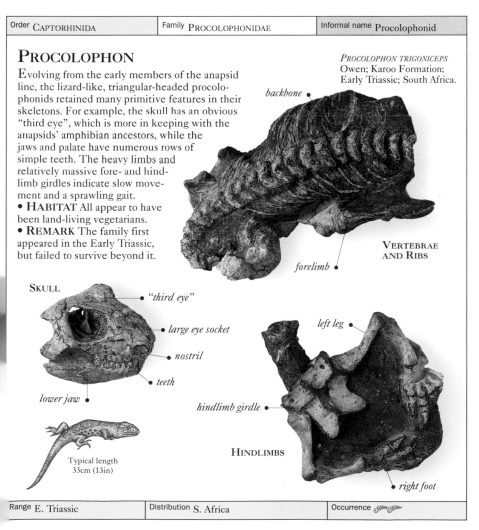

backbone •

VERTEBRAE AND RIBS

forelimb •

SKULL

• "third eye"

• large eye socket

• nostril

• teeth

lower jaw •

left leg •

hindlimb girdle •

HINDLIMBS

Typical length 33cm (13in)

• right foot

Range E. Triassic	Distribution S. Africa	Occurrence

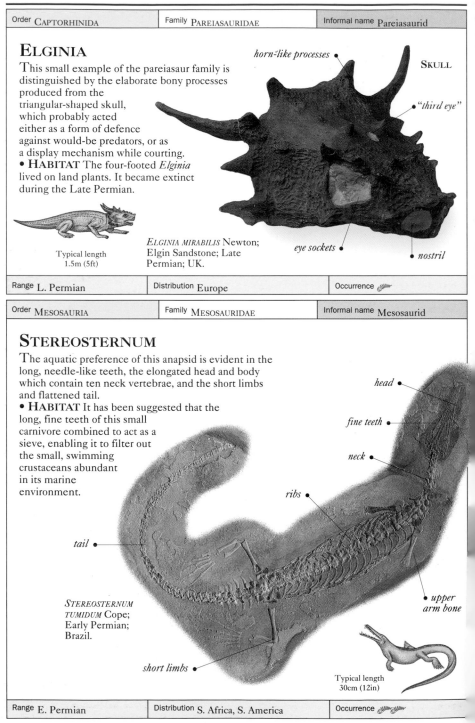

Order CAPTORHINIDA	Family PAREIASAURIDAE	Informal name Pareiasaurid

ELGINIA

This small example of the pareiasaur family is distinguished by the elaborate bony processes produced from the triangular-shaped skull, which probably acted either as a form of defence against would-be predators, or as a display mechanism while courting.

• HABITAT The four-footed *Elginia* lived on land plants. It became extinct during the Late Permian.

Typical length
1.5m (5ft)

horn-like processes

SKULL

"third eye"

eye sockets

nostril

ELGINIA MIRABILIS Newton; Elgin Sandstone; Late Permian; UK.

Range L. Permian	Distribution Europe	Occurrence

Order MESOSAURIA	Family MESOSAURIDAE	Informal name Mesosaurid

STEREOSTERNUM

The aquatic preference of this anapsid is evident in the long, needle-like teeth, the elongated head and body which contain ten neck vertebrae, and the short limbs and flattened tail.

• HABITAT It has been suggested that the long, fine teeth of this small carnivore combined to act as a sieve, enabling it to filter out the small, swimming crustaceans abundant in its marine environment.

head

fine teeth

neck

ribs

tail

upper arm bone

short limbs

STEREOSTERNUM TUMIDUM Cope; Early Permian; Brazil.

Typical length
30cm (12in)

Range E. Permian	Distribution S. Africa, S. America	Occurrence

Order CHELONIA	Family PROGANOCHELYDAE	Informal name Primitive turtle

PROGANOCHELYS

Turtles and tortoises are recognizable by their large eye sockets, toothless jaws with horny coverings forming a beak, and bony shells. *Proganochelys* displays its primitiveness in retaining tooth-like denticles on the palate, as well as nasal bones. It has an extra series of peripheral plates in the carapace.
• HABITAT This semi-aquatic form fed on plants.

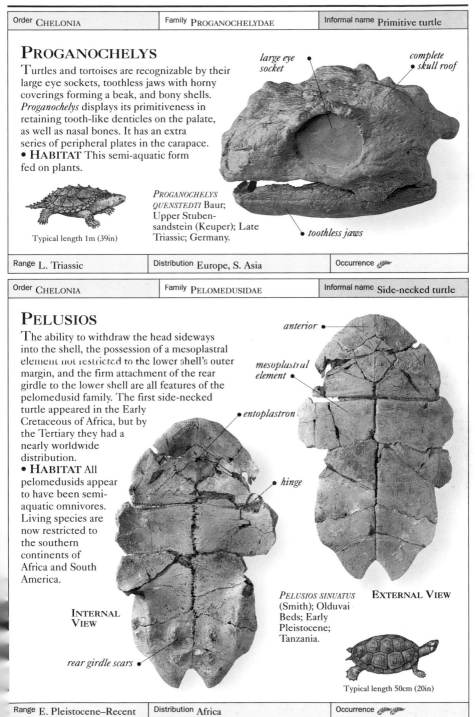

large eye socket

complete skull roof

toothless jaws

PROGANOCHELYS QUENSTEDTI Baur; Upper Stuben-sandstein (Keuper); Late Triassic; Germany.

Typical length 1m (39in)

Range L. Triassic	Distribution Europe, S. Asia	Occurrence

Order CHELONIA	Family PELOMEDUSIDAE	Informal name Side-necked turtle

PELUSIOS

The ability to withdraw the head sideways into the shell, the possession of a mesoplastral element not restricted to the lower shell's outer margin, and the firm attachment of the rear girdle to the lower shell are all features of the pelomedusid family. The first side-necked turtle appeared in the Early Cretaceous of Africa, but by the Tertiary they had a nearly worldwide distribution.
• HABITAT All pelomedusids appear to have been semi-aquatic omnivores. Living species are now restricted to the southern continents of Africa and South America.

anterior

mesoplastral element

entoplastron

hinge

INTERNAL VIEW

rear girdle scars

PELUSIOS SINUATUS (Smith); Olduvai Beds; Early Pleistocene; Tanzania.

EXTERNAL VIEW

Typical length 50cm (20in)

Range E. Pleistocene–Recent	Distribution Africa	Occurrence

| Order CHELONIA | Family MEIOLANIIDAE | Informal name Horned tortoise |

MEIOLANIA

The bizarre head of this tortoise could not be retracted into its shell because of its large size and the bony spikes that adorn the skull roof. The tail was heavily armoured and club-like, an adaptation that probably helped when defending its territory.

• **HABITAT** *Meiolania* belonged to a family of tortoises that were omnivorous and lived on land.

• **REMARK** It is believed that this family may have had its origins in the Late Cretaceous of South America, as a similar genus occurred there at an earlier period.

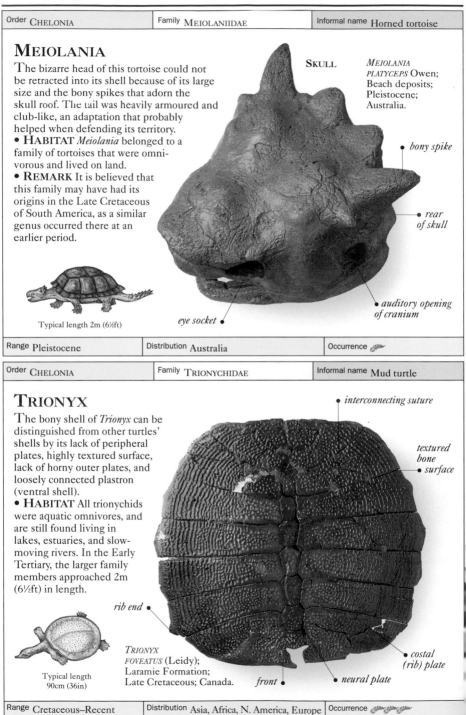

SKULL

MEIOLANIA PLATYCEPS Owen; Beach deposits; Pleistocene; Australia.

• *bony spike*

• *rear of skull*

• *auditory opening of cranium*

eye socket •

Typical length 2m (6½ft)

| Range Pleistocene | Distribution Australia | Occurrence ⟨⟩ |

| Order CHELONIA | Family TRIONYCHIDAE | Informal name Mud turtle |

TRIONYX

The bony shell of *Trionyx* can be distinguished from other turtles' shells by its lack of peripheral plates, highly textured surface, lack of horny outer plates, and loosely connected plastron (ventral shell).

• **HABITAT** All trionychids were aquatic omnivores, and are still found living in lakes, estuaries, and slow-moving rivers. In the Early Tertiary, the larger family members approached 2m (6½ft) in length.

• *interconnecting suture*

textured bone
• *surface*

rib end •

TRIONYX FOVEATUS (Leidy); Laramie Formation; Late Cretaceous; Canada.

front •

• *neural plate*

• *costal (rib) plate*

Typical length 90cm (36in)

| Range Cretaceous–Recent | Distribution Asia, Africa, N. America, Europe | Occurrence ⟨⟩ |

Order CHELONIA	Family CHELONIIDAE	Informal name Marine turtle

PUPPIGERUS

This genus has characteristic adaptations for an aquatic existence: large eye-sockets, with a secondary skull roof behind them, and a fully formed secondary palate. The latter was especially important, for it prevented an unwanted intake of water while feeding below the surface. In adults, the shell is fully ossified, with an outer margin of peripheral plates, while the plastron (ventral shell) comprises four paired elements and one centrally placed, all of which are loosely connected by finger-like projections in the midline. The forelimbs developed into flippers.

• HABITAT *Puppigerus* was a marine turtle, and, like its modern counterparts, fed on sea grasses. Its hindlimbs were less flipper-like, a condition that possibly indicates a greater mobility on land.

• REMARK Like modern sea turtles, females would have buried their eggs on sandy beaches.

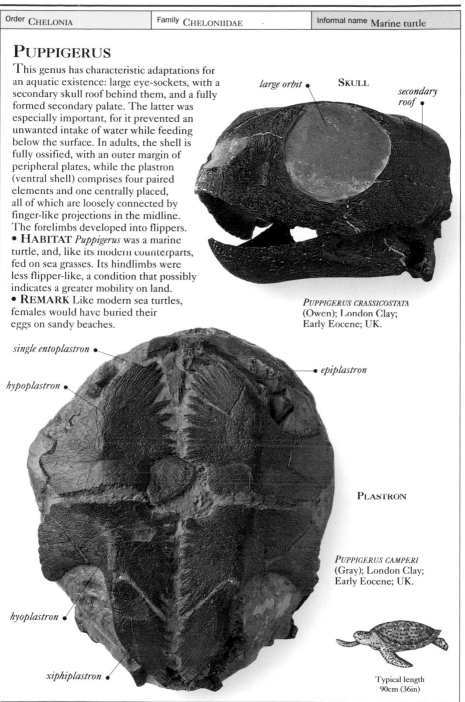

large orbit • SKULL *secondary roof* •

PUPPIGERUS CRASSICOSTATA (Owen); London Clay; Early Eocene; UK.

single entoplastron •

hypoplastron •

• *epiplastron*

PLASTRON

PUPPIGERUS CAMPERI (Gray); London Clay; Early Eocene; UK.

hyoplastron •

xiphiplastron •

Typical length 90cm (36in)

Range Eocene	Distribution Europe	Occurrence

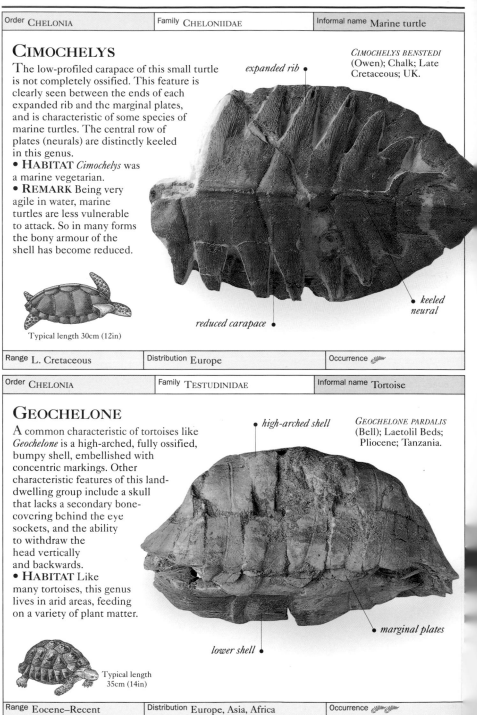

Order CHELONIA	Family CHELONIIDAE	Informal name Marine turtle

CIMOCHELYS

The low-profiled carapace of this small turtle is not completely ossified. This feature is clearly seen between the ends of each expanded rib and the marginal plates, and is characteristic of some species of marine turtles. The central row of plates (neurals) are distinctly keeled in this genus.
• **HABITAT** *Cimochelys* was a marine vegetarian.
• **REMARK** Being very agile in water, marine turtles are less vulnerable to attack. So in many forms the bony armour of the shell has become reduced.

CIMOCHELYS BENSTEDI (Owen); Chalk; Late Cretaceous; UK.

expanded rib •

• keeled neural

• reduced carapace

Typical length 30cm (12in)

Range L. Cretaceous	Distribution Europe	Occurrence

Order CHELONIA	Family TESTUDINIDAE	Informal name Tortoise

GEOCHELONE

A common characteristic of tortoises like *Geochelone* is a high-arched, fully ossified, bumpy shell, embellished with concentric markings. Other characteristic features of this land-dwelling group include a skull that lacks a secondary bone-covering behind the eye sockets, and the ability to withdraw the head vertically and backwards.
• **HABITAT** Like many tortoises, this genus lives in arid areas, feeding on a variety of plant matter.

• high-arched shell

GEOCHELONE PARDALIS (Bell); Laetolil Beds; Pliocene; Tanzania.

• marginal plates

lower shell •

Typical length 35cm (14in)

Range Eocene–Recent	Distribution Europe, Asia, Africa	Occurrence

DIAPSID REPTILES

T HE SECOND MAJOR DIVISION of the reptiles, the Diapsida, evolved during the Carboniferous, shortly after the evolution of the anapsid reptiles from the amphibians. Diapsid reptiles are characterized by the possession of two skull openings behind the eye sockets, but this condition is often obscured by modifications evolved to accommodate the various life styles of different species. Within the Diapsida are all modern forms, except turtles, and the majority of extinct species. The group reached maximum diversity during the Mesozoic Era, when its members – dinosaurs, various marine reptiles, and pterosaurs – ruled land, sea, and air.

Order SPHENODONTA	Family SPHENODONTIDAE	Informal name Sphenodontid

HOMEOSAURUS

A small, lizard-like reptile, *Homeosaurus* resembles the last surviving member of its order – the tuatara of New Zealand – in many details. The group to which it belongs differs from the lizards by having skulls with a rigid articulation bone (quadrate). Also characteristic is the attachment of the few marginal teeth, which are firmly fused to the edge of the jaws. These were not replaced when worn, but were added at the rear as growth continued. Further teeth are present in the palate, and the snout is turned down to produce a chisel-like cutting edge.
• **HABITAT** *Homeosaurus* was probably a land dweller, living on plants and insects.
• **REMARK** First appearing during the Triassic, the order became widespread during the early part of the Mesozoic, before declining to the single species still alive today.

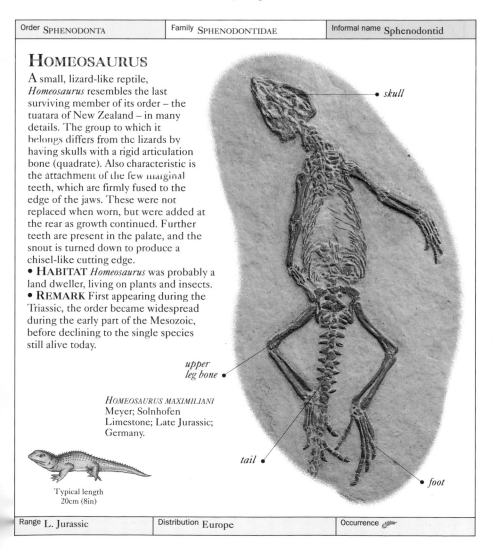

skull

upper leg bone

HOMEOSAURUS MAXIMILIANI Meyer; Solnhofen Limestone; Late Jurassic; Germany.

tail

foot

Typical length 20cm (8in)

Range L. Jurassic	Distribution Europe	Occurrence

Order SQUAMATA	Family KUEHNEOSAURIDAE	Informal name Flying lizard

KUEHNEOSUCHUS

This primitive, gliding, lizard-like diapsid had very long, fixed ribs, giving a "wing-span" of about 30cm (12in). It is thought that these ribs were attached to each other by tissue, thus forming a continuous membrane, which would have acted as a gliding surface, reminiscent of the present-day "flying lizards" such as *Draco*.

• HABITAT *Kuehneosuchus* is thought to have been insectivorous, and lived in open woodland.

three vertebrae

KUEHNEOSUCHUS LATISSIMUS Robinson; Fissure fill; Late Triassic; UK.

long, hollow rib

rib

upper thigh bone

fragments

Typical "wing-span" 30cm (12in)

Range L. Triassic	Distribution Europe	Occurrence

Order SQUAMATA	Family AMPHISBAENIDAE	Informal name Worm lizard

LYSTROMYCTER

This worm-like lizard had a characteristically robust, wedge-shaped skull with simple, peg-like teeth, and with one tooth centrally positioned in the front of the upper jaw. Living species of this family of burrowers have weak eye-sight and legless bodies.

• HABITAT Living species of *Lystromycter* have a preference for burrowing into loose soil, while actively hunting worms and insects.

SIDE VIEW OF SKULL

eye socket

shovel-like snout

LYSTROMYCTER LEAKEYI Charig & Gans; Rusinga Beds; Early Miocene; Kenya.

tooth row

palate

median tooth

UNDERSIDE OF SKULL

Typical length 30cm (12in)

Range E. Miocene	Distribution E. Africa	Occurrence

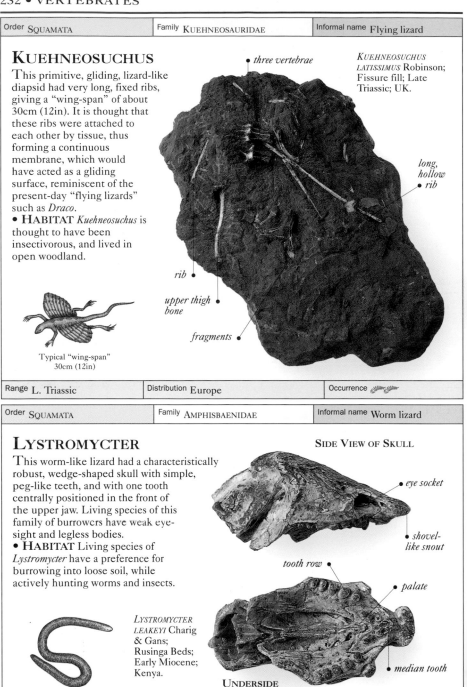

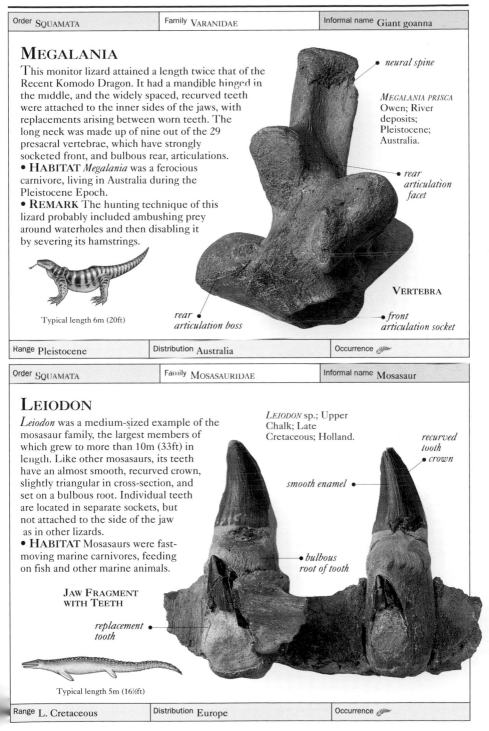

Order SQUAMATA	Family VARANIDAE	Informal name Giant goanna

MEGALANIA

This monitor lizard attained a length twice that of the Recent Komodo Dragon. It had a mandible hinged in the middle, and the widely spaced, recurved teeth were attached to the inner sides of the jaws, with replacements arising between worn teeth. The long neck was made up of nine out of the 29 presacral vertebrae, which have strongly socketed front, and bulbous rear, articulations.
• HABITAT *Megalania* was a ferocious carnivore, living in Australia during the Pleistocene Epoch.
• REMARK The hunting technique of this lizard probably included ambushing prey around waterholes and then disabling it by severing its hamstrings.

neural spine

MEGALANIA PRISCA Owen; River deposits; Pleistocene; Australia.

rear articulation facet

VERTEBRA

Typical length 6m (20ft)

rear articulation boss

front articulation socket

Range Pleistocene	Distribution Australia	Occurrence

Order SQUAMATA	Family MOSASAURIDAE	Informal name Mosasaur

LEIODON

Leiodon was a medium-sized example of the mosasaur family, the largest members of which grew to more than 10m (33ft) in length. Like other mosasaurs, its teeth have an almost smooth, recurved crown, slightly triangular in cross-section, and set on a bulbous root. Individual teeth are located in separate sockets, but not attached to the side of the jaw as in other lizards.
• HABITAT Mosasaurs were fast-moving marine carnivores, feeding on fish and other marine animals.

JAW FRAGMENT WITH TEETH

LEIODON sp.; Upper Chalk; Late Cretaceous; Holland.

recurved tooth
crown

smooth enamel

bulbous root of tooth

replacement tooth

Typical length 5m (16½ft)

Range L. Cretaceous	Distribution Europe	Occurrence

Order SQUAMATA	Family MOSASAURIDAE	Informal name Mosasaur

TYLOSAURUS

The mosasaurs had large, lightly built skulls, armed with recurved teeth set in sockets and a lower jaw hinged in the middle. Their necks were short, with seven vertebrae, while the remainder of their bodies was elongate. Individual vertebrae had socket-and-ball articulations, allowing considerable sideways movement. The limbs were reduced and paddle-like, used for steering not propulsion.

• **HABITAT** The mosasaurs evolved from land forms that later returned to an aquatic environment. The group appears to be related to the varanid lizards living today. They actively hunted an assortment of marine organisms in shallow seas.

• **REMARK** Although a short-lived group, appearing and becoming extinct during the Late Cretaceous, the mosasaurs were the most important and widespread of the marine carnivores living at that time. Their remains have been recovered from around the world.

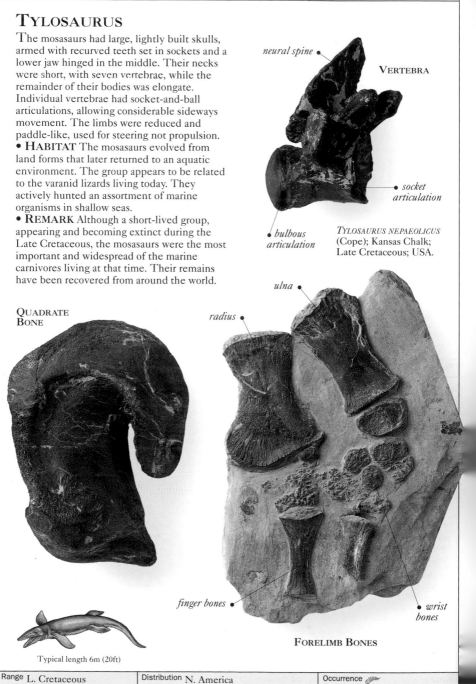

neural spine •

VERTEBRA

• socket articulation

• bulbous articulation

TYLOSAURUS NEPAEOLICUS (Cope); Kansas Chalk; Late Cretaceous; USA.

ulna •

QUADRATE BONE

radius •

finger bones •

• wrist bones

FORELIMB BONES

Typical length 6m (20ft)

Range L. Cretaceous	Distribution N. America	Occurrence

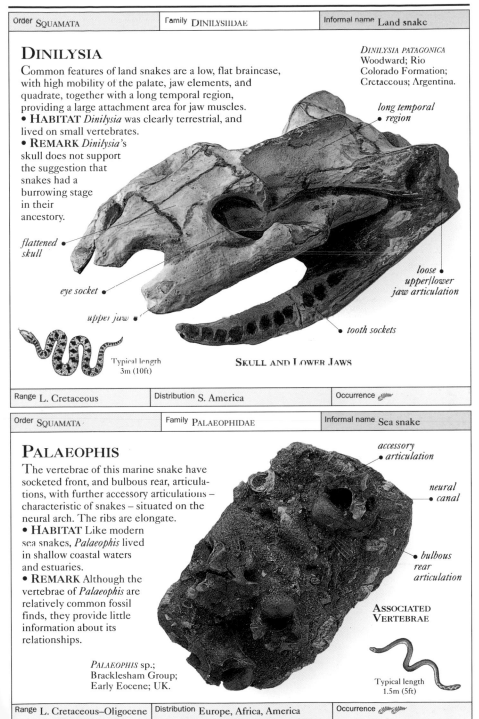

| Order SQUAMATA | Family DINILYSIIDAE | Informal name Land snake |

DINILYSIA

Common features of land snakes are a low, flat braincase, with high mobility of the palate, jaw elements, and quadrate, together with a long temporal region, providing a large attachment area for jaw muscles.
• HABITAT *Dinilysia* was clearly terrestrial, and lived on small vertebrates.
• REMARK *Dinilysia*'s skull does not support the suggestion that snakes had a burrowing stage in their ancestry.

DINILYSIA PATAGONICA Woodward; Rio Colorado Formation; Cretaceous; Argentina.

long temporal region

flattened skull

eye socket

upper jaw

loose upper/lower jaw articulation

tooth sockets

Typical length 3m (10ft)

SKULL AND LOWER JAWS

| Range L. Cretaceous | Distribution S. America | Occurrence |

| Order SQUAMATA | Family PALAEOPHIDAE | Informal name Sea snake |

PALAEOPHIS

The vertebrae of this marine snake have socketed front, and bulbous rear, articulations, with further accessory articulations – characteristic of snakes – situated on the neural arch. The ribs are elongate.
• HABITAT Like modern sea snakes, *Palaeophis* lived in shallow coastal waters and estuaries.
• REMARK Although the vertebrae of *Palaeophis* are relatively common fossil finds, they provide little information about its relationships.

PALAEOPHIS sp.; Bracklesham Group; Early Eocene; UK.

accessory articulation

neural canal

bulbous rear articulation

ASSOCIATED VERTEBRAE

Typical length 1.5m (5ft)

| Range L. Cretaceous–Oligocene | Distribution Europe, Africa, America | Occurrence |

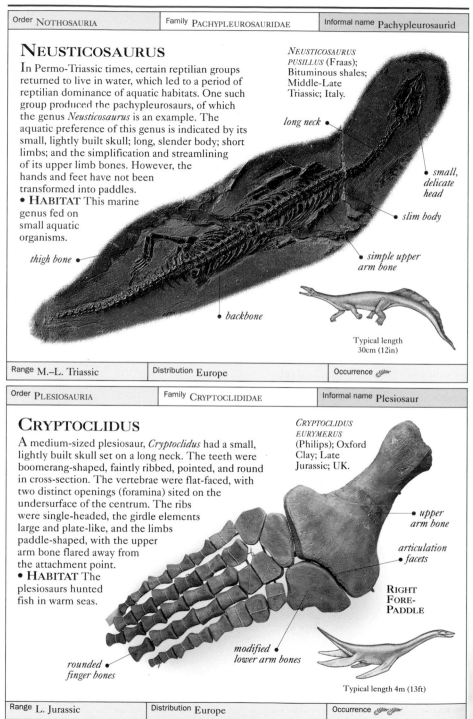

Order NOTHOSAURIA	Family PACHYPLEUROSAURIDAE	Informal name Pachypleurosaurid

NEUSTICOSAURUS

In Permo-Triassic times, certain reptilian groups returned to live in water, which led to a period of reptilian dominance of aquatic habitats. One such group produced the pachypleurosaurs, of which the genus *Neusticosaurus* is an example. The aquatic preference of this genus is indicated by its small, lightly built skull; long, slender body; short limbs; and the simplification and streamlining of its upper limb bones. However, the hands and feet have not been transformed into paddles.

• HABITAT This marine genus fed on small aquatic organisms.

NEUSTICOSAURUS PUSILLUS (Fraas); Bituminous shales; Middle-Late Triassic; Italy.

long neck •

• small, delicate head

• slim body

• simple upper arm bone

thigh bone •

• backbone

Typical length 30cm (12in)

Range M.–L. Triassic	Distribution Europe	Occurrence

Order PLESIOSAURIA	Family CRYPTOCLIDIDAE	Informal name Plesiosaur

CRYPTOCLIDUS

A medium-sized plesiosaur, *Cryptoclidus* had a small, lightly built skull set on a long neck. The teeth were boomerang-shaped, faintly ribbed, pointed, and round in cross-section. The vertebrae were flat-faced, with two distinct openings (foramina) sited on the undersurface of the centrum. The ribs were single-headed, the girdle elements large and plate-like, and the limbs paddle-shaped, with the upper arm bone flared away from the attachment point.

• HABITAT The plesiosaurs hunted fish in warm seas.

CRYPTOCLIDUS EURYMERUS (Philips); Oxford Clay; Late Jurassic; UK.

• upper arm bone

articulation • facets

RIGHT FORE-PADDLE

rounded • finger bones

modified • lower arm bones

Typical length 4m (13ft)

Range L. Jurassic	Distribution Europe	Occurrence

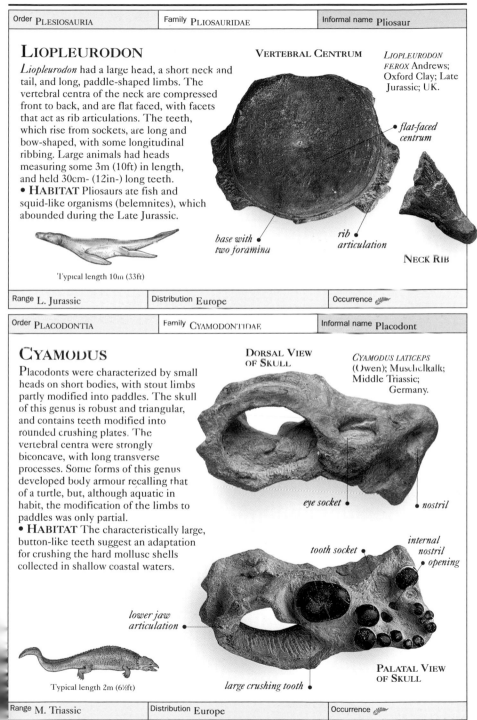

Order PLESIOSAURIA	Family PLIOSAURIDAE	Informal name Pliosaur

LIOPLEURODON

Liopleurodon had a large head, a short neck and tail, and long, paddle-shaped limbs. The vertebral centra of the neck are compressed front to back, and are flat faced, with facets that act as rib articulations. The teeth, which rise from sockets, are long and bow-shaped, with some longitudinal ribbing. Large animals had heads measuring some 3m (10ft) in length, and held 30cm- (12in-) long teeth.
• HABITAT Pliosaurs ate fish and squid-like organisms (belemnites), which abounded during the Late Jurassic.

VERTEBRAL CENTRUM

LIOPLEURODON FEROX Andrews; Oxford Clay; Late Jurassic; UK.

• *flat-faced centrum*

base with • two foramina

rib • articulation

NECK RIB

Typical length 10m (33ft)

Range L. Jurassic	Distribution Europe	Occurrence

Order PLACODONTIA	Family CYAMODONTIDAE	Informal name Placodont

CYAMODUS

Placodonts were characterized by small heads on short bodies, with stout limbs partly modified into paddles. The skull of this genus is robust and triangular, and contains teeth modified into rounded crushing plates. The vertebral centra were strongly biconcave, with long transverse processes. Some forms of this genus developed body armour recalling that of a turtle, but, although aquatic in habit, the modification of the limbs to paddles was only partial.
• HABITAT The characteristically large, button-like teeth suggest an adaptation for crushing the hard mollusc shells collected in shallow coastal waters.

DORSAL VIEW OF SKULL

CYAMODUS LATICEPS (Owen); Muschelkalk; Middle Triassic; Germany.

eye socket •   *• nostril*

internal nostril • opening

tooth socket •

lower jaw articulation •

PALATAL VIEW OF SKULL

Typical length 2m (6½ft)

large crushing tooth •

Range M. Triassic	Distribution Europe	Occurrence

Order ICHTHYOPTERYGIA	Family MIXOSAURIDAE	Informal name Ichthyosaur

MIXOSAURUS

The body of *Mixosaurus* is stream-lined and dolphin-like, with a tail that kinks downwards. The long-snouted skull is filled with teeth set in sockets, while the limbs are paddle-shaped, with disc-like finger elements.
• HABITAT Ichthyosaurs were adapted to a marine existence, and even gave birth to live young at sea. They were fast-swimming, fish-eating carnivores.

tail

paddle-like forelimb

MIXOSAURUS sp.; Bituminous Shales; Middle Triassic; Switzerland.

nostril

long, multi-toothed snout

round cranium with large eye

Typical length 1m (39in)

Range M. Triassic	Distribution Europe, E. Indies, USA, Asia	Occurrence

Order ICHTHYOPTERYGIA	Family ICHTHYOSAURIDAE	Informal name Ichthyosaur

ICHTHYOSAURUS

Typical ichthyosaur features are: numerous teeth set in a groove within the long jaws; each eye held in a ring of bony plates; the reduction of the pelvic girdle components and associated paddle; a tail kinked downwards to support a lower tail lobe; and subdivided finger rows.
• HABITAT The ring of strengthening bones around an ichthyosaur's eye indicates it was capable of diving to considerable depths in pursuit of fish.

ICHTHYOSAURUS COMMUNIS Conybeare; Lower Lias; Early Jurassic; UK.

SKULL

jaws

teeth

nostril

ring of bony plates

Typical length 2m (6½ft)

Range E. Jurassic	Distribution Europe, Greenland	Occurrence

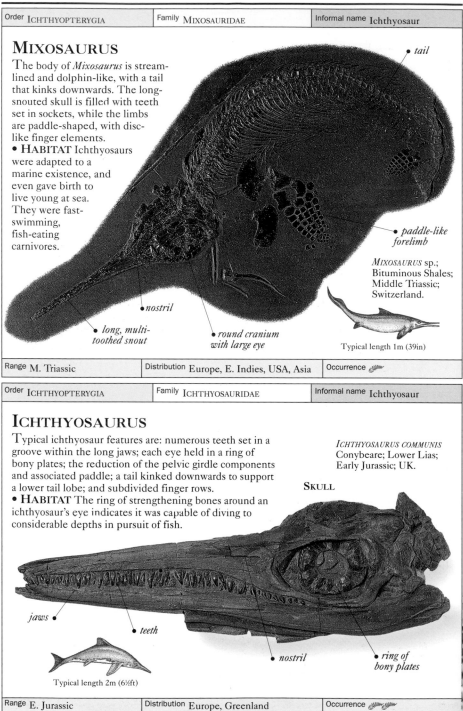

Order ICHTHYOPTERYGIA	Family LEPTOPTERYGIIDAE	Informal name Ichthyosaur

PLATYPTERYGIUS

Platypterygius had a heavy beaked, multi-toothed head, and paddle-like forelimbs with eight to nine digital rows. As in all ichthyosaurs, the vertebral centra are short and biconcave, with no fusion of the neural arch, which has no transverse processes. The double-headed rib articulates via two indistinct bosses on the centrum.
• **HABITAT** *Platypterygius* was a marine reptile, living on fish.

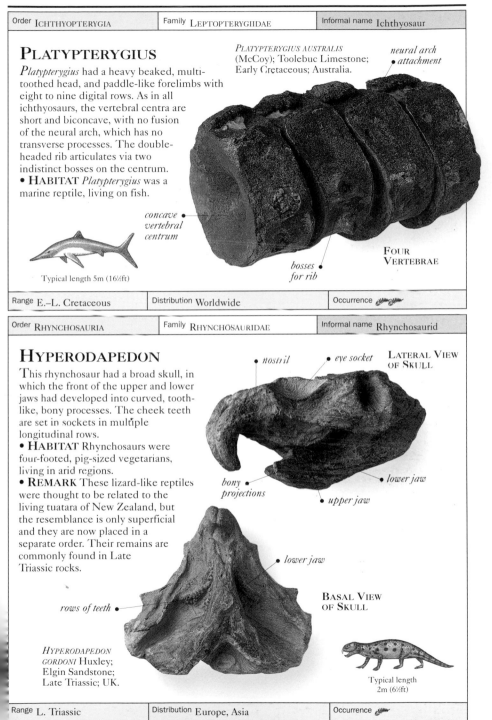

PLATYPTERYGIUS AUSTRALIS (McCoy); Toolebuc Limestone; Early Cretaceous; Australia.

neural arch attachment

concave vertebral centrum

bosses for rib

FOUR VERTEBRAE

Typical length 5m (16½ft)

Range E.–L. Cretaceous	Distribution Worldwide	Occurrence

Order RHYNCHOSAURIA	Family RHYNCHOSAURIDAE	Informal name Rhynchosaurid

HYPERODAPEDON

This rhynchosaur had a broad skull, in which the front of the upper and lower jaws had developed into curved, tooth-like, bony processes. The cheek teeth are set in sockets in multiple longitudinal rows.
• **HABITAT** Rhynchosaurs were four-footed, pig-sized vegetarians, living in arid regions.
• **REMARK** These lizard-like reptiles were thought to be related to the living tuatara of New Zealand, but the resemblance is only superficial and they are now placed in a separate order. Their remains are commonly found in Late Triassic rocks.

nostril

eye socket

LATERAL VIEW OF SKULL

bony projections

lower jaw

upper jaw

lower jaw

BASAL VIEW OF SKULL

rows of teeth

HYPERODAPEDON GORDONI Huxley; Elgin Sandstone; Late Triassic; UK.

Typical length 2m (6½ft)

Range L. Triassic	Distribution Europe, Asia	Occurrence

Order THECODONTIA	Family ORNITHOSUCHIDAE	Informal name Ornithosuchid

RIOJASUCHUS

The head of *Riojasuchus* is large, but lightly built, with the upper jaw curved down over the lower. There is a skull opening just before the eye socket, and the teeth are large, blade-like, compressed sideways, and recurved. The hip joint is only partly open, and the head of the thigh bone only slightly turned in. There are three pairs of sacral ribs.
• **HABITAT** All ornithosuchids were land-dwellers, mainly four-footed, and living on a flesh diet.
• **REMARK** This family is a member of the great archosaur assemblage, which includes dinosaurs, pterosaurs, and crocodiles.

RIOJASUCHUS TENUISCEPS
Bonaparte; Los Colorados Formation; Late Triassic; Argentina.

downcurved upper jaw •

• *anterior orbital opening*

• *eye socket*

Typical length 3m (10ft)

Range L. Triassic	Distribution S. America	Occurrence

Order THECODONTIA	Family PHYTOSAURIDAE	Informal name Phytosaurid

BELODON

Outwardly, the body of this phytosaur resembled that of our modern, long-snouted crocodiles, having short legs, an ornate sculptured surface to the skull, and considerable body armour. In detail, however, the ankle joint and the plate-like elements of the hindlimb girdle indicate a more primitive condition, and thus a more awkward gait. The nostrils being situated on top of the head just forward of the eye sockets, rather than at the tip of the snout as in crocodiles, provides an instant identification

BELODON PLIENINGERI
Meyer; Keuper Sandstone; Late Triassic; Germany.

nostril • *openings*

• *eye socket*

• *long, hooked snout*

tooth row •

jaw articulation •

feature. These nostril openings are also elevated above the other skull bones, so that they could protrude above the water when the remainder of the body was submerged.
• **HABITAT** The long snout suggests a fish-eater, but preserved stomach contents show *Belodon* fed upon a variety of reptiles.

Typical length 3m (10ft)

Range L. Triassic	Distribution Europe	Occurrence

| Order CROCODYLIA | Family METRIORHYNCHIDAE | Informal name Marine crocodile |

METRIORHYNCHUS

The metriorhynchid family is the most specialized of all known crocodiles, and is perhaps the only archosaur group to become fully aquatic. Changes in its original habit are clearly reflected in its skeleton, for the forelimbs were transformed into paddles, the neck was shortened, the tail bent downwards at the end to support a large caudal fin, and the body armour lost. In contrast to their more terrestrial crocodilian cousins, the skull is long and lightly built – this was another require-ment for a fully aquatic mode of life.
• **HABITAT** Species of *Metriorhynchus* were particularly common in the Jurassic seas of Europe, where they hunted for fish and squid-like animals which shared the same habitat. It may be that they only came to land to lay their eggs, in the manner of modern turtles. It is also possible that they hauled themselves on to sand banks to bask after hunting for fish.
• **REMARK** The metriorhynchids belong to the primitive mesosuchian suborder of crocodiles, which appeared in the Triassic but finally became extinct in the earliest part of the Tertiary, some 60 million years ago.

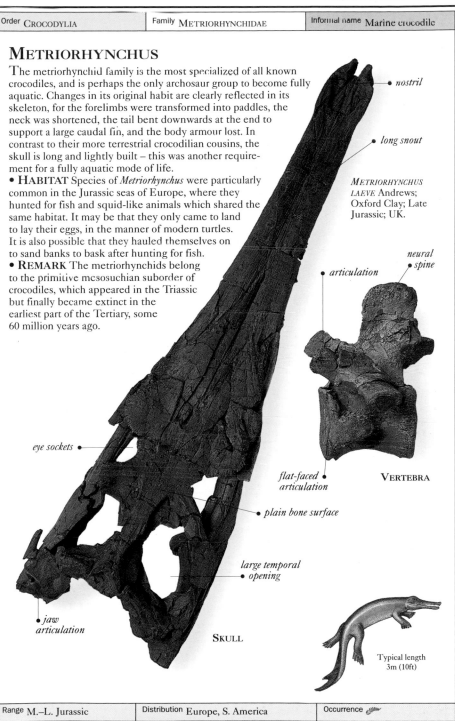

nostril

long snout

METRIORHYNCHUS LAEVE Andrews; Oxford Clay; Late Jurassic; UK.

neural spine

articulation

eye sockets

flat-faced articulation

VERTEBRA

plain bone surface

large temporal opening

jaw articulation

SKULL

Typical length 3m (10ft)

| Range M.–L. Jurassic | Distribution Europe, S. America | Occurrence |

Order CROCODYLIA	Family GONIOPHOLIDIDAE	Informal name Crocodile

GONIOPHOLIS

Goniopholids had strongly built, low-profiled skulls, with ornamented bone surfaces and patterned body armour, thus differing from the metriorhynchids. Like their marine cousins, however, they had nearly flat-faced centra to their vertebrae, which contrasts with the socket-and- ball development found in the more modern forms.
• HABITAT Like most unspecialized crocodiles, *Goniopholis* lived a semi-aquatic existence, feeding upon a mixture of animal and plant matter.

DORSAL ARMOUR

GONIOPHOLIS CRASSIDENS Owen; Wealden Beds; Early Cretaceous; UK.

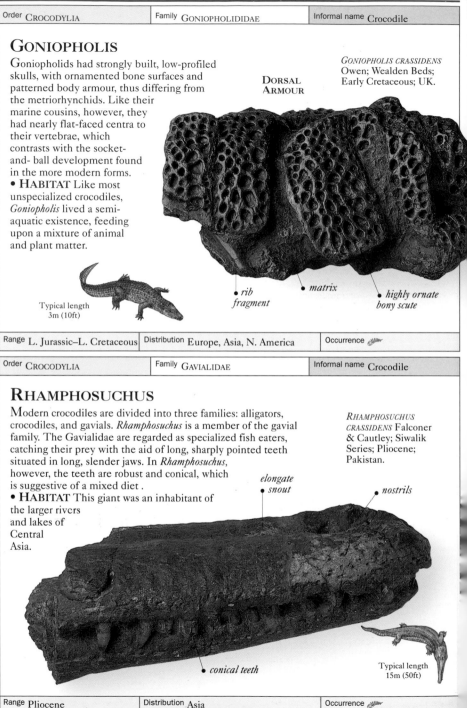

Typical length
3m (10ft)

• *rib fragment*

• *matrix*

• *highly ornate bony scute*

Range L. Jurassic–L. Cretaceous	Distribution Europe, Asia, N. America	Occurrence

Order CROCODYLIA	Family GAVIALIDAE	Informal name Crocodile

RHAMPHOSUCHUS

Modern crocodiles are divided into three families: alligators, crocodiles, and gavials. *Rhamphosuchus* is a member of the gavial family. The Gavialidae are regarded as specialized fish eaters, catching their prey with the aid of long, sharply pointed teeth situated in long, slender jaws. In *Rhamphosuchus*, however, the teeth are robust and conical, which is suggestive of a mixed diet .
• HABITAT This giant was an inhabitant of the larger rivers and lakes of Central Asia.

RHAMPHOSUCHUS CRASSIDENS Falconer & Cautley; Siwalik Series; Pliocene; Pakistan.

elongate • *snout*

• *nostrils*

• *conical teeth*

Typical length
15m (50ft)

Range Pliocene	Distribution Asia	Occurrence

Order CROCODYLIA	Family ALLIGATORIDAE	Informal name Alligator

DIPLOCYNODON

Alligators like the medium-sized *Diplocynodon* can be distinguished from true crocodiles by the absence of a pit to house the fourth tooth of the lower jaw. In other respects, the skull anatomy of the modern families is basically similar, having a strongly buttressed skull with a highly ornate bony surface, a jaw articulation set well back to facilitate the wide opening of the mouth, and a variety of rounded to sharply pointed teeth placed in deep sockets in the jaws. The remainder of the crocodilian skeleton is even more conservative, for its basic plan has been unchanged since the Triassic.
• **HABITAT** Unlike Recent species, *Diplocynodon* had a distribution that encompassed both North America and Europe. Although alligators are now restricted to America, this genus was particularly common in the swamps of Europe in Oligocene times. It had a mixed diet of animal and plant matter.
• **REMARK** The crocodiles survived the great extinction at the end of the Mesozoic, becoming even more numerous and widespread during the warmer periods of the Tertiary. But their more primitive mesosuchian cousins became extinct at the start of this era.

DIPLOCYNODON HANTONIENSIS Wood; Lower Headon Beds; Late Eocene; UK.

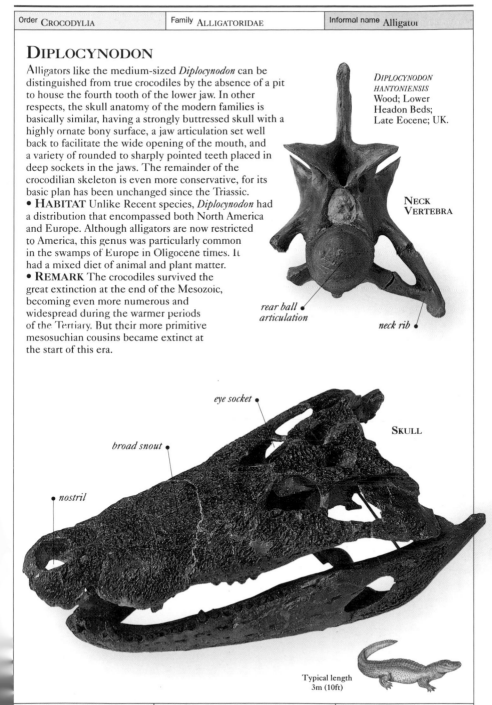

NECK VERTEBRA

rear ball articulation

neck rib

eye socket

SKULL

broad snout

nostril

Typical length 3m (10ft)

Range Eocene–Pliocene	Distribution Europe, N. America	Occurrence

Order PTEROSAURIA	Family PTERODACTYLIDAE	Informal name Pterosaur

PTERODACTYLUS

Pterodactylus is thought to have been a small-toothed insectivore, belonging to an order of archosaurs characterized by: delicate skulls with lightly built skeletons; paper-thin, hollow bones; greatly extended first fingers, supporting a wing membrane; and short legs. All family members had short tails and long skulls.

PTERODACTYLUS KOCHI Wagner; Solnhofen Limestone; Late Jurassic; Germany.

• **HABITAT** The pterosaurs were the only reptiles to develop powered flight, chasing and catching their prey on the wing, in a manner similar to that of certain birds.

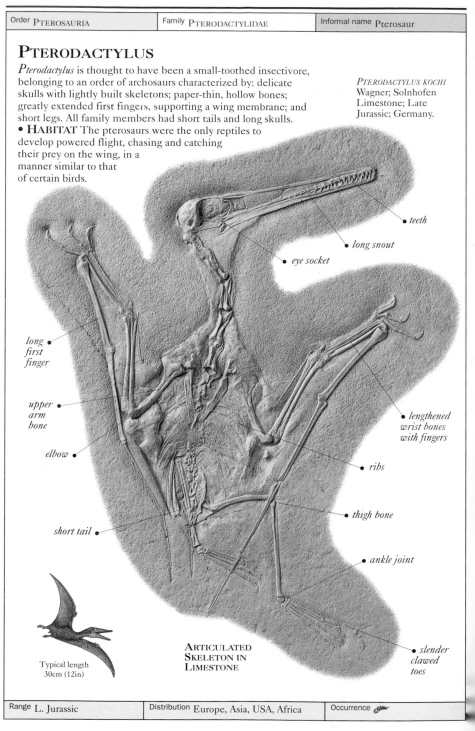

teeth

long snout

eye socket

long first finger

upper arm bone

elbow

short tail

lengthened wrist bones with fingers

ribs

thigh bone

ankle joint

slender clawed toes

Typical length 30cm (12in)

ARTICULATED SKELETON IN LIMESTONE

Range L. Jurassic	Distribution Europe, Asia, USA, Africa	Occurrence

DINOSAURS

T HIS SUCCESSFUL DIAPSID group, made up mainly of land-dwelling reptiles, first appeared about 225 million years ago, having evolved from the closely related thecodontian archosaurs. They are divided into two orders: the reptile-hipped Saurischia, in which the pubic bone faces forwards; and the bird-hipped Ornithischia, in which it faces backwards. Included in the Saurischia are the great four-footed herbivores and the two-footed flesh-eaters, while the Ornithischia contains the remaining plant-eaters. The rise to dominance of the dinosaurs has been attributed to modifications of the limbs and girdle bones, which so improved their stance and gait that they were able to adapt to new habitats. Their largely unexplained extinction at the end of the Mesozoic Era, along with most of the great aquatic reptiles, brought to an end 150 million years of domination.

Order SAURISCHIA	Family COMPSOGNATHIDAE	Informal name Compsognathid

COMPSOGNATHUS

This small, chicken-sized dinosaur had recurved, serrated teeth set in a lightly built skull. The limbs are long, slender, and hollow, and the pubic bone faces forwards.

• **HABITAT** This highly mobile, bipedal carnivore preyed upon insects and small, lizard-like creatures, which it stalked and snatched from the ground.

• **REMARK** Its hunting habit, therefore, could have been in direct competition with those suggested for the similar-sized bird *Archaeopteryx*.

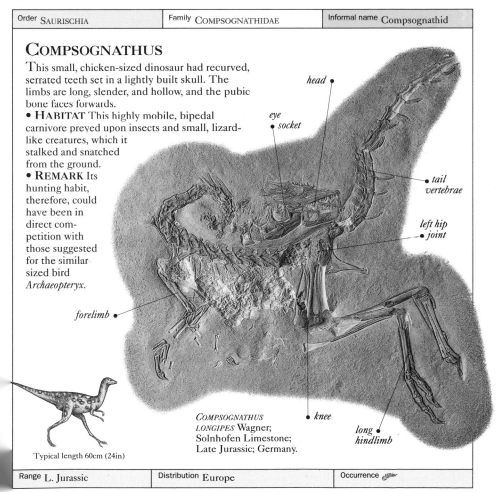

COMPSOGNATHUS LONGIPES Wagner; Solnhofen Limestone; Late Jurassic; Germany.

Typical length 60cm (24in)

Range L. Jurassic	Distribution Europe	Occurrence

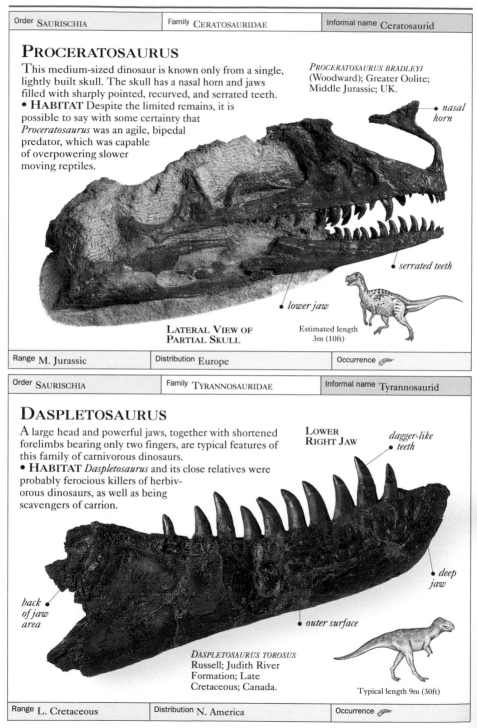

| Order SAURISCHIA | Family CERATOSAURIDAE | Informal name Ceratosaurid |

PROCERATOSAURUS

This medium-sized dinosaur is known only from a single, lightly built skull. The skull has a nasal horn and jaws filled with sharply pointed, recurved, and serrated teeth.
• HABITAT Despite the limited remains, it is possible to say with some certainty that *Proceratosaurus* was an agile, bipedal predator, which was capable of overpowering slower moving reptiles.

PROCERATOSAURUS BRADLEYI (Woodward); Greater Oolite; Middle Jurassic; UK.

nasal horn

serrated teeth

lower jaw

LATERAL VIEW OF PARTIAL SKULL

Estimated length 3m (10ft)

| Range M. Jurassic | Distribution Europe | Occurrence |

| Order SAURISCHIA | Family TYRANNOSAURIDAE | Informal name Tyrannosaurid |

DASPLETOSAURUS

A large head and powerful jaws, together with shortened forelimbs bearing only two fingers, are typical features of this family of carnivorous dinosaurs.
• HABITAT *Daspletosaurus* and its close relatives were probably ferocious killers of herbivorous dinosaurs, as well as being scavengers of carrion.

LOWER RIGHT JAW

dagger-like teeth

deep jaw

back of jaw area

outer surface

DASPLETOSAURUS TOROSUS Russell; Judith River Formation; Late Cretaceous; Canada.

Typical length 9m (30ft)

| Range L. Cretaceous | Distribution N. America | Occurrence |

Order SAURISCHIA	Family ORNITHOMIMIDAE	Informal name Ostrich dinosaur

GALLIMIMUS

The ostrich dinosaurs were long-limbed, lightly built, small-headed reptiles, with a tendency to become toothless. In *Gallimimus*, the toothless jaws were covered by a horny beak.
• HABITAT Although presumed to be a carnivore, it has been suggested that *Gallimimus* also raided the nests of other reptiles for their eggs.

large eye • *socket*

jaw • *articulation*

• *toothless beak*

GALLIMIMUS BULLATUS
Ronicwicz & Barsbold;
Upper Nemegt Beds; Late
Cretaceous; Mongolia.

• *nostril*

Typical length
4m (13ft)

Range L. Cretaceous	Distribution Asia	Ooourronoc

Order SAURISCHIA	Family CETIOSAURIDAE	Informal name Sauropod

CETIOSAURUS

The small head, long neck and tail, and solid limb bones of this giant show it to be a member of the reptile-footed dinosaurs. Its banjo-like vertebrae are characteristic.
• HABITAT *Cetiosaurus* was a plant-eater, but it is not certain whether it inhabited the margins of lakes and rivers, or was a plains wanderer. The latter suggestion is the most favoured at present.

VERTEBRA

• *neural spine*

• *articulation process*

• *neural canal*

flat-faced • *centrum*

CETIOSAURUS LEEDSI
Hulke; Oxford Clay;
Middle Jurassic; UK.

• *transverse process*

Typical length
20m (65ft)

Range M.–L. Jurassic	Distribution Europe	Occurrence

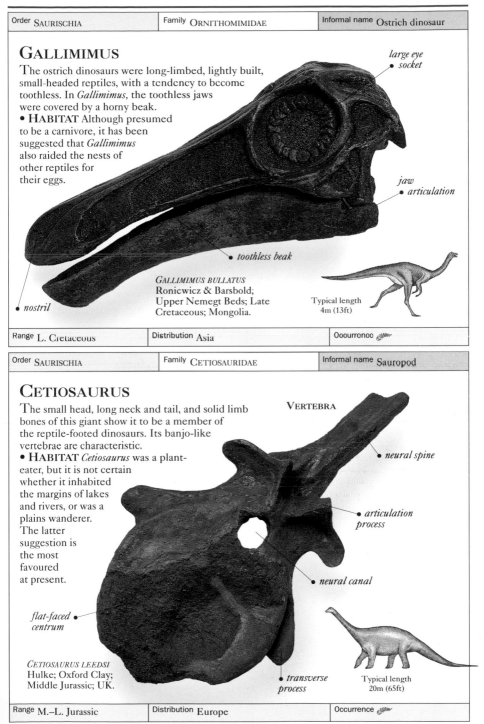

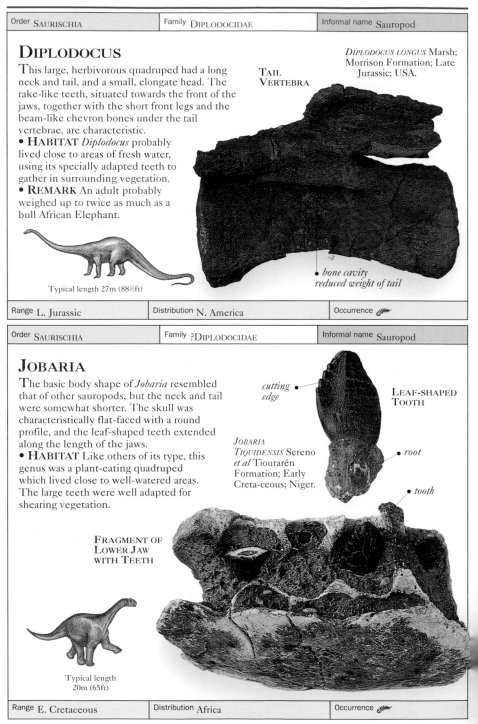

Order SAURISCHIA	Family DIPLODOCIDAE	Informal name Sauropod

DIPLODOCUS

This large, herbivorous quadruped had a long neck and tail, and a small, elongate head. The rake-like teeth, situated towards the front of the jaws, together with the short front legs and the beam-like chevron bones under the tail vertebrae, are characteristic.

• **HABITAT** *Diplodocus* probably lived close to areas of fresh water, using its specially adapted teeth to gather in surrounding vegetation.

• **REMARK** An adult probably weighed up to twice as much as a bull African Elephant.

TAIL
VERTEBRA

DIPLODOCUS LONGUS Marsh; Morrison Formation; Late Jurassic; USA.

bone cavity reduced weight of tail

Typical length 27m (88½ft)

Range L. Jurassic	Distribution N. America	Occurrence

Order SAURISCHIA	Family ?DIPLODOCIDAE	Informal name Sauropod

JOBARIA

The basic body shape of *Jobaria* resembled that of other sauropods, but the neck and tail were somewhat shorter. The skull was characteristically flat-faced with a round profile, and the leaf-shaped teeth extended along the length of the jaws.

• **HABITAT** Like others of its type, this genus was a plant-eating quadruped which lived close to well-watered areas. The large teeth were well adapted for shearing vegetation.

cutting edge

LEAF-SHAPED TOOTH

JOBARIA TIQUIDENSIS Sereno *et al* Tiourarén Formation; Early Creta-ceous; Niger.

root

tooth

FRAGMENT OF LOWER JAW WITH TEETH

Typical length 20m (65ft)

Range E. Cretaceous	Distribution Africa	Occurrence

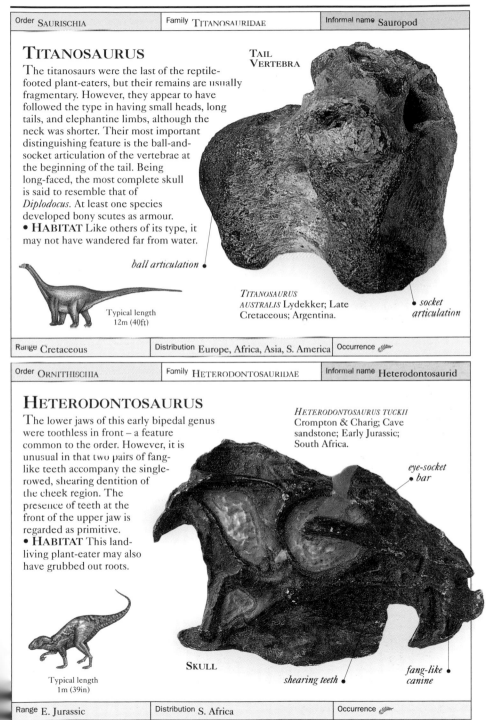

Order SAURISCHIA	Family TITANOSAURIDAE	Informal name Sauropod

TITANOSAURUS

TAIL VERTEBRA

The titanosaurs were the last of the reptile-footed plant-eaters, but their remains are usually fragmentary. However, they appear to have followed the type in having small heads, long tails, and elephantine limbs, although the neck was shorter. Their most important distinguishing feature is the ball-and-socket articulation of the vertebrae at the beginning of the tail. Being long-faced, the most complete skull is said to resemble that of *Diplodocus*. At least one species developed bony scutes as armour.
• **HABITAT** Like others of its type, it may not have wandered far from water.

ball articulation

Typical length
12m (40ft)

TITANOSAURUS AUSTRALIS Lydekker; Late Cretaceous; Argentina.

socket articulation

Range Cretaceous	Distribution Europe, Africa, Asia, S. America	Occurrence

Order ORNITHISCHIA	Family HETERODONTOSAURIDAE	Informal name Heterodontosaurid

HETERODONTOSAURUS

The lower jaws of this early bipedal genus were toothless in front – a feature common to the order. However, it is unusual in that two pairs of fang-like teeth accompany the single-rowed, shearing dentition of the cheek region. The presence of teeth at the front of the upper jaw is regarded as primitive.
• **HABITAT** This land-living plant-eater may also have grubbed out roots.

HETERODONTOSAURUS TUCKII Crompton & Charig; Cave sandstone; Early Jurassic; South Africa.

eye-socket bar

Typical length
1m (39in)

SKULL

shearing teeth

fang-like canine

Range E. Jurassic	Distribution S. Africa	Occurrence

Order ORNITHISCHIA	Family HYPSILOPHODONTIDAE	Informal name Hypsilophodontid

HYPSILOPHODON

The hypsilophodonts were medium-sized, light-bodied, land-dwelling bipeds. They show their primitiveness in having teeth situated in the front of the upper jaws, and by the extreme length of the backward-facing pubic rod. The cheek teeth were of the shearing type, arranged in a single row and replaced in batches of three. The feet were four-toed, each terminating in a pointed hoof.
• HABITAT *Hypsilophodon* fed upon the fern and cycad-like plants that dominated the early Cretaceous.

socket articulation

SINGLE TOE

tendon attchment

ball articulation

pointed hoof

HYPSILOPHODON FOXII
Huxley; Hypsilophodon
Bed; Early Cretaceous; UK.

Typical length 2.5m (8ft)

Range L. Jurassic–E. Cretaceous	Distribution Europe, N. America	Occurrence

Order ORNITHISCHIA	Family IGUANODONTIDAE	Informal name Iguanodontid

IGUANODON

This genus is made up of large, heavily-built, land-dwelling semi-bipeds. The skull was rather long in profile and lacked teeth at the front of the beak-like jaws. The cheek teeth were arranged in a single row, and were leaf-shaped when new, chisel-shaped when worn. The forelimb was heavy, with the first digit of the hand ending in a spike.
• HABITAT *Iguanodon* was common in Europe during the early part of the Cretaceous. It fed on plants.

single-rowed, leaf-like teeth

muscle attachment area

LOWER JAW

front of jaw

inner surface

IGUANODON HOLLINGTONIENSIS
Lydekker; Wealden Clays; Early
Cretaceous; UK.

Typical length 9m (30ft)

Range E. Cretaceous	Distribution Europe, Asia, Africa, N. America	Occurrence

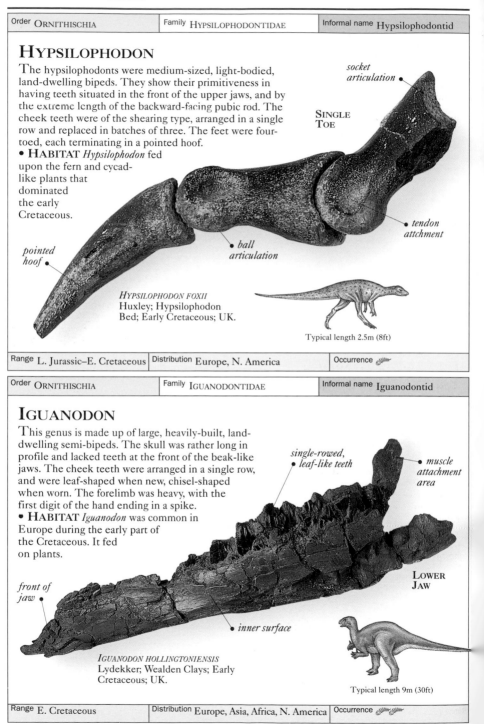

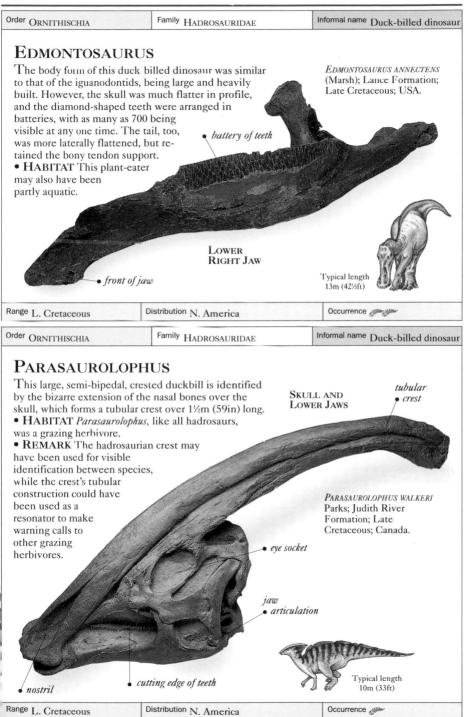

| Order ORNITHISCHIA | Family HADROSAURIDAE | Informal name Duck-billed dinosaur |

EDMONTOSAURUS

The body form of this duck billed dinosaur was similar to that of the iguanodontids, being large and heavily built. However, the skull was much flatter in profile, and the diamond-shaped teeth were arranged in batteries, with as many as 700 being visible at any one time. The tail, too, was more laterally flattened, but retained the bony tendon support.
• **HABITAT** This plant-eater may also have been partly aquatic.

EDMONTOSAURUS ANNECTENS (Marsh); Lance Formation; Late Cretaceous; USA.

• *battery of teeth*

LOWER RIGHT JAW

• *front of jaw*

Typical length 13m (42½ft)

| Range L. Cretaceous | Distribution N. America | Occurrence |

| Order ORNITHISCHIA | Family HADROSAURIDAE | Informal name Duck-billed dinosaur |

PARASAUROLOPHUS

This large, semi-bipedal, crested duckbill is identified by the bizarre extension of the nasal bones over the skull, which forms a tubular crest over 1½m (59in) long.
• **HABITAT** *Parasaurolophus*, like all hadrosaurs, was a grazing herbivore.
• **REMARK** The hadrosaurian crest may have been used for visible identification between species, while the crest's tubular construction could have been used as a resonator to make warning calls to other grazing herbivores.

SKULL AND LOWER JAWS

tubular
• *crest*

PARASAUROLOPHUS WALKERI Parks; Judith River Formation; Late Cretaceous; Canada.

• *eye socket*

jaw
• *articulation*

• *nostril*

• *cutting edge of teeth*

Typical length 10m (33ft)

| Range L. Cretaceous | Distribution N. America | Occurrence |

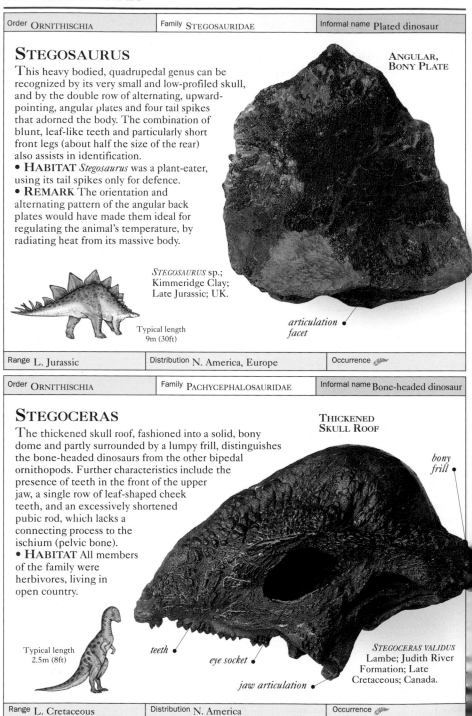

Order ORNITHISCHIA	Family STEGOSAURIDAE	Informal name Plated dinosaur

STEGOSAURUS

This heavy bodied, quadrupedal genus can be recognized by its very small and low-profiled skull, and by the double row of alternating, upward-pointing, angular plates and four tail spikes that adorned the body. The combination of blunt, leaf-like teeth and particularly short front legs (about half the size of the rear) also assists in identification.

• HABITAT *Stegosaurus* was a plant-eater, using its tail spikes only for defence.

• REMARK The orientation and alternating pattern of the angular back plates would have made them ideal for regulating the animal's temperature, by radiating heat from its massive body.

ANGULAR, BONY PLATE

STEGOSAURUS sp.; Kimmeridge Clay; Late Jurassic; UK.

Typical length
9m (30ft)

articulation
facet

Range L. Jurassic	Distribution N. America, Europe	Occurrence

Order ORNITHISCHIA	Family PACHYCEPHALOSAURIDAE	Informal name Bone-headed dinosaur

STEGOCERAS

The thickened skull roof, fashioned into a solid, bony dome and partly surrounded by a lumpy frill, distinguishes the bone-headed dinosaurs from the other bipedal ornithopods. Further characteristics include the presence of teeth in the front of the upper jaw, a single row of leaf-shaped cheek teeth, and an excessively shortened pubic rod, which lacks a connecting process to the ischium (pelvic bone).

• HABITAT All members of the family were herbivores, living in open country.

THICKENED SKULL ROOF

bony frill

Typical length
2.5m (8ft)

teeth

eye socket

jaw articulation

STEGOCERAS VALIDUS Lambe; Judith River Formation; Late Cretaceous; Canada.

Range L. Cretaceous	Distribution N. America	Occurrence

| Order ORNITHISCHIA | Family ANKYLOSAURIDAE | Informal name Armoured dinosaur |

EUOPLOCEPHALUS

END OF TAIL

This tank-like quadruped can be identified by its skull, protected by a series of scutes fused to its surface, and by its body, covered by a mosaic of flat and keel-shaped, interlocking, bony plates which narrow to a tail that terminates in a huge club.
• HABITAT This genus probably lived in arid areas.

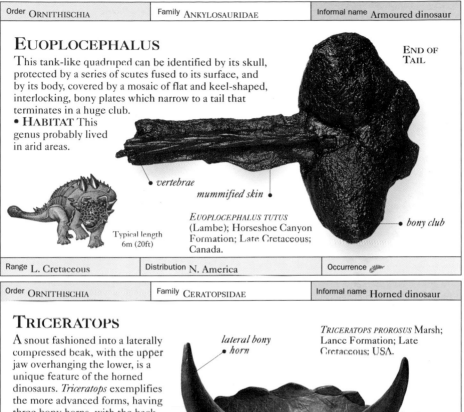

vertebrae

mummified skin

EUOPLOCEPHALUS TUTUS (Lambe); Horseshoe Canyon Formation; Late Cretaceous; Canada.

bony club

Typical length 6m (20ft)

| Range L. Cretaceous | Distribution N. America | Occurrence |

| Order ORNITHISCHIA | Family CERATOPSIDAE | Informal name Horned dinosaur |

TRICERATOPS

TRICERATOPS PROROSUS Marsh; Lance Formation; Late Cretaceous; USA.

A snout fashioned into a laterally compressed beak, with the upper jaw overhanging the lower, is a unique feature of the horned dinosaurs. *Triceratops* exemplifies the more advanced forms, having three bony horns, with the back of the skull extended into a huge bony frill.
• HABITAT This was a large, quadrupedal herbivore, which used its powerful beak to slice through the tougher stems of plants. It may have lived in more open habitats, forming small herds in a similar fashion to many present-day plains mammals.

lateral bony horn

bony frill

eye socket

nostril

SKULL

single tooth row

toothless beak

lower jaw

Typical length 9m (30ft)

| Range L. Cretaceous | Distribution N. America | Occurrence |

Order ORNITHISCHIA	Family PROTOCERATOPSIDAE	Informal name Horned dinosaur

PROTOCERATOPS

This small, stocky quadruped is characterized by a horny beak, a small nose horn, leaf-like cheek teeth set in a single line, and a much reduced neck frill containing large perforations.

• HABITAT *Protoceratops* probably lived in open areas, where it fed upon plant stems which it cut off with its powerful beak. The stems were then sheared into smaller pieces by the cheek teeth.

• REMARK In the1920s, an American expedition to Mongolia discovered numerous *Protoceratops* nests and eggs, some containing partly developed young. This provided palaeontologists with their first insight into the social behaviour of the dinosaurs. It was evident that the eggs had been deliberately arranged in neat, concentric rings, before being buried by the adults. Numerous adult bones were also encountered, suggesting that they nested in loose colonies and stood guard over their nesting sites.

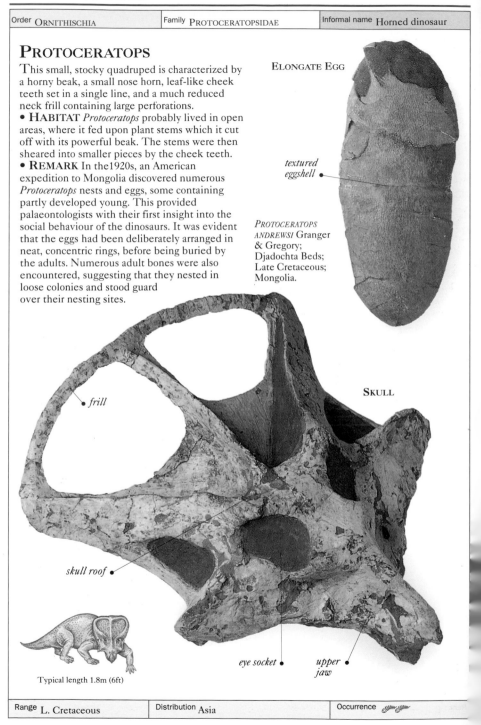

ELONGATE EGG

textured eggshell

PROTOCERATOPS *ANDREWSI* Granger & Gregory; Djadochta Beds; Late Cretaceous; Mongolia.

SKULL

frill

skull roof

Typical length 1.8m (6ft)

eye socket

upper jaw

Range L. Cretaceous	Distribution Asia	Occurrence

SYNAPSID REPTILES

THE SUBCLASS SYNAPSIDA, more popularly referred to as the mammal-like reptiles, is the third major division of the class Reptilia. It is characterized by the possession of a single opening in the skull roof, together with a unique configuration of the associated bones behind the eye socket. The first synapsids appeared during the Carboniferous, 300 million years ago. Although early examples were small and lizard-like, they were highly successful and developed numerous varieties. By the Permian they were the dominant land forms, but were then unable to compete with the newly evolved and more agile thecodonts, crocodiles, and dinosaurs in the late Triassic. They became extinct at the beginning of the Jurassic, but not before they had given rise to the line that produced mammals.

| Order PELYCOSAURIA | Family SPHENACODONTIDAE | Informal name Sail-backed lizard |

DIMETRODON

The most spectacular feature of this genus was the huge dorsal sail, the result of the extreme elongation of the vertebral neural spines, which characteristically remain smooth along their length. The skull is deep, has dagger-like teeth, with the lower jaw articulation situated well below, and behind, the tooth row. In comparison with other sail-backs, the quadrupedal *Dimetrodon* had lightly built limbs.
• **HABITAT** This relatively fast-moving, carnivorous reptile preyed upon less agile species in arid environments.
• **REMARK** It was this group of pelycosaurs that acquired the adaptations that eventually developed fully in mammals.

DIMETRODON LOOMISI
Romer; Arroyo Formation; Early Permian; USA.

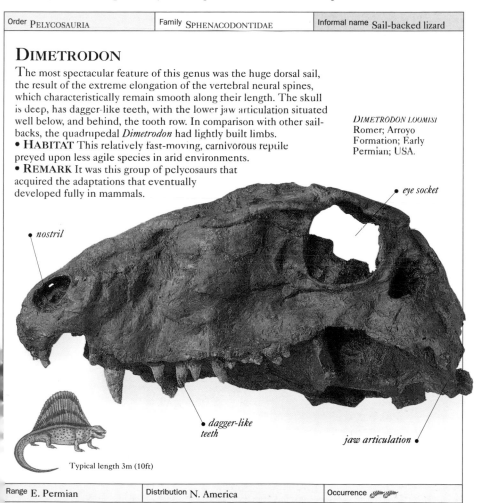

nostril

eye socket

dagger-like teeth

jaw articulation

Typical length 3m (10ft)

| Range E. Permian | Distribution N. America | Occurrence |

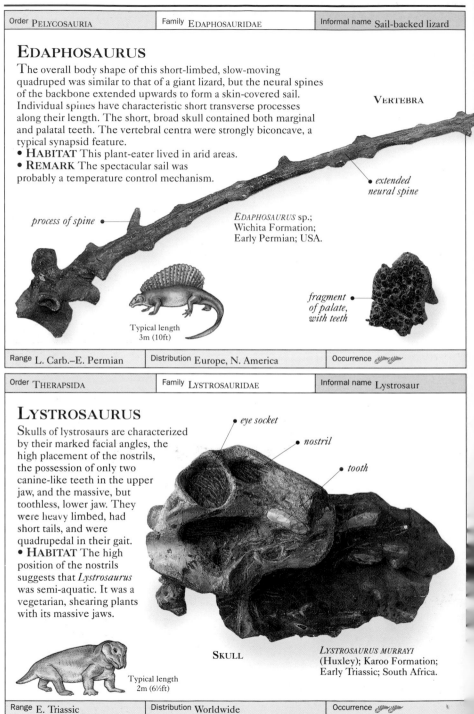

| Order PELYCOSAURIA | Family EDAPHOSAURIDAE | Informal name Sail-backed lizard |

EDAPHOSAURUS

The overall body shape of this short-limbed, slow-moving quadruped was similar to that of a giant lizard, but the neural spines of the backbone extended upwards to form a skin-covered sail. Individual spines have characteristic short transverse processes along their length. The short, broad skull contained both marginal and palatal teeth. The vertebral centra were strongly biconcave, a typical synapsid feature.

• **HABITAT** This plant-eater lived in arid areas.

• **REMARK** The spectacular sail was probably a temperature control mechanism.

VERTEBRA

extended neural spine

process of spine

EDAPHOSAURUS sp.; Wichita Formation; Early Permian; USA.

fragment of palate, with teeth

Typical length 3m (10ft)

| Range L. Carb.–E. Permian | Distribution Europe, N. America | Occurrence |

| Order THERAPSIDA | Family LYSTROSAURIDAE | Informal name Lystrosaur |

LYSTROSAURUS

Skulls of lystrosaurs are characterized by their marked facial angles, the high placement of the nostrils, the possession of only two canine-like teeth in the upper jaw, and the massive, but toothless, lower jaw. They were heavy limbed, had short tails, and were quadrupedal in their gait.

• **HABITAT** The high position of the nostrils suggests that *Lystrosaurus* was semi-aquatic. It was a vegetarian, shearing plants with its massive jaws.

eye socket

nostril

tooth

SKULL

LYSTROSAURUS MURRAYI (Huxley); Karoo Formation; Early Triassic; South Africa.

Typical length 2m (6½ft)

| Range E. Triassic | Distribution Worldwide | Occurrence |

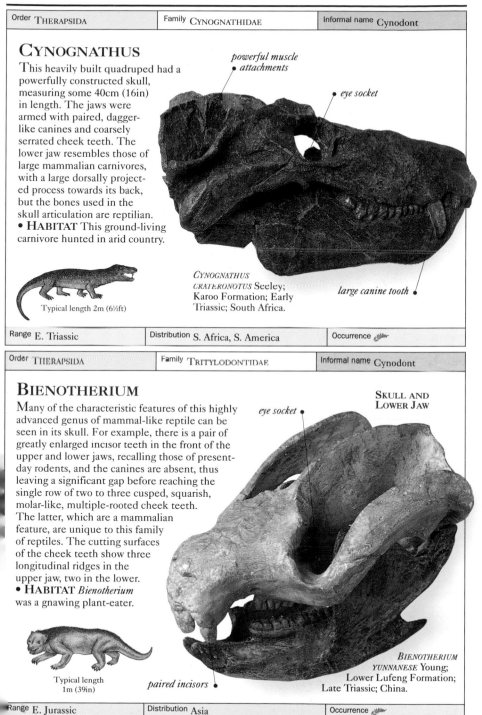

| Order THERAPSIDA | Family CYNOGNATHIDAE | Informal name Cynodont |

CYNOGNATHUS

This heavily built quadruped had a powerfully constructed skull, measuring some 40cm (16in) in length. The jaws were armed with paired, dagger-like canines and coarsely serrated cheek teeth. The lower jaw resembles those of large mammalian carnivores, with a large dorsally project-ed process towards its back, but the bones used in the skull articulation are reptilian.
• **HABITAT** This ground-living carnivore hunted in arid country.

powerful muscle attachments

eye socket

Typical length 2m (6½ft)

CYNOGNATHUS CRATERONOTUS Seeley; Karoo Formation; Early Triassic; South Africa.

large canine tooth

| Range E. Triassic | Distribution S. Africa, S. America | Occurrence |

| Order THERAPSIDA | Family TRITYLODONTIDAE | Informal name Cynodont |

BIENOTHERIUM

SKULL AND LOWER JAW

Many of the characteristic features of this highly advanced genus of mammal-like reptile can be seen in its skull. For example, there is a pair of greatly enlarged incisor teeth in the front of the upper and lower jaws, recalling those of present-day rodents, and the canines are absent, thus leaving a significant gap before reaching the single row of two to three cusped, squarish, molar-like, multiple-rooted cheek teeth. The latter, which are a mammalian feature, are unique to this family of reptiles. The cutting surfaces of the cheek teeth show three longitudinal ridges in the upper jaw, two in the lower.
• **HABITAT** *Bienotherium* was a gnawing plant-eater.

eye socket

Typical length 1m (39in)

paired incisors

BIENOTHERIUM YUNNANESE Young; Lower Lufeng Formation; Late Triassic; China.

| Range E. Jurassic | Distribution Asia | Occurrence |

BIRDS

THE CLASS AVES is divided into four subclasses: Archaeornithes, Odontornithes, Enantiornithes, and Neornithes, with only the last surviving beyond the onset of the Cenozoic Era. Most specialists now agree that birds evolved from one of the carnivorous dinosaur families. Exactly when this occurred is unclear, but the first clearly identifiable remains were found in Late Jurassic rocks. Following its appearance, the class seems to have been slow in establishing itself as an important group until the end of the Cretaceous, when many reptile types became extinct and ceased to be the dominant vertebrates. At this juncture, birds of the neorthine type quickly diversified and started the progression towards the 8,600 or so species included in the modern avifauna.

| Order ARCHAEOPTERYGIFORMES | Family ARCHAEOPTERYGIDAE | Informal name Archaeopteryx |

ARCHAEOPTERYX

The chicken-sized *Archaeopteryx* can be readily identified by the great proportion of reptilian features in its skeleton. For example, the lightly built skull possesses true teeth, set in sockets in the jaws; the breastbone is small and lacks a keel; the forelimb skeleton retains three functional fingers, and lacks the reductions and fusions present in other birds; the hindlimb girdle, although modified, is distinctly dinosaurian in character; and there is a long, bony tail. Other uncharacteristic avian features include almost flat-faced vertebrae, belly ribs, and an incomplete fusion of the lower leg bones. Impressions of feathers, associated with the five known skeletons, confirm that this creature was a bird.
• **HABITAT** *Archaeopteryx* was certainly capable of flight, but probably chased and seized insects and reptiles on the ground, near the shores of inland seas.

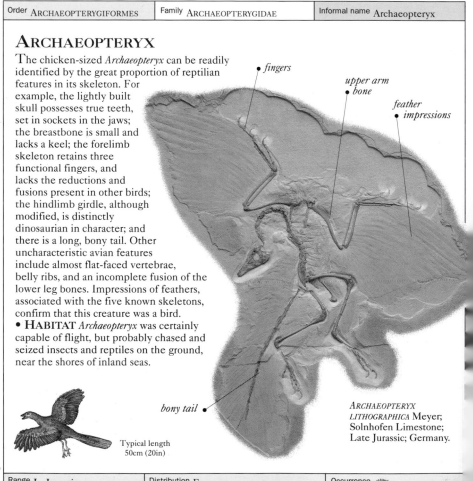

fingers

upper arm bone

feather impressions

bony tail

Typical length
50cm (20in)

ARCHAEOPTERYX LITHOGRAPHICA Meyer;
Solnhofen Limestone;
Late Jurassic; Germany.

| Range L. Jurassic | Distribution Europe | Occurrence |

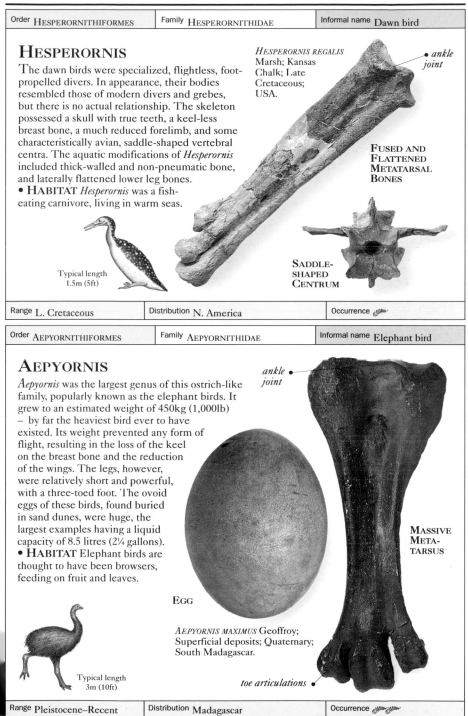

| Order HESPERORNITHIFORMES | Family HESPERORNITHIDAE | Informal name Dawn bird |

HESPERORNIS

The dawn birds were specialized, flightless, foot-propelled divers. In appearance, their bodies resembled those of modern divers and grebes, but there is no actual relationship. The skeleton possessed a skull with true teeth, a keel-less breast bone, a much reduced forelimb, and some characteristically avian, saddle-shaped vertebral centra. The aquatic modifications of *Hesperornis* included thick-walled and non-pneumatic bone, and laterally flattened lower leg bones.
• HABITAT *Hesperornis* was a fish-eating carnivore, living in warm seas.

HESPERORNIS REGALIS
Marsh; Kansas Chalk; Late Cretaceous; USA.

• ankle joint

FUSED AND FLATTENED METATARSAL BONES

SADDLE-SHAPED CENTRUM

Typical length 1.5m (5ft)

| Range L. Cretaceous | Distribution N. America | Occurrence |

| Order AEPYORNITHIFORMES | Family AEPYORNITHIDAE | Informal name Elephant bird |

AEPYORNIS

Aepyornis was the largest genus of this ostrich-like family, popularly known as the elephant birds. It grew to an estimated weight of 450kg (1,000lb) – by far the heaviest bird ever to have existed. Its weight prevented any form of flight, resulting in the loss of the keel on the breast bone and the reduction of the wings. The legs, however, were relatively short and powerful, with a three-toed foot. The ovoid eggs of these birds, found buried in sand dunes, were huge, the largest examples having a liquid capacity of 8.5 litres (2¼ gallons).
• HABITAT Elephant birds are thought to have been browsers, feeding on fruit and leaves.

ankle • joint

MASSIVE META-TARSUS

EGG

AEPYORNIS MAXIMUS Geoffroy; Superficial deposits; Quaternary; South Madagascar.

toe articulations •

Typical length 3m (10ft)

| Range Pleistocene–Recent | Distribution Madagascar | Occurrence |

| Order SPHENISCIFORMES | Family SPHENISCIDAE | Informal name Penguin |

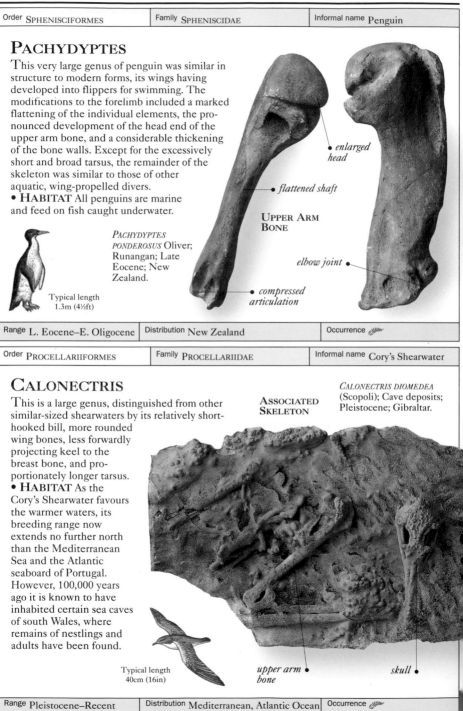

PACHYDYPTES

This very large genus of penguin was similar in structure to modern forms, its wings having developed into flippers for swimming. The modifications to the forelimb included a marked flattening of the individual elements, the pronounced development of the head end of the upper arm bone, and a considerable thickening of the bone walls. Except for the excessively short and broad tarsus, the remainder of the skeleton was similar to those of other aquatic, wing-propelled divers.
• **HABITAT** All penguins are marine and feed on fish caught underwater.

PACHYDYPTES PONDEROSUS Oliver; Runangan; Late Eocene; New Zealand.

Typical length 1.3m (4½ft)

• *enlarged head*

• *flattened shaft*

UPPER ARM BONE

elbow joint •

• *compressed articulation*

| Range L. Eocene–E. Oligocene | Distribution New Zealand | Occurrence |

| Order PROCELLARIIFORMES | Family PROCELLARIIDAE | Informal name Cory's Shearwater |

CALONECTRIS

This is a large genus, distinguished from other similar-sized shearwaters by its relatively short-hooked bill, more rounded wing bones, less forwardly projecting keel to the breast bone, and proportionately longer tarsus.
• **HABITAT** As the Cory's Shearwater favours the warmer waters, its breeding range now extends no further north than the Mediterranean Sea and the Atlantic seaboard of Portugal. However, 100,000 years ago it is known to have inhabited certain sea caves of south Wales, where remains of nestlings and adults have been found.

ASSOCIATED SKELETON

CALONECTRIS DIOMEDEA (Scopoli); Cave deposits; Pleistocene; Gibraltar.

Typical length 40cm (16in)

upper arm bone •

skull •

| Range Pleistocene–Recent | Distribution Mediterranean, Atlantic Ocean | Occurrence |

Order PELECANIFORMES	Family ODONTOPTERYGIDAE	Informal name Bony-toothed bird

ODONTOPTERYX

The bony-toothed birds were long-winged seabirds, with unique tooth-like projections along the cutting edge of the jaws. In the diminutive *Odontopteryx*, these projections have a distinct forward slant, and are set in a 15cm- (6in-) long skull, similar in form and size to that of the living gannet. The larger species are thought to have had a wing-span of about 5m (16½ft).

ODONTOPTERYX TOLIAPICA Owen; London Clay; Early Eocene; UK.

SKULL

• HABITAT *Odontopteryx* was certainly a fish-eater, perhaps snatching its prey from the sea as it glided over the surface.
• REMARK *Odontopteryx* is sometimes classified with pelicans and cormorants.

Typical length
90cm (36in)

bony tooth •

• *lower jaw*

Range E. Eocene	Distribution Europe	Occurrence

Order GRUIFORMES	Family PHORUSRHACIDAE	Informal name Phorusrhacid

PHORUSRHACUS

The most outstanding feature of this large, flightless genus is its gigantic hooked bill, which resembles that of a powerful eagle. It has been suggested that it is related to the present-day cranes.
• HABITAT It probably hunted over open plains country.
• REMARK The family first appeared during the Oligocene in South America, where they evolved and became the dominant carnivore. The superiority lasted until about four million years ago, when they became extinct before the end of the Pliocene.

PHORUSRHACUS INFLATUS Ameghino; Santa Cruz Formation; Miocene; Argentina.

nostril •

SKULL

Typical length
1.5m (5ft)

eye socket •

Range Miocene	Distribution S. America	Occurrence

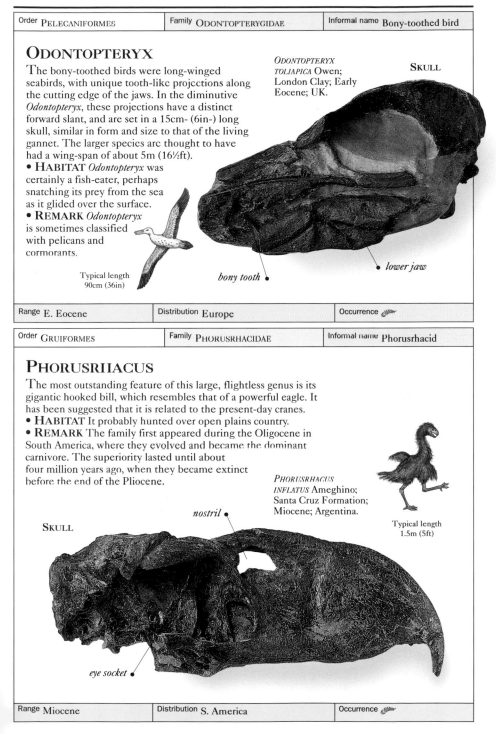

Order APODIFORMES	Family AEGIALORNITHIDAE	Informal name Swift

PRIMAPUS

The upper arm bone of this genus exhibits structures clearly adapted for a specialized aerial mode of life. For example, it is short and stout, the head is highly developed, the bicipital surface and deltoid crest are well formed. All these characteristics suggest a bird that had considerable powers of flight, and it is with the modern swifts that the closest match occurs.
• HABITAT The successful early evolution of the swifts probably resulted from the increase in flowering plants and their insect pollinators. The latter provided an ample source of food for this insect predator.

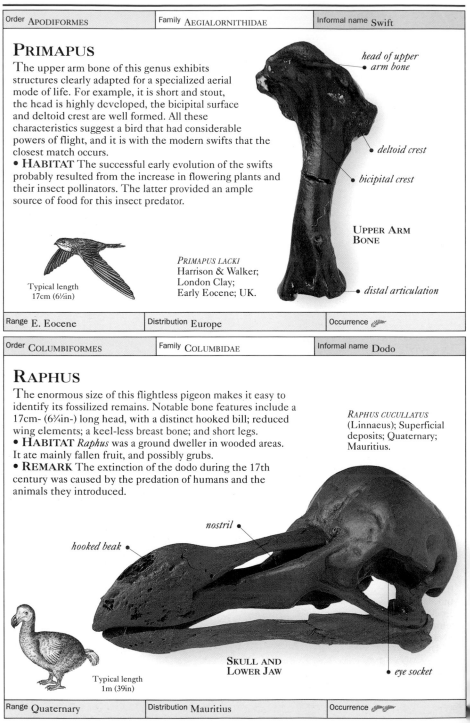

head of upper
• arm bone

• deltoid crest

• bicipital crest

UPPER ARM
BONE

Typical length
17cm (6½in)

PRIMAPUS LACKI
Harrison & Walker;
London Clay;
Early Eocene; UK.

• distal articulation

Range E. Eocene	Distribution Europe	Occurrence

Order COLUMBIFORMES	Family COLUMBIDAE	Informal name Dodo

RAPHUS

The enormous size of this flightless pigeon makes it easy to identify its fossilized remains. Notable bone features include a 17cm- (6¾in-) long head, with a distinct hooked bill; reduced wing elements; a keel-less breast bone; and short legs.
• HABITAT *Raphus* was a ground dweller in wooded areas. It ate mainly fallen fruit, and possibly grubs.
• REMARK The extinction of the dodo during the 17th century was caused by the predation of humans and the animals they introduced.

RAPHUS CUCULLATUS
(Linnaeus); Superficial
deposits; Quaternary;
Mauritius.

nostril •

hooked beak •

Typical length
1m (39in)

SKULL AND
LOWER JAW

• eye socket

Range Quaternary	Distribution Mauritius	Occurrence

MAMMALS

MAMMALS ARE A VERY successful group. From terrestrial origins they have colonized most of the habitable areas of the Earth's surface, the oceans, and the air. The main identifying features of mammals, such as the possession of hair, milk-producing mammary glands, and the details of their reproductive system, are rarely preserved as fossils. To the palaeontologist, the most vital mammalian identification feature is the jaw articulation between the dentary bone (the only bone in the lower jaw) and the squamosal bone in the skull. The quadrate and articular bones, forming the articulation in other vertebrates, became associated with mammalian hearing, and survive today as the incus and malleus of the middle ear.

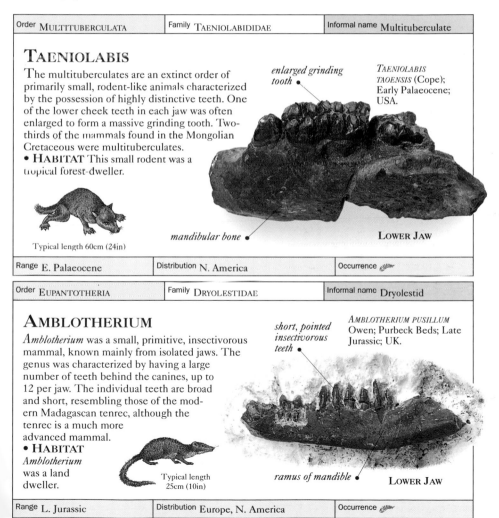

Order MULTITUBERCULATA	Family TAENIOLABIDIDAE	Informal name Multituberculate

TAENIOLABIS

The multituberculates are an extinct order of primarily small, rodent-like animals characterized by the possession of highly distinctive teeth. One of the lower cheek teeth in each jaw was often enlarged to form a massive grinding tooth. Two-thirds of the mammals found in the Mongolian Cretaceous were multituberculates.

• **HABITAT** This small rodent was a tropical forest-dweller.

enlarged grinding tooth •

TAENIOLABIS TAOENSIS (Cope); Early Palaeocene; USA.

mandibular bone • **LOWER JAW**

Typical length 60cm (24in)

Range E. Palaeocene	Distribution N. America	Occurrence

Order EUPANTOTHERIA	Family DRYOLESTIDAE	Informal name Dryolestid

AMBLOTHERIUM

Amblotherium was a small, primitive, insectivorous mammal, known mainly from isolated jaws. The genus was characterized by having a large number of teeth behind the canines, up to 12 per jaw. The individual teeth are broad and short, resembling those of the modern Madagascan tenrec, although the tenrec is a much more advanced mammal.

• **HABITAT**
Amblotherium
was a land
dweller.

short, pointed insectivorous teeth •

AMBLOTHERIUM PUSILLUM Owen; Purbeck Beds; Late Jurassic; UK.

Typical length 25cm (10in)

ramus of mandible • **LOWER JAW**

Range L. Jurassic	Distribution Europe, N. America	Occurrence

Order DIDELPHIMORPHIA	Family DIDELPHIDAE	Informal name Opossum

DIDELPHIS

SKULL

Opossums are mouse- to cat-sized marsupials with up to 50 teeth, a long snout, and small eyes. The pouch (or marsupium) is variably developed. Opossums have hands and feet well adapted for grasping; there are usually five digits on each foot, with the big toe acting as an opposable digit. While most species are climbers, some are not, and one is aquatic. Many species have prehensile tails.

• HABITAT Opossums are arboreal, feeding on a wide variety of animal and vegetable matter.

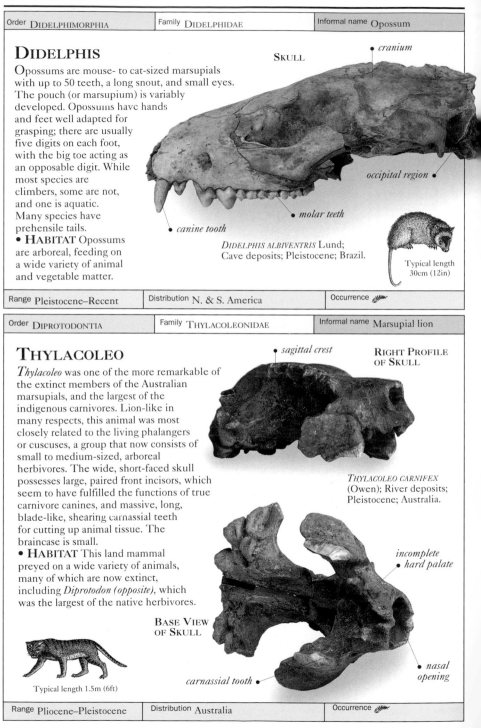

cranium

occipital region

molar teeth

canine tooth

DIDELPHIS ALBIVENTRIS Lund; Cave deposits; Pleistocene; Brazil.

Typical length 30cm (12in)

Range Pleistocene–Recent	Distribution N. & S. America	Occurrence

Order DIPROTODONTIA	Family THYLACOLEONIDAE	Informal name Marsupial lion

THYLACOLEO

sagittal crest

RIGHT PROFILE OF SKULL

Thylacoleo was one of the more remarkable of the extinct members of the Australian marsupials, and the largest of the indigenous carnivores. Lion-like in many respects, this animal was most closely related to the living phalangers or cuscuses, a group that now consists of small to medium-sized, arboreal herbivores. The wide, short-faced skull possesses large, paired front incisors, which seem to have fulfilled the functions of true carnivore canines, and massive, long, blade-like, shearing carnassial teeth for cutting up animal tissue. The braincase is small.

• HABITAT This land mammal preyed on a wide variety of animals, many of which are now extinct, including *Diprotodon (opposite)*, which was the largest of the native herbivores.

THYLACOLEO CARNIFEX (Owen); River deposits; Pleistocene; Australia.

incomplete hard palate

BASE VIEW OF SKULL

nasal opening

Typical length 1.5m (6ft)

carnassial tooth

Range Pliocene–Pleistocene	Distribution Australia	Occurrence

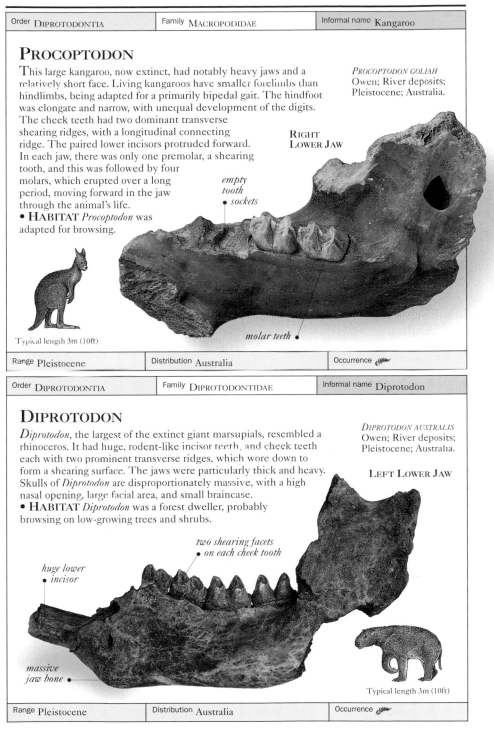

| Order DIPROTODONTIA | Family MACROPODIDAE | Informal name Kangaroo |

PROCOPTODON

This large kangaroo, now extinct, had notably heavy jaws and a relatively short face. Living kangaroos have smaller forelimbs than hindlimbs, being adapted for a primarily bipedal gait. The hindfoot was elongate and narrow, with unequal development of the digits. The cheek teeth had two dominant transverse shearing ridges, with a longitudinal connecting ridge. The paired lower incisors protruded forward. In each jaw, there was only one premolar, a shearing tooth, and this was followed by four molars, which erupted over a long period, moving forward in the jaw through the animal's life.
• HABITAT *Procoptodon* was adapted for browsing.

PROCOPTODON GOLIAH
Owen; River deposits;
Pleistocene; Australia.

RIGHT
LOWER JAW

empty tooth sockets

molar teeth

Typical length 3m (10ft)

| Range Pleistocene | Distribution Australia | Occurrence |

| Order DIPROTODONTIA | Family DIPROTODONTIDAE | Informal name Diprotodon |

DIPROTODON

Diprotodon, the largest of the extinct giant marsupials, resembled a rhinoceros. It had huge, rodent-like incisor teeth, and cheek teeth each with two prominent transverse ridges, which wore down to form a shearing surface. The jaws were particularly thick and heavy. Skulls of *Diprotodon* are disproportionately massive, with a high nasal opening, large facial area, and small braincase.
• HABITAT *Diprotodon* was a forest dweller, probably browsing on low-growing trees and shrubs.

DIPROTODON AUSTRALIS
Owen; River deposits;
Pleistocene; Australia.

LEFT LOWER JAW

two shearing facets on each cheek tooth

huge lower incisor

massive jaw bone

Typical length 3m (10ft)

| Range Pleistocene | Distribution Australia | Occurrence |

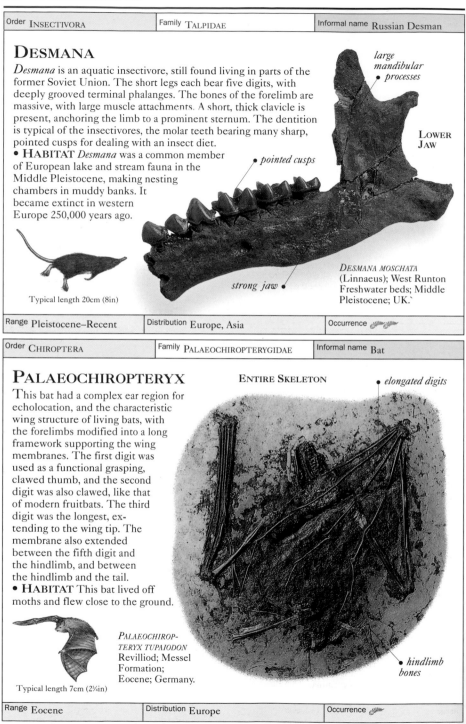

| Order INSECTIVORA | Family TALPIDAE | Informal name Russian Desman |

DESMANA

Desmana is an aquatic insectivore, still found living in parts of the former Soviet Union. The short legs each bear five digits, with deeply grooved terminal phalanges. The bones of the forelimb are massive, with large muscle attachments. A short, thick clavicle is present, anchoring the limb to a prominent sternum. The dentition is typical of the insectivores, the molar teeth bearing many sharp, pointed cusps for dealing with an insect diet.
• HABITAT *Desmana* was a common member of European lake and stream fauna in the Middle Pleistocene, making nesting chambers in muddy banks. It became extinct in western Europe 250,000 years ago.

large mandibular processes

LOWER JAW

pointed cusps

strong jaw

Typical length 20cm (8in)

DESMANA MOSCHATA (Linnaeus); West Runton Freshwater beds; Middle Pleistocene; UK.`

| Range Pleistocene–Recent | Distribution Europe, Asia | Occurrence |

| Order CHIROPTERA | Family PALAEOCHIROPTERYGIDAE | Informal name Bat |

PALAEOCHIROPTERYX

This bat had a complex ear region for echolocation, and the characteristic wing structure of living bats, with the forelimbs modified into a long framework supporting the wing membranes. The first digit was used as a functional grasping, clawed thumb, and the second digit was also clawed, like that of modern fruitbats. The third digit was the longest, extending to the wing tip. The membrane also extended between the fifth digit and the hindlimb, and between the hindlimb and the tail.
• HABITAT This bat lived off moths and flew close to the ground.

ENTIRE SKELETON

elongated digits

PALAEOCHIROPTERYX TUPAIODON Revilliod; Messel Formation; Eocene; Germany.

hindlimb bones

Typical length 7cm (2¾in)

| Range Eocene | Distribution Europe | Occurrence |

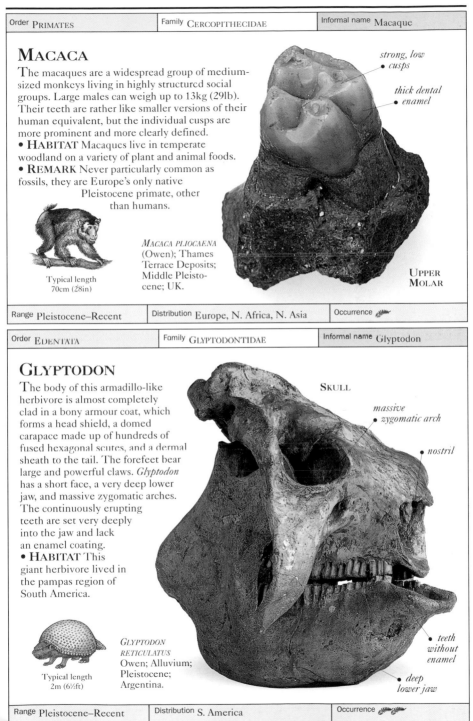

MACACA

The macaques are a widespread group of medium-sized monkeys living in highly structured social groups. Large males can weigh up to 13kg (29lb). Their teeth are rather like smaller versions of their human equivalent, but the individual cusps are more prominent and more clearly defined.

• **HABITAT** Macaques live in temperate woodland on a variety of plant and animal foods.

• **REMARK** Never particularly common as fossils, they are Europe's only native Pleistocene primate, other than humans.

strong, low
• cusps

thick dental
• enamel

MACACA PLIOCAENA
(Owen); Thames
Terrace Deposits;
Middle Pleisto-
cene; UK.

Typical length
70cm (28in)

UPPER
MOLAR

Range Pleistocene–Recent | Distribution Europe, N. Africa, N. Asia | Occurrence

GLYPTODON

The body of this armadillo-like herbivore is almost completely clad in a bony armour coat, which forms a head shield, a domed carapace made up of hundreds of fused hexagonal scutes, and a dermal sheath to the tail. The forefeet bear large and powerful claws. *Glyptodon* has a short face, a very deep lower jaw, and massive zygomatic arches. The continuously erupting teeth are set very deeply into the jaw and lack an enamel coating.

• **HABITAT** This giant herbivore lived in the pampas region of South America.

SKULL

massive
• zygomatic arch

• nostril

*GLYPTODON
RETICULATUS*
Owen; Alluvium;
Pleistocene;
Argentina.

Typical length
2m (6½ft)

• teeth
without
enamel

• deep
lower jaw

Range Pleistocene–Recent | Distribution S. America | Occurrence

Order EDENTATA	Family MEGATHERIIDAE	Informal name Giant ground sloth

MEGATHERIUM

CLAW-BEARING PHALANGE

This giant sloth, now extinct, had a massive but short and high skull, with a high nasal opening and very deep jaws. It had very thick skin, armoured throughout with small ossicles of bone, and huge, powerful claws on all four feet. Its very simple teeth, lacking in dental enamel, consisted of a battery of continuously growing square columns, deeply set in each jaw.
• HABITAT This giant sloth lived on a wide range of vegetation.

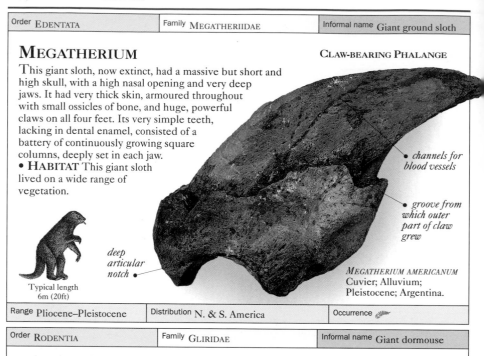

• channels for blood vessels

• groove from which outer part of claw grew

deep articular notch •

Typical length 6m (20ft)

MEGATHERIUM AMERICANUM
Cuvier; Alluvium; Pleistocene; Argentina.

Range Pliocene–Pleistocene	Distribution N. & S. America	Occurrence

Order RODENTIA	Family GLIRIDAE	Informal name Giant dormouse

LEITHIA

UNDERSIDE OF SKULL

Dormice are a primitive group of rodents, with very low-crowned grinding teeth which suit their mixed plant-food diet. Their teeth have biting surfaces divided into transverse ridges, which grind the food as if between two files. In common with many other herbivores, there is a long gap (or diastema) between the incisor teeth and the cheek teeth, dividing the mouth into two distinct functional regions, one dealing with procurement of food, the other with mastication.
• HABITAT Probably nocturnal, this giant dor-mouse lived in woodland and dense scrub. It is likely to have hibernated in caves and holes in the ground.

• diastema (gap between incisors and cheek teeth)

• transverse enamel ridges

cheek teeth •

Typical length 50cm (20in)

LEITHIA MELITENSIS
Falconer; Cave breccia; Pleistocene; Malta.

Range Pleistocene	Distribution Malta	Occurrence

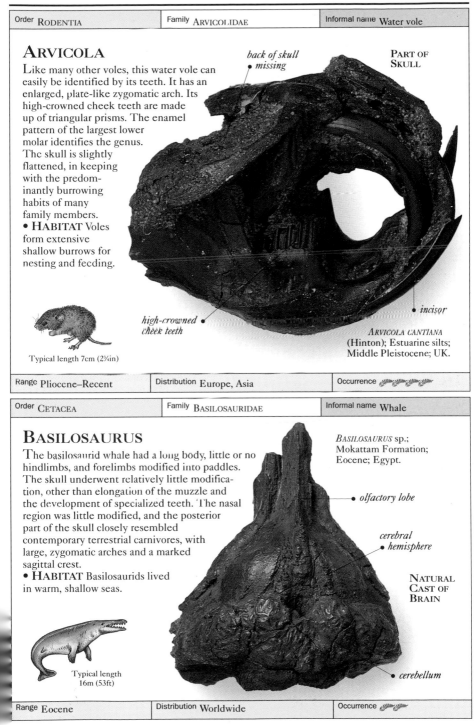

Order RODENTIA	Family ARVICOLIDAE	Informal name Water vole

ARVICOLA

Like many other voles, this water vole can easily be identified by its teeth. It has an enlarged, plate-like zygomatic arch. Its high-crowned cheek teeth are made up of triangular prisms. The enamel pattern of the largest lower molar identifies the genus. The skull is slightly flattened, in keeping with the predominantly burrowing habits of many family members.
• HABITAT Voles form extensive shallow burrows for nesting and feeding.

back of skull • missing

PART OF SKULL

• incisor

high-crowned • cheek teeth

Typical length 7cm (2¾in)

ARVICOLA CANTIANA (Hinton); Estuarine silts; Middle Pleistocene; UK.

Range Pliocene–Recent	Distribution Europe, Asia	Occurrence

Order CETACEA	Family BASILOSAURIDAE	Informal name Whale

BASILOSAURUS

The basilosaurid whale had a long body, little or no hindlimbs, and forelimbs modified into paddles. The skull underwent relatively little modification, other than elongation of the muzzle and the development of specialized teeth. The nasal region was little modified, and the posterior part of the skull closely resembled contemporary terrestrial carnivores, with large, zygomatic arches and a marked sagittal crest.
• HABITAT Basilosaurids lived in warm, shallow seas.

BASILOSAURUS sp.; Mokattam Formation; Eocene; Egypt.

• olfactory lobe

cerebral • hemisphere

NATURAL CAST OF BRAIN

Typical length 16m (53ft)

• cerebellum

Range Eocene	Distribution Worldwide	Occurrence

Order CETACEA	Family BALAENIDAE	Informal name Right whale

BALAENA

Balaena has developed a highly specialized filtration system to replace its dentition. The filter is composed of baleen plates – like the bristles of a huge brush – and is used to filter out small sea creatures, such as krill. The nasal opening has migrated to a position high on the forehead to form a closeable blowhole. There is no trace of a rear limb, and the front limb is modified into a huge paddle, articulated on a very short humerus. Whales have distinctive tympanic (ear) bones, quite commonly found as fossils. In baleen whales, these actually resemble a large ear.
• HABITAT *Balaena* lives in temperate to Arctic seas.

EAR BONE
(TYMPANIC)

BALAENA PRIMIGENIA
Van Beneden; Red
Crag; Pliocene; UK.

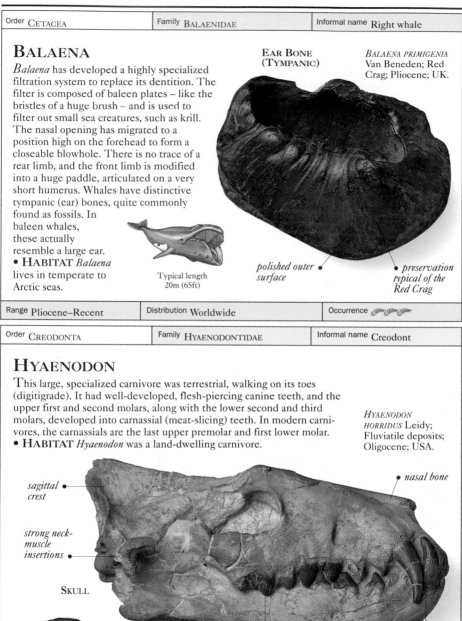

Typical length
20m (65ft)

polished outer •
surface

• preservation
typical of the
Red Crag

Range Pliocene–Recent	Distribution Worldwide	Occurrence

Order CREODONTA	Family HYAENODONTIDAE	Informal name Creodont

HYAENODON

This large, specialized carnivore was terrestrial, walking on its toes (digitigrade). It had well-developed, flesh-piercing canine teeth, and the upper first and second molars, along with the lower second and third molars, developed into carnassial (meat-slicing) teeth. In modern carnivores, the carnassials are the last upper premolar and first lower molar.
• HABITAT *Hyaenodon* was a land-dwelling carnivore.

*HYAENODON
HORRIDUS* Leidy;
Fluviatile deposits;
Oligocene; USA.

• nasal bone

sagittal •
crest

strong neck-
muscle
insertions •

SKULL

canine •
tooth

molar with shearing •
blade in upper jaw

Typical length
2m (6½ft)

Range M. Eocene–M. Miocene	Distribution Europe, N. America, Asia	Occurrence

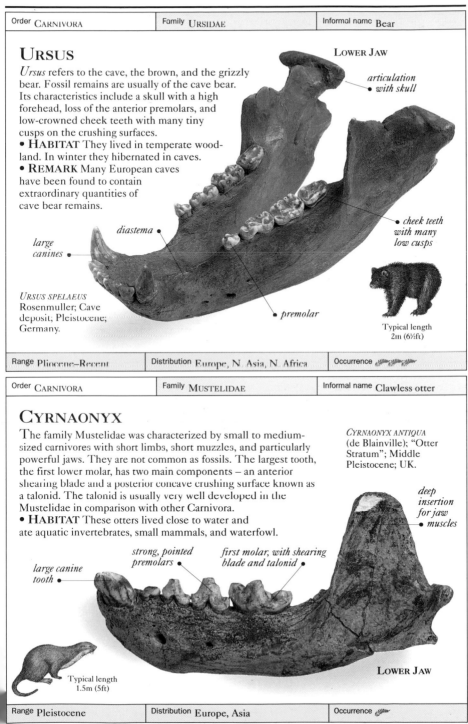

| Order CARNIVORA | Family URSIDAE | Informal name Bear |

URSUS

Ursus refers to the cave, the brown, and the grizzly bear. Fossil remains are usually of the cave bear. Its characteristics include a skull with a high forehead, loss of the anterior premolars, and low-crowned cheek teeth with many tiny cusps on the crushing surfaces.
• **HABITAT** They lived in temperate woodland. In winter they hibernated in caves.
• **REMARK** Many European caves have been found to contain extraordinary quantities of cave bear remains.

LOWER JAW

articulation with skull

cheek teeth with many low cusps

diastema

large canines

URSUS SPELAEUS Rosenmuller; Cave deposit; Pleistocene; Germany.

premolar

Typical length 2m (6½ft)

| Range Pliocene–Recent | Distribution Europe, N. Asia, N. Africa | Occurrence |

| Order CARNIVORA | Family MUSTELIDAE | Informal name Clawless otter |

CYRNAONYX

The family Mustelidae was characterized by small to medium-sized carnivores with short limbs, short muzzles, and particularly powerful jaws. They are not common as fossils. The largest tooth, the first lower molar, has two main components – an anterior shearing blade and a posterior concave crushing surface known as a talonid. The talonid is usually very well developed in the Mustelidae in comparison with other Carnivora.
• **HABITAT** These otters lived close to water and ate aquatic invertebrates, small mammals, and waterfowl.

CYRNAONYX ANTIQUA (de Blainville); "Otter Stratum"; Middle Pleistocene; UK.

deep insertion for jaw muscles

strong, pointed premolars

first molar, with shearing blade and talonid

large canine tooth

Typical length 1.5m (5ft)

LOWER JAW

| Range Pleistocene | Distribution Europe, Asia | Occurrence |

Order CARNIVORA	Family FELIDAE	Informal name Big cat

PANTHERA

The first lower molar of this large cat has a highly efficient flesh-shearing notch that works against the blade of the corresponding last upper premolar. The canine tooth is large and conical, with two prominent parallel grooves in its enamel surface, typical of the family.
• **HABITAT** *Panthera* was an open-country predator.
• **REMARK** Fossil lions are closely associated with fossil horses, and as the horses of the Middle Pleistocene were large, so, too, were the lions.

PANTHERA LEO (Linnaeus); Fluviatile deposits; Middle Pleistocene; UK.

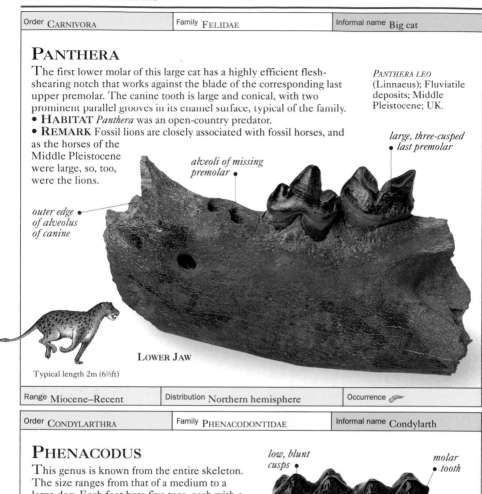

large, three-cusped last premolar

alveoli of missing premolar •

outer edge • of alveolus of canine

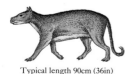

LOWER JAW

Typical length 2m (6½ft)

Range Miocene–Recent	Distribution Northern hemisphere	Occurrence

Order CONDYLARTHRA	Family PHENACODONTIDAE	Informal name Condylarth

PHENACODUS

This genus is known from the entire skeleton. The size ranges from that of a medium to a large dog. Each foot bore five toes, each with a small hoof. The teeth had low, blunt cusps, suitable for a diet consisting mainly of fruit. The family is considered close to the stem of the Perissodactyla (horses, rhinoceroses, and tapirs), the Proboscidea (elephants), and the Sirenia (sea cows).
• **HABITAT** *Phenacodus* was a ground dweller that fed mainly on fallen fruit.

PHENACODUS VORTMANI (Cope); Willwood Formation; Early Eocene; USA.

low, blunt cusps •

molar • tooth

FRAGMENT OF LOWER JAW

Typical length 90cm (36in)

Range L. Palaeocene–M. Eocene	Distribution N. America, Europe	Occurrence

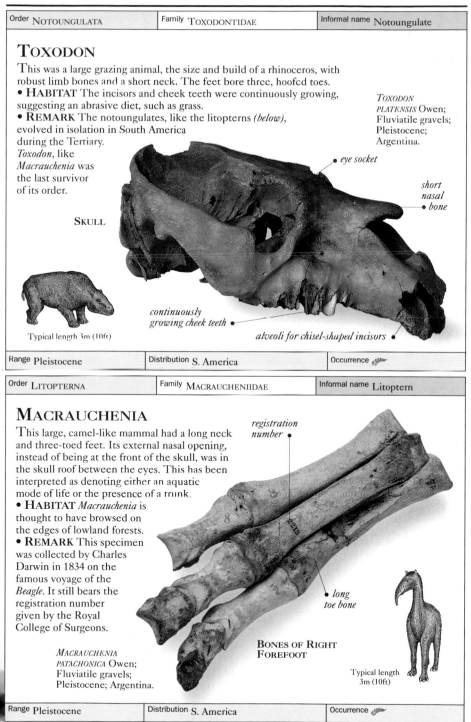

| Order NOTOUNGULATA | Family TOXODONTIDAE | Informal name Notoungulate |

TOXODON

This was a large grazing animal, the size and build of a rhinoceros, with robust limb bones and a short neck. The feet bore three, hoofed toes.
• **HABITAT** The incisors and cheek teeth were continuously growing, suggesting an abrasive diet, such as grass.
• **REMARK** The notoungulates, like the litopterns *(below)*, evolved in isolation in South America during the Tertiary. *Toxodon*, like *Macrauchenia* was the last survivor of its order.

TOXODON PLATENSIS Owen; Fluviatile gravels; Pleistocene; Argentina.

• *eye socket*

short nasal • *bone*

SKULL

continuously growing cheek teeth •

Typical length 3m (10ft)

alveoli for chisel-shaped incisors •

| Range Pleistocene | Distribution S. America | Occurrence |

| Order LITOPTERNA | Family MACRAUCHENIIDAE | Informal name Litoptern |

MACRAUCHENIA

This large, camel-like mammal had a long neck and three-toed feet. Its external nasal opening, instead of being at the front of the skull, was in the skull roof between the eyes. This has been interpreted as denoting either an aquatic mode of life or the presence of a trunk.
• **HABITAT** *Macrauchenia* is thought to have browsed on the edges of lowland forests.
• **REMARK** This specimen was collected by Charles Darwin in 1834 on the famous voyage of the *Beagle*. It still bears the registration number given by the Royal College of Surgeons.

registration number •

• *long toe bone*

MACRAUCHENIA PATACHONICA Owen; Fluviatile gravels; Pleistocene; Argentina.

BONES OF RIGHT FOREFOOT

Typical length 3m (10ft)

| Range Pleistocene | Distribution S. America | Occurrence |

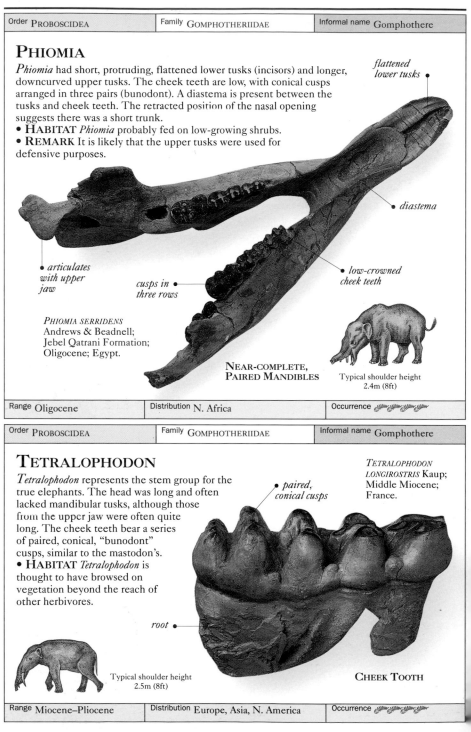

Order PROBOSCIDEA	Family GOMPHOTHERIIDAE	Informal name Gomphothere

PHIOMIA

Phiomia had short, protruding, flattened lower tusks (incisors) and longer, downcurved upper tusks. The cheek teeth are low, with conical cusps arranged in three pairs (bunodont). A diastema is present between the tusks and cheek teeth. The retracted position of the nasal opening suggests there was a short trunk.
• HABITAT *Phiomia* probably fed on low-growing shrubs.
• REMARK It is likely that the upper tusks were used for defensive purposes.

flattened lower tusks

diastema

articulates with upper jaw

cusps in three rows

low-crowned cheek teeth

PHIOMIA SERRIDENS
Andrews & Beadnell;
Jebel Qatrani Formation;
Oligocene; Egypt.

NEAR-COMPLETE, PAIRED MANDIBLES

Typical shoulder height 2.4m (8ft)

Range Oligocene	Distribution N. Africa	Occurrence

Order PROBOSCIDEA	Family GOMPHOTHERIIDAE	Informal name Gomphothere

TETRALOPHODON

Tetralophodon represents the stem group for the true elephants. The head was long and often lacked mandibular tusks, although those from the upper jaw were often quite long. The cheek teeth bear a series of paired, conical, "bunodont" cusps, similar to the mastodon's.
• HABITAT *Tetralophodon* is thought to have browsed on vegetation beyond the reach of other herbivores.

paired, conical cusps

TETRALOPHODON LONGIROSTRIS Kaup; Middle Miocene; France.

root

Typical shoulder height 2.5m (8ft)

CHEEK TOOTH

Range Miocene–Pliocene	Distribution Europe, Asia, N. America	Occurrence

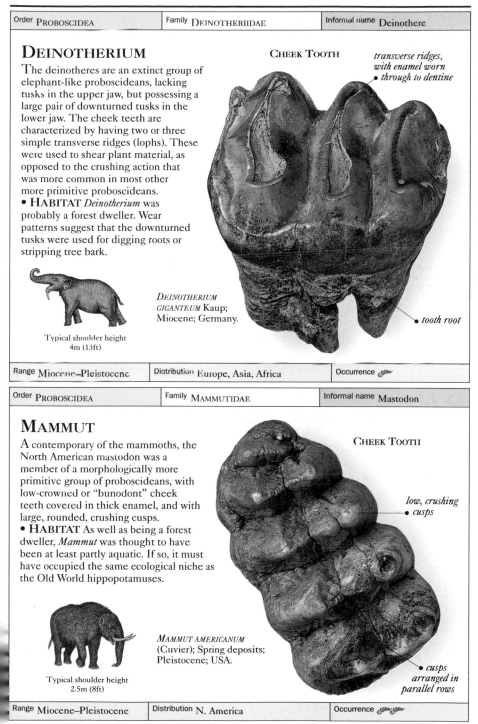

Order PROBOSCIDEA	Family DEINOTHERIIDAE	Informal name Deinothere

DEINOTHERIUM

The deinotheres are an extinct group of elephant-like proboscideans, lacking tusks in the upper jaw, but possessing a large pair of downturned tusks in the lower jaw. The cheek teeth are characterized by having two or three simple transverse ridges (lophs). These were used to shear plant material, as opposed to the crushing action that was more common in most other more primitive proboscideans.
• HABITAT *Deinotherium* was probably a forest dweller. Wear patterns suggest that the downturned tusks were used for digging roots or stripping tree bark.

CHEEK TOOTH

transverse ridges, with enamel worn • through to dentine

DEINOTHERIUM GIGANTEUM Kaup; Miocene; Germany.

• tooth root

Typical shoulder height 4m (13ft)

Range Miocene–Pleistocene	Distribution Europe, Asia, Africa	Occurrence

Order PROBOSCIDEA	Family MAMMUTIDAE	Informal name Mastodon

MAMMUT

A contemporary of the mammoths, the North American mastodon was a member of a morphologically more primitive group of proboscideans, with low-crowned or "bunodont" cheek teeth covered in thick enamel, and with large, rounded, crushing cusps.
• HABITAT As well as being a forest dweller, *Mammut* was thought to have been at least partly aquatic. If so, it must have occupied the same ecological niche as the Old World hippopotamuses.

CHEEK TOOTH

low, crushing • cusps

MAMMUT AMERICANUM (Cuvier); Spring deposits; Pleistocene; USA.

• cusps arranged in parallel rows

Typical shoulder height 2.5m (8ft)

Range Miocene–Pleistocene	Distribution N. America	Occurrence

Order PROBOSCIDEA	Family ELEPHANTIDAE	Informal name Mammoth

MAMMUTHUS

Although smaller than an African elephant, mammoths must have proved a formidable prey for early human hunters. Mammoths first appeared in the African Pliocene and rapidly spread to Europe and Asia. Their evolution can most readily be traced through their tooth structure. The teeth of a mammoth consist of a series of plates composed of enamel surrounding a dentine core. These are held together in a matrix of dental cement. Each tooth erupted from the back of the jaw and slowly moved forward as it wore, to be replaced by another tooth from behind. The thickness and number of tooth plates are important identification criteria.

• HABITAT Mammoths are thought to have grazed on grasses and low shrubs. Whole frozen carcasses have been found in the Siberian Arctic. The carcasses confirm the accuracy of drawings of long-haired mammoths in European caves.

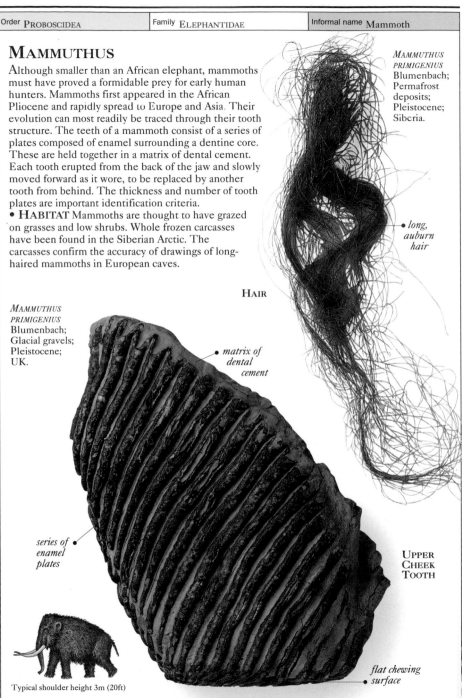

MAMMUTHUS PRIMIGENIUS Blumenbach; Permafrost deposits; Pleistocene; Siberia.

• *long, auburn hair*

HAIR

MAMMUTHUS PRIMIGENIUS Blumenbach; Glacial gravels; Pleistocene; UK.

• *matrix of dental cement*

• *series of enamel plates*

UPPER CHEEK TOOTH

• *flat chewing surface*

Typical shoulder height 3m (20ft)

Range Pliocene–E. Holocene	Distribution Europe	Occurrence

Order HYRACOIDEA	Family PLIOHYRACIDAE	Informal name Giant hyrax

TITANOHYRAX

Resembling a very large guinea pig, *Titanohyrax* was the largest known species of hyrax, about the size of a modern tapir. The incisor teeth were enlarged for nibbling, the cheek teeth were rhinoceros-like and quadrate, with a thick enamel coat and prominent lophs.
• HABITAT It is probable that *Titanohyrax* browsed on scrub vegetation.

TITANOHYRAX ULTIMUS
Matsumoto;
Jebel Qatrani
Formation;
Oligocene;
Egypt.

UPPER CHEEK TOOTH

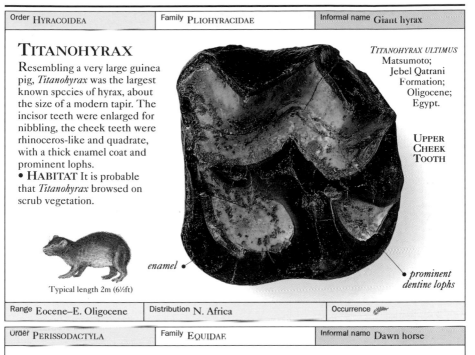

Typical length 2m (6½ft)

enamel •

• *prominent dentine lophs*

Range Eocene–E. Oligocene	Distribution N. Africa	Occurrence

Order PERISSODACTYLA	Family EQUIDAE	Informal name Dawn horse

HYRACOTHERIUM

Classically considered as the "dawn horse", the genus is related to the true horses, which evolved in North America, and the palaeotheres, which evolved in isolation in Europe and became extinct in the Oligocene. *Hyracotherium* had four toes on the forefeet and three toes on the hind feet, each of which bore a small hoof. It was adapted for running but its gait was less erect than that of a modern horse. Its teeth were low-crowned with low cusps, which enabled it to live off a diet of both fruit and soft leaves.
• HABITAT *Hyracotherium* is thought to have lived in a tropical forest environment.

HYRACOTHERIUM CRASPEDOTUM
Cope; Wind River Formation;
Early Eocene;
USA.

MAXILLA WITH CHEEK TEETH

simple, low-crowned tooth •

• *fragment of upper jaw*

Typical shoulder height 40cm (16in)

Range L. Palaeocene–E. Eocene	Distribution Europe, N. America	Occurrence

Order PERISSODACTYLA	Family EQUIDAE	Informal name Horse

EQUUS

Among the best known of all the mammals, the horse is nearly extinct in the wild – but survives in domestication. A grazing, terrestrial herbivore, the horse has square, high-crowned cheek teeth with complex enamel patterns. The feet are heavily modified, being reduced to a single, elongate metapodial with a short phalange terminating on a prominent hoof, thus adapting them for rapid forward movement on hard ground. The anatomy and physiology of the digestive system, with a large caecum and colon, enables horses to subsist upon high-fibre diets with a low protein content.
• **HABITAT** Modern horses and their relatives have teeth and limbs that are adapted for a grazing, plains-dwelling life.
• **REMARK** The genus *Equus* first appeared in North America in the Pliocene and rapidly spread to every continent except Australia and Antarctica. Cave paintings dating from the Palaeolithic period indicate that the Late Pleistocene forms resembled the extant Przewalskii's horse, with a mane of short, stiff, upwardly pointing hair.

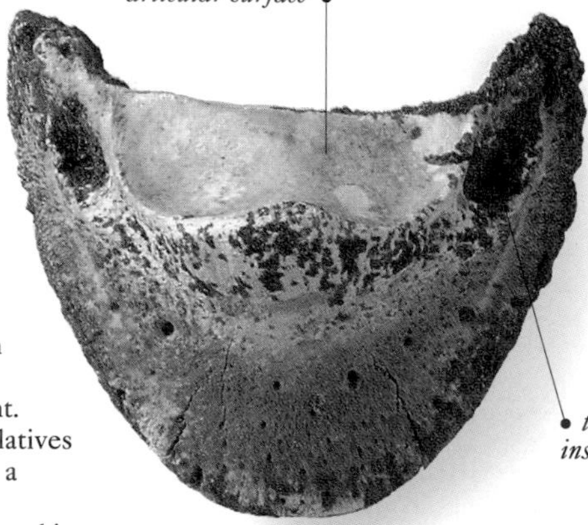

HOOF BONE
(THIRD PHALANGE)

articular surface •

• *tendon insertion*

EQUUS FERUS Boddaert; Cave earth; Late Pleistocene; UK.

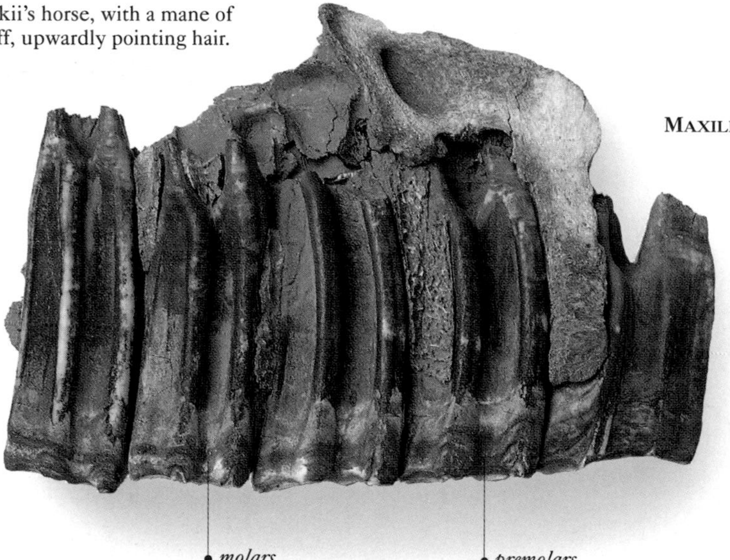

MAXILLA

• *molars*   • *premolars*

Typical shoulder height
1.5m (5ft)

Range Pliocene–Recent	Distribution Worldwide	Occurrence

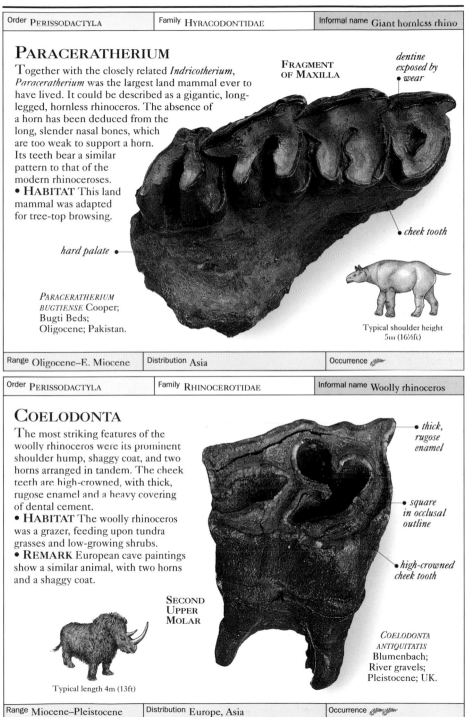

| Order PERISSODACTYLA | Family HYRACODONTIDAE | Informal name Giant hornless rhino |

PARACERATHERIUM

Together with the closely related *Indricotherium*, *Paraceratherium* was the largest land mammal ever to have lived. It could be described as a gigantic, long-legged, hornless rhinoceros. The absence of a horn has been deduced from the long, slender nasal bones, which are too weak to support a horn. Its teeth bear a similar pattern to that of the modern rhinoceroses.
• **HABITAT** This land mammal was adapted for tree-top browsing.

FRAGMENT OF MAXILLA

dentine exposed by wear

cheek tooth

hard palate

PARACERATHERIUM BUGTIENSE Cooper; Bugti Beds; Oligocene; Pakistan.

Typical shoulder height 5m (16½ft)

| Range Oligocene–E. Miocene | Distribution Asia | Occurrence |

| Order PERISSODACTYLA | Family RHINOCEROTIDAE | Informal name Woolly rhinoceros |

COELODONTA

The most striking features of the woolly rhinoceros were its prominent shoulder hump, shaggy coat, and two horns arranged in tandem. The cheek teeth are high-crowned, with thick, rugose enamel and a heavy covering of dental cement.
• **HABITAT** The woolly rhinoceros was a grazer, feeding upon tundra grasses and low-growing shrubs.
• **REMARK** European cave paintings show a similar animal, with two horns and a shaggy coat.

thick, rugose enamel

square in occlusal outline

high-crowned cheek tooth

SECOND UPPER MOLAR

COELODONTA ANTIQUITATIS Blumenbach; River gravels; Pleistocene; UK.

Typical length 4m (13ft)

| Range Miocene–Pleistocene | Distribution Europe, Asia | Occurrence |

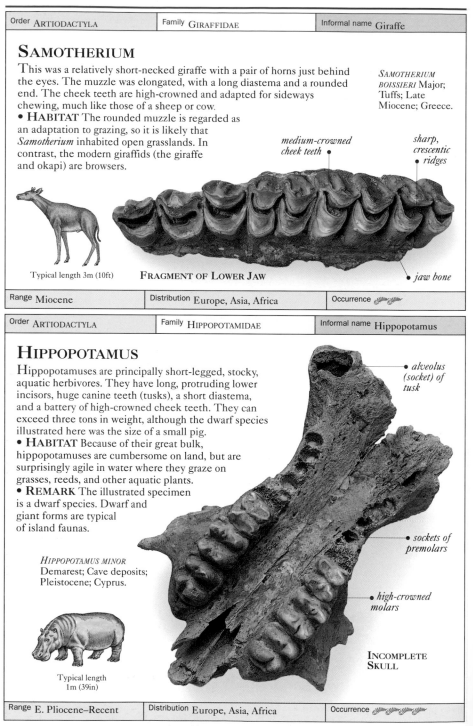

| Order ARTIODACTYLA | Family GIRAFFIDAE | Informal name Giraffe |

SAMOTHERIUM

This was a relatively short-necked giraffe with a pair of horns just behind the eyes. The muzzle was elongated, with a long diastema and a rounded end. The cheek teeth are high-crowned and adapted for sideways chewing, much like those of a sheep or cow.
• HABITAT The rounded muzzle is regarded as an adaptation to grazing, so it is likely that *Samotherium* inhabited open grasslands. In contrast, the modern giraffids (the giraffe and okapi) are browsers.

SAMOTHERIUM BOISSIERI Major; Tuffs; Late Miocene; Greece.

medium-crowned cheek teeth

sharp, crescentic ridges

Typical length 3m (10ft)

FRAGMENT OF LOWER JAW

jaw bone

| Range Miocene | Distribution Europe, Asia, Africa | Occurrence |

| Order ARTIODACTYLA | Family HIPPOPOTAMIDAE | Informal name Hippopotamus |

HIPPOPOTAMUS

Hippopotamuses are principally short-legged, stocky, aquatic herbivores. They have long, protruding lower incisors, huge canine teeth (tusks), a short diastema, and a battery of high-crowned cheek teeth. They can exceed three tons in weight, although the dwarf species illustrated here was the size of a small pig.
• HABITAT Because of their great bulk, hippopotamuses are cumbersome on land, but are surprisingly agile in water where they graze on grasses, reeds, and other aquatic plants.
• REMARK The illustrated specimen is a dwarf species. Dwarf and giant forms are typical of island faunas.

alveolus (socket) of tusk

sockets of premolars

HIPPOPOTAMUS MINOR Demarest; Cave deposits; Pleistocene; Cyprus.

high-crowned molars

Typical length 1m (39in)

INCOMPLETE SKULL

| Range E. Pliocene–Recent | Distribution Europe, Asia, Africa | Occurrence |

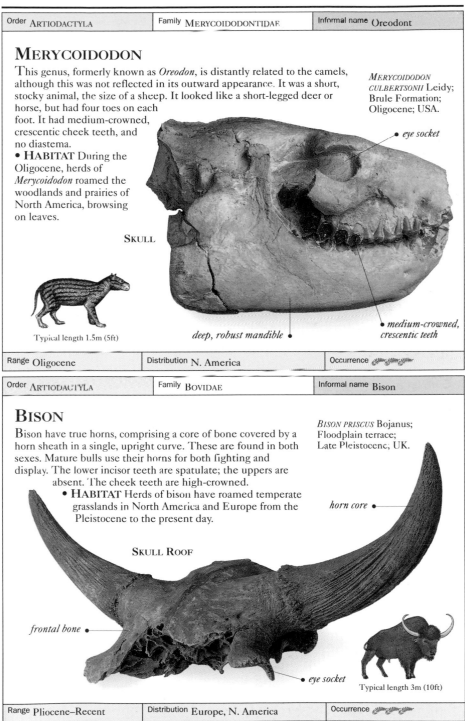

Order ARTIODACTYLA	Family MERYCOIDODONTIDAE	Informal name Oreodont

MERYCOIDODON

This genus, formerly known as *Oreodon*, is distantly related to the camels, although this was not reflected in its outward appearance. It was a short, stocky animal, the size of a sheep. It looked like a short-legged deer or horse, but had four toes on each foot. It had medium-crowned, crescentic cheek teeth, and no diastema.
• HABITAT During the Oligocene, herds of *Merycoidodon* roamed the woodlands and prairies of North America, browsing on leaves.

MERYCOIDODON CULBERTSONII Leidy; Brule Formation; Oligocene; USA.

• *eye socket*

SKULL

Typical length 1.5m (5ft)

deep, robust mandible •

• *medium-crowned, crescentic teeth*

Range Oligocene	Distribution N. America	Occurrence

Order ARTIODACTYLA	Family BOVIDAE	Informal name Bison

BISON

Bison have true horns, comprising a core of bone covered by a horn sheath in a single, upright curve. These are found in both sexes. Mature bulls use their horns for both fighting and display. The lower incisor teeth are spatulate; the uppers are absent. The cheek teeth are high-crowned.
• HABITAT Herds of bison have roamed temperate grasslands in North America and Europe from the Pleistocene to the present day.

BISON PRISCUS Bojanus; Floodplain terrace; Late Pleistocene, UK.

horn core •

SKULL ROOF

frontal bone •

• *eye socket*

Typical length 3m (10ft)

Range Pliocene–Recent	Distribution Europe, N. America	Occurrence

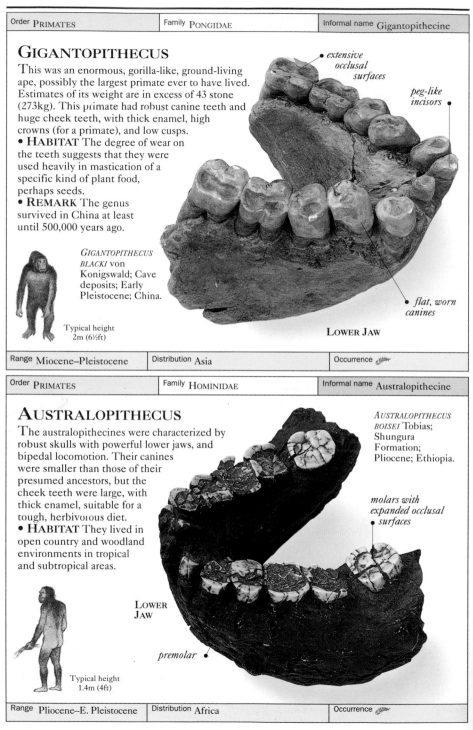

| Order PRIMATES | Family PONGIDAE | Informal name Gigantopithecine |

GIGANTOPITHECUS

This was an enormous, gorilla-like, ground-living ape, possibly the largest primate ever to have lived. Estimates of its weight are in excess of 43 stone (273kg). This primate had robust canine teeth and huge cheek teeth, with thick enamel, high crowns (for a primate), and low cusps.
• **HABITAT** The degree of wear on the teeth suggests that they were used heavily in mastication of a specific kind of plant food, perhaps seeds.
• **REMARK** The genus survived in China at least until 500,000 years ago.

• *extensive occlusal surfaces*

peg-like incisors •

GIGANTOPITHECUS BLACKI von Konigswald; Cave deposits; Early Pleistocene; China.

• *flat, worn canines*

LOWER JAW

Typical height
2m (6½ft)

| Range Miocene–Pleistocene | Distribution Asia | Occurrence |

| Order PRIMATES | Family HOMINIDAE | Informal name Australopithecine |

AUSTRALOPITHECUS

The australopithecines were characterized by robust skulls with powerful lower jaws, and bipedal locomotion. Their canines were smaller than those of their presumed ancestors, but the cheek teeth were large, with thick enamel, suitable for a tough, herbivorous diet.
• **HABITAT** They lived in open country and woodland environments in tropical and subtropical areas.

AUSTRALOPITHECUS BOISEI Tobias; Shungura Formation; Pliocene; Ethiopia.

molars with expanded occlusal • *surfaces*

LOWER JAW

premolar •

Typical height
1.4m (4ft)

| Range Pliocene–E. Pleistocene | Distribution Africa | Occurrence |

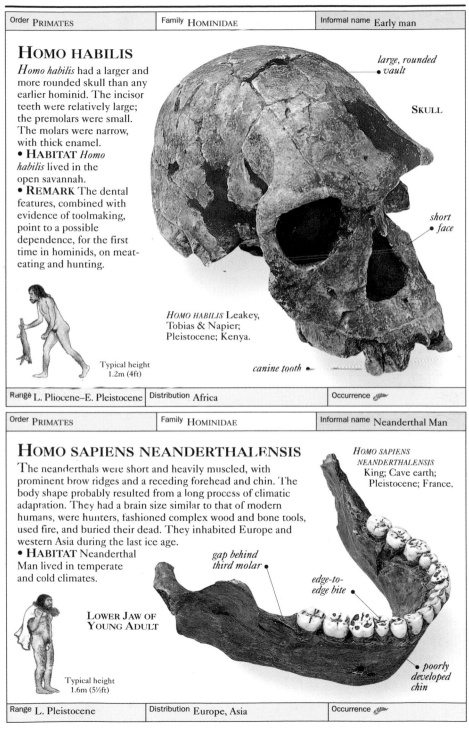

| Order PRIMATES | Family HOMINIDAE | Informal name Early man |

HOMO HABILIS

Homo habilis had a larger and more rounded skull than any earlier hominid. The incisor teeth were relatively large; the premolars were small. The molars were narrow, with thick enamel.
• **HABITAT** *Homo habilis* lived in the open savannah.
• **REMARK** The dental features, combined with evidence of toolmaking, point to a possible dependence, for the first time in hominids, on meat-eating and hunting.

large, rounded vault

SKULL

short face

HOMO HABILIS Leakey, Tobias & Napier; Pleistocene; Kenya.

Typical height 1.2m (4ft)

canine tooth

| Range L. Pliocene–E. Pleistocene | Distribution Africa | Occurrence |

| Order PRIMATES | Family HOMINIDAE | Informal name Neanderthal Man |

HOMO SAPIENS NEANDERTHALENSIS

The neanderthals were short and heavily muscled, with prominent brow ridges and a receding forehead and chin. The body shape probably resulted from a long process of climatic adaptation. They had a brain size similar to that of modern humans, were hunters, fashioned complex wood and bone tools, used fire, and buried their dead. They inhabited Europe and western Asia during the last ice age.
• **HABITAT** Neanderthal Man lived in temperate and cold climates.

HOMO SAPIENS NEANDERTHALENSIS King; Cave earth; Pleistocene; France.

gap behind third molar

edge-to-edge bite

LOWER JAW OF YOUNG ADULT

poorly developed chin

Typical height 1.6m (5½ft)

| Range L. Pleistocene | Distribution Europe, Asia | Occurrence |

Order PRIMATES	Family HOMINIDAE	Informal name Modern man

HOMO SAPIENS SAPIENS

Modern humans are taller than the neanderthals, with more gracile bones, more prominent chins and more domed foreheads. Their teeth are similar, though the incisors are less protruding.
• **HABITAT** Although once restricted to warm climates, the acquisition of the skills to make clothing and construct shelters allowed modern humans to colonize more hostile environments. Co-operative hunting, armed with simple stone and wood weapons, allowed them to exploit prey that would otherwise have eluded them.
• **REMARK** Modern humans manufactured a variety of tools with specific functions, as distinct from the multi-purpose axes of their forbears. The bone, flint, and antler tools shown opposite are often found associated with fossil human remains, although not strictly speaking fossils themselves. Although of different ages and degrees of sophistication, they indicate a level of culture rather than a specific date.

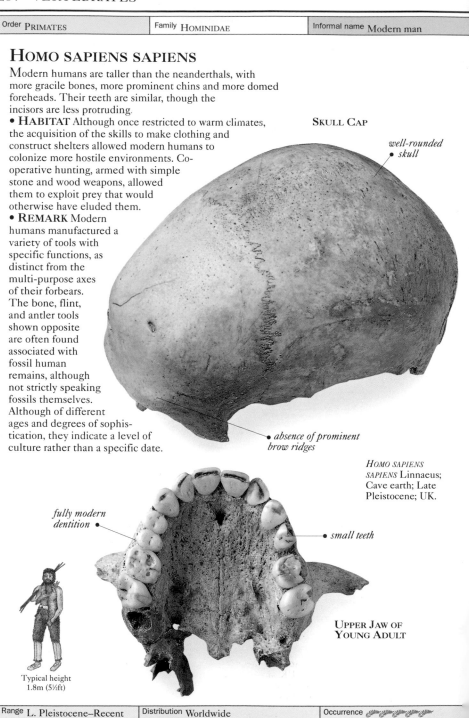

SKULL CAP

well-rounded skull

absence of prominent brow ridges

HOMO SAPIENS SAPIENS Linnaeus; Cave earth; Late Pleistocene; UK.

fully modern dentition

small teeth

UPPER JAW OF YOUNG ADULT

Typical height 1.8m (5½ft)

Range L. Pleistocene–Recent	Distribution Worldwide	Occurrence

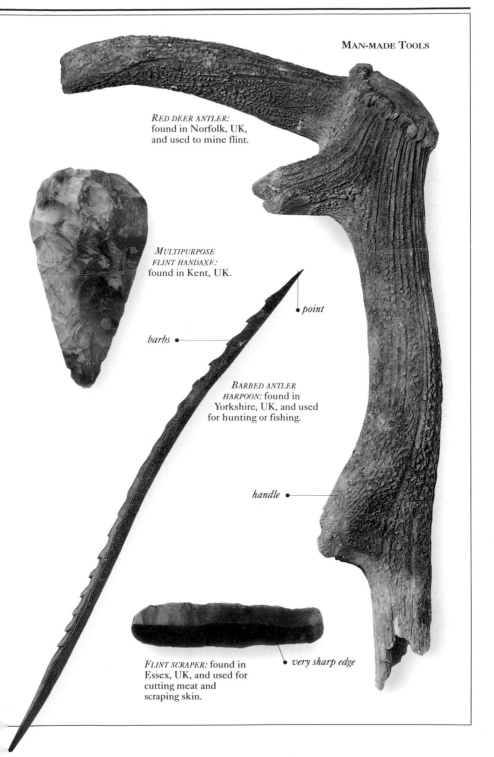

MAN-MADE TOOLS

RED DEER ANTLER:
found in Norfolk, UK,
and used to mine flint.

MULTIPURPOSE
FLINT HANDAXE:
found in Kent, UK.

point

barbs

BARBED ANTLER
HARPOON: found in
Yorkshire, UK, and used
for hunting or fishing.

handle

FLINT SCRAPER: found in
Essex, UK, and used for
cutting meat and
scraping skin.

very sharp edge

PLANTS

ALGAE

T HE ALGAE HAVE A fossil record that extends from the Precambrian to the present day. Some algae are important age indicators and are used extensively in the oil industry. They present a wide range of form, from simple unicells to complex multi-cellular plants. Fossil remains are usually limited to those which produce structures impregnated with silica or forms of calcium carbonate, or which developed tough-walled cysts. As algae released oxygen into the atmosphere, they were responsible for a critical change in atmospheric composition during the Precambrian.

Order CYANOPHYTA	Family Unclassified	Informal name Stromatolites

COLLENIA

Part of the stromatolite group, this genus has a conical to cylindrical structure composed of limestone and/or silica. This structure is always layered, sometimes with alternating light and dark bands. The minute algal threads of which it is composed can be seen under the microscope. These threads bound to-gether detrital sands and muds in a bed of lime produced by the algae.
• HABITAT Like living stroma-tolitic algae, *Collenia* inhabited tropical intertidal zones.

COLLENIA sp.;
Stromatolitic Limestone;
Precambrian; USA.

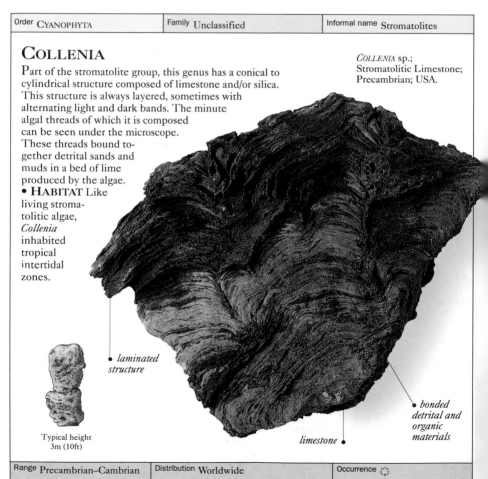

• *laminated structure*

Typical height
3m (10ft)

limestone •

• *bonded detrital and organic materials*

Range Precambrian–Cambrian	Distribution Worldwide	Occurrence ⌂

PLANTS • 287

Order DASYCLADALES	Family DASYCLADACEAE	Informal name Green alga

MASTOPORA

The genus is characterized by clusters of thalli originating from a central axis. The resulting globular structure was covered by a calcified mucillage, which helped it to be preserved as a fossil. The reticulum was formed by primary branches radiating from a central axis; each branch terminated bluntly and secreted a protective limestone covering. The fossils have a characteristic hexagonal honeycomb pattern on the surface. Each hexagon has a raised border with a depressed centre, imparting a rough surface to the fossil.
• HABITAT *Mastopora* are usually associated with fossil coral reefs, brachiopods, and bryozoans.
• REMARK This genus of plants was previously and inaccurately classified as an animal (proto-zoan or sponge).

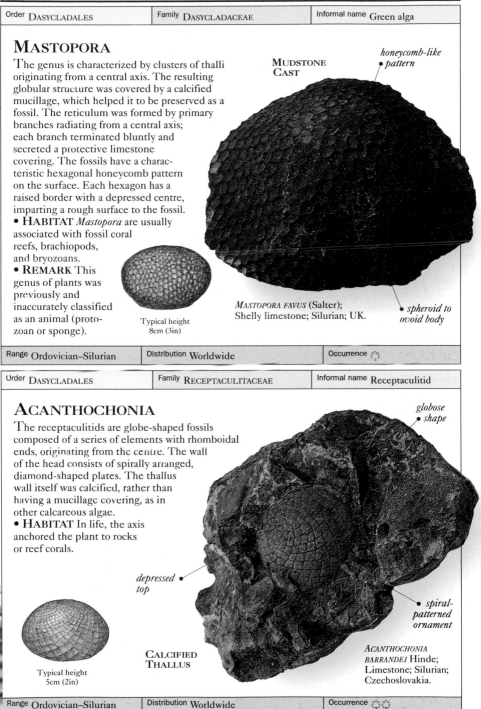

MUDSTONE CAST

honeycomb-like pattern

Typical height 8cm (3in)

MASTOPORA FAVUS (Salter); Shelly limestone; Silurian; UK.

spheroid to ovoid body

Range Ordovician–Silurian	Distribution Worldwide	Occurrence

Order DASYCLADALES	Family RECEPTACULITACEAE	Informal name Receptaculitid

ACANTHOCHONIA

The receptaculitids are globe-shaped fossils composed of a series of elements with rhomboidal ends, originating from the centre. The wall of the head consists of spirally arranged, diamond-shaped plates. The thallus wall itself was calcified, rather than having a mucillage covering, as in other calcareous algae.
• HABITAT In life, the axis anchored the plant to rocks or reef corals.

globose shape

depressed top

spiral-patterned ornament

Typical height 5cm (2in)

CALCIFIED THALLUS

ACANTHOCHONIA BARRANDEI Hinde; Limestone; Silurian; Czechoslovakia.

Range Ordovician–Silurian	Distribution Worldwide	Occurrence

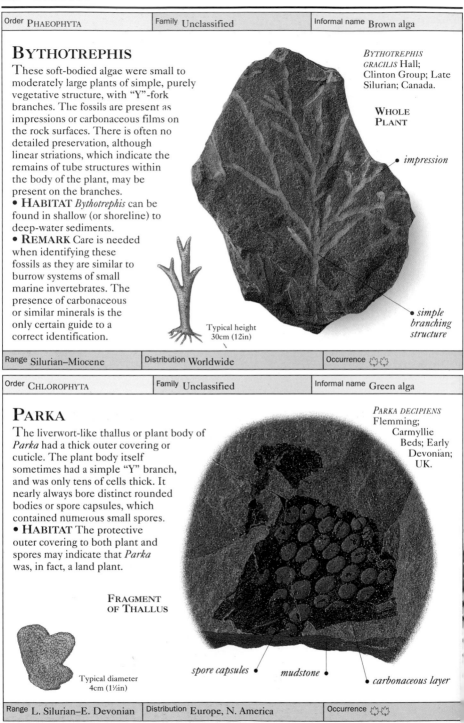

| Order PHAEOPHYTA | Family Unclassified | Informal name Brown alga |

BYTHOTREPHIS

These soft-bodied algae were small to
moderately large plants of simple, purely
vegetative structure, with "Y"-fork
branches. The fossils are present as
impressions or carbonaceous films on
the rock surfaces. There is often no
detailed preservation, although
linear striations, which indicate the
remains of tube structures within
the body of the plant, may be
present on the branches.
• HABITAT *Bythotrephis* can be
found in shallow (or shoreline) to
deep-water sediments.
• REMARK Care is needed
when identifying these
fossils as they are similar to
burrow systems of small
marine invertebrates. The
presence of carbonaceous
or similar minerals is the
only certain guide to a
correct identification.

*BYTHOTREPHIS
GRACILIS* Hall;
Clinton Group; Late
Silurian; Canada.

WHOLE
PLANT

• *impression*

• *simple
branching
structure*

Typical height
30cm (12in)

| Range Silurian–Miocene | Distribution Worldwide | Occurrence |

| Order CHLOROPHYTA | Family Unclassified | Informal name Green alga |

PARKA

The liverwort-like thallus or plant body of
Parka had a thick outer covering or
cuticle. The plant body itself
sometimes had a simple "Y" branch,
and was only tens of cells thick. It
nearly always bore distinct rounded
bodies or spore capsules, which
contained numerous small spores.
• HABITAT The protective
outer covering to both plant and
spores may indicate that *Parka*
was, in fact, a land plant.

PARKA DECIPIENS
Flemming;
Carmyllie
Beds; Early
Devonian;
UK.

FRAGMENT
OF THALLUS

spore capsules •   *mudstone* •   • *carbonaceous layer*

Typical diameter
4cm (1½in)

| Range L. Silurian–E. Devonian | Distribution Europe, N. America | Occurrence |

EARLY LAND PLANTS

THE FIRST INDISPUTABLE land plants are characterized by a mechanical supporting tissue which provided rigidity, a perforated cuticle which allowed the plant to "breathe", and spores resistant to desiccation, due to a tough spore coat, which helped them to survive and germinate on land. Spore-bearing capsules were borne either at the ends of thin branches, singly or in bunches, or along the sides. These plants ranged from small, scrambling types to spiny-stemmed varieties one metre (3ft) tall.

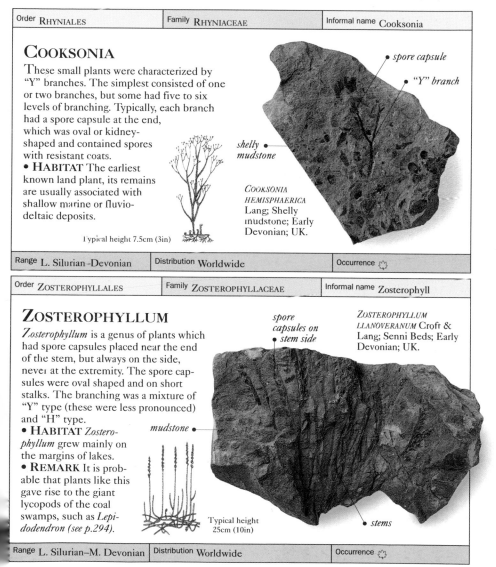

Order RHYNIALES	Family RHYNIACEAE	Informal name Cooksonia

COOKSONIA

These small plants were characterized by "Y" branches. The simplest consisted of one or two branches, but some had five to six levels of branching. Typically, each branch had a spore capsule at the end, which was oval or kidney-shaped and contained spores with resistant coats.
• **HABITAT** The earliest known land plant, its remains are usually associated with shallow marine or fluvio-deltaic deposits.

Typical height 7.5cm (3in)

spore capsule

"Y" branch

shelly mudstone

COOKSONIA HEMISPHAERICA Lang; Shelly mudstone; Early Devonian; UK.

Range L. Silurian–Devonian	Distribution Worldwide	Occurrence ☼

Order ZOSTEROPHYLLALES	Family ZOSTEROPHYLLACEAE	Informal name Zosterophyll

ZOSTEROPHYLLUM

Zosterophyllum is a genus of plants which had spore capsules placed near the end of the stem, but always on the side, never at the extremity. The spore capsules were oval shaped and on short stalks. The branching was a mixture of "Y" type (these were less pronounced) and "H" type.
• **HABITAT** Zostero-phyllum grew mainly on the margins of lakes.
• **REMARK** It is probable that plants like this gave rise to the giant lycopods of the coal swamps, such as *Lepidodendron (see p.294)*.

spore capsules on stem side

mudstone

Typical height 25cm (10in)

stems

ZOSTEROPHYLLUM LLANOVERANUM Croft & Lang; Senni Beds; Early Devonian; UK.

Range L. Silurian–M. Devonian	Distribution Worldwide	Occurrence ☼

HEPATOPHYTES

HEPATOPHYTES OR LIVERWORTS are small plants, with flat (thalloid) or leafy bodies. They reproduce by spores contained in capsules borne on wiry stems. They usually have either prone growth (thalloid liverworts), or only limited vertical growth (leafy liverworts). They have a poor fossil record. Today these plants are found in damp environments worldwide.

Order MARCHANTIALES	Family MARCHANTIACEAE	Informal name Liverwort

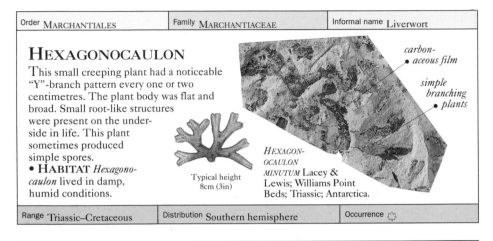

HEXAGONOCAULON

This small creeping plant had a noticeable "Y"-branch pattern every one or two centimetres. The plant body was flat and broad. Small root-like structures were present on the under-side in life. This plant sometimes produced simple spores.
• **HABITAT** *Hexagono-caulon* lived in damp, humid conditions.

Typical height 8cm (3in)

carbon-aceous film

simple branching plants

HEXAGON-OCAULON MINUTUM Lacey & Lewis; Williams Point Beds; Triassic; Antarctica.

Range Triassic–Cretaceous	Distribution Southern hemisphere	Occurrence

SPHENOPSIDS

THE FOSSIL HISTORY of sphenopsids can be traced back to the Late Devonian. Commonly known as horsetails, these plants have jointed stems and leaves produced in whorls about the stem. The spores are produced in spore capsules, which are tightly grouped into cones.

Order EQUISETALES	Family EQUISETACEAE	Informal name Horsetail

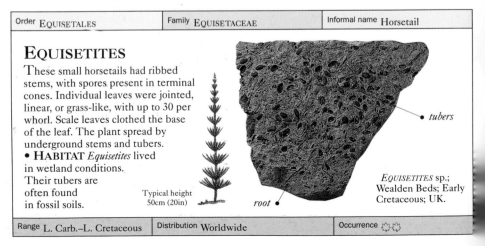

EQUISETITES

These small horsetails had ribbed stems, with spores present in terminal cones. Individual leaves were jointed, linear, or grass-like, with up to 30 per whorl. Scale leaves clothed the base of the leaf. The plant spread by underground stems and tubers.
• **HABITAT** *Equisetites* lived in wetland conditions. Their tubers are often found in fossil soils.

Typical height 50cm (20in)

root

tubers

EQUISETITES sp.; Wealden Beds; Early Cretaceous; UK.

Range L. Carb.–L. Cretaceous	Distribution Worldwide	Occurrence

Order EQUISETALES	Family CALAMOSTACHYACEAE	Informal name Horsetail

ASTEROPHYLLITES

This horsetail was actually tree-sized. The stem was ribbed and derived
its strength from an outer cylinder of wood-like tissue (as seen in
bamboo), protecting a spongy interior. The branches were arranged
in whorls about the thick main stem. The leaves were sword-shaped,
with a single, central vein, and arranged in whorls about the branch,
which gave a dense, almost ornamental-conifer look to the mature
plant. It spread by underground runners, or by spores produced in
terminal cones formed from tight aggregations of whorled spore
capsules and cone leaves.

*ASTEROPHYLLITES
EQUISETIFORMIS*
(Brongniart); Coal
Measures; Late
Carboniferous; UK.

• HABITAT *Asterophyllites* was one of several primitive
plant groups to reach gigantic sizes in the Late
Carboniferous swamps.

branch

jointed stems

leaves
in whorls

carbonized leaves

shale

Typical height
10m (33ft)

Range L. Carb.–E. Permian	Distribution Worldwide	Occurrence 🍁🍁🍁

FERNS

THIS LARGE GROUP of plants has a fossil record extending back to the Middle Devonian. Ferns have leaves, called fronds, which usually consist of leaflets, although some have entire or undivided fronds. Reproduction is by spores produced in a variety of spore capsule types, found either on the underside of fronds or, more rarely, produced on specialized fronds. Sizes vary from large tree ferns to minute filmy ferns. They live in a wide range of habitats, ranging from the tropics to cold, temperate regions.

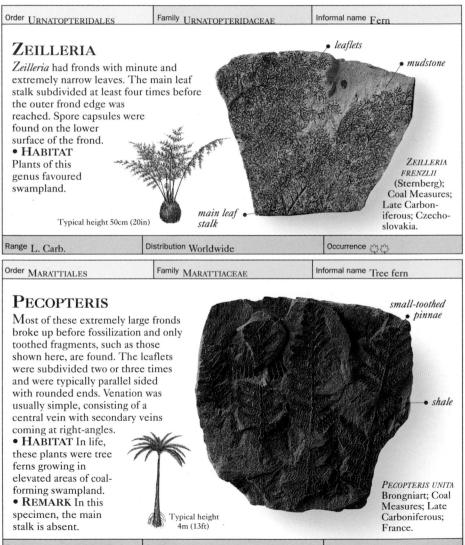

Order URNATOPTERIDALES	Family URNATOPTERIDACEAE	Informal name Fern

ZEILLERIA

Zeilleria had fronds with minute and extremely narrow leaves. The main leaf stalk subdivided at least four times before the outer frond edge was reached. Spore capsules were found on the lower surface of the frond.
• HABITAT Plants of this genus favoured swampland.

Typical height 50cm (20in)

leaflets

mudstone

main leaf stalk

ZEILLERIA FRENZLII (Sternberg); Coal Measures; Late Carboniferous; Czechoslovakia.

Range L. Carb.	Distribution Worldwide	Occurrence ⚘⚘

Order MARATTIALES	Family MARATTIACEAE	Informal name Tree fern

PECOPTERIS

Most of these extremely large fronds broke up before fossilization and only toothed fragments, such as those shown here, are found. The leaflets were subdivided two or three times and were typically parallel sided with rounded ends. Venation was usually simple, consisting of a central vein with secondary veins coming at right-angles.
• HABITAT In life, these plants were tree ferns growing in elevated areas of coal-forming swampland.
• REMARK In this specimen, the main stalk is absent.

Typical height 4m (13ft)

small-toothed pinnae

shale

PECOPTERIS UNITA Brongniart; Coal Measures; Late Carboniferous; France.

Range L. Carb.–E. Permian	Distribution Worldwide	Occurrence ⚘⚘⚘

Order OSMUNDALES	Family OSMUNDACEAE	Informal name Royal fern

OSMUNDA

This is a fern with a short stem, large ordinary fronds, and specialized spore-bearing fronds. The stem, where present, has a fibrous structure with many leaf bases passing through it to the outside. The ordinary fronds bear large leaflets with complex netted venation. Spore-bearing fronds either have no leaflets or they are only present at the leaf-stalk end.
• HABITAT It is probable that, like its modern counterpart, fossil plants of this genus were to be found near water, often in tropical or warm, temperate, wetland areas.

OSMUNDA DOWKERI (Carruthers); Thanet Formation; Palaeocene; UK.

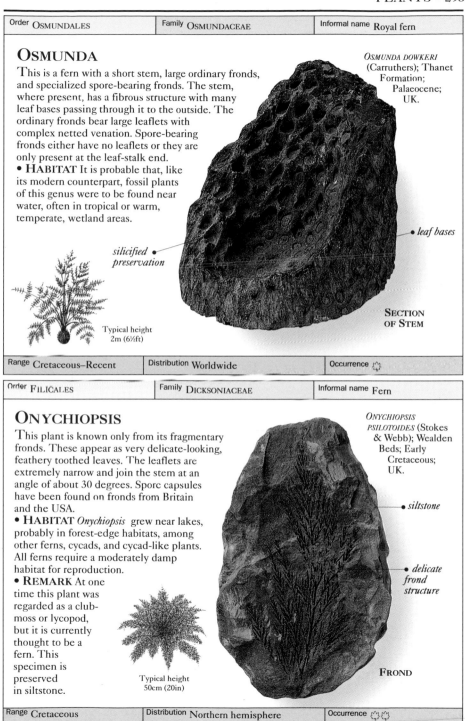

leaf bases

silicified preservation

Typical height 2m (6½ft)

SECTION OF STEM

Range Cretaceous–Recent	Distribution Worldwide	Occurrence

Order FILICALES	Family DICKSONIACEAE	Informal name Fern

ONYCHIOPSIS

This plant is known only from its fragmentary fronds. These appear as very delicate-looking, feathery toothed leaves. The leaflets are extremely narrow and join the stem at an angle of about 30 degrees. Spore capsules have been found on fronds from Britain and the USA.
• HABITAT *Onychiopsis* grew near lakes, probably in forest-edge habitats, among other ferns, cycads, and cycad-like plants. All ferns require a moderately damp habitat for reproduction.
• REMARK At one time this plant was regarded as a club-moss or lycopod, but it is currently thought to be a fern. This specimen is preserved in siltstone.

ONYCHIOPSIS PSILOTOIDES (Stokes & Webb); Wealden Beds; Early Cretaceous; UK.

siltstone

delicate frond structure

Typical height 50cm (20in)

FROND

Range Cretaceous	Distribution Northern hemisphere	Occurrence

LYCOPODS

THE LYCOPODS OR CLUB-MOSSES have a long fossil history, stretching back to the Late Silurian. They reached their peak in the Late Carboniferous, and today they are represented by only a handful of genera. All plants have spirally arranged leaves with spore capsules in the leaf axil, or aggregated into distinct terminal cones. In the Carboniferous, many lycopods were tree-sized, with branches clothed in long, grass-like foliage and cones containing spores. Today, lycopods are small herbaceous plants.

Order LEPIDODENDRALES	Family LEPIDODENDRACEAE	Informal name Giant club-moss

LEPIDODENDRON

These tree-sized lycopods or club-mosses are notable for their scale-like bark. From the base upwards the plant was anchored in shallow soil by several "Y"-branch rooting organs called stigmaria. These had spirally arranged, finger-sized roots coming from them. A pole-like trunk, unbranched for most of its length, and up to 40m (130ft) or more in height, supported a crown of simple branches. Much of the trunk was covered in diamond-shaped leaf bosses, the familiar *Lepidodendron* fossil. Grass-like leaves, spirally arranged, clothed the upper branches, terminating in cigar-shaped cones (*Lepidostrobus*). These contained, depending on the species, only small spores, large spores, or both.
• **HABITAT** *Lepidodendron* grew in hot and humid swampland.

LEPIDODENDRON ACULEATUM Sternberg; Coal Measures; Late Carboniferous; UK.

BARK

• *scale-like surface*

ironstone nodule •

diamond-shaped • *pattern*

• *cast*

LEPIDOSTROBUS VARIABILIS Lindley & Hutton; Coal Measures; Late Carboniferous; Locality Unknown.

CIGAR-SHAPED CONE

Typical height 30m (100ft)

Range Carb.	Distribution Worldwide	Occurrence ✿✿✿✿

Order DREPANOPHYCALES	Family DREPANOPHYCACEAE	Informal name Club-moss

BARAGWANATHIA

These were prostrate or low-growing, soft-bodied (herbaceous) plants, with a simple "Y"-branch structure. The stems were always entirely clothed in fine leaves about one centimetre (⅜ in) in length. Spore capsules were present where the leaf joined the main stem (axil). The capsules were organized into zones up the stem, but not into cones.

• HABITAT *Baragwanathia* grew in lowland areas and flood-plains.

• REMARK Much debate has arisen from *Baragwanathia* appearing in the fossil record as early as the Late Silurian, given that it is such an "advanced" plant in comparison to its contemporaries.

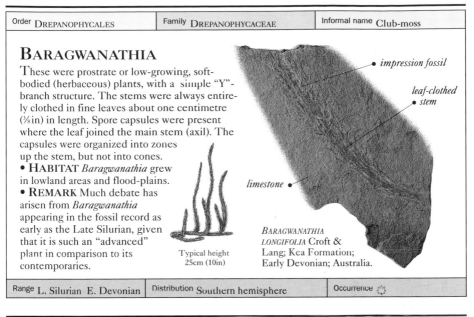

impression fossil

leaf-clothed stem

limestone

Typical height 25cm (10in)

BARAGWANATHIA LONGIFOLIA Croft & Lang; Kea Formation; Early Devonian; Australia.

Range L. Silurian–E. Devonian	Distribution Southern hemisphere	Occurrence

PTERIDOSPERMS

T HIS DIVERSE GROUP of plants was at its height during the Late Palaeozoic and most of the Mesozoic. Pteridosperms were popularly called seed ferns, after the Carboniferous forms that had foliage seemingly indistinguishable from some ferns. Evidence of seed association, discovered earlier this century, has now placed them within their own group.

Order MEDULLOSALES	Family MEDULLOSACEAE	Informal name Seed fern

PARIPTERIS

The illustrated pollen-bearing organ of *Paripteris* is called a potoniea. Bell-shaped, it was produced upon separate candelabra-like structures at the base of the frond. Each potoniea had many finger-like pollen-producing structures.

• HABITAT *Paripteris* was an inhabitant of elevated regions of hot, humid, swampland.

ironstone nodule

compression fossil

pollen organ

Typical height 5m (16½ft)

PARIPTERIS GIGANTEA (Sternberg) Gothan; Late Carboniferous; UK.

Range L. Carb.	Distribution Worldwide	Occurrence

| Order MEDULLOSALES | Family MEDULLOSACEAE | Informal name Seed fern |

MEDULLOSA

These were seed-bearing plants, growing up to 5m (16½ft) in height. The stem or trunk consisted partially of old leaf bases, similar to the sago palm (cycad), with prop-roots coming off near the base. They bore enormous fronds of various types: some toothed, others with rounded leaflets. All reproduced by seeds, which were often quite large.
• HABITAT This was a typical plant of Late Carboniferous swamps.
• REMARK The genus *Medullosa* may, in fact, represent a number of similar genera.

MEDULLOSA NOEI Steidtmann; Coal Measures; Late Carboniferous; USA.

Typical height 5m (16½ft)

COAL-BALL SECTION

preservation of fine detail

| Range L. Carb.–E. Permian | Distribution Worldwide | Occurrence |

| Order MEDULLOSALES | Family MEDULLOSACEAE | Informal name Seed fern |

ALETHOPTERIS

This plant was characterized by large fronds with toothed leaflets. Typically, the thick, robust individual leaflets were not separated from one another but connected by leaf tissue running between them. Venation was simple: a central vein with smaller veins coming off it at, or near to, right-angles.
• HABITAT *Alethopteris* grew in elevated areas of hot swamps.
• REMARK This genus name applies to the foliage, which was was borne on *Medullosa* stems. The name *Alethopteris* is used for a number of plants with a similar frond shape, which may not, in fact, be closely related.

ALETHOPTERIS SERLII Brongniart; Coal Measures; Late Carboniferous; USA.

cast

thick, strong-veined leaflets

ironstone nodule

Typical height 5m (16½ft)

frond part

| Range L. Carb–E. Permian | Distribution Worldwide | Occurrence |

| Order GLOSSOPTERIDALES | Family GLOSSOPTERIDACEAE | Informal name Gondwana Tree |

GLOSSOPTERIS

These were tree-sized pteridosperms with rosettes of small to very large leaves. The leaves varied in shape from very narrow to broad, and were similar in shape to banana leaves. The venation consisted of a broad central vein which was made up of many smaller veins. From this, a fine reticulum (or net) of minor veins spread, dividing the leaf surface into small lozenge shapes. The wood was of softwood type, with evidence of growth rings, indicating a seasonal climate. Fructifications were borne on specialized leaves, such as pollen-bearing capsules or seed-bearing structures.
• HABITAT *Glossopteris* grew in warm, damp lowlands.

SLAB OF
LEAF BED

GLOSSOPTERIS
sp.; Red beds;
Permian; India.

shale

net venation

*sword-shaped
leaves*

*straight leaf
margins*

Typical height
8m (26ft)

| Range Permian | Distribution Southern hemisphere | Occurrence |

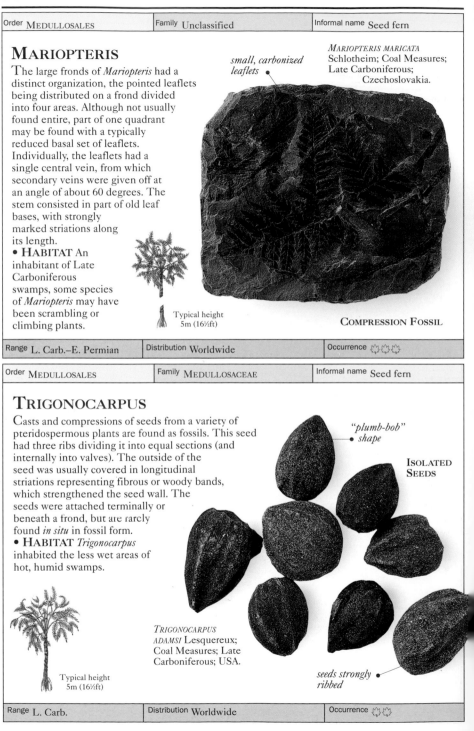

| Order MEDULLOSALES | Family Unclassified | Informal name Seed fern |

MARIOPTERIS

The large fronds of *Mariopteris* had a distinct organization, the pointed leaflets being distributed on a frond divided into four areas. Although not usually found entire, part of one quadrant may be found with a typically reduced basal set of leaflets. Individually, the leaflets had a single central vein, from which secondary veins were given off at an angle of about 60 degrees. The stem consisted in part of old leaf bases, with strongly marked striations along its length.
• HABITAT An inhabitant of Late Carboniferous swamps, some species of *Mariopteris* may have been scrambling or climbing plants.

small, carbonized leaflets

MARIOPTERIS MARICATA Schlotheim; Coal Measures; Late Carboniferous; Czechoslovakia.

Typical height
5m (16½ft)

COMPRESSION FOSSIL

| Range L. Carb.–E. Permian | Distribution Worldwide | Occurrence ♧♧♧ |

| Order MEDULLOSALES | Family MEDULLOSACEAE | Informal name Seed fern |

TRIGONOCARPUS

Casts and compressions of seeds from a variety of pteridospermous plants are found as fossils. This seed had three ribs dividing it into equal sections (and internally into valves). The outside of the seed was usually covered in longitudinal striations representing fibrous or woody bands, which strengthened the seed wall. The seeds were attached terminally or beneath a frond, but are rarely found *in situ* in fossil form.
• HABITAT *Trigonocarpus* inhabited the less wet areas of hot, humid swamps.

"plumb-bob" shape

ISOLATED SEEDS

TRIGONOCARPUS ADAMSI Lesquereux; Coal Measures; Late Carboniferous; USA.

Typical height
5m (16½ft)

seeds strongly ribbed

| Range L. Carb. | Distribution Worldwide | Occurrence ♧♧ |

Order CAYTONIALES	Family CORYSTOSPERMACEAE	Informal name Seed fern

DICROIDIUM

This large plant, a notable constituent of some Triassic floras of the southern hemisphere, was actually of shrub to small-tree stature. The fronds had unusual "Y"-forked branches, with opposite leaflets along the complete length. Palaeo-botanists know little about the plant as a whole; however, by association with other plant fossils, they believe it was likely to have been seed bearing.
• **HABITAT** *Dicroidium* was an inhabitant of tropical tree-fern forests.

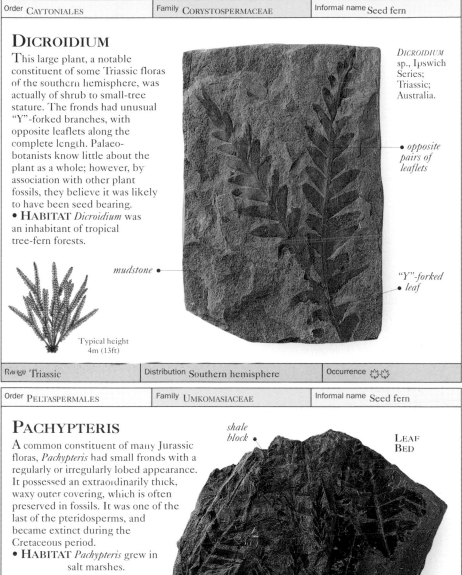

DICROIDIUM sp., Ipswich Series; Triassic; Australia.

• *opposite pairs of leaflets*

mudstone •

"Y"-forked leaf

Typical height 4m (13ft)

Range Triassic	Distribution Southern hemisphere	Occurrence 🌿🌿

Order PELTASPERMALES	Family UMKOMASIACEAE	Informal name Seed fern

PACHYPTERIS

A common constituent of many Jurassic floras, *Pachypteris* had small fronds with a regularly or irregularly lobed appearance. It possessed an extraordinarily thick, waxy outer covering, which is often preserved in fossils. It was one of the last of the pteridosperms, and became extinct during the Cretaceous period.
• **HABITAT** *Pachypteris* grew in salt marshes.

shale block •

LEAF BED

PACHYPTERIS sp.; Shemshak Formation; Jurassic; Iran.

Typical height 2m (6½ft)

smallest, lobed leaflets •

• *compression fossil*

Range Triassic–Cretaceous	Distribution Worldwide	Occurrence 🌿🌿

BENNETTITES

THE BENNETTITES or cycadeoids were very similar in appearance to sago palms or cycads. They were distinguished by their star-shaped flowers, of which several types are known. The form of the plants varied from globular stumps to branching trees, all with palm-like foliage.

Order BENNETTITALES	Family Unclassified	Informal name Cycadeoid

WILLIAMSONIA

This plant resembled a shrub or small tree, with diamond-patterned bark and palm-like leaves. Its most interesting aspect was its large, star-shaped flowers. One type contained spore capsules, while the other produced seeds.
• **HABITAT** *Williamsonia* grew in tropical tree-fern forest.

Typical height 3m (10ft)

WILLIAMSONIA GIGAS (Lindley & Hutton); Estuarine Series; Middle Jurassic; UK.

• *carbonized flower*

Range Jurassic–Cretaceous	Distribution Worldwide	Occurrence

PROGYMNOSPERMS

THIS GROUP IS BELIEVED to be ancestral to all seed plants. Appearing in the Devonian, some were moderately large trees, while others were like tree ferns. They began to produce both small and large spores, and determined spore and seed reproduction during the Late Devonian.

Order ARCHAEOPTERIDALES	Family ARCHAEOPTERIDACEAE	Informal name Archaeopteris

ARCHAEOPTERIS

Archaeopteris was one of the first trees on Earth. Trees of this genus were small to medium in size, with leafy foliage reminiscent of some conifers. The leafy shoots occurred in opposite arrangement in a single plane. The leaves overlapped one another and were subcircular to nearly wedge shaped. Leaves were replaced by spore capsules on fertile branches.
• **HABITAT** This genus grew in flood-plain woodland.

Typical height 10m (33ft)

compression • *fossil*

leafy shoots off • *axis*

• *limestone*

ARCHAEOPTERIS sp.; Kiltorcan Beds; Late Devonian; USA.

Range Devonian	Distribution Worldwide	Occurrence

CORDAITALES

MEMBERS OF THIS GROUP of plants were ancestors of the conifers. They were distinguished by long, leathery leaves, spirally arranged, with many parallel veins. Their reproductive structures were loosely aggregated cones, producing flat seeds with a membranous outer "skirt".

Order CORDAITANTHALES	Family CORDAITACEA	Informal name Cordaite

CORDAITES

An ancestor of the true conifers, *Cordaites* was a tree-sized plant that bore huge, strap-shaped leaves in tight spirals about the stem. The leaves have distinctive linear venation. The cones were loose, terminal aggregations of spore capsules or seeds. Some members of the genus were thought to be mangroves, with arching stilt roots.

• **HABITAT** *Cordaites* was an inhabitant of mangrove swamps and elevated hummocks.

CORDAITES ANGULOSTRIATUS Grand Eury; Coal Measures; Late Carboniferous; UK.

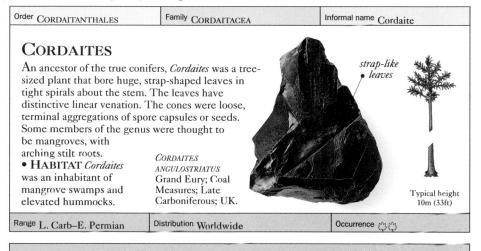

strap-like leaves

Typical height 10m (33ft)

Range L. Carb–E. Permian	Distribution Worldwide	Occurrence 🍁🍁

CONIFERS

THESE ARE USUALLY shrubs or trees distinguished by the production of woody cones of various shapes and sizes. The leaves are often needle-shaped in temperate and subtropical genera, but are flat and broad in tropical podocarps. The seeds are produced mainly in cones.

Order CONIFERALES	Family PINACEAE	Informal name Pine

PITYOSTROBUS

The form-genus represents the cones of various pine-like trees common in the Jurassic and Cretaceous periods. They were about three times longer than broad. The cones were woody, with the curved to reflexed cone leaves or bracts arranged helically about a central axis. Seeds were attached to the bract bases and fell out of the cone when mature.

• **HABITAT** *Pityostrobus* grew in sub-tropical forests.

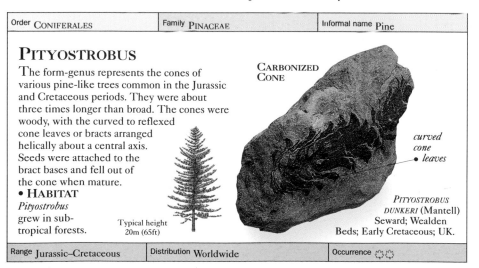

CARBONIZED CONE

curved cone leaves

Typical height 20m (65ft)

PITYOSTROBUS DUNKERI (Mantell) Seward; Wealden Beds; Early Cretaceous; UK.

Range Jurassic–Cretaceous	Distribution Worldwide	Occurrence 🍁🍁

Order CONIFERALES	Family TAXODIACEAE	Informal name Coast Redwood

SEQUOIA

This genus includes very large trees also known as coast redwoods. Small, very globular cones are a feature of these plants. The woody cone leaves (or bracts) are arranged helically about a central axis, and have a seed with a scale-leaf on the upper surface, near the base or point of attachment. The cones do not often disintegrate (as disassociated bracts), even as fossils, but open to let the seeds fall out.
• **HABITAT** Redwoods once formed extensive forests in subtropical regions of the world. These forests, as found today in California, are of an open nature, with few other tree species present.

globular shape •

PINE CONES

ironstone •

carbonized • interior

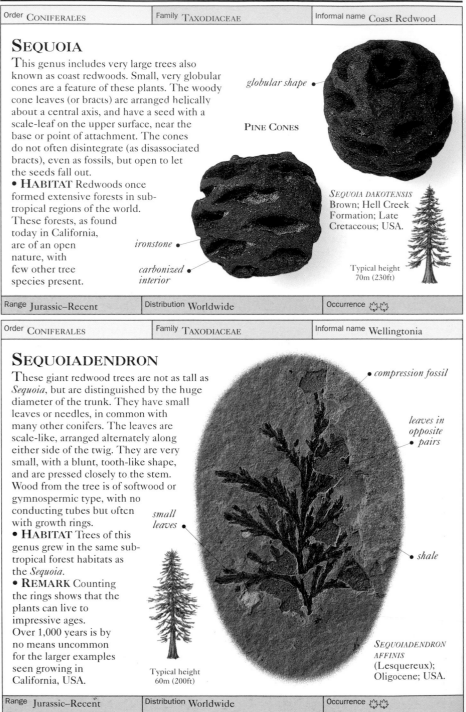

SEQUOIA DAKOTENSIS
Brown; Hell Creek Formation; Late Cretaceous; USA.

Typical height 70m (230ft)

Range Jurassic–Recent	Distribution Worldwide	Occurrence 〽〽

Order CONIFERALES	Family TAXODIACEAE	Informal name Wellingtonia

SEQUOIADENDRON

These giant redwood trees are not as tall as *Sequoia*, but are distinguished by the huge diameter of the trunk. They have small leaves or needles, in common with many other conifers. The leaves are scale-like, arranged alternately along either side of the twig. They are very small, with a blunt, tooth-like shape, and are pressed closely to the stem. Wood from the tree is of softwood or gymnospermic type, with no conducting tubes but often with growth rings.
• **HABITAT** Trees of this genus grew in the same subtropical forest habitats as the *Sequoia*.
• **REMARK** Counting the rings shows that the plants can live to impressive ages. Over 1,000 years is by no means uncommon for the larger examples seen growing in California, USA.

• compression fossil

leaves in opposite • pairs

small leaves •

• shale

Typical height 60m (200ft)

SEQUOIADENDRON AFFINIS
(Lesquereux); Oligocene; USA.

Range Jurassic–Recent	Distribution Worldwide	Occurrence 〽〽

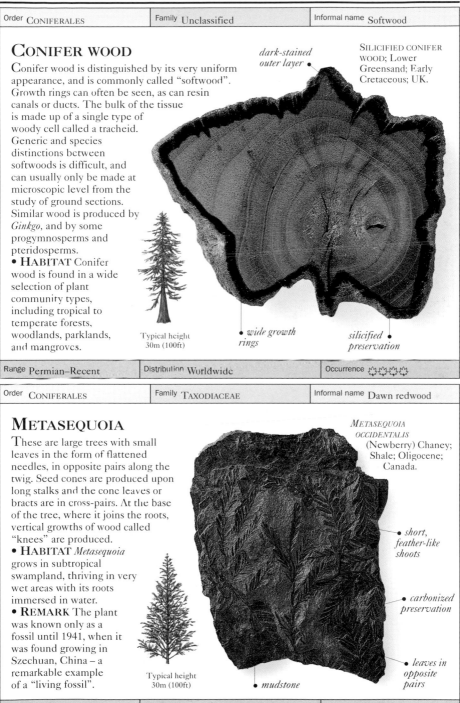

| Order CONIFERALES | Family Unclassified | Informal name Softwood |

CONIFER WOOD

Conifer wood is distinguished by its very uniform appearance, and is commonly called "softwood". Growth rings can often be seen, as can resin canals or ducts. The bulk of the tissue is made up of a single type of woody cell called a tracheid. Generic and species distinctions between softwoods is difficult, and can usually only be made at microscopic level from the study of ground sections. Similar wood is produced by *Ginkgo*, and by some progymnosperms and pteridosperms.
• HABITAT Conifer wood is found in a wide selection of plant community types, including tropical to temperate forests, woodlands, parklands, and mangroves.

dark-stained outer layer •

SILICIFIED CONIFER WOOD; Lower Greensand; Early Cretaceous; UK.

Typical height 30m (100ft)

• *wide growth rings*

silicified • *preservation*

| Range Permian–Recent | Distribution Worldwide | Occurrence 🌿🌿🌿🌿 |

| Order CONIFERALES | Family TAXODIACEAE | Informal name Dawn redwood |

METASEQUOIA

These are large trees with small leaves in the form of flattened needles, in opposite pairs along the twig. Seed cones are produced upon long stalks and the cone leaves or bracts are in cross-pairs. At the base of the tree, where it joins the roots, vertical growths of wood called "knees" are produced.
• HABITAT *Metasequoia* grows in subtropical swampland, thriving in very wet areas with its roots immersed in water.
• REMARK The plant was known only as a fossil until 1941, when it was found growing in Szechuan, China – a remarkable example of a "living fossil".

METASEQUOIA OCCIDENTALIS (Newberry) Chaney; Shale; Oligocene; Canada.

• *short, feather-like shoots*

• *carbonized preservation*

Typical height 30m (100ft)

• *mudstone*

• *leaves in opposite pairs*

| Range Cretaceous–Recent | Distribution Northern hemisphere | Occurrence 🌿🌿 |

Order CONIFERALES	Family ARAUCARIACEAE	Informal name Monkey Puzzle

ARAUCARIA

This genus of large trees includes the Monkey Puzzle Tree and Norfolk Island Pine. The leaves are small and tooth-like, spirally arranged, and closely pressed to the twig, hiding it completely. The cones are large, almost spherical, and very spiny. The surface is formed of the closely packed woody ends of cone leaves or bracts. Seeds are present at the base of the bracts.

• **HABITAT** This genus grew in subtropical mountain forests. Recent genera are restricted to the southern hemisphere.

• **REMARK** The famous fossil forest buried by volcanic ash at Cerro Cuadrado, Patagonia, is made up of *Araucaria* trees. Silicified twig, cone, and wood remains from there are common.

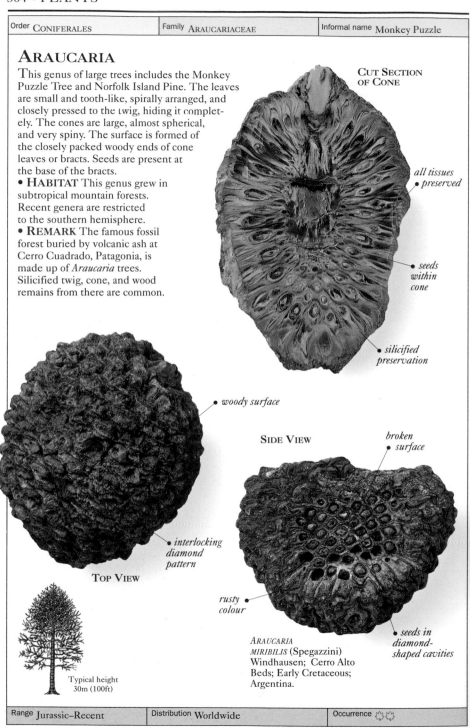

CUT SECTION OF CONE

all tissues preserved

seeds within cone

silicified preservation

woody surface

SIDE VIEW

broken surface

interlocking diamond pattern

TOP VIEW

rusty colour

seeds in diamond-shaped cavities

Typical height 30m (100ft)

ARAUCARIA MIRIBILIS (Spegazzini) Windhausen; Cerro Alto Beds; Early Cretaceous; Argentina.

Range Jurassic–Recent	Distribution Worldwide	Occurrence

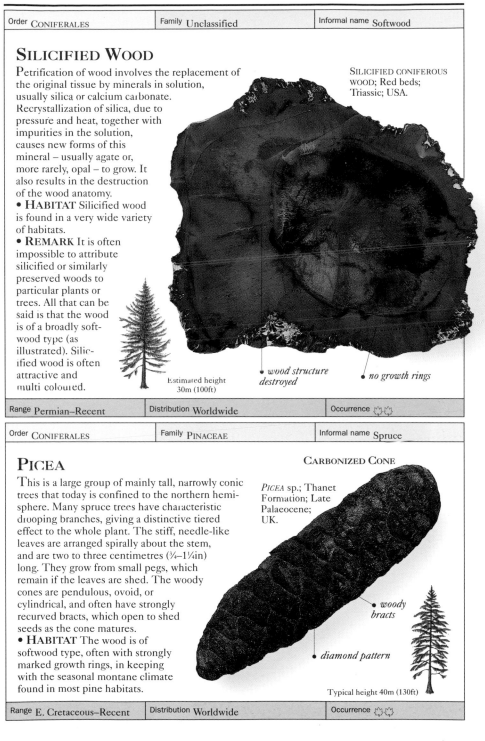

Order CONIFERALES	Family Unclassified	Informal name Softwood

SILICIFIED WOOD

Petrification of wood involves the replacement of the original tissue by minerals in solution, usually silica or calcium carbonate. Recrystallization of silica, due to pressure and heat, together with impurities in the solution, causes new forms of this mineral – usually agate or, more rarely, opal – to grow. It also results in the destruction of the wood anatomy.

• **HABITAT** Silicified wood is found in a very wide variety of habitats.

• **REMARK** It is often impossible to attribute silicified or similarly preserved woods to particular plants or trees. All that can be said is that the wood is of a broadly softwood type (as illustrated). Silicified wood is often attractive and multi coloured.

SILICIFIED CONIFEROUS WOOD; Red beds; Triassic; USA.

Estimated height 30m (100ft)

• *wood structure destroyed*

• *no growth rings*

Range Permian–Recent	Distribution Worldwide	Occurrence

Order CONIFERALES	Family PINACEAE	Informal name Spruce

PICEA

This is a large group of mainly tall, narrowly conic trees that today is confined to the northern hemisphere. Many spruce trees have characteristic drooping branches, giving a distinctive tiered effect to the whole plant. The stiff, needle-like leaves are arranged spirally about the stem, and are two to three centimetres (¾–1¼in) long. They grow from small pegs, which remain if the leaves are shed. The woody cones are pendulous, ovoid, or cylindrical, and often have strongly recurved bracts, which open to shed seeds as the cone matures.

• **HABITAT** The wood is of softwood type, often with strongly marked growth rings, in keeping with the seasonal montane climate found in most pine habitats.

CARBONIZED CONE

PICEA sp.; Thanet Formation; Late Palaeocene; UK.

• *woody bracts*

• *diamond pattern*

Typical height 40m (130ft)

Range E. Cretaceous–Recent	Distribution Worldwide	Occurrence

Order CONIFERALES	Family Not applicable	Informal name Amber

AMBER AND COPAL

Amber is fossilized resin or gum produced by
some fossil plants. The earliest recorded fossil
resins are of Carboniferous age, but ambers do
not occur until the Early Cretaceous. Famous
amber deposits include those from the Baltic
region and the Dominican Republic. It is likely
that ambers were mainly ancient gymnosperm
(probably conifer) resins, but today such gums are
also produced by flowering plants. Baltic amber
occasionally contains insect and plant remains. It
is supposed to have been formed in forests of a
primitive species of pine, *Pinus succinifera*. Recent
and semi-fossil copal resins differ from amber in
that they are still readily soluble in organic
solvents. Resins are exuded from within the tree
when it is traumatized due to attack or growth
splits. Today they are gathered commercially,
one example being the copals derived from
Kauri pine in New Zealand. Baltic amber is
used in jewelry; copals in varnish manufacture.

KAURI GUM;
Pleistocene;
New Zealand.

• *stalactitic
flow*

MIXED
CLEAR AND
CLOUDY
AMBER

• *cloudy
area rich
in succinic
acid*

BALTIC AMBER
(Succinite); Late
Eocene; Denmark.

CLEAR GEM-
QUALITY AMBER

ROLLED
AMBER
PEBBLE

• *red
patina*

TREE
(*PINUS* sp.)

Typical height
30m (100ft)

Range E. Cretaceous–Recent	Distribution Worldwide	Occurrence

GINKGOS

T HIS WAS FORMERLY an extensive group of plants, but it is now represented by a solitary relict genus, the *Ginkgo* or maidenhair tree. The group appeared during the Early Permian and was at its height during the Jurassic. All members had characteristic fan-shaped leaf architecture.

Order GINKGOALES	Family GINKGOACEAE	Informal name Maidenhair tree

GINKGO

These very tall trees have a distinctive fan- or wedge-shaped foliage. The leaves may be notched or almost entire. The trees produce spherical seeds.
• **HABITAT** A "living" fossil, the *Ginkgo*'s natural habitat is China, but it has been introduced as an ornamental tree in many parks and gardens.

Typical height 35m (115ft)

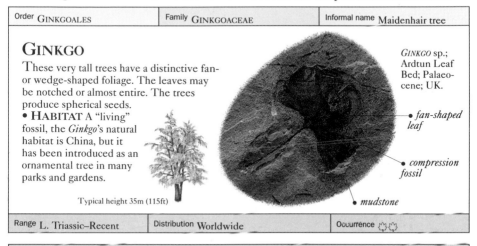

GINKGO sp.; Ardtun Leaf Bed; Palaeocene; UK.

• *fan-shaped leaf*

• *compression fossil*

• *mudstone*

Range L. Triassic–Recent	Distribution Worldwide	Occurrence

DICOTYLEDONOUS ANGIOSPERMS

T HESE FLOWERING PLANTS are distinguished by having two seed leaves. Ordinary leaves have a variety of simple to compound shapes. Plants range from herbaceous to tree types. All reproduce sexually by seeds. The earliest record of the group is from Early Cretaceous pollen.

Order HAMAMELIDALES	Family BETULACEAE	Informal name Birch

BETULITES

The leaves of this genus have some similarity to those of *Betula* or the birch family. They were round, oval, or heart-shaped, and always had teeth along the margin. Venation consisted of a central vein, with secondary veins coming off at about 45 degrees. They are usually found disassociated from twigs, which indicates that at least some were dropped seasonally.
• **HABITAT** This genus grew in temperate climates and usually damp habitats.

Typical height 10m (33ft)

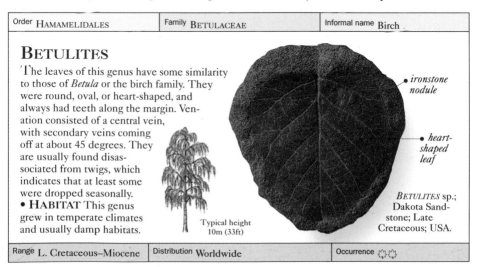

• *ironstone nodule*

• *heart-shaped leaf*

BETULITES sp.; Dakota Sandstone; Late Cretaceous; USA.

Range L. Cretaceous–Miocene	Distribution Worldwide	Occurrence

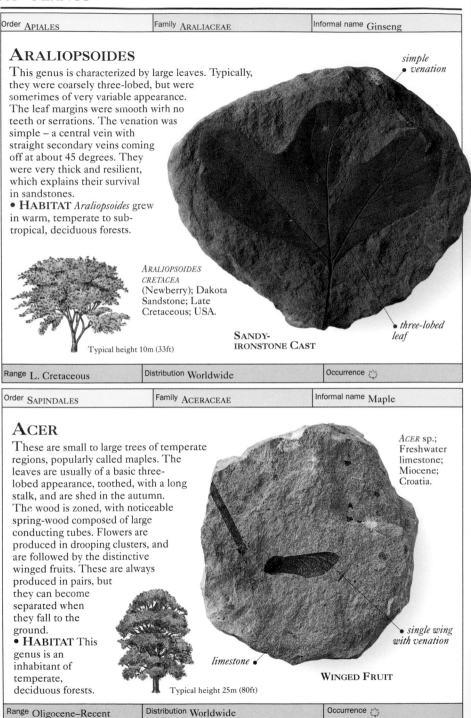

Order APIALES	Family ARALIACEAE	Informal name Ginseng

ARALIOPSOIDES

This genus is characterized by large leaves. Typically, they were coarsely three-lobed, but were sometimes of very variable appearance. The leaf margins were smooth with no teeth or serrations. The venation was simple – a central vein with straight secondary veins coming off at about 45 degrees. They were very thick and resilient, which explains their survival in sandstones.

• **HABITAT** *Araliopsoides* grew in warm, temperate to sub-tropical, deciduous forests.

simple venation

ARALIOPSOIDES CRETACEA (Newberry); Dakota Sandstone; Late Cretaceous; USA.

Typical height 10m (33ft)

SANDY-IRONSTONE CAST

three-lobed leaf

Range L. Cretaceous	Distribution Worldwide	Occurrence

Order SAPINDALES	Family ACERACEAE	Informal name Maple

ACER

These are small to large trees of temperate regions, popularly called maples. The leaves are usually of a basic three-lobed appearance, toothed, with a long stalk, and are shed in the autumn. The wood is zoned, with noticeable spring-wood composed of large conducting tubes. Flowers are produced in drooping clusters, and are followed by the distinctive winged fruits. These are always produced in pairs, but they can become separated when they fall to the ground.

• **HABITAT** This genus is an inhabitant of temperate, deciduous forests.

ACER sp.; Freshwater limestone; Miocene; Croatia.

single wing with venation

limestone

WINGED FRUIT

Typical height 25m (80ft)

Range Oligocene–Recent	Distribution Worldwide	Occurrence

Order HAMAMELIDALES	Family MORACEAE	Informal name Fig

FICUS

A large genus of shrubs and trees, the figs have thick, oval to fiddle-shaped leaves, with a noticeable central vein. The fruit is a globular, flat-topped, and stalked structure, with seeds embedded in a fleshy surround. One species, the Strangler Fig, is a parasite of other trees. Germinating in a branch crook, it gradually constricts its host until it dies.
• HABITAT This is a tropical to temperate genus.

Typical height
30m (100ft)

FICUS sp.; Early Eocene; USA.

• pointed end

woody • covering

• blunt end

• striations

FRUITS

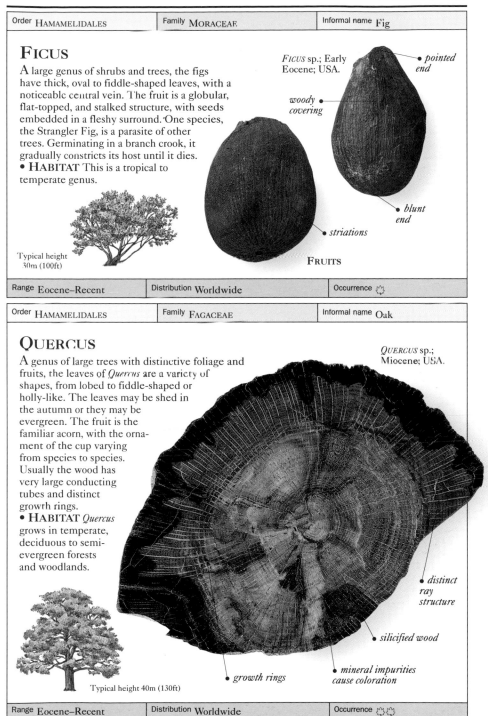

Range Eocene–Recent	Distribution Worldwide	Occurrence �

Order HAMAMELIDALES	Family FAGACEAE	Informal name Oak

QUERCUS

A genus of large trees with distinctive foliage and fruits, the leaves of *Quercus* are a variety of shapes, from lobed to fiddle-shaped or holly-like. The leaves may be shed in the autumn or they may be evergreen. The fruit is the familiar acorn, with the ornament of the cup varying from species to species. Usually the wood has very large conducting tubes and distinct growth rings.
• HABITAT *Quercus* grows in temperate, deciduous to semi-evergreen forests and woodlands.

QUERCUS sp.; Miocene; USA.

• distinct ray structure

• silicified wood

• mineral impurities cause coloration

• growth rings

Typical height 40m (130ft)

Range Eocene–Recent	Distribution Worldwide	Occurrence ☐☐

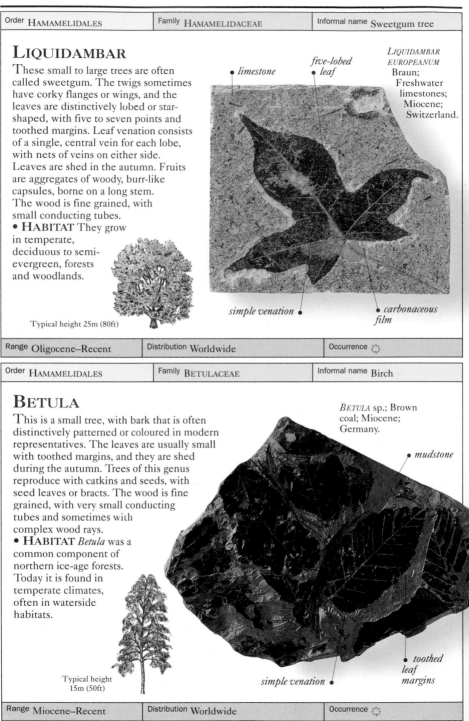

| Order HAMAMELIDALES | Family HAMAMELIDACEAE | Informal name Sweetgum tree |

LIQUIDAMBAR

These small to large trees are often called sweetgum. The twigs sometimes have corky flanges or wings, and the leaves are distinctively lobed or star-shaped, with five to seven points and toothed margins. Leaf venation consists of a single, central vein for each lobe, with nets of veins on either side. Leaves are shed in the autumn. Fruits are aggregates of woody, burr-like capsules, borne on a long stem. The wood is fine grained, with small conducting tubes.
• HABITAT They grow in temperate, deciduous to semi-evergreen, forests and woodlands.

Typical height 25m (80ft)

limestone

five-lobed leaf

LIQUIDAMBAR EUROPEANUM Braun; Freshwater limestones; Miocene; Switzerland.

simple venation

carbonaceous film

| Range Oligocene–Recent | Distribution Worldwide | Occurrence ⌂ |

| Order HAMAMELIDALES | Family BETULACEAE | Informal name Birch |

BETULA

This is a small tree, with bark that is often distinctively patterned or coloured in modern representatives. The leaves are usually small with toothed margins, and they are shed during the autumn. Trees of this genus reproduce with catkins and seeds, with seed leaves or bracts. The wood is fine grained, with very small conducting tubes and sometimes with complex wood rays.
• HABITAT *Betula* was a common component of northern ice-age forests. Today it is found in temperate climates, often in waterside habitats.

Typical height 15m (50ft)

BETULA sp.; Brown coal; Miocene; Germany.

mudstone

simple venation

toothed leaf margins

| Range Miocene–Recent | Distribution Worldwide | Occurrence ⌂ |

MONOCOTYLEDONOUS ANGIOSPERMS

THIS IMPORTANT GROUP of plants is characterized by their mode of germination — with a single seed leaf — and by leaves with parallel venation. Included in the group are grasses, narcissi, sedges, rushes, orchids, lilies, irises, and palms — all of them with a bewildering range of flowers and reproduction strategies. Fossil forms are recognized from the Late Cretaceous as palms and rushes, while grasses do not appear until the Early Cenozoic Era. A possible monocot is recorded from the Triassic of America.

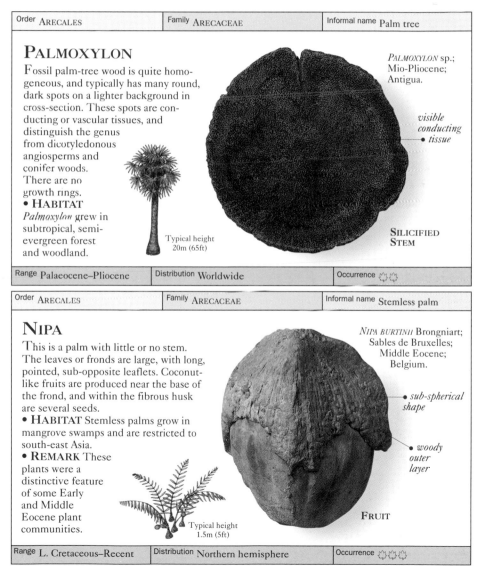

Order ARECALES	Family ARECACEAE	Informal name Palm tree

PALMOXYLON

Fossil palm-tree wood is quite homogeneous, and typically has many round, dark spots on a lighter background in cross-section. These spots are conducting or vascular tissues, and distinguish the genus from dicotyledonous angiosperms and conifer woods. There are no growth rings.
• **HABITAT** *Palmoxylon* grew in subtropical, semi-evergreen forest and woodland.

PALMOXYLON sp.; Mio-Pliocene; Antigua.

visible conducting tissue

SILICIFIED STEM

Typical height 20m (65ft)

Range Palaeocene–Pliocene	Distribution Worldwide	Occurrence

Order ARECALES	Family ARECACEAE	Informal name Stemless palm

NIPA

This is a palm with little or no stem. The leaves or fronds are large, with long, pointed, sub-opposite leaflets. Coconut-like fruits are produced near the base of the frond, and within the fibrous husk are several seeds.
• **HABITAT** Stemless palms grow in mangrove swamps and are restricted to south-east Asia.
• **REMARK** These plants were a distinctive feature of some Early and Middle Eocene plant communities.

NIPA BURTINII Brongniart; Sables de Bruxelles; Middle Eocene; Belgium.

sub-spherical shape

woody outer layer

FRUIT

Typical height 1.5m (5ft)

Range L. Cretaceous–Recent	Distribution Northern hemisphere	Occurrence

GLOSSARY

THE USE OF SOME technical expressions is unavoidable in a book of this nature. Commonly used technical words are often defined in the text itself, and many terms are explained by the annotated illustrations. The definitions given below have been simplified and generalized, and are appropriate for this book only. Words in bold type are explained elsewhere in the glossary.

• **ADDUCTOR MUSCLES**
The muscles controlling the valves of bivalves and brachiopods.
• **ADIPOSE FIN**
In fish, a fleshy **dorsal** fin.
• **ALATE PLATE**
A flap-like extension on the interior hinge line of the **brachial valve** of a brachiopod.
• **ALVEOLUS**
A tooth socket in vertebrates; a cavity containing **phragmocone** in belemnites.
• **AMBULACRA**
The plated zones of echinoderms associated with tube feet.
• **ANAL FIN**
An unpaired **posterior** fish fin.
• **ANAL TUBE**
The projecting part of the arm that carries the anus in crinoids.
• **ANTENNULES**
The sensory appendages towards the front of a trilobite.
• **ANTERIOR**
Towards the front.
• **APERTURE**
The opening surrounded by the shell margin in molluscs.
• **APICAL DISC**
The upper central disc of a sea urchin, from which the **ambulacra** radiate.
• **APTIAN STAGE**
The fifth out of the six stages in the Early Cretaceous.
• **ARAGONITE**
A crystalline form of calcium carbonate.
• **ARISTOTLE'S LANTERN**
The five-sided feeding and locomotor structure sited around the mouth of sea urchins.
• **ARTICULAR BONES**
The bones incorporated in the articulation between the skull and lower jaw in some vertebrates.
• **AURICLES**
The ear-like structure on a bivalve shell.
• **AVICULARIA**
The defensive individuals in a bryozoan colony.

• **AXIAL BOSS**
The raised node at the centre of the **corallites** in corals.
• **AXIS**
In trilobites, the ridge that runs from **anterior** to **posterior**, down the midline; in vertebrates, the first or second element of the backbone.
• **BARBEL**
A slim, sensitive process near the mouth of some fish.
• **BASAL**
At, or pertaining to, the base.
• **BEAK**
A prominent curved structure: in bivalves, the extremity of the **umbo**; in cephalopods and vertebrates, a part of the jaw structure.
• **BENTHONIC**
Living on the sea floor.
• **BICIPITAL SURFACE**
A bulbous surface at the **proximal** end of the upper arm bone in vertebrates.
• **BICONIC**
Pointed at both ends.
• **BOREAL**
Suggesting a fauna with preference for a cold climate.
• **BOSS**
A protuberance.
• **BRACHIAL VALVE**
One of the two valves that form the brachiopod shell.
• **BRACHIOLE**
An arm-like appendage to a brachiopod.
• **BRACT**
A modified leaf associated with plant reproductive structures.
• **BUNODONT**
A condition in which molar teeth possess rounded **cusps** and **tubercles**.
• **BYSSAL NOTCH**
The notch near to the **hinge** of some bivalve shells, associated with attachment threads.
• **BYSSUS**
The attachment threads of a bivalve.

• **CALICE**
The upper portion of a coral skeleton.
• **CALLUM**
The dome of calcite in molluscs.
• **CALCAREOUS**
Made of calcium carbonate; chalky.
• **CALYX**
In crinoids, a cup-shaped structure to which the arms are attached; in plants, the outer circle of a flower made up of sepals.
• **CAPITILUM**
A portion of a crustacean or chelicerate, usually composed of armoured plates, protecting the food-gathering organs.
• **CARAPACE**
In crustaceans and chelicerates, the external shield covering head and trunk; in vertebrates, the upper shell.
• **CARDINAL TEETH**
The articulating structures on the **hinge** of a brachiopod.
• **CARINA** (*pl.* **CARINAE**)
A ridge- or keel-shaped structure.
• **CARNASSIAL TOOTH**
A molar or premolar specialized for cutting.
• **CARTILAGE**
Highly specialized tissue that is hard but flexible.
• **CAST**
The filling of a **mould**.
• **CAUDAL FIN**
The tail fin of a vertebrate.
• **CENOZOIC**
The fourth era of time in the history of the Earth, 65 to 2 million years ago.
• **CENTRUM** (*pl.* **CENTRA**)
The main body of a **vertebra**.
• **CEPHALON**
The head of a trilobite.
• **CEPHALOTHORAX**
The combined head and trunk region of an arthropod.
• **CERCI**
The sensory appendages at the **posterior** of the abdomen of insects.

• **CHELA** (*pl.* **CHELAE**)
The pincer-like end of limb of crustaceans or chelicerates.

• **CHELICERAE**
The biting appendages of spiders.

• **CHEVRON BONES**
In reptiles, the pair of bones, often fused to form a "Y", that hang below the tail **vertebrae**.

• **CHITIN**
A horny substance, forming all or part of the skeleton of arthropods.

• **CILIA**
Tiny, hair-like structures on a cell.

• **CIRRI**
A tendril-like animal appendage; the jointed **thoracic** appendages of barnacles.

• **CLASPERS**
The specialized pelvic fins of sharks, rays, and rabbitfishes.

• **COENOSTEUM**
The **calcareous** skeleton of a bryozoan and some corals.

• **COLONY**
An assemblage of connected organisms that have grown from an individual.

• **COLUMELLA**
The column that surrounds the shell's **axis** in gastropods.

• **COLUMNAL**
The stem **ossicles** in crinoids.

• **COMMISSURE**
The line along which two valves of a shell meet.

• **COMPRESSION FOSSIL**
A flattened fossil.

• **CORALLITE**
In corals, an individual **polyp**'s skeleton.

• **CORNUA**
A horn-like structure in fish.

• **COSTAE**
Fine, concentrically arranged ribbing.

• **COXA** (*pl.* **COXAE**)
The **proximal** or base region of a limb, which articulates with the body in insects and some other arthropods.

• **CRANIUM**
The part of the skull enclosing the brain.

• **CUSP**
A projection on the chewing surface of a tooth.

• **CUSPLET**
A small **cusp**.

• **CUTICLE**
The hardened outer surface of the external skeleton of arthropods.

• **CYST**
A thick-walled cell in plants.

• **DEGENERATE**
Not fully formed.

• **DELTOID**
A "V"-shaped plate in the cup of a blastoid.

• **DELTOID CREST**
The projection of the upper arm bone for the attachment of muscles in vertebrates.

• **DEMOSPONGE**
A sponge with a skeleton possessing one- to four-rayed sponge fibres.

• **DENTARY**
The bone of the lower jaw in vertebrates.

• **DENTICLE**
A small, tooth-like structure.

• **DENTICULATE**
Serrated; housing **denticles**.

• **DENTINE**
The bone-like substance that makes up the bulk of a tooth.

• **DERMAL ARMOUR**
The bony plates situated in the skin of some vertebrates.

• **DERMAL DENTICLE**
A tooth-like structure found in the skin of sharks.

• **DETRITUS**
Fine particles of organic matter.

• **DIAGENESIS**
The process involved in turning sediment into a rock.

• **DIASTEMA**
The space between two types of teeth.

• **DISCOIDAL**
Disc-shaped.

• **DISSEPIMENT**
In corals, a vertical plate sited between **septa**.

• **DORSAL**
The upper surface or back.

• **DORSAL FIN**
A midline, unpaired, vertical fin sited on the back of aquatic vertebrates.

• **DORSO-VENTRALLY FLATTENED**
Compressed from top to bottom.

• **ELYTRA**
The modified **anterior** wings that act as protective covers for the membranous hindwings in beetles.

• **ENTOPLASTRON**
The **anterior**, median bony plate of the lower shell in turtles.

• **EPIDERMIS**
The bloodless, non-sensitive portion of the skin in vertebrates.

• **EPIPLANKTONIC**
The area of the sea from the surface to about 100 fathoms.

• **EPIPLASTRON**
One of the **anterior** pair of bony plates of the lower shell in turtles.

• **EPISTOME**
The area covering the mouth and second antennae, and the plate covering this region, in crustaceans.

• **ESCUTCHEON**
A depression found behind the **umbones** of a bivalve shell.

• **EVOLUTE**
Loosely coiled.

• **EXOSKELETON**
The hard outer casing of arthropods.

• **EXTERNAL MOULD**
An impression of the outside of an organism.

• **FACIAL SUTURE**
A line on the head of a trilobite along which splitting occurred during moulting.

• **FENESTRULE**
An opening located between the branches of a bryozoan colony.

• **FILTER FEEDER**
An organism that gains nutrition by filtering particles from the water.

• **FLAGELLUM**
A whip-like appendage.

• **FOOT**
In invertebrates, the base from which the organism grows, or by which it is cemented to the substrate.

• **FORAMEN**
(*pl.* **FORAMINAE**)
A small opening or perforation in brachiopods.

• **FORM-GENUS**
A genus containing many similar species but which may not actually be related.

• **FRONTAL BONE**
In vertebrates, one of a pair of bones situated in the skull.

• **FUSIFORM**
Tapering at each end.

• **GENAL ANGLE**
The angle between the back and lateral margins of a trilobite's head.

• **GENAL SPINE**
A trilobite's cheek spine.

• **GIRDLE**
In chitons, the outer portion of the **mantle**; in vertebrates, the hoop-like group of bones that support the limbs.

• **GLABELLA**
In trilobites, the central region of the head; in vertebrates, the prominent front bone which joins the ridges above the eyes.

- **GLAUCONITIC**
Containing the mineral glauconite, the presence of which indicates that a sediment was deposited in marine conditions.
- **GONADS**
Sex glands.
- **GRACILE**
Lightly built.
- **GROWTH LINES**
The dividing lines between periods of growth.
- **GUARD**
A massive, bullet-shaped calcite structure in belemnites.
- **HADROSAURIAN CREST**
A bony crest found on the skulls of hadrosaurian dinosaurs.
- **HALTERES**
The pair of structures representing hindwings in flies.
- **HETEROCERCAL TAIL**
The tail of a fish with unequal-sized lobes.
- **HINGE**
The linear area along which a mollusc shell articulates.
- **HINGE PLATE**
In molluscs, the portion of valve that supports the **hinge teeth**; in brachiopods, the socket-bearing portion of the **dorsal** valve.
- **HINGE TEETH**
Articulating structures in mollusc shells.
- **HOLDFAST**
A **basal** structure that attaches a plant to the substrate.
- **HOMOCERCAL TAIL**
A symmetrical fish tail.
- **HYOPLASTRON**
The paired, second lateral, bony plate of the lower shell of a turtle.
- **HYPOCERCAL TAIL**
A type of fish tail in which the **notochord** ends in the extended lower lobe.
- **HYPOPLASTRON**
The paired, third lateral, bony plate of the lower shell of a turtle.
- **INCUS**
The central of the three bones of the inner ear of vertebrates.
- **INTERAMBULACRAL**
The area between two radial plates, along which the tube feet of echinoids are arranged.
- **INTERAREA**
The flat area on a brachiopod shell between the **hinge** line and **beak** areas.
- **INTERNAL MOULD**
An impression of the inside of an organism.

- **LABIAL**
Pertaining to the lips.
- **LABIAL SPINES**
Spines sited at the aperture of certain gastropod shells.
- **LIVING FOSSIL**
An animal or plant species that has remained almost unchanged for millions of years.
- **LOCALLY OCCURING**
Found only at certain, specific localities.
- **LOPH**
A crest or ridge.
- **LUNULE**
A crescent-shaped structure or mark in the **test** of some sea urchins.
- **MACROCONCH**
The larger form of a shell in a species in which males and females differ.
- **MALLEUS**
The outermost bone of the inner ear in vertebrates.
- **MANDIBLE**
In vertebrates, the lower jaw; in invertebrates, the various mouth-parts which hold or bite food.
- **MANTLE**
The external body wall, lining the shell of some invertebrates.
- **MANTLE CAVITY**
The space between the body and **mantle** of a bivalve.
- **MARINE INDICATORS**
Characteristics denoting saltwater conditions.
- **MARL**
A **calcareous** mudstone.
- **MATRIX**
The material on which an organism rests or is embedded.
- **MAXILLARY LOBES**
A part of the mouth of an arthropod.
- **MEDIAN TOOTH**
A tooth placed in the midline of the mouth.
- **MESIAL TOOTH**
A tooth placed near the middle of the jaw.
- **MESOPLASTRON**
In turtles, one of a pair of bony plates forming the lower shell.
- **MESOSUCHIAN**
A primitive crocodile.
- **MESOZOIC**
The second era of the Phanerozoic aeon, from 248 to 65 million years ago.
- **METAMORPHISM**
A change in an organism's structure during development.

- **METATARSAL**
Pertaining to the bones in the ankle.
- **MICROCONCH**
The smaller form of a shell in a species in which males and females differ in size.
- **MICROSCULPTURE**
Small patterns of ornamentation.
- **MONTANE CLIMATE**
Hilly areas below the timberline.
- **MONTICULE**
A hummock on the surface of a bryozoan colony.
- **MORPHOLOGY**
The structure and form of plants and animals.
- **MOULD**
An impression obtained from an original form.
- **MUCILLAGE**
A carbohydrate found in certain plants, which can be secreted.
- **MUCRON**
A short tip or **process**.
- **MUCRONATE**
Ended by a short tip or **process**.
- **NACRE**
An iridescent internal layer of a mollusc shell.
- **NACREOUS**
Made of **nacre**.
- **NEMA**
The attachment thread found in some graptolites.
- **NEOTONY**
A condition in which development is terminated at a pre-adult stage but sexual maturity is reached.
- **NEURAL PLATE**
A series of bony plates sited in the midline of the upper shell of turtles.
- **NEURAL ARCH**
The upper portion of a **vertebra**.
- **NEURAL CANAL**
The channel through which the spinal cord passes.
- **NEURAL SPINE**
The blade- or prong-like structure located on the **dorsal** aspect of a **vertebra**.
- **NODES**
Bumps or protruberances; in plants, the attachment point of leaf stem.
- **NOTOCHORD**
A skeletal rod located above the nerve chord of fish.
- **NUTRITIVE GROOVE**
Food channel.
- **NYMPH**
An immature insect, or, in bivalves, the narrow ledge on the **hinge** behind the **umbo**.

- **OCCIPITAL**
A bone at the rear of the skull which articulates with the spinal column.
- **OCCLUSAL**
The cutting or grinding surface of a tooth.
- **OPERCULUM**
The structure attached to a gastropod's foot, used to close the shell's **aperture**.
- **ORAL TEETH**
Teeth situated in the mouth, as opposed to on the rostrum.
- **ORBIT**
An eye socket.
- **ORNITHOPOD**
A group of dinosaurs with bird-like feet.
- **OSSICLES**
In invertebrates, the **calcareous bodies** that make up the skeleton.
- **OSSIFIED**
Turned to bone.
- **OTOLITH**
A **calcareous** concretion in a vertebrate's ear.
- **PALAEOZOIC**
The first era of the Phanerozoic aeon, 545 to 248 million years ago.
- **PALLETS**
The burrowing structure of molluscs.
- **PALLIAL LINE**
In bivalves, an impressed line inside the valve, parallel to the margin, caused by the attachment of the **mantle**.
- **PECTORAL FIN**
One of a pair of forward-pointing fins in fish.
- **PEDICLE**
A **cuticle**-covered appendage for the attachment of a brachiopod shell to the **substrate**.
- **PEDIPALPS**
The first pair of post-oral appendages in chelicerates.
- **PEDUNCLE**
In some invertebrates, the stalk that supports most of the body.
- **PELVIC FIN**
In fish, one of a pair of fins placed towards the back.
- **PEN**
The horny internal skeleton of squids.
- **PERIDERM**
A horny, cuticular covering.
- **PHRAGMOCONE**
In belemnites and other molluscs, the cone-like internal shell that is

divided into chambers by **septa** and perforated by a **siphuncle**.
- **PINNAE**
Small leaflets on plants.
- **PINNULE**
A part of the fan-like structure of the arms of a crinoid.
- **PLANISPIRAL**
Coiled in one plane.
- **PLANKTON**
Weak-swimming or passively floating animals or plants.
- **PLASTRON**
The lower bony shell of turtles.
- **PLEOTELSON**
In crustaceans and chelicerates, the plate formed by the fusion of tail plates with abdominal segments.
- **PLEURAL LOBES**
The lateral parts of the **thoracic** segments of trilobites.
- **PLEURAL SPINE**
The body spine of a trilobite.
- **PNEUMATIC BONE**
In birds, the bones connected by canals to the respiratory system.
- **POLYMORPHIC**
A species with more than one form.
- **POLYP**
An individual member of a coral colony.
- **POSTERIOR**
Towards the rear.
- **PRESACRAL VERTEBRAE**
Part of the backbone in front of the hindlimb girdle.
- **PRISMATIC**
A shell structure of minute, columnar prisms.
- **PROBOSCIS**
In insects, a tubular feeding structure; in mammals, a flexible, elongated snout.
- **PROCESS**
An extension or appendage to a organism.
- **PUSTULE**
A small, rounded protuberance, smaller than a **node**.
- **PRONOTUM**
The back of the first body segment in insects.
- **PRO-OSTRACUM**
The thin, tongue-like extension in front of the **guard** in belemnites.
- **PROPARIAN**
A form of **suture** in trilobites that reaches the edge in front of the **genal angle**.
- **PROP-ROOT**
A root that helps to support a plant.
- **PROXIMAL**
At or towards the near, inner, or attached end.

- **PSEUDOPELAGIC**
Refers to the life style of organisms that live attached to floating objects in the sea.
- **PUBIC BONE**
One of the paired girdle bones in vertebrates.
- **PUSTULE**
A small, raised mound or **tubercle**.
- **PYGIDIUM**
The tail of a trilobite.
- **PYRITE**
Gold-coloured mineral composed of iron sulphide.
- **QUADRATE**
The bone that produces the **articulation** of the skull and lower jaw in some vertebrates.
- **RADIAL**
Diverging from the centre.
- **RADULA**
A horny or tooth-like structure located in the mouth of all molluscs, except bivalves.
- **RAMUS**
A **process** projecting from a bone.
- **RECURVED**
Curved backwards.
- **REFLEXED**
Turned backwards.
- **RETICULUM**
A fine network.
- **RIBS**
In invertebrates, raised ornamental bands; in vertebrates, part of the **thoracic** skeleton.
- **ROCK-FORMER**
Animals that occur in sufficient abundance and frequency as to form the major bulk of a rock.
- **ROSTRAL PLATE**
One of the plates covering a barnacle (also known as a rostrum).
- **RUGAE**
Wrinkles on a shell surface.
- **SACCULITH**
The largest **otolith** in the inner ear.
- **SACRAL**
Associated with the hip girdle.
- **SAGITTAL CREST**
The median crest sited on the posterior portion of the skull.
- **SANDSTONE**
A rock made from coarse mineral grains, principally quartz.
- **SCALE-LEAF**
A tough, membranous leaf that often has a protective function.
- **SCLEROSPONGE**
A calcified **demosponge**.
- **SCLEROTIC RING**
A ring of bony plates around the eye socket in reptiles and birds.

- **SCULPTURE**
Ornament on bone surface.
- **SCUTE**
The bony, scale-like structure found in reptiles.
- **SELENIZONE**
A groove in a gastropod shell.
- **SEPTUM** (*pl.* **SEPTA**)
A thin dividing wall.
- **SEXUAL DIMORPHISM**
A condition in which the sexes differ in form.
- **SHELF SEA**
Shallow seas around land masses.
- **SICULA**
The cone-shaped skeleton of a graptolite colony.
- **SILTSTONE**
A rock formed from silt deposits.
- **SINUS**
A cavity or recess in gastropods.
- **SIPHON**
A tubular element used for the intake of water in molluscs.
- **SIPHUNCLE**
A tubular extension of the **mantle** passing through all chambers of shelled cephalopods.
- **SOMITE**
A body segment of a crustacean.
- **SPICULE**
A spike-like supporting structure in many invertebrates, especially sponges.
- **SPINNERET**
An organ that spins fibre from the secretion of silk glands.
- **SPINULE**
A small, spine-like **process**.
- **SPIRE**
A complete set of **whorls** of a spiral shell.
- **SPRING WOOD**
The part of an annual ring formed mainly in the growing season in plants.
- **SQUAMOSAL**
A skull bone situated behind the ear in many vertebrates.
- **STERNITE**
The **ventral** plate in an arthropod segment.
- **STERNUM**
The breast bone of vertebrates.
- **STILT-ROOT**
The aerial roots that help to support trees such as mangroves.
- **STIPE**
A branch supporting a colony of individuals.
- **STRIAE**
Minute lines, grooves, or channels.
- **STROMATOLITE**
A cushion-like, algal growth.

- **SUB-CHELATE**
Having a claw without a fixed finger, and a movable finger operating against a short outgrowth of the hand.
- **SUBSTRATE**
The base on which an animal or plant lives.
- **SULCUS**
A depression on a shell's surface.
- **SUSPENSION FEEDER**
An organism that derives its nourishment from food particles suspended in water.
- **SUTURE**
A line on gastropod shells where **whorls** connect.
- **SYMBIOSIS**
The mutually beneficial inter-relationship between two different species.
- **SYMPHYSEAL TOOTH**
A tooth located in the midline, near the apex of the jaw.
- **TABULA**
A transverse **septum** that shuts off the lower region of a **polyp** cavity in some extinct corals.
- **TABULATE**
Flat, table-like.
- **TALONID**
The posterior part of the lower molar tooth in certain mammals.
- **TEGMEN** (*pl.* **TEGMINA**)
The thickened forewing of certain insects, such as beetles.
- **TELSON**
In crustaceans, the last segment of the body, containing the anus and/or spines.
- **TERMINAL MOUTH**
Mouth placed at the front in fish.
- **TEST**
A hard external covering or shell.
- **TETHYS OCEAN**
An ancient seaway which stretched from Europe to eastern Asia.
- **THALLUS**
A plant body consisting of a single cell or a complex multi-cellular structure.
- **THECA**
In graptolites, the organic-walled tubes housing **zooids**.
- **THORACIC**
Pertaining to the **thorax**.
- **THORAX**
In certain arthropods, the middle of the three main divisions of the body; in vertebrates, the chest region.
- **TRACHEID**
An elongate plant cell with thickened secondary walls.

- **TRITORS**
Specialized dentine in certain fish.
- **TUBE FEET**
Tentacle-like structures found in sea urchins.
- **TUBER**
A thickened underground stem or root of a plant.
- **TUBERCLE**
A raised mound or bump.
- **TUMID**
Raised, swollen.
- **TYMPANIC BONES**
Bones of the ear.
- **ULNA**
In vertebrates, one of the lower arm bones.
- **UMBILICUS**
The first-formed region of a coiled shell.
- **UMBO** (*pl.* **UMBONES**)
The beak-like first-formed region of a bivalve shell.
- **UROPOD**
A limb on the sixth trunk segment of crustaceans; generally fan-like.
- **VENTER**
In arthropods, the undersurface of the abdomen; in molluscs, the external, convex part of a curved or coiled shell.
- **VENTRAL**
Towards the underside.
- **VERTEBRA**
(*pl.* **VERTEBRAE**)
One bone in the series that makes up the backbone in vertebrates.
- **VISCERA**
The organs within the body cavities of an animal.
- **WATER COLUMN**
Water depth from surface to bed.
- **WEBERIAN OSSICLES**
A chain of three to four bones that connect the swim bladder to the inner ear of some fish.
- **WHORL**
One complete turn of a shell.
- **XIPHIPLASTRON**
A paired, bony plate of the lower shell of a turtle.
- **ZONAL MARKER**
See **Zone Fossil**.
- **ZONE FOSSIL**
A fossil species that characterizes a particular layer of the Earth's crust and is restricted to it in time.
- **ZOOID**
An individual of a colonial animal, such as corals, graptolites, and bryozoans.
- **ZYGOMATIC ARCH**
In mammals, a bony bar located on the side of the face below the eye.

INDEX

A

ACKNOWLEDGMENTS

THIS BOOK COULD not have been completed without the help, material and otherwise, of a number of people and institutions. The authors and publisher are greatly indebted to the following: Dr Robin Cocks and Dr Hugh Owen for permitting access to the collection at the Natural History Museum, London, UK; Dr Noel Morris, Dr Peter Forey, Mr Steve Baker, Mr David Lewis, and Mr Cedric Shute for help and general assistance within the collection. The authors would also like to thank the Shop Manager of The Geological Museum (The British Museum) for providing specimens and equipment. Thanks also go to Tim Parmenter and Harry Taylor of the photographic unit, for their time and expertise. Further specimens, which were not available in the Natural History Museum, were kindly provided by Bob Weist, Frank and Becky Hyne, and Dr Neville Hollingworth.

The authors wish to thank the staff and freelancers at Dorling Kindersley, Richmond, especially Susie Behar, Peter Cross, Jonathan Metcalf, Mary-Clare Jerram, Gill Della Casa, and Clive Hayball for their guidance and encouragement. David Ward would like to thank Mrs Alison Ward for all her support.

Dorling Kindersley would like to thank the following: Elaine Hewson, Alastair Wardle, Kevin Ryan, and Ian Callow for design help; Alison Edmonds, Angeles Gavira, and Andrea Fair for editorial help; Ailsa Allaby for editorial guidance; Michael Allaby for compiling the index and glossary; Janos Marffy for airbrush artwork; Andy Farmer for the illustrations on pp.14, 15, and 11; Adam Moore for computer back-up; and Ziggy and Nina at the Right Type.

Photography by Colin Keates, except: Frank Lane Picture Agency / W. Broadhurst p.17 *(top right)* / E. J. Davis p.17 *(centre)* / M. J. Thomas p.16 *(bottom)*; The Natural History Museum p.22 *(top)*; Nature Photographers / Paul Sterry p.16 *(top)*. Dorling Kindersley / Colin Keates p.13 *(top)* / p.17 *(top left)* / p.22 *(bottom left)* / p.23 *(top)* / p.25 *(top right)* / p.240 *(top left)* / p.254 *(top)* / p.258 *(bottom right)*.

Endpaper illustrations by Caroline Church.